Oliver Krüger
Virtual Immortality –
God, Evolution, and the Singularity in Post- and Transhumanism

Cultures of Society | Volume 41

Oliver Krüger is professor for the Study of Religions at Fribourg University (Switzerland). His Ph.D. which he completed in 2002 at the University of Bonn was awarded by the German Association for the History of Religions. He then researched rituals of the Wicca movement as a postdoc at the University of Heidelberg. This was followed by a project at Princeton University on funeral rituals in the United States. Since 2007, Krüger has been teaching and researching at Fribourg University, primarily on sociology of religion and new media and science in relation to religion. He also served as president of the Swiss Society for the Study of Religions.

Oliver Krüger

**Virtual Immortality –
God, Evolution, and the Singularity
in Post- and Transhumanism**

Translated from German by Ali Jones and Paul Knight

[transcript]

The translation of this work was funded by the Faculty of Humanities (Fribourg University) and by Geisteswissenschaften International – Translation Funding for Work in the Humanities and Social Sciences from Germany, a joint initiative of the Fritz Thyssen Foundation, the German Federal Foreign Office, the collecting society VG WORT, and the Börsenverein des Deutschen Buchhandels (German Publishers & Booksellers Association).

Bibliographic information published by the Deutsche Nationalbibliothek
The Deutsche Nationalbibliothek lists this publication in the Deutsche Nationalbibliografie; detailed bibliographic data are available in the Internet at http://dnb.d-nb.de

© 2021 transcript Verlag, Bielefeld

All rights reserved. No part of this book may be reprinted or reproduced or utilized in any form or by any electronic, mechanical, or other means, now known or hereafter invented, including photocopying and recording, or in any information storage or retrieval system, without permission in writing from the publisher.

Cover layout: Maria Arndt, Bielefeld
Cover illustration: Graphic based on the poster for »Metropolis« by Fritz Lang
Translation: Ali Jones and Paul Knight
Proofread: Graeme Currie

Print-ISBN 978-3-8376-5059-4
PDF-ISBN 978-3-8394-5059-8
https://doi.org/10.14361/9783839450598
ISSN of series: 2703-0040
eISSN of series: 2703-0059

Contents

Foreword to the English Edition 11

A *Who is Who?* of Post- and Transhumanism 15

1. Virtuality, Media, and Immortality. An Introduction 19

Part I
Humans and Media

2. Virtuality 29
2.1 Virtuality and Time 31
2.2 Virtuality and Space 37
2.3 Virtuality and Corporeality 40
2.4 Virtuality, Reality, and the Imaginary 43

3. Promethean Shame 51
3.1 Human Beings and Technology in the Work of Günther Anders 51
3.2 Virtuality and Death 55

Part II
Technological Posthumanism

4. Transhumanism 61
4.1 Post- and Transhumanism 61
4.2 Intellectual Predecessors and the Transhuman 62
4.3 Early Transhumanism: Ettinger, FM-2030, Leary 68
4.4 The Extropy Institute and the (Vita-)Mores 75
4.5 The World Transhumanist Association / humanity+ 78
4.6 Other Actors and Institutions 82
4.7 Religious and Spiritual Transhumanism 87

4.8	Conclusion	89
5.	**Technological Posthumanism**	**91**
5.1	The Posthuman and Posthumanism	92
5.2	The Face of Posthumanism	95
	Frank Tipler	95
	Marvin Minsky	98
	Hans Moravec	100
	Ray Kurzweil	103
5.3	Posthumanism and Art	105
6.	**A History of Technological Posthumanism**	**115**
6.1	Writing the "History of the Future"	115
6.2	How We Became Posthuman	118
	L'Homme Machine	120
	Simulation and Identity	129
	The Cybernetic Paradigm	140
	The Measure of Perfection: Work and Knowledge	151
6.3	Annihilation or Infinite Progress	158
	Death, Entropy, and the Annihilation of All Life	158
	The Sacrifice of Humankind	164
	Progress and Perfectibility	170
	Evolution and the Emergence of Life	177
	Frank Tipler's Physico-Theology	190
6.4	Singularities	197
	Cosmological Singularity and Black Holes	199
	The Technological Singularity	201
	The Law of Progress and the *Endless Frontier*	212
6.5	Immortality	218
	Posthuman and Immortal	218
	From Longevity to Computer-Aided Immortalization	224
	Immortality in Science Fiction	236
	Cryonics and the Suspension of Death	244
	Technological Immortality	257
6.6	The Transcendental Superintelligence	260
	Transcendence and the Superhuman	260
	Mind, Genius, and Superintelligence	263
6.7	Omega	276
	The Cosmic Consciousness	276
	Teilhard de Chardin, McLuhan, and the Noosphere	281
7.	**Virtuality. Immortality in the Age of Digital Media**	**291**
7.1	Economy	292
7.2	Control and Contingency	297
7.3	Secular Progress and Christian Salvation History	301

7.4   The End of the Affronts 310

Appendix

List of Abbreviations 317

Bibliography..319
    a) Literature 319
    b) Movies, TV series, and documentaries 345
    c) Videos (online) 346

Index of Names..348

in memoriam
David Lavery (1949-2016)
who left too early for the stars

Foreword to the English Edition

The problem with this book, and perhaps with all books, is that we are not *Tralfamadorians*. As American author Kurt Vonnegut explains, the characteristic feature of Tralfamadorian books is that we do not read them word for word or sentence for sentence. Instead, on every page a cluster of signs creates the experience of a feeling, of a situation, or of an idea as *a whole*.[1] In this book I have had to resort to traditional methods of authorship in an effort to analyze the highly complex ramifications of virtuality and immortality and to explain the interrelation between the various discourses in their historical dimensions.

This book was based initially on my doctoral thesis written from 1999 to 2004.[2] In the following years I regarded posthumanism and transhumanism mainly as a phenomenon that euphorically celebrated the new digital technologies at the turn of the millennium. However, I soon realized that there was far more to it. The future never dies. The future is an inexhaustible resource, both for religions and for technological prophecies. Thus, academic, media, and popular culture interest in post- and transhumanism did not wane over the years. In 2019 I published the second German edition, which was the fruit of three years of further research and reading.[3] After that, I received several enquiries from the United States and the United Kingdom encouraging me to attempt an English version of my book. This project has now come to fruition thanks to the support of the *Börsenverein des Deutschen Buchhandels*.

Compared with my time as a student around the turn of the century, few new ideas and protagonists have appeared on the posthumanist scene. However, there has been a clear shift in the topics and the direction of the visions. In the year 2000 when I visited the transhumanist congress in London (*Transvision MM*), the name Ray Kurzweil was completely unknown to all the participants that I spoke to. I even wondered at the time whether it would be legitimate to include Kurzweil in my analyses. His writings were not

---

1 See Vonnegut 1991, 88.
2 See Krüger 2004.
3 See Krüger 2019. The bibliography for the English edition, which originally amounted to over 50 pages, has now been limited to the main sources and literature. All the Internet addresses quoted in the list of sources and in the footnotes were available, unless stated otherwise, on 12/15/2020.

particularly innovative compared to those of Frank Tipler, Hans Moravec, and Marvin Minsky. Ten years ago, I had even suspected that posthumanism and transhumanism would turn out to be short-lived phenomena, as a large number of networks and organizations had already disappeared. But then Ray Kurzweil dramatically revived the debate with his 2005 book *The Singularity is Near* and the subsequent founding of the Singularity University. Today Kurzweil is undoubtedly the central figure in this discussion. Moravec is now working mainly as an entrepreneur, Minsky died in January 2016, and Tipler is still a marginal figure, although his central idea of cosmic evolution is now widely accepted. More than in the past, religious and secular elements of progress theories are becoming intermingled. My main focus now is on the issue of singularity, the all-embracing superintelligence, and their contextualization in cultural history.

The English version of my book was written in 2019 and 2020. In the United States, where Kurzweil's supporters are proclaiming the imminent arrival of a super intelligence, the drug crisis has brought about a decline in overall life expectancy in recent years. By March 2021 the Corona pandemic has led to well over 500,000 deaths in the US. Politics in the country is rife with conspiracy theories, while scientific findings about climate change were denied by the US government under the Trump presidency and the opinions of critical scientists were ignored. The situation is reminiscent of the end of *The War of the Worlds* by H. G. Wells, in which the technically superior Martians are killed off by a common cold.

Progress is not a mathematical quantity but depends on social developments and on the structure of social knowledge. The same applies to theories of progress such as posthumanism and transhumanism, which are analyzed in this book. Their message of exponential growth can be likened to dicing with death as it finds its most radical expression in a period when the ecological and social consequences of the relentless exploitation of natural and human resources are becoming more visible and tangible every day. Perhaps this is also no coincidence.

As an academic *homo viator* (a human on a journey), I have experienced the complexity of this subject in many different libraries, and a large number of people have contributed in various ways to the success of this book. This reflects the complexity of the subject discussed here on a social level. Without the constant support of family, friends, and scholars in other disciplines this book would never have been possible in its present form.

I would like to thank the following friends and colleagues for their unwavering encouragement, for many stimulating conversations, recommendations on relevant literature, collected newspaper articles, philological advice, artistic and philosophical reflections: Hatice Çiğdem, Stefanie Elbern, Ulrike Gergaut, Stefan Guschker, Carla Hagen, Michael Hagemeister, Manfred Hammes (†), Sabine Haupt, Silja Joneleit-Oesch, Alice Kaiser, Alexandra Kraatz, Elisabeth Krüger, Janina Loh, Stephanie Majerus, Elias Maya, Karin Meiner, Susann Mende, Adriano Montefusco, Refika Sariönder, Markus Sauer, Brigitte Schön, Renate Schoch, Frank Schüller, Ricarda Stegmann, Ulrich Vollmer, Jochen Walter, Dagmar Wujastyk, Han Yan, and Helmut Zander.

I would also like to thank Frank Tipler, Max More, and Torsten Nahm (*De:Trans*) for kindly answering my questions in connection with the first edition of this book.

For their stimulating ideas and continuous support for my dissertation I would like to thank my supervisors Karl Hoheisel (†) and Gregor Ahn as well as Jan Assmann, Wolfgang Gantke, David Lavery (†), Jan Snoek, and Rudolf Wagner (†).

My special thanks go to Ralf Hoffmann, Dardo Lessmann, and Sonja Pruhs. For the first edition they accompanied the entire process of writing my thesis and enriched it with their constructive comments and discussions.

Working with my two translators Ali Jones and Paul Knight proved to be an enjoyable intellectual exchange which I greatly appreciated. I thank Graeme Currie for his solid proofreading. Finally, I would like to thank Edelgard Spaude and Torang Sinaga of the *Rombach Verlag* as well as Annika Linnemann and Dagmar Buchwald of the publishing house *transcript* for their excellent cooperation.

Oliver Krüger
Bern, Winter 2020

A *Who is Who?* of Post- and Transhumanism

Bernal, John D. (1901-1971), pioneer and prophet of transhumanist ideas. Main publication: *The World, the Flesh, and the Devil* (1929).

Bostrom, Nick (born 1973), initiator of the transhumanist movement in the 1990s, from 1998 to 2008 coordinator / chairman of the *World Transhumanist Association*, since 2005 founder and director of the Future of Humanity Institute. Main publication: *Superintelligence: Paths, Dangers, Strategies* (2014).

Brown, Bernadeane (born 1937), since the 1960s, together with Charles Paul Brown and James Russel Strole, has headed various associations such as *Eternal Flame* or *People Unlimited Inc.*, all advocating the overcoming of death.

Esfandiary, Fereidoun M. / FM-2030 (1930-2000), since the 1970s a central figure and advocate of transhumanist ideas. Main publication: *Are you a Transhuman?* (1989).

Ettinger, Robert C. W. (1918-2011), founder of cryonics. Main publication: *The Prospect of Immortality* (1964).

De Grey, Aubrey (born 1963), gerontologist with ambitious claims about aging. Head of the *SENS Research Foundation*. Main publication: *Ending Aging* (2008).

Drexler, K. Eric (born 1955), nanotechnologist, co-founder of the Foresight Institute (1986). Main publication: *Engines of Creation* (1986).

Faloon, William (Bill) (born 1954), co-founder of the *Life Extension Foundation* (1980) and the *Church of Perpetual Life* (2013), which promote the sale of supplements and advocate cryonics.

Goertzel, Ben (born 1966), IT entrepreneur, head of *humanity+* (2008-2010, and since 2018). Main publication: *A Cosmist Manifesto* (2010).

Haldane, John B. S. (1892-1964), evolutionary biologist, early prophet of transhumanist ideas. Main publication: *Daedalus; or, Science and the Future* (1924)

Hughes, James J. (born 1961), Sociologist, executive director of the *World Transhumanist Association* from 2004 to 2006, founder and head of the Institute for Ethics and Emerging Technologies (2004). Main publication: *Citizen Cyborg* (2004).

Huxley, Julian (1887-1975), evolutionary biologist, eugenicist, first director of UNESCO, early prophet of transhumanist ideas. Main publication: *Transhumanism* (1957).

Istvan, Zoltan (born 1973), American transhumanist activist whose candidature for the US presidency in 2016 attracted considerable media attention.

Kent, Saul (born 1940), cryonics specialist and co-founder of the *Life Extension Foundation* (1980).

Kurzweil, Raymond (born 1948), IT entrepreneur, since 2012 a Director of Engineering for Google, co-founder of the *Singularity University* (2008), author of futurological and life help books, leading representative of trans- and posthumanism. Main publication: *The Singularity is Near* (2005).

Leary, Timothy (1920-1996), psychologist, LSD researcher, prophet, and networker in early transhumanism. Main publication: *Chaos and Cyber Culture* (1994).

Merkle, Ralph (born 1952), computer scientist, nanotechnologist, cryonics specialist.

Minsky, Marvin (1927-2016), AI researcher at MIT, teacher of many transhumanists, leading representative of technological posthumanism.

Moravec, Hans (born 1948), roboticist. His advocacy of the abolition of human beings in favor of artificial intelligence and of robots was the founding act for technological posthumanism. He popularized the idea of the immortalization of the human mind by means of a brain scan. Main publication: *Mind Children* (1988).

More, Max (born 1964), transhumanist and cryonics specialist. Founder and head of the Extropy Institute (1991-2006), from 2011 to 2021 he served as president and CEO of cryonics company *Alcor*. Main publication: *Transhumanism* (1990).

Neumann, John von (1903-1959), American-Hungarian mathematician and computer scientist who is seen by many transhumanists as the originator of the singularity idea.

O'Neill, Gerard K. (1927-1992), physicist and prophet of space colonization, he played a key role in the founding of the L5 Society in which many later transhumanists met. Main publication: *The High Frontier* (1977).

Pearce, David, co-founder of the *World Transhumanist Association* (1998).

Prisco, Giulio (born 1957), transhumanist and cryonics specialist, co-founder of the *Order of Cosmic Engineers* (2008-2012).

Rothblatt, Martine (born 1954), entrepreneur in the fields of biotechnologies and space travel. Transhumanist and transgender activist. Main publication: *Virtually Human* (2014).

Sandberg, Anders (born 1972), neurologist, co-founder, and chairman of the *Swedish Transhumanist Association* (1996-1998), staff member of the Future of Humanity Institute (Oxford).

Sorgner, Stefan L. (born 1973), philosopher, founder of metahumanism. Main publication (as editor): *Beyond Humanism: Trans- and Posthumanism* book series (since 2014).

Stock, Gregory (born 1949), physicist and entrepreneur in the field of biotechnologies. Main publication: Metaman (1993).

Strole, James (born 1949), since the 1960s, together with Charles Paul and Bernadeane Brown, he has headed various associations such as Eternal Flame and People Unlimited Inc. In 2016 he founded the *RAADfest (Revolution Against Aging and Death)*.

Teilhard de Chardin, Pierre (1881-1955), Jesuit philosopher and paleontologist, advocate of eugenics, influential due to his ideas on the future of the universe in the divine Omega Point and the notion of the planetary noosphere in which all thinking converges. Main book: *The Phenomenon of Man* (1959).

Vinge, Vernor (born 1944), science fiction author, played a central role in developing the concept of technological singularity.

Vita-More, Natasha (born 1950), artist and transhumanist activist since the 1980s. Main publication: *The Transhumanist Reader* (ed. with Max More, 2013).

Walford, Roy L. (1924-2004), popular dietician promising to enormously prolong the natural life span. Main publication: *Maximum Life Span* (1983).

Warwick, Kevin (born 1954), cyberneticist who claims to have become the first cyborg in human history thanks to a chip implant. Main publication: *March of the Machines* (1997).

Yudkowsky, Eliezer (born 1979), AI researcher, co-founder of the Machine Intelligence Research Institute (2000). Main publication: *Singularitarian Principles* (2000).

1. Virtuality, Media, and Immortality. An Introduction

> **human** (ˊhyü-men) adj. 1. of, belonging to, or typical of the extinct species *Homo sapiens* <the human race> 2. what consisted of or was produced by *Homo sapiens* <human society> n. an extinct biped, *Homo sapiens*, characterized by carbon-based anatomy: also HUMAN BEING.[1]
> *Wired*, April 2000

The most recent surveys of media use in the United States show that the average adult spends about 12 hours a day on the consumption of media products. Six and a half of these are spent on digital media and three and a half hours on classical television.[2] There can be no doubt whatsoever that media experiences have become an integral part of everyday social life. Moreover, the experience of those with whom we interact in society is increasingly shaped by forms of virtual reproduction, whether this takes the form of fictional formats, livestreams, social media, or smartphones.

Every technological innovation is, of course, accompanied by practical considerations in which the pros and cons of the applications are weighed up alongside the costs. At the same time, a social and cultural discussion of the merits and effects of the new technology begins. This process is heterogeneous and dynamic, which means that what emerges is not a uniform and static interpretation but rather a variety of opinions that are highly contentious, that develop over time, and that are subject to further changes.

Media hermeneutics is an approach that seeks to capture these dynamic processes in the framework of sociological hermeneutics and media research. As far back as 1962, sociologists Elihu Katz and David Foulkes said that " ... the question (is) not 'what do the media do to people?' but, rather, 'What do people do with the media.' "[3] This implies rejecting claims that a certain medium has a determined effect on society, searching rather for different modes of use and reception among social groups (age,

---

1   Cover of *Wired* 8.04.
2   Dolliver 2019.
3   Katz / Foulkes 1962, 378.

gender, education, cultural / religious background), and taking historical dynamics into account. Here, media research becomes a social science. Media hermeneutics focuses on media praxis, the production, and reception of specific media contents as well as general, cultural interpretative processes of certain media.[4]

In the case of audiovisual media innovations, ranging from photography in the 19th century to the digital media of our days, virtual images and simulations of human beings have raised new questions. How should the relationship between virtuality and reality be interpreted? How do technical images change our relationship to space, time, and the body? Do these media change our ideals and the values connected to being human?

Technological posthumanism is probably the most extreme interpretation of recent media. It is extreme because it projects the utopia of a future immortality from the comparison of biological human beings with their virtual reproduction, which ultimately leads to the dissolution of the previous human being. It is also extreme because it derives a cybernetic definition of life by comparing human beings with advanced computer technology – a definition involving a technocentric re-interpretation of evolution. On this basis, posthumanism formulates an inescapable universal claim of a cosmic history of salvation. The opening quotation, in the form of a crumpled encyclopedia article on the cover of *Wired* in April 2000, reflects the scope of this ideology.

It is more than 30 years since the American roboticist Hans Moravec in his sensational work *Mind Children. The Future of Robot and Human Intelligence* formulated the vision of immortality in computers as the normative goal of human progress. The ideas of technological posthumanism and transhumanism have now found their way into literature, art, film, television, and journalism. Films such as *Transcendence* (2014) and television series such as *Altered Carbon* (2018) present dramatic scenarios of the specific possibility of computer-assisted immortalization. Michel Houellebecq's utterly bleak social analysis in his novel *Les particules élémentaires* (1998) and Dan Brown's novels *Inferno* (2013) and *Origin* (2017) have made the logics of eugenic transhumanism known to a wide audience.[5] Presently, IT entrepreneur, author, and Google employee Ray Kurzweil has exploited the posthumanist concept of singularity in line with the capitalist market to found his eponymous *Singularity University*. His ideas are now even being taught in German classrooms.

My aim in this book is to understand and explain how the posthumanist idea of immortality emerged and developed around the turn of the 21st century. This study focuses exclusively on *technological* or *speculative posthumanism*.[6]

This type of posthumanism must be distinguished from *philosophical* or *critical posthumanism*, which has also emerged in the past three decades. This variant has incorporated approaches from post-structuralist literary studies and adapted them to

---

4   See Krüger 2018, 2; Krüger / Rota 2015, 75-80; Ayaß 2012.
5   See Pfister 2014; Kalogridis 2018; Houellebecq 2000; Brown 2013, 2017.
6   I prefer the term *technological posthumanism* as this is always technocentric, i.e. according to posthumanist reasoning technological progress determines the value and the goals of life, not the other way around.

criticize Eurocentric and androcentric humanism. Stefan Herbrechter was one of the first authors to introduce the term *critical posthumanism*. Its main exponents today are Rosi Braidotti, Karen Barad, Cary Wolfe, Pramod K. Nayar, Elaine L. Graham, and Neil Badmington.[7]

The initial spark for critical posthumanism was provided by feminist thinker Donna Haraway in her 1985 publication *A Cyborg Manifesto*. In her collection of essays *Simians, Cyborgs, and Women* she discusses the "human being" as the primary focus of traditional humanism and uses the image of the cyborg, among others, to deconstruct the essentialist determinations of the "humanistic" human being.[8] The British artist Robert Pepperell declared in his 1985 *Posthuman Manifesto* that an era was now beginning in which the arrogant belief in the superiority and uniqueness of human beings would be transcended. He viewed *post-humanism* as a consequence of feminism, the fight against slavery, and the advocacy of human rights. He seeks to set limits to the exploitation of human beings and their environment: "Post-Humanism is about how we live, how we conduct our exploitation of the environment, animals, and each other ... The fact that all these movements exist suggests the gradual overturning of a hu*man*-centered world is well underway."[9]

Critical posthumanism aims above all to bring about a reform of language, science, and the epistemologies underlying them. It deals only marginally with the actual technologization of modern societies and their social consequences.[10] In her systematic analysis of critical posthumanism, Janina Loh stresses that the representatives of this movement (mostly women) are united more by their criticism of humanism than by their counter-projects.[11] Rosi Braidotti sums up the critical potential of posthumanism as follows:

> The starting point for me is the anti-humanist death of Wo/Man, which marks the decline of some of the fundamental premises of the Enlightenment, namely the progress of mankind through a self-regulatory and teleological ordained use of reason and of secular scientific rationality allegedly aimed at the perfectibility of 'Man'.[12]

These few remarks already indicate that, technological posthumanism, with its insistence on the rational perfectibility of human beings, and critical posthumanism have diametrically opposed views of the overcoming of the human being and of humanism. Loh regards the passivation of human beings as the key distinction with transhumanism. Human beings are thus degraded to the status of passive material requiring further perfection. This is particularly true of the reproductive enhancement

---

7 See Herbrechter 2013.
8 For a long time, this playing with elements of techno utopias hampered the formation of a clear distinction between technological and critical posthumanism. See Haraway 1985, 1991; Graham 2002, 200-220.
9 Pepperell 1995, 176. See ibid., 160-177.
10 A good example of this is *Posthuman Bodies* edited by Ira Livingston and Judith Halberstam. The articles in this book discuss the posthuman *gender* issue in relation to postmodern literature, film, and popular culture. See Halberstam / Livingston 1995.
11 See Loh 2018, 80-109; Braidotti 2013, 13-104; Wolfe 2010, XI-XXXIV.
12 Braidotti 2013, 37.

of unborn offspring, who can never be asked if they consent.[13] This is why Cary Wolfe also makes a clear demarcation between critical posthumanism and transhumanism: "In this respect, my sense of posthumanism is the opposite of transhumanism, and in this light, transhumanism should be seen as an intensification of humanism."[14]

The utopias of technological posthumanism were first noted in cultural studies at the beginning of the 1990s, both in discussions about art and in the reports mainly of American journalists and scientists about the wide-ranging visions of Silicon Valley's technophile subculture. In 1992 Jeffrey Deitch organized the exhibition *Post Human* about all forms of body transformation – from Michael Jackson to the plastic surgery staged by the French artist ORLAN. This was followed in 1996 by the two volumes of *Kunstforum International* edited by Florian Rötzer entitled *Die Zukunft des Körpers (The Future of the Body)*, which contained numerous articles explicitly referring to the ideas of technological posthumanism.[15] Besides artists, philosophers, art and media scholars, representatives of posthumanism such as Hans Moravec, Luc Steels, and performance artist Stelarc also expressed their viewpoints.[16] The publication of this widely read two-volume edition of *Kunstforum* likely triggered the extensive discussion of transhumanism in German.[17]

During the same period in the United States, certain journalists reported on the colorful utopias of cryonics, nanotechnologists, and the representatives of the new cyber culture, which all corresponded to various elements of posthumanist philosophy. In his 1990 *Great Mambo Chicken and the Transhuman Condition. Science Slightly over the Edge*, Ed Regis produced a wide-ranging overview of the efforts of American researchers to achieve omnipotence – efforts he regarded as symptomatic of human hubris. In 1996 Mark Dery in *Escape Velocity* and media scientist and journalist Gundolf Freyermuth provided a more detailed analyses of the futuristic vision of the computer culture in *Cyberland*.[18] More recent publications, such as *Radical Evolution* (2006) by journalist Joel Garreau and *Transcendence. The Disinformation Encyclopedia of Transhumanism and the Singularity* (2015) by cyber activist R. U. Sirius and journalist Jay Cornell, supplemented these descriptive overviews with more up-to-date insights.[19] David Lavery, a keen analyst of postmodern popular culture whose work I greatly appreciate, discussed the dreams of a space age connected with posthumanism in his 1992 book *Late for the Sky*. Many visionaries regarded the advent of the posthuman age as a precondition for the departure of earthly life into space.[20]

If we discount philosophical and art-historical works, that address the posthumanist theory of the overcoming of the human body in general terms,[21]

---

13   See Loh 2018, 54, 51-57.
14   Wolfe 2010, XV. See Bernstein 2019, 19-22.
15   See Deitch 1996, 112-115.
16   See Rötzer 1996a; Moravec 1996a; Steels 1996; Stelarc 1996.
17   See Randow 1998; Herbrechter 2009; Irrgang 2005; Sanders 2014; Krysmanski 2014; Meyer-Drawe 2014; Kluge 2014; Baedtke / Brandt / Lessing 2015; Sorgner 2016; Loh 2018.
18   See Regis 1990; Dery 1996; Freyermuth 1998.
19   See Garreau 2006; Sirius / Cornell 2015.
20   See Lavery 1992.
21   See Kroker / Kroker 1996; Davis 1998; Kamper 1999; Richard 2000; Schröter 2002; Kröner 2020.

the number of cultural studies investigations of technological posthumanism to date remains manageable. Journalist Franz Rottensteiner has done pioneering work in this area, notably in his 1997 essay on immortality in the computer, in which he pointed out that the posthumanist image of the human being was ultimately derived from cybernetic theory.[22] The following period saw the publication of a whole series of works dealing with the relationship between science fiction and general motifs in posthumanism. The monograph *How We Became Posthuman* by American literary scholar N. Katherine Hayles, which analyzes the interaction between cybernetics and science fiction, is particularly noteworthy in this connection.[23] In his anthology on singularity, philosopher Amnon H. Eden made a major contribution to the cultural study of technological posthumanism. Philosophers of technology Reinhard Heil and Christopher Coenen of the Karlsruhe Institute of Technology have enriched the debate with a number of stimulating articles on transhumanism.[24] Anthropologist Anya Bernstein has produced an outstanding book on transhumanism in Russia today. She supplements the material of her fieldwork with thorough descriptions of its overall historical and philosophical context.[25]

The most extensive discussion of posthumanism now takes place in the disciplines of philosophy and ethics, which deal with many practical issues around human enhancement. In 2001 literary scholar Raimar Zons formulated *Die Zeit des Menschen. Zur Kritik des Posthumanismus* (*The Time of Humankind. A Criticism of Posthumanism*), a philosophical response to the goals of this future utopia. The following year saw the publication of *Our Posthuman Future: Consequences of the Biotechnology Revolution* by the American political scientist Francis Fukuyama, a critical account of the social consequences of genetic engineering.[26]

In contrast to Zons und Fukuyama, Israeli philosopher Yuval Harari selectively adapts elements of the posthumanist idea of progress in his 2015 work *Homo Deus*. He envisions the development of an all-powerful, immortal human being and adapts this for his philosophical speculations on the future of humankind. In his view, the present is the dawning of the age of the Anthropocene, an age in which hunger and diseases have been eliminated, and human beings are taking creation into their own hands. As a result, immortality and divinity will develop. The world will be conquered not by Islamic fundamentalism but by techno religions, because they promise salvation through algorithms and genes. Harari sees two possible variants: One is data religion, which propagates the replacement of human beings by artificial intelligence, while the other is techno-humanism, which seeks to transform *homo sapiens* into *homo deus* (thanks to technical upgrades of the brain and of consciousness).[27]

---

22 See Rottensteiner 1997.
23 See Hayles 1999; Flessner 2000a, 2000b; Graham 2002, 38-108; Gräfrath 2000; Schenkel 2000; Tabbert 2004.
24 See Heil 2010a, 2010b; Heil / Coenen 2014; Coenen 2010; see also the collection of essays *Die Debatte über "Human Enhancement"* (Coenen et al. 2010).
25 See Bernstein 2019.
26 See Zons 2001; Fukuyama 2002.
27 See Harari 2016, 372-402.

The German philosopher Stefan L. Sorgner is even closer to the transhumanist movement.[28] Since 2014 he has edited for the publisher Peter Lang the series *Beyond Humanism: Trans- and Posthumanism / Jenseits des Humanismus: Trans- und Posthumanismus*, which now comprises nine volumes. The books in this series tend to align themselves with transhumanist discourses and tackle specific elements of transhumanist utopias in philosophical terms.[29]

The New Zealand philosopher Nicholas Agar has produced subtle analyses of many of the specific aspects of bio and neuro technologies that have characterized the ethical debate about transhumanist visions in the past two decades. While his early writings were notable for their pragmatic optimism about progress, it is now clear that he is increasingly skeptical about technocentric promises. In the splendid transhumanist scenarios, Agar notes above all the absence of a moral discussion that would enable us to make decisions about the future of humankind.[30]

In their recent publications, sociologists Fréderic Vandenberghe and Thomas Wagner and film-maker Philipp von Becker have introduced a new perspective into the debate by pointing out the parallels between transhumanist utopias and capitalist market systems.[31]

The two parts of this study focus on the posthumanist idea of immortality in virtuality. The first section, entitled *Humans and Media*, outlines the technological conditions in which posthumanism appeared on the scene at the end of the 20th century. This philosophy is not only the result of trends in cultural history, but also presupposes media experiences that have only been consolidated in recent decades. I certainly do not regard these experiences of virtuality as deterministic, but they undoubtedly exert an influence on our interpretations of time, space, and corporeality (chapter 2). The utopian, future-oriented interpretation of computers and media as carried out by technological posthumanism is itself part of this diversity of interpretation. The philosopher Günther Anders first expressed the key motif of later posthumanism when he coined the term "Promethean shame" – the feeling of inferiority and worthlessness of human beings when confronted with their perfect technological creations (chapter 3).

Many academic references in both chapters invoke the work of German- and French-speaking authors, such as postmodernist philosophers Jean-Franois Lyotard and Jean Baudrillard, media theoretician and sociologist Götz Großklaus, Dietmar Kamper, Christoph Wulf, Polish philosopher and science fiction author Stanisław Lem, and the German philosopher Günther Anders. Some of these authors have not yet been translated into English. I can only speculate at this point about why such approaches do not yet exist in English and why they have attracted relatively little interest. One reason is probably an institutional one: Media Studies in Germany has been strongly influenced by literary scholarship, art, and German studies, whereas Anglo-Saxon communication

---

28 See chapter 4.
29 See beyondhumanism.org.
30 See Agar 2010; Agar 2015.
31 See Becker 2015; Wagner 2015; Vandenberghe 2006.

studies have been and remain more focused on electronic media. The former discipline is more philosophical in its approach while the latter tends to be more pragmatic.

In addition, many of the authors mentioned overstep disciplinary boundaries and subject areas – I include myself among them. Posthumanism is an unusual research topic for a scholar of the Study of Religions. However, these phenomena, in which technological, philosophical, literary, and religious ideas intermingle, can only be adequately explored if the author is prepared to remain open to a wide variety of sources.

Posthumanism did not arise *ex nihilo*. Experiences with advanced media and computer technology have long been embedded in established cultural interpretation models, which are based above all on the European and American theory of progress, on elements of Christian salvation history, and on a cybernetic understanding of human beings. After short introductions to transhumanism (chapter 4) and technological posthumanism (chapter 5), the second part of the book focuses on the study of central aspects of technological posthumanism in the history of ideas (chapter 6). These comprise the posthumanist conception of human beings in cybernetics, followed by several aspects of progress ideology and salvation history, such as the understanding of evolution, entropy, singularity, immortality, the transcendent superintelligence, and finally the Omega Point as the ultimate goal of cosmic developments.

This study was not originally intended to be a philosophical or ethical evaluation of posthumanism, transhumanism, or even of certain computer- and biotechnologies. However, this analytical overview of the history of ideas could provide a basis for such a philosophical approach. This kind of foundational hermeneutic research sharpens our awareness of the motifs, interpretations, and values of posthumanist reasoning within their historical contexts. Our future is written here and now, just as other generations wrote theirs in the past.

Part I
Humans and Media

2. Virtuality

> IMAGES ARE IMMORTAL. BODIES ARE
> EPHEMERAL ... THE BODY NOW PERFORMS
> BEST AS ITS IMAGE.[1]
> *Stelarc*

It seems that the concept of virtuality rivals the notion of reality in the multiplicity of its meanings. Virtuality is found in cybersex machines, in the data-gloves used by surgeons, in remote-controlled military drones, in virtual dressing rooms, and in the vast numbers of selfies on social media.[2] In contrast to *cyberspace*, most authors define *virtual reality* as *each and every* form of technologically generated artificial reality.[3] In their view, the term virtual reality covers not only the usual suspects such as flight simulators and computer games but also television, radio, and music apps on smartphones. It does not matter at this stage whether these virtual realities reproduce fictional (e.g. the fantastic worlds of computer games) or actual events (e.g. television broadcasts).

In the English-speaking world, the author William Gibson is cited as the originator of virtual reality and of cyberspace.[4] However, if we trace the emergence of this concept we will inevitably be confronted with the *Summa Technologiae* published by Polish philosopher Stanisław Lem in 1964.[5] In his first work of philosophy Lem not only coined the term "phantomology" to describe the possibilities of a technologically generated artificial reality, he also conceived the idea of screen glasses, a forerunner of today's Google Glass.[6]

Lem points out that, in encounters with virtual reality, a divergence always opens up between external action and internal experience. Regardless of whether a filmgoer bursts into tears at the virtual death of a movie hero or a student pilot breaks out in a

---

1   Stelarc 1998, 123.
2   Flessner 1997a, 7-8.
3   See Baudrillard 1994; Flusser 2011; Flessner 1997a; Lem 2010, 191-234.
4   The term *cyberspace* first appeared in 1984 in William Gibson's novel *Neuromancer*. See Gibson 2000.
5   Flessner 1996, 7.
6   Lem terms the screen glass an "anti-eye". See Lem 2010, 191-234; Flessner 1996, 8.

nervous sweat when operating a flight simulator, there is always a bifurcation between inner experience and external action in the cinema or the flight simulator:

> A bifurcation would occur within his sensations – between what he is feeling and observing and what he is doing. This bifurcation would be a consequence of the separation of his current motor activity from his earlier sentient activity recorded by us.[7]

This would mean that the starting point for determining virtuality would not be a simplistic opposition between reality and virtual illusions. Rather, it would have its origin in the nature of human perception itself – in the concept of an anthropology of the senses as developed by Helmuth Plessner:

> In human experience, the world consists of senses: the sense of color in the eyes, the sense of sound in the ears, the sense of touch on the surface of their body and of our limbs. Our knowledge of the world comes from the sensations of our senses.[8]

The Canadian media theoretician Marshall McLuhan first connected the question of the media's impact to the conditions of perception: the senses of human beings. He regarded media as a kind of extension of the human body. Transcending time and space, media can produce mainly visual or acoustic perceptions of an event for a recipient by means of imitation (painting) or technical simulation (computers, television). As a result, the nature of our physical senses is permanently transformed.[9]

> If a technology is introduced either from within or from without a culture, and if it gives new stress or ascendancy to one or another of our senses, the ratio among all of our senses is altered. We no longer feel the same, nor do our eyes and ears and other senses remain the same.[10]

At this point, I would like to introduce a concept that will perhaps make certain distinctions easier to grasp as they appear over the coming pages. As a counterpart to the concept of life-world (*Lebenswelt*) developed by Alfred Schütz, the world of experience (*Erlebniswelt*) marks the area of reality which the waking and "normal" adult, adopting a common sense approach, does *not* perceive as simply given, for it eludes immediate sense perception. The concept of the world of experience describes everything that is objectively present in one form or another but is not fundamentally given and "real".[11]

The brief examples above illustrate two points: Virtual realities are not realities that spring from the exuberant imagination of an individual, nor are they realities that are immediately accessible to our everyday life-world, i.e. that which *can be experienced* visibly, tangibly, or spatially. Virtual reality nowadays refers to the visual, acoustic and, less frequently, haptic simulation of *real* or *fictional* experiences. These perceptions no longer depend primarily on the physical constitution of the individual, but rather on

---

7   See Lem 2010, 194.
8   Plessner 1980, 25, trans. by PK.
9   See McLuhan 1994, 7-21; McLuhan 2002, 5-7.
10 McLuhan 2002, 28-29.
11 See Schutz / Luckmann 1974, 25-44.

technology. In this context, Bernd Flessner aptly refers to *world prostheses* as opposed to *prosthetic worlds*.[12]

Within the relevant literature virtual reality has not yet been explicitly contrasted with virtuality as such. We can think of "virtual reality" more as a particular "reality" or experience world – for example the virtual reality of the Grand Canyon as experienced in the simulation of a VR headset. In contrast, virtuality can be understood as the totality of virtual realities available in a specific medium, for example the virtuality of the Internet or of television.

After these more general remarks, it is now necessary to look in greater detail at those aspects of virtuality that have a decisive impact on human perception. Virtuality alters our interpretation and perception of time, space, and bodies. It constitutes a specific interpretation framework for reality and for the imaginary, a framework that favors certain interpretations of media. These aspects will be discussed in the following chapters.

2.1 Virtuality and Time

> Media reality turns out to be a construct in time; media reality is created strictly in the present.[13]
> *Götz Großklaus*

What role does the time of virtuality – media time – play in the development of human consciousness of time? We are interested more specifically in the structural conditions for the representation of temporality – the transitory nature of human beings in electronic media – especially in television and in computer-assisted media applications. Berlin sociologist Dietmar Kamper once wrote that all media are "time machines in disguise". The following reflections are based on sociological theories of time formulated by Alfred Schütz, Norbert Elias, Armin Nassehi, Klaus Beck, and Götz Großklaus. These social theories of time that ultimately also analyze the specific relationship between media and time are based on a lengthy philosophical development in which the philosophers Henri Bergson, Helmuth Plessner, and Edmund Husserl are central figures. A brief outline of their theories is given in the following paragraphs.[14]

There is no doubt that all human activity, and hence all forms of human experience, are inextricably linked with the existence of time. Time can be understood here as physically measurable and evenly distributed (Newton). Against the background of quantitative-scientific and qualitative-hermeneutic perceptions, the French philosopher Henri Bergson introduced the crucial distinction between external and internal time, which would remain valid for all subsequent philosophies of time. In Bergson's view, duration (*durée*) is not something that is intrinsic to objects, but

---

12 See Flessner 1991.
13 Großklaus 1997, 45, trans. by PK.
14 See Kamper 1995; Nassehi 1993; Beck 1994; Großklaus 1997.

rather is a product of the human process of consciousness that cannot be reduced to the quantitative aspect of spatialized time. Bergson's theory of time maintains that the temporal structure of consciousness not only generates experience but is also generated *by* experience. Bergson's dichotomy between quantitative and qualitative time was important for the sociology of time. But his philosophy of the consciousness of time, which conceptualizes time as a free, natural, and constitutive element of personal experience, is relevant only within his specific school of thought, the philosophy of life (*Lebensphilosophie*).[15]

Helmuth Plessner interpreted the *durée* of natural time, which was postulated by Bergson in its continuous becoming and unbecoming through the flow of experience, as a pre-Christian consciousness of time. This presupposes a cyclical unity between passing, return, and survival. He argues that it is only the emergence of the Judeo-Christian consciousness of time, with its individual and collective eschatology, that gives form to the notion of the definitive and transitory nature of the present. Thanks to the idea of resurrection, the linear conception of time in Christianity makes the present absolutely irretrieveable. For Plessner, time in its Christian linearity means, above all, the transience of the present.[16]

In his phenomenology of the inner consciousness of time, Edmund Husserl focuses exclusively on the role of the human subject in the perception and experience of temporal manifestations:

> Just as the actual thing, the actual world, is not a phenomenological datum, neither is world time, the real time, the time of nature in the sense of natural science and even in the sense of psychology as the natural science of the psychic.[17]

Husserl directs the epistemological question of the possibility and nature of the experience of time toward those manifesting themselves in the psychic subject. Subjective time cannot be grasped as a measurable quantity that elapses evenly. Rather, it is a phenomenon that originates in the consciousness and has a multi-layered structure.[18]

The sociologist Alfred Schütz explicitly invokes Edmund Husserl and Henri Bergson's ideas when he connects the question of the meaning of social action with the problem of time. He concludes that it is only the creation of unity in the flow of consciousness in time that produces meaning. The meaning of an experience thus consists in the integration of this particular experience in the given overall context of experiences, which then operates as an interpretation model for new experiences. The problem of meaning thus becomes a temporal problem, because the latter becomes a condition for the production of internal duration. Like Bergson, Schütz distinguishes between internal and external time, and refers to the connection between this concept of time and the sociological theory of action:

---

15   See Nassehi 1993, 35-58.
16   See Plessner 1952, 355-362.
17   Husserl 1991, 4-5. See ibid., 4-8.
18   See ibid.

Inner time and world-time are both irreversible. But thinking, an action located exclusively in inner time, is revocable in a way that does not hold true for operation. Operation engages in the outside world and takes place in world-time: what has happened, has happened.[19]

For Schütz, the temporal structure of our inter-subjective experiences, "social time", becomes particularly evident given the inevitable approach of death:

The expectation of my death as a definitive departure (from the life-world) also arises out of my existence in the intersubjective world. Others become older, die, and the world continues on (and I in it). It is indeed one of my basic experiences that I become older. I become older; thus I know that I will die and I know that the world will continue. I know that there are limits to my duration.[20]

Even though Alfred Schütz did not explicitly define a sociological theory of time, his observations on the theory of time remain an important contribution to an interactionist and thus a sociological reflection on time.[21]

Sociologist Norbert Elias adopted a similar approach in his essay *Time*, arguing that the increasing consciousness of time, the experience of and feeling for time, and the various acts of representing time are embedded in the overall process of the civilization of humanity.[22] For Elias time is a social construction: "Time is an expression of the fact that people try to define positions, the duration of intervals, the speed of changes and suchlike for the purpose of orientation."[23]

With a clear nod in the direction of Schütz, and taking up George Herbert Mead's action theory and Alfred North Whitehead's process theory, sociologist Armin Nassehi develops a concept of social time that seeks to avoid the trap of being one-sidedly derived from so-called objective or cosmic time, or remaining dependent upon the temporality of intentional first-person subjects. This operative time presupposes present actions as final temporal units that join forces as they emerge. According to Nassehi, the "primordial presents" of the emerging flow of time are not the experiences of consciousness (Bergson, Husserl) but rather actions themselves.[24]

It is noteworthy in this context that the sociologist Niklas Luhmann reminded us of a largely forgotten theory of time that is of fundamental importance in our context, as elaborated in the 18th century by the philosopher Luc de Clapiers, Marquis de Vauvenargues.[25] In contrast to current theories of interaction that seek to understand action in terms of the meaning intended by the actors and the motives of the subject, Vauvenargues proposes that we define action as a counter-movement to the flow of time:

---

19   Schutz / Luckmann 1989, 18.
20   Schutz / Luckmann 1974, 47.
21   See ibid., 45-58; Schutz / Luckmann 1989, 14-18; Nassehi 1993, 84-98.
22   See Elias 1993, 1-36.
23   Ibid., 36.
24   See Nassehi 1993, 126-130.
25   See Luhmann 1979.

> It is not possible to condemn the activity without accusing the natural order. It is wrong to claim that it is our anxiety that conceals the present from us; the present escapes us of its own accord and annihilates itself despite our efforts. All our thoughts are mortal and we cannot hold them back; and if our soul were not aided by this tireless activity, which repairs the perpetual flow of our spirit, we would not last for a moment ... We cannot hold back the present except by an action that breaks free of the present ... this activity, which destroys the present, also recalls it, reproduces it and charms the evils of life.[26]

When Vauvenargues identifies action as a countermovement to the transience of time,[27] this already indicates the important role that media play in the social construction of temporality, as well as the transience of human life. Media theoretician Klaus Beck therefore stresses the role of *media action* in the mediation of social time as an element of social knowledge:

> Media use and reception in terms of interaction theory can be understood as *media action*, which, like all actions, has a time and a meaning structure ... media action can be read as a mediation process of social time in which the media action of the communicators and of the users / recipients intertwine because both actors perceive their partners and their actions in a highly typified and anonymized form.[28]

According to Klaus Beck, human communication is inextricably linked to the construction of meaning and the reciprocal construction of the Other, whether this construction takes a direct form or occurs via medial communication. From Beck's constructivist perspective, objective physical time is not reproduced and depicted by our perception, but rather is constructively generated. The time modes of present, future, and past as well as the time qualities of duration, repetition, and sequence are cognitive constructions because they are determined by the structure of our perception and not by the nature of the external world.[29]

The significance of the experience of time in relation to virtuality becomes clear when we consider Hans Michael Baumgartner's supposition that the origin of human temporal experience is closely connected to existential loss.[30] However, media negate the life-world conditions of human temporal experience, thus opening up a third escape route from the dilemma of the irretrievable present, in addition to the cyclic and the progressive interpretations of time.

The invention of writing makes a new temporal experience of past events possible, which extends beyond the purely mental act of remembering. Jan Assmann and Peter Gendolla explicitly regard the invention of writing as the act of overcoming death: an attempt to capture an individual's glorious life and endow it with immortality.[31] Readers of written documents know that these items were produced in the past, yet they can

---

26 Vauvenargues 1857, 94-95, trans. by PK. See Luhmann 1979, 65.
27 See Vauvenargues 1857, 94-95; Luhmann 1979, 65-66.
28 Beck 1994, 114, trans. by PK.
29 See ibid., 43-44, 71.
30 See Baumgartner 1994, 210.
31 See Assmann 1993, 64-66; Gendolla 1992b, 22-26.

also be read as if they were statements in the present. Readers and writers create a – literally medial – present by pretending that readers and writers are actually present.[32] Thomas Luckmann points out that in societies without writing systems, borderlines are not sharply established between the abstract categories of time and the social time of "pure intersubjectivity". By contrast, in societies that have developed written systems, the abstract temporal categories have become completely divorced from immediate everyday experience and have instead become part of scientific or religious specialist knowledge. Thanks to modern technology – calendars, watches, smartphones, and smartwatches – abstract categories of time now permeate all levels of social life, even including social interaction and control.[33]

Photography, the first technical medium for images that visually simulates past events, radically disconnects us from the natural time cycle of our neuro-physiological perceptions, and it does so in two ways: by means of accelerated temporal access, as well as by freezing an instant in time. Photography involves a new kind of present in regard to the temporal capture of a moment and its preservation: "arrested, the past present extends into the present that we are living at this moment – as an image."[34] Photography acquires its relevance through the simulation of past (visual) contexts of experience:

> The advantage of photography is that it enables the representation of the intensive past moment to be repeated at will, and in the secondary perception of the image it makes possible the simulation of a primary experience that may well have been insignificant.[35]

Photography thus enforces a new codification of space and time because the photographic image, through the material trace left behind by the "real", confirms the authenticity of what "really happened". It shows us the technical simulation of real persons and spaces in a "past condition", but now as manifestations of real presence.[36]

Roland Barthes regards photographs as "emanations of past realities". He argues that, given the disappearance of a historical interval, the present act of looking can be described as concentration – an accumulation of interval time.[37] No other scholar has so effectively stressed the subtle connection between death and photography as Barthes in his essay *La Chambre Claire*. The photograph provides momentary access to what once was, which means that the individual history of the bourgeoisie can be visually captured. The family album is thus considered a private "miniature museum". In this context, Günther Anders refers to "immortality in one's lifetime", which the average citizen realizes through photographs, but which film stars – such as the *immortal Garbo* – have already perfected.[38]

---

32 See Beck 1994, 171.
33 See ibid., 113; Luckmann 1986.
34 Großklaus 1997, 17, trans. by PK.
35 Ibid., 19, trans. by PK.
36 See ibid., 33; Barthes 1981, 76-77.
37 See Barthes 1981, 85-89.
38 See ibid., 92-97; Großklaus 1997, 18; Anders 1983, 57-58.

In contrast to capturing a moment in a photo, film and, subsequently, television, video, and digital film media produce a succession of individual images, and hence the sequence of an event. In this filmic representation (expansion, compression, time leaps) time becomes visible.[39] It is only with the advent of film that it becomes possible to simulate the *course* of time: "It is with film that what could be called the mimesis of time begins. The course of time and temporality – in contrast to the photographically frozen moment – now become visible for the first time."[40] Nevertheless, temporality is conserved in this medium too – Thomas Macho aptly refers to the preservation of our dead in the medium of television.[41] Götz Großklaus sums this up with regard to television and computer media: "If we constantly transfer the past into the present of media reality – and the future into the present of computer simulation – then we are increasingly living in an artificial present of moments without distance ... ".[42]

Computer simulations and virtual realities as programmed models of objects, events, and sequences can create three different relations to real time. They simulate that which no longer exists (but was "real"); that which does not yet exist (but is "really" possible); and that which does not exist (but is possible as a "simulation").[43] Großklaus argues that computers will ultimately realize the goal of the modernist project, i.e. the elimination of temporal and spatial distances. Current scenarios produce simulations of past and future sequences of events and endow them with the visibility of the present.[44] Similarly, at the beginning of the 1990s, before the Internet became widely used, Klaus Beck wrote that, thanks to the influence of the new electronic mass media, indications were emerging of a tendency towards the expansion of the present and hence of a "shrinking of the past".[45]

But what does the medial construction of time mean for the human consciousness of time? Do we historicize our present by the historical relation to real and fictional worlds of virtuality? With regard to this question, I agree with Götz Großklaus:

> I think that the tendency of the entire modernization process is to abolish temporal and spatial distance, and to expand and compress the field of the present. Everything is moving in the direction of being the present, to be here, to happen now... In the case of photography we are at the beginning of this development. Photography does not tolerate the emergence of the past, it does not allow the emergence of distance or that something moves away. Again and again, the image insists that we bring to mind the past ...[46]

In virtuality, past, future, and fictional worlds are *presented*, thus creating a time of its own that emerges from real time and is independent of its contents. A distinction could

---

39 See Großklaus 1997, 22-30.
40 Ibid., 22, trans. by PK.
41 See Macho 1994, 433.
42 Großklaus 1997, 45, trans. by PK.
43 See ibid., 53-54.
44 See ibid., 53-57.
45 See Beck 1994, 344.
46 Großklaus 1997, 21, trans. by PK. Günther Anders interprets photography similarly. See Anders 1983, 179-181.

be made here between the time of the social life-world, as opposed to the experiential time induced by the media. This difference is perceived all the more intensively the more our attention is absorbed by media action. Computer games or endlessly surfing YouTube lead players and users to quickly forget the social time of the life-world.

Vauvenargues believed that action is a necessary countermovement to the irretrievability of the present. The visualization of real, real-possible, and fictional action and, more importantly, of emotional experience in virtuality, provides a further opportunity to forget the transience of the present within a conception of time dominated by linearity. Media specialist Götz Großklaus argues that tendencies toward the dissolution of the western linear conception of time are reflected in the specific features of virtual media.[47]

In light of human mortality, the media-induced experience of time makes possible the replacement of subjective temporality and the sense of human finitude. Really "being" means the possibility of being present at any time. Here we have to read Günther Anders' idea of denial of the human "uniqueness" as the subject in terms of Vauvenargues' notion of temporal uniqueness: "It [the medial reproduction] is a large-scale counter-measure designed to destroy the general belief that 'I am unique'."[48] "Reality is produced by reproduction. Being exists only in the plural, in the serial form – or conversely: Just once does not count; the merely unique does not exist; the singular still belongs to the category of non-being."[49]

The electronic media, which has ceased to imitate real human beings mimetically but – to our audio-visual perception – simulates real human beings only technically, provides our social knowledge with an *image* of the human being released from the temporal conditionality. Götz Großklaus has aptly described this development as follows: "The history of the media is a history of increasing symbolic control of non-present distant times and distant places."[50] However, this also implies symbolic control of non-present people from distant times and spaces. The next chapter is devoted to these non-present spaces.

2.2 Virtuality and Space

> It once again made an enormous impression on me when they put on the radio and leaped from London to Rome, from Rome to Moscow, etc. The concepts of time and space are annihilated. One must become a mystic.[51]
>
> *Victor Klemperer*

---

47   See Großklaus 1997, 40-42; McLuhan 2002, 334-335.
48   Anders 1983, 57, trans. by PK.
49   Ibid., 180, trans. by PK.
50   Großklaus 1997, 33, trans. by PK.

To understand virtuality, it is also essential to study its spatial aspects. For human beings, space is not perceived as a mathematical-Euclidean, immaterial abstraction, but rather as a social experience of the limits and movements of our bodies in space – an experienced space that as *homo viator* we literally pass through. As the philosopher Otto Friedrich Bollnow puts it "In order to conceptualize these conditions, we must speak of an experienced space, by which we mean the space that opens up to concrete human life."[52] The perception of our own bodies in space is constitutive both for the motor control of the parts of the body, and in a higher sense for human identity:

> It is about ... the relationship between human beings and their space, and thus about the structure of human existence itself, insofar as this is determined by its relation to space. In this sense, we speak of the spatiality of human existence.[53]

Human beings perceive space visually, acoustically, haptically, and olfactorily. Proximity and distance are constructed by means of complex receptive mechanisms, as well as from a vast collection of existing experiential values. The new technologies of movement that have emerged since the 19th century have fundamentally altered our perception of space. Indeed, the opening of space by roads and paths, and medieval modes of transport such as horses and carriages, were soon rapidly superseded by railways hosting trains. As a method of "space shrinkage" this made a strong impression on the 19th century poet Heinrich Heine.[54] Götz Großklaus points out that the invention of these technologies of movement coincided with the discovery of a new technical medium:

> Simultaneously from the 1830s and 1840s onwards, the new movement machines (railway, steamship) and the new pictorial and communication media (photography, telegraphy, phonography) eliminate spatial distances and interstices and obliterate temporal-historical intervals. This has the dual effect of temporal-spatial contraction and the creation of concentrated points – or the expansion and networking of these points to form time and space fields. In these fields or networks, the old intervals have become short switch-points, super-fast signal run times, instantaneous access and retrieval processes, they have in fact shrunk to live and real-time processes with simultaneous expansion of the networks.[55]

It is obvious that, at the latest with the invention of telegraphy and the railway, traditional distinctions between various civilizations, between near and far, and between public and private space start to be shaken up.[56]

The impact of the invention of new transmission and reproduction media was to prove even more dramatic than the acceleration of human movement through space. Firstly, the experience of space increasingly became dissociated from actual movement

---

51 Klemperer 1998, 139.
52 Bollnow 1997, 18, trans. by PK.
53 Ibid., 22. See ibid., 13-25.
54 See ibid., 96-101; Großklaus 1997, 72-79; Schivelbusch 1977, 37.
55 Großklaus 1997, 37, trans. by PK.
56 See ibid., 72-102.

in space. Secondly, it was now possible to technologically simulate images of spaces, i.e. to visually capture spatiality. Admittedly, in paintings and in mosaics of antiquity there were a number of surprisingly successful representations of three-dimensional space,[57] but it was not until the middle of the 19th century with the invention of the Daguerreotype (1837) that the technical reproduction of visual spatiality became possible. Nature is no longer imitated in a mimetic process by the subjective talent of an artist, but rather its physical qualities are objectively captured and made visible by the lens of a camera, with the aid of suitable storage and reproduction media (photographic paper, film, magnetic tapes, television and computer screens, smartphone displays) whose methods are constantly improving. Spatiality is now simulated by technology. In the same year that Louis Daguerre made his great discovery, Samuel Morse developed the telegraph, making the transmission of news independent of a material carrier and a messenger who had to move physically through space. Information could be transmitted by means of energy differences. In this way, images of spaces gradually detached themselves from actual space.[58]

> With the emergence of new and modern media, with photography, film, radio, and television, every real event, no matter where or when it happens, can become a close-up event thanks to its medial image.[59]

Through film and later through television, the Internet and mobile telephony, not only single images but entire image sequences could now simulate human action and movement in space. Without the need for a single movement by the observer in real space, television and live streaming online bring the world into our living rooms or studies, thus overcoming all spatial distance and, in the presence of those who are absent, replacing presence by presentation. Günther Anders recognized this principle.[60] The spatial distance between the viewer and the object can be further artificially reduced by altering the camera distance.

In line with the preceding distinctions, the perception of virtual reality becomes characterized by the coexistence of a "living space" in the life-world and an "experience space" in the virtual medium. Both spaces may really exist – as for example in the transmission of a football match. But for the live-streaming viewer in question, only the room in which he or she is located can be really experienced, whereas the experience space is mediated by technology, and the temporal and spatial presence of the observer is virtually available, but no social preconditions are imposed for participating in the event.

In a wider cultural and historical context, British sociologist Anthony Giddens argues that the transition from the traditional to the modern world is marked by an increasing disjunction between space and time, a process he calls *disembedding*. As a result, habits and practices are freed from their local constraints, and numerous possibilities of change emerge alongside with the onset of modernity: "By disembedding

---

57   The panopticon is the culmination of this pre-technological representation of spatiality.
58   See Hammel 1994, 62-70.
59   Großklaus 1997, 97, trans. by PK.
60   See Anders 1983, 114-134.

I mean the 'lifting out' of social relations from local contexts of interaction and their restructuring across indefinite spans of space-time."[61] From this perspective, media experiences are generally independent of their original social space. The ability to perceive spatial and acoustic signals makes "tele-present" participation in distant and perhaps socially inaccessible events possible – for example sessions of the UK Parliament. Communication and interaction – and hence sociality and identity – become detached from their local and social constraints but also from their original, identity-forming spatial community.[62]

2.3 Virtuality and Corporeality

> The central event of the 20th century is the overthrow of matter. In technology, economics, and the politics of nations, wealth – in the form of physical resources – has been losing value and significance. The powers of mind are everywhere ascendant over the brute force of things.[63]
> *The Magna Carta of Cyberspace*

The above reflections on the changes to our experience of time and space brought about by electronic media have also clearly shown that these changes go hand in hand with alterations to the perception of the materiality and corporeality of our environment. Soon after the discovery of telegraphy and photography, the American doctor and poet Oliver Wendell Holmes Sr. drew some thoroughly postmodern conclusions in an essay of 1859:

> *Form is henceforth divorced from matter.* In fact, matter as a visible object is of no great use any longer, except as the mould on which form is shaped. Give us a few negatives of a thing worth seeing, taken from different points of view, and that is all we want of it. Pull it down or burn it up, if you please. We must, perhaps, sacrifice some luxury in the loss of color; but form and light and shade are the great things, and even color can be added, and perhaps by and by may be got direct from Nature ... There is only one Coliseum or Pantheon; but how many millions of potential negatives have they shed, representatives of billions of pictures, since they were erected! Matter in large masses must always be fixed and dear; form is cheap and transportable. We have got the fruit of creation now, and need not trouble ourselves with the core.[64]

Holmes' reflections are relevant for considering experiences of materiality and concrete corporeality as increasingly shaped by electronic media. The human body itself is a

---

61 Giddens 1990, 21. See ibid., 21-29.
62 See ibid., 26-29.
63 Dyson et al. 1994, 1.
64 Holmes 1859, 747.

product of our perceptions, while simultaneously being our cognitive apparatus. The psychologist Jean Piaget stressed the physical aspect in the development of intelligence, and the philosopher Arnold Gehlen attributed the higher development of human beings to their physical conditionality. Wilhelm Dilthey argued that our belief in the reality of the external world is partly based upon our experience of the material resistance of the world. Human cognition and identity are, to a large degree, dependent on the material form of the human body, its perceptual possibilities, as well as our own perceptions of the body. According to art theoretician Karlheinz Lüdeking, the perception of bodies on television, the Internet, and computer games differs considerably from that of everyday life in the real world.[65]

> The spatial anchoring of our bodies in the here and now is increasingly being eroded by the sensory and motor limitations of our bodies. Even without robots or virtual dolls we transcend our sensory and motor limitations in every new form of technology and in every man-machine system. Our experience, which is always dependent on our body, changes thanks to these extensions or prostheses. Our body no longer ends with our skin when we drive a car or move a remote-controlled robot ... Our body image is shaped by what we experience and feel through our bodies and by what we do (and must do) with it.[66]

French philosopher Jean-François Lyotard identified the immateriality of reality via the spread of electronic media as one of the essential characteristics of postmodernism. In *Immaterialität und Postmoderne* from 1985 he explains:

> Research and development in techno-science, art and technology, even politics nowadays creates the impression that reality, whatever it may be, is constantly becoming more and more ungraspable, that it can never be directly controlled ... Moreover, we hardly ever intervene in the reality that we wish to transform. Work at home or in the workplace requires more and more equipment (*matériels*). Manual, visual and olfactory contact with material is disappearing ... It is as if a filter had been placed between ourselves and objects, a screen of numbers ... With the coding and decoding systems we learn that there are realities that are intangible in the new way... Reality consists of elements that are organized according to structural laws (matrices), according to time criteria that no longer bear any relation to human space and time scales.[67]

Compared to the present situation, Lyotard is only describing a transitional phase. In the 1980s, philosophy acknowledged that *perception* and *change* of reality were increasingly being shaped by immaterial media, such as television or computers. During and after the 1990s, humankind found itself embarking upon a new type of existence in which an ever-greater part of experience was made not *through* but *with* immaterial, virtual realities. Today, to a greater extent than ever before, actions seek to make changes *in* virtual areas of experience – instead of making changes in the

---

65 See Hayles 1999, 220-221; Gebauer 1984, 234-235.
66 Lüdeking 1996, 66, trans. by PK.
67 Lyotard et al. 1985, 10-11, trans. by PK; published only in German.

material world *through* immaterial media. The like/dislike culture of social media largely relates only to digitally optimized images – the real-world events to which these images refer are not actually consequential, or in fact often even anything close to their online portrayal.

A crucial aspect of this new understanding of reality is the changed perception of the human body, as Lüdeking has already emphasized. Here in most cases corporeal experience refers not so much to the experience of one's own body as to the perception or interactive control of other real or fictitious bodies. Even though haptic and movement-responsive simulations such as those made possible by Nintendo Wii are now available and omnipresent acoustic virtualization began with the invention of the phonograph, the most important forms of virtuality in television, computers, Internet, and mobile telephony remain dominated by images.[68]

With the intellectual Enlightenment of Europe, the eye – imitating the supervising Baroque eye of God – assumed increasing dominance. This led to a serious narrowing down of perception, until practically monopolized by the sense of sight. The ability to experience the world as a whole with all our senses has been superseded by the visually dominated world, as well as by self-perception, which transforms the sensation of one's own presence in the body's sensory reaction to the world of objects. However, the eye's power fails precisely in the differentiation between reality and phantasms.[69] Vilém Flusser emphasizes this dominance of images in European cultural history:

> What we can no longer challenge is the dominance of technical images in this future society … This essay is about the universe of technical images, the universe that for the past few decades has been making use of photographs, films, videos, television screens, and computer terminals to take over the task formerly served by linear texts, that is, the task of transmitting information crucial to society and to individuals. It is concerned with a cultural revolution whose scope and implications we are just beginning to suspect.[70]

A technical image simulates a visually perceptible reality. According to Flusser, artistic images are abstractions of phenomena, while technical images are concretizations of objective abstractions.[71] The technical image corresponds to the reality that we *could* perceive with our eyes. It does not require any imagination on the part of the subject, who would have to engage in a thought process to construct sensually perceptible images from abstract, linguistic symbols. Unlike artistic images, technical images do not leave empty spaces for exercising the subjective imagination. The technically generated image of the body now de-contextualizes the body, stripping it of its material context. As image telegraphy and the subsequent digitalization of visual representations develop in the 20th century, the image of the body becomes the sum of

---

68 See McLuhan 2002, 275-283.
69 See Wulf 1984, 22-23.
70 Flusser 2011, 4-5.
71 Technical images as defined by Flusser refer to photographs and to images on television and on computers. They do not refer to artistic images (even those that are created using computers). See Flusser 2011, 5-23.

mathematically defined states. The image of the body becomes immaterial – it becomes information.

Through this altered perception of the body, this technical image creates a new relation to time and space. This occurs because such images are arbitrarily reproducible in time and space: "The images take on a life of their own, creating 'de-spatialized spaces' and 'de-temporalized temporality', into which they draw the viewer."[72]

Sociologist Dietmar Kamper places this development of technical images and the related emergence of a new understanding of the body into a wider historical context. He understands the history of civilization as the planned appropriation of nature – as the (intellectual) generalization of the (physical) specific. However, he also interprets it as the unstoppable abstraction and formalization of all content: the mindless corporeal subsumed under a bodiless mind.[73] Posthumanist and corporeal utopias enabled by genetics thus appear as a continuation of the modern discourse on the body, as formulated in various aspects, particularly those of Norbert Elias and Michel Foucault. Increasing control of the body is a characteristic of the bourgeois society of the 19th century, whereas older, moral perspectives have been largely replaced today by criteria such as efficiency or the variety of experience.[74] The removal of the human body by means of linguistic abstractions, repression, law, and prohibition or, more recently, by normative image abstraction, serves as a means of finding one's bearings in the world. Bodies are reduced from their original multiplicity to zero dimensionality – from presence to absence.[75] The stages of this abstraction are marked firstly by bodiless language, secondly by the speechless image, and finally by the imageless sign in its digital reproducibility.[76]

Technical images appear to be freed from their material carriers (in fact they depend on electronic hardware, whose production has enormous physical consequences for human beings and for the environment). At the same time, these technical images are mathematically completely determinable and controllable. In principle, this means that body images are also technically completely determinable and controllable. They can be manipulated at will. The free choice and design of virtual bodies (avatars) in computer games and in certain online communication and gaming applications suggest hope for the ability to construct new versions of our own corporeal identity in virtual space.

2.4 Virtuality, Reality, and the Imaginary

> We live in a society of coffee without caffeine, chocolate without sugar and virtuality as reality without reality.[77]
> *Slavoj Žižek*

---

72 Wulf 1984, 42, trans. by PK.
73 See Kamper 1976, 8.
74 See Elias 1982; Schröter 2002, 88-89.
75 See Kamper 1999, 7.
76 See ibid., 145-146.

The change of meaning that accompanies electronic media culminates in the dissolution of the traditional concept of reality. The interpenetration of virtual experiences and the real life-world makes it hard to distinguish between virtuality and reality. Nobody foresaw the media's erosion of the traditional concept of reality more lucidly than Günther Anders in his 1956 essay *Die Welt als Phantom und Matrize* (*The World as Phantom and Matrix*).

> Just as life is conceived as a dream, and dreams are conceived of as life, today all reality appears as a phantom and every phantom seems real. Where every real event acquires an illusory character by its transmission, the illusory action is bound to lose its specific aesthetic character ... in transmission.[78]

Stanisław Lem also dramatized and bizarrely exaggerated this phenomenon of dwindling reality in 1971 in *The Futurological Congress*.[79] After Günther Anders and Stanisław Lem, the dissolution of reality by virtual worlds has often been invoked almost hyperbolically.[80] The resumé of writer and computer artist Herbert W. Franke tends in a similar direction, but also involves a useful distinction:

> Regardless of positive or negative expectations, this technology confronts us with questions of a quite different kind, for example the distinction between reality and appearance ... Up to now we have known only the virtual spaces of our imagination, and statements made about these problems are based on psychological experiences that we have had in our perceptions and in mental images. But now a third possibility opens up in the shape of virtual spaces ... [81]

Franke refers here to our perceptions of the world, our statements about it, and finally to virtuality. On the basis of this approach, I would like to propose a heuristic model that distinguishes between reality, virtuality, and the imaginary. This is not an attempt to produce a new ontology – that would raise a huge number of additional philosophical and psychological issues. Rather, the object of this exercise is simply to arrive at a more precise definition of virtuality via the relationship between reality and the imaginary. Adopting a variety of approaches, I will try to delineate these three aspects more precisely. The crucial question here is: What is the significance of the experience of and with virtuality? This question will focus specifically upon the quality of human sensory perception.[82]

Reality here means the life-world that can be immediately experienced using human senses.[83] The fact that constructivist and sociolinguistic theories argue that there is no

---

77 *Funkhausgespräche* (radio broadcast WDR5) with Oskar Negt and Slavoj Žižek of 9/20/2001.
78 Anders 1983, 143, trans. by PK.
79 See Lem 1974.
80 See Lyotard 1985; Kamper 1995; Flusser 2011, 5-15; Baudrillard 1994, 9-10.
81 Franke 1997, 366.
82 The perception of the world by animals or by means of physical measurements is not relevant for the question of virtuality. This is because virtuality is part of media experiences that are produced especially for the sensory perceptive capacities of human beings.
83 The alternative of defining reality as "everything that can be understood independently of human perception" would seem to imply that statements about the world can be made based on objective

objective world independent of the observer's activity is not relevant for this heuristic model. If all world and media experience is regarded as a linguistic, psychic, or media-technological construction, there is neither an applicable possibility of distinguishing between the imaginary, reality, and virtuality, nor is there any resultant gain in knowledge. This objective reality can be perceived by our visual, acoustic, olfactory, and haptic senses. Reality in this context presupposes an observer and stands in a temporal, spatial and material relation to the life-world. In the case of a photograph, the life-world reality of this image consists of the photographic paper, the colors applied, the specific smell, etc. at a specific time, as well as the specific physical place in the life-world that this photo occupies.

The imaginary is to be understood here as the imagination of perception, memory, and representation as produced by the human subject. The Germanist Wolfgang Iser's reflections may be useful here. He argues for the abolition of the bipolar opposition between reality and fiction in literary scholarship. Iser makes a distinction between the real, the imaginary, and fiction. By imaginary, he means those psychic forms of operations that arise spontaneously and involuntarily, including manifestations of the imaginary as fantasy, imaginative power, and imagination. By the intentional act of pretending, which the imaginary undergoes in a work of literature, it thus becomes a work of fiction.[84] Life-world reality and the imaginary unite in fiction, which in the case of literature becomes fixed in writing.[85] The imaginary is thus the product of the purely subjective imagination – i.e. the visual, acoustic, or other sensory imaginative capacities of human beings. Actions, experiences, fantasies, or thoughts about future and past events are imagined – pictorially in most cases – and are thus in part already linguistically abstracted. In this context, the imaginary presupposes the subjective imagination. It operates in a temporal, spatial, and material context within the subject's psychic experience. In the case of photography, the picture's imaginary aspect consists of the thoughts, emotions, and imagined memories and fantasies that an observer develops internally.

Virtuality can thus be defined as the simulation of human sensory perceptions of reality or of the imaginary. Virtual reality simulates the body's visual, acoustic and, less often, olfactory or haptic sensual experiences. Virtuality always presupposes a simulation technology. It occurs in a temporal, spatial and material context in the life-world. In the case of photography, the virtual aspect of the image consists of the technical simulation of a photographed scene, for example a landscape.

French sociologist and philosopher Jean Baudrillard made a major contribution to the question of the relationship between reality, the media, and virtuality. He divides the history of the West according to the nature of the relation between the sign and the signified. By sign, Baudrillard means everything that reproduces reality in codified form: language, numbers, images, clothes, and the like. In hierarchical medieval societies, the sign as a symbolic ordering of society always retained its reference to

---

criteria. However, that is never the case, as all statements about the world that are available to us are always already filtered and understood via our being human.
84   See Iser 1990, 23-30; Iser 1991, 24-59.
85   See Sill 1997, 141-145.

the real. However, the Renaissance marked the beginning of the end of the imposed sign:[86]

> Competitive democracy succeeds the endogamy of signs proper to status-based orders. With the transit of values or signs of prestige from one class to another, we simultaneously and necessarily enter into the age of the *counterfeit*. For from a limited order of signs, the 'free' production of which is prevented by a prohibition, we pass into a proliferation of signs according to demand.[87]

The imitation of signs, which as a mere simulacrum now only mimic a reference to the real, acquires a new quality with the advent of the industrial revolution and the mass production of signs. As all signs as industrial simulacra are equivalently repeatable, the imitation of those signs connected to their original reference loses its meaning in light of the production of new signs. The reference to the model thus supersedes the reference to reality. The sign itself generates meaning and no longer competes primarily with other signs or with the references of these signs.

According to Baudrillard, the determining schema of our age is simulation, which, in its digital codification of signs with no reference to reality, gives birth to hyperreality: "At the end of this process of reproducibility, the real is not only that which can be reproduced, but *that which is always already reproduced*: the hyperreal."[88] Signs constitute their own reality and thus resolve the contradiction between the real and the imaginary. "Irreality no longer belongs to the dream or the phantasm, to a beyond or a hidden interiority, but to *the hallucinatory resemblance of the real to itself*."[89] Signs no longer represent reality – by means of simulation they now create hyperreality.[90]

In his philosophical analysis, Baudrillard posits a relation between virtuality and the imaginary, the meaning of which he regards as equivalent to illusion. He condemns the simulation of the world in virtuality as the perfect crime. This crime is no less than the murder of the world by its simulation, which is accompanied by the destruction of the radical illusion of the world. For Baudrillard, illusion is not deceptive appearance. Rather, it is the vitally necessary utopian spirit, the autonomous creativity of human beings (and therefore corresponds to the imaginary as defined above according to Iser):[91]

> Thought becomes an arithmetical operation and all doubt, all distance, every unpredictable eventuality, every game and every illusion of thought is suppressed – just as the body as illusion disappears in its genetic inscription, just as the world as illusion disappears in its technical artifact ... All this, artificial intelligence, real time, tele-sensoriality, means the final suppression of illusion. The wild illusion of thought, scene, passion, intelligence, the illusion of the world, the vision of the world (not its

---

86 In the Middle Ages, each estate had its own identifying signs or symbols (clothes, language, code of behavior, etc.). See Baudrillard 1993, 87-99.
87 Ibid., 51.
88 Ibid., 73.
89 Ibid., 72.
90 See ibid., 101-124.
91 See Baudrillard 1996, 8-35.

representation and analytical cognition) ... , the contemplation of good and evil ... , true and false, the wild illusion of death, or of life at all costs – all this evaporates in tele-reality, in all technologies that trap us in the virtual, which is the opposite of illusion – total disillusionment.[92]

If we take Baudrillard's ideas on board, virtuality can, in principle, be taken to mean the simulation both of reality or of "illusion" (i.e. for Iser the imaginary). The view that virtuality itself no longer refers to reality and that signs merely *designate* themselves is not immediately convincing. Like Herbert W. Franke and Wolfgang Iser, Baudrillard produces a tripartite model consisting of the real world, the illusion of the world, and virtuality. All three thinkers distinguish between firstly the level of objectively existing reality, secondly the subjectively constructed imaginary, and thirdly the medial simulation of reality and the imaginary through virtuality. It is at this point – the transfer of the subjective imaginary to linguistic or pictorial simulation – that Iser's concept of the fictional proves useful.[93]

In light of these reflections, it is clear that virtuality does not mean mere illusiveness or the opposite of reality, a notion that Günther Anders was trying to express with his paradox of phantomization, i.e. real yet not real.[94] A plane crash on television may be a live broadcast or a dramatic visualization in a feature film. The broadcast presents a real event, the feature film a fictional one (i.e. a virtualization of the imaginary), yet both are only virtually existent for the television viewer.

Virtuality, then, can only be interpreted from the viewpoint of the perceiving subject. Events are not virtual in themselves; it is their perception from the perspective of a specific observer that makes them virtual. An illuminating experience for me personally was a campaign speech by the then German Chancellor Helmut Kohl 1998 on the main square of the city of Bonn. As a chance visitor at the edge of a crowd, I had to accept that the speaker in front of the town hall was standing a long way away from me, but a tourist was filming the scene with his video camera just in front of me with his viewfinder screen open. It was much easier to recognize Kohl on the small screen than if I had looked directly at the rostrum. Both Kohl and I were actually present at the same time on the market square in Bonn. The camera screen in front of me was not creating an illusion, but rather was technically simulating sensory experiences (in this case those of visual proximity) that were not accessible to me. However, in the same way – but without electronics – my spectacles were already producing a better image of the speaker. My real life-world and the virtual experience of the camera screen were almost identical – but only *almost*.

Beyond the distinction between the real life-world and the virtual experience, which is based on the specific situation of media use, there is no definitive demarcation between phenomena of virtuality as opposed to those of reality. All additional distinctions are gradual in nature, and depend on the extent to which a technical

---

92   Baudrillard 1994, 19-21, trans. by PK.
93   The imaginary is a psychological process within the subject, whereas fiction combines the purely mental imaginary with the real in the form of a text, a film, an image, a sculpture, or a computer program. The imaginary in materialized fiction is also accessible to outside observers.
94   See Anders 1983, 129-31; Heim 1993, 109-110.

simulation of inaccessible perceptions is taking place. Glasses, or a telescope, just like a smartphone live-stream, produce virtual spatial proximity by making available, in this case visually, a reality that is inaccessible to the senses.[95] It is impossible to answer in general terms which medium involves greater degrees of virtuality. This depends on the heterogeneous contents of the medium, which influences the viewer's involvement in and concentration on the virtually perceived event.

Nevertheless, it is clear that the more total the technical simulation of corporeal-sensory experiences is, the more it detaches itself from the real experiential possibilities of our body and our person in the real life-world, in the here and now, the greater the degree of technically generated virtuality becomes in its spatial and temporal aspects.

Absolute reality, as defined by Vladimir Cherniavsky,[96] must therefore be contrasted with absolute virtuality. In absolute virtuality, the simulation of the real is so perfect and so total that we cannot recognize the simulation as such, as we do not have a point of reference for a higher level of reality. Absolute virtuality therefore cannot be distinguished from absolute reality. Posthumanist Frank Tipler transfigures this as a vision of the continued existence of humanity. Rainer Werner Fassbinder in his film *Welt am Draht* (*World on a Wire*) and the *Matrix* trilogy problematize the dissolution of the real in face of this perfect simulation.[97]

The more perfect and total a simulation is, the smaller the creative, i.e. imaginary – contribution of human beings becomes, as all emotional dispositions and possible options for action are pre-programmed and planned. Christoph Wulf and Nicholas Negroponte emphasize this loss of subjective imagination, which results from the interlinked unity of sound and image in film, television, and computer games:[98]

> Interactive multimedia leaves very little to the imagination. Like a Hollywood film, multimedia narrative includes such a specific representation that less and less is left to the mind's eye. By contrast, the written word sparks images and evokes metaphors that get much of their meaning from the reader's imagination and experiences. When you read a novel, much of the color, sound, and motion come from you.[99]

After these observations on the relation between reality, the imaginary, virtuality, and the corresponding temporal, spatial, and corporeal aspects, we are again confronted with the question: What is virtuality?

The medieval logician John Duns Scotus (1266-1308) considered the Latin term *virtualiter* as a term indicating that an object not only possessed empirically observable

---

95 See Lem 2010, 217-221.
96 For Cherniavsky, absolute reality is a reality whose existence does not depend on us. It is one that is immediately accessible to us through our senses. Apart from this, Cherniavsky's philosophical-mathematical concept of virtuality is scarcely applicable to virtuality in media theory, because it connects virtuality to categories of logical truth affirmations and thus ignores major aspects of the fictional. See Cherniavsky 1994, 4, 383.
97 In *The Matrix* and *Welt am Draht* (*World on a Wire*) all our sensory experiences are part of a gigantic computer program. See Fassbinder 1973; Lem 2010, 206-211; Wachowsky / Wachowsky 1999.
98 See Hammel 1994, 73-78; Wulf 1984, 42.
99 Negroponte 1996, 8.

qualities, but also ones that were virtually existent though not simultaneously actual.[100] If we look at the history of the French and English terms *virtualité* and *virtuality* and *virtuel/-le* and *virtual*, we notice that the characteristics of virtuality discussed above are partially present in the various historical meanings of this word. The Middle English word *vertualyte* denotes power and ability in what was originally a religious context. From the 17th century onwards, the modern English word *virtuality* denotes the true essence of a thing or a person, which exists independently of its or his material embodiment. In the 15th century in French and from the 19th century in English, *virtualité*, *virtuality* and their corresponding adjectives designate a possible state, a potential capacity that is not actually realized. Today, the various meanings of virtuality in philosophy, literature, religion, optics, and computer science converge in a focus upon virtual reality.[101]

It is obvious from this discussion so far that the term virtuality cannot be limited to computer-aided simulation techniques, to the context of *virtual reality* outlined by Jaron Lanier, or to the metaphor of *cyberspace*. It is also clear that further temporal, spatial and material aspects that involve non-electronic media need to be considered. Previous attempts to grasp the essence of the term virtuality have tended to focus only on certain aspects. For example, N. Katherine Hayles highlights the role of information in her study of cybernetics and science fiction:

> *Virtuality is the cultural perception that material objects are interpenetrated by information patterns* ... Virtual reality technologies are fascinating because they make visually immediate the perception that a world of information exists parallel to the 'real' world.[102]

By contrast, Dietmar Kamper and Vilém Flusser provide a more pragmatic and no less plausible interpretation when they regard virtuality as a space of possibility. According to Flusser, the virtual space created by computers as a universal medium leads to a large number of alternative worlds. It creates new fields of possibility that are so plural and so singular that they change into the real and become specific. However, in Kamper's view this opening up of new possibilities also involves the elimination of the real world.[103]

> The virtual is the possible, the possible at all times, everywhere, and even in different ways. It is a farewell to the corporeal because it negates the conditions of time and space, and thus denies its own genesis.[104]

We can understand virtuality in the context of media theory by saying that something is potentially present but is not actually there. It is present in the sense that our

---

100 See Heim 1993, 132-133; Williams 2001.
101 The Latin root *virtus* and *virtualis* meaning power, strength, virtue, and capacity, refer only indirectly to the later meaning. In the sense of possibilities that are not actually realized, modern usages such as *foyer virtuelle* (1757) and *virtual focus* (1704) are derived from optics, while *virtual memory* (1959) is from information technology. See Trésor 1994, 1186-1187; Simpson / Weiner 1989, Vol. 19, 674-675.
102 Hayles 1999, 14.
103 See Flusser 1993, 70.
104 Kamper 1999, 22, trans. by PK.

visual, acoustic and possibly other sense perceptions of a phenomenon are simulated. Virtuality is not merely the opposite of reality, nor is it identical with illusion or with the subjective imaginary. Virtuality may mean the simulation of reality as well as of the imaginary. In the process of technical simulation, electronic media imply the idea of an information pattern behind reality. In my view, these observations lead to the following, only approximate, media-theoretical definition of the concept of virtuality.

Virtuality is the availability of the non-available. Unavailable here means the spatial, temporal and material-corporeal unavailability of real or imaginary experiences. Availability means the simulation of the sensory perception of these experiences. The more independent these virtual experiences are of time, space, and bodies, the greater their dependence on technology becomes. In the context of media theory, virtuality makes the visual, acoustic or even haptic and olfactory actualization of events possible, which are spatially, temporally, and actually (for our body) not available in the real life-world or in imaginary or fictional worlds.

Virtuality does not simulate space, or time, or bodies. Rather, it simulates our *perceptions* of space, time, and bodies. As Stanisław Lem points out in the *Summa Technologiae*, as long as human beings remain human beings and are not part of a computer, we retain the ability to unmask virtuality by means of our corporeality: by our observing bodies. If Wilhelm Dilthey concludes that it is only the resistance of the material world that give us our identity and orientation, Dietmar Kamper points out that in the computer age our back pain is the only – albeit clearly perceptible – remaining memory of the world and the body. [105]

Media experiences of virtuality are experiences of the availability of time, space, and bodies. Our relation to media actors, computer game characters, or virtual presentations of ourselves offers us the partial experience of independence of time, space and our physical limits. Virtuality, in its ability to make the past present, also gains control over the transience of life. In the context of the social life-world – rather than just that of media reality – real human beings are confronted with simulations of human beings that are ostensibly removed from all temporality, spatiality, and corporeality.

---

105   See ibid., 58-59; Lem 2010, 195-203; Kamper 1999, 22.

3. Promethean Shame

> In my mind I call it "Promethean Shame"; and by this I mean "Shame at the 'shamingly' high quality of things made by human beings."[1]
> *Günther Anders*

3.1 Human Beings and Technology in the Work of Günther Anders

Günther Anders (1902-1992) was one of the most remarkable figures of 20th century German intellectual history. Born Günther Stern, he came from an educated middle-class Jewish family in Breslau. Influenced at an early age by the horrors of the First World War, he espoused pacifism as well as the idea of a united Europe. He studied philosophy under Ernst Cassirer, Martin Heidegger, and Edmund Husserl in Freiburg, where he obtained his PhD in 1923 with a dissertation on philosophical phenomenology. After graduating, he worked as a freelance journalist and lecturer, and during this period adopted the pseudonym Günther Anders ("anders" means "other" in German), which he used in all his publications thereafter. From 1929 to 1937 he was married to the philosopher Hannah Arendt. After the National Socialists seized power in Germany, he went into exile, first in Paris, and from 1936 in the United States.

While living there, in addition to his journalism he also had to work as a laborer, in museums, and in factories to make ends meet. After the Second World War he moved to Vienna. The publication of his two-volume magnum opus *Die Antiquiertheit des Menschen* (*The Obsolescence of Humankind*) in 1956 and 1980 established his reputation as one of the leading critics of contemporary technology and industrial society. In this work, he laid the foundations for a philosophy of technology and media. In the 1950s he also became a prominent advocate for the German peace movement in its opposition to nuclear weapons. If the following pages seem to quote Anders extensively, this only reflects my own amazement at the exceptional aptitude he shows for interpretations of human beings and technology, as would later be articulated in posthumanism.

---

1   Anders 1983, 23.

When visiting a technology exhibition in 1942 during his American exile, Anders "discovered" a new motif, which, in his view, had never previously existed: *Promethean Shame*. He begins by describing how *homo faber*, in the process of increasing industrialization and alienation from the fruits of his labor, loses his sense of pride in those products. Anders illustrates his point with reference to the most complex machine of his time: the cybernetic *computing machine*. He argues that human beings feel inferior and consider themselves to be defective constructions when confronted with products that have lost their quality of being created – products that simply *are*. They thus feel shame at their own inferiority:

> Human beings are inferior to their apparatuses in terms of power, precision, and speed. It is an undeniable fact that their intellectual abilities compare poorly with those of their 'computing machines'.[2]

Human beings perceive themselves as badly constructed compared to these machines, which are superior in so many respects. Humans thus remain painfully aware of their many imperfections and their own defective bodies. Meanwhile, machines themselves are becoming increasingly perfect:

> What about us? What about our bodies? There is no daily improvement ... They are morphologically constant; in moral terms they are: unfree, unruly, and stubborn; seen from the perspective of the machines they are: conservative, unprogressive, antiquated, unimprovable, a dead weight hampering the rise of machines. In short, the subjects of freedom and unfreedom have been exchanged. It is things that are free and human beings that are unfree.[3]

In the presence of accelerating technological progress, the physical limitations of human beings make their bodies seem antiquated and obsolete when compared to these machines. Humans are saboteurs of their own work. To avoid accepting their inferiority, backwardness, and the "stubbornness of the body", they follow the promising path of *human engineering* by shifting to the realm of the hybrid and the artificial:

> The aim of the experiments is to subject physis, which (apart from magic and medicine) had always been considered a "fatum", to a metamorphosis; to relieve it of its fatality – which also means to ... eliminate all its fatal and shameful aspects.[4]

More than 30 years before the first normative posthumanist texts were published, Anders had already outlined a theory of posthumanism that I would like to expand upon here. The relevance and topicality of Anders' brilliant reflections is greater than ever, as it illustrates the connections between recent developments in genetic technology and posthumanist dreams of fusing human beings with computers.[5]

Philosopher Johannes Rohbeck adopts Anders and Arendt's ideas, and has recently added a fourth affront to Sigmund Freud's classification of three challenges to

---

2 Ibid., 32, trans. by PK.
3 Ibid., 33, trans. by PK.
4 Ibid., 38, trans. by PK.
5 See ibid., 23-50.

human beings, including: the cosmological affront (Copernicus), the biological affront (Darwin), and the psychological affront (psychoanalysis), which have all shattered human self-confidence:

> I believe that we could add a fourth affront to these three: the technological affront. This means that human beings discover that they are no longer the lords of their own creations but are in fact controlled by their own contrivances. Like the sorcerer's apprentice, they have created something that has gone on to develop a dynamism of its own.[6]

According to Anders, human beings are inferior to machines not only because of their "morphological pre-formation". "Although they are more stubborn than their products, they are also shorter-lived and more mortal than their products."[7] Individual human beings are confronted with the quasi-immortal serial existence of industrial products and their models: "Has it not become 'eternal' by virtue of its substitutability, by reproduction technology? Death, where is thy sting?"[8] Human beings seek to escape from this second form of inferiority by what Anders terms *iconomania*, by which they multiply themselves in photographs, films, "television phantoms", and posters:

> One of the main reasons for what has aptly been described as hypertrophic image production is that human beings can obtain the chance to create "spare-pieces" of themselves; to show that the notion of their unbearable uniqueness is false ... They are not only equally widespread [as film stars and serial products], they have also overcome their mortality in the same way: both can continue to exist after death in their reproductions.[9]

Anders defines *Promethean Shame* as the sense of disorientation and despair when people realize the limited nature of human freedom and individuation, and as they become aware of their helplessness and failure: " 'Feeling shame' in this context means: *being unable to do anything about being unable to do anything.*"[10] He does not regard *Promethean Shame* as a metaphor but as an actual experience of shame in our world of machines:

> Those who have never had the experience of making the wrong move on a machine and standing silent and incredulous as the conveyor belt rolled on ... who have never felt disconcerted as they looked at their hands, whose clumsiness, obsolescence and incorrigible incompetence caused their failure – those who have never experienced this do not know what the shame of today is, a shame that emerges thousands of times every day.[11]

There have been several attempts in cultural theory to establish a link between the idea of the machine with the rational disciplining and behavioral control applied to

---

6   Rohbeck 1993, 10, trans. by PK.
7   Anders 1983, 50.
8   Ibid., 51.
9   Ibid., 57. See ibid., 50-64.
10 Ibid., 70. See ibid., 64-95.
11 Ibid., 95.

human beings over the process of civilization. Following Norbert Elias' impressive description, Peter Gendolla and Wolfgang Schivelbusch saw the Enlightenment as an ideal rationalization of social behavior. In an ever-more differentiated society, the machine embodies the ideal of the exact interlocking of all individual parts under conditions of increasing complexity. This illustrates the necessity of the rationality of individual and collective *rules* of behavior in social life.[12]

In her book *Die Achse Avantgarde – Faschismus* (*The Avantgarde – Fascism Axis*) Eva Hesse emphasizes the question of the connection between the rise of eugenics, i.e. the optimization of the human body, and the process of increasing industrialization at the end of the 19th century. To what extent did the encounter with the "perfect machine" influence the idea of a racist or genetic optimization of human beings? Why was there no place in racist and fascist ideologies for the weak, the imperfect – or simply the merely human?[13]

At the turn of the century, connections were already being made between the eugenic optimization of human beings and technological progress. The doctor and later race fanatic Ludwig Woltmann described attempts to achieve biological optimization in light of the rapid perfecting of machines as follows:

> But here there are no survivors and no self-reproducing best human beings. Only one thing is becoming perfect and that is the machine that is making human power superfluous, not the individual, personal human being ... And this is why the capitalist competitive struggle produces this extra-human and technical result, because the economic forces in the machine are detached from individual people and represent a social labor force.[14]

The "new human being" is the project of the social and psychological visions of the 19th and 20th centuries, which have dedicated themselves to the control and optimization of human action, from humanism to race theories. These brief glimpses illustrate the range and depth of Anders' concept of *Promethean Shame* in its historical dimension, which also provides a starting point for the current debate on transhumanism. In fact, it was Anders who first unmasked eugenics, human engineering, or genetic engineering as the first step towards the cyborgization of human beings.

> "Human Engineering" experiments are actually the initiation rites of the robotic age; and the guinea pigs in this experiment are the candidates and finally the neophytes who are now proud of having put their "childhood" behind them and of having completed the "Education of the Human Race" that is required today. But when manufactured objects are considered to be "adult", then "putting childhood behind you" and "Education of the Human Race" mean: "putting being human behind you".[15]

---

12 See Elias 1982, 363-348; Gendolla 1992a, 16-29, 52-59; Schivelbusch 1977, 149-173.
13 While many Futurists, including Marinetti, opposed antisemitism, strong ideological links nonetheless remained between *Avant garde* art and Fascism, especially in the 1920s at the inception of both movements. See Hesse 1992, 227-233, 281-336.
14 Ludwig Woltmann: *Die Darwinsche Theorie und der Sozialismus*. Düsseldorf 1899, 30. Quoted from Bolle 1962, 154. See ibid., 144-157, trans. by PK.
15 Anders 1983, 41.

Although, in addition to his concept of *Promethean Shame* Anders also developed a "Phenomenology of Television" regarding machines and devices, the connections between these two areas remain marginal in his work and are not further elaborated. However, Anders' example of the immortality of film stars in their infinite serial reproducibility in photo, film, and cosmetic self-reification testifies to the potential that the combination of media and machine theory still contains.[16]

3.2 Virtuality and Death

> All those young photographers who are at work in the world, determined upon the capture of actuality, do not know that they are agents of Death.[17]
> Roland Barthes

Since the Enlightenment, religion is no longer the sole source of meaning offered in the face of death. Medical utopias promising an almost unlimited life span have been repeatedly articulated by progressive thinkers over the past three centuries. Technological and medial visions of immortalization begin to appear around the end of the 19th century.[18] In fact, the relationship between death, media, and the longing for immortality has been astonishingly persistent over the course of human cultural history. In his study of ancient Egyptian ideas of immortality, the Egyptologist Jan Assmann concluded that, in addition to stone buildings, sculpture, and mummification, the use of writing in Egyptian tombs must be seen as a crucial expression of the aspiration for immortality. The tomb inscriptions of Egyptian graves record the lives of the deceased, thus overcoming the limitations of life by the act of remembering. The medium of writing as the first systematic abstraction of reality makes mortals immortal:[19]

> Human beings have left behind the orders of nature because of their excess of knowledge and must now create an artificial world in which they can live. This is culture. Culture arises from knowledge of death and immortality. It represents the attempt to create a space and a time in which human beings can think beyond their limited life horizon. Where they can extend the lines of their activity, experience, and planning to other horizons and dimensions of fulfilment. In which their need for meaning can be satisfied and the painful, indeed unbearable consciousness of their existential limitation and fragmentation finds peace. Human beings cannot live ... without fantasies of immortality.[20]

---

16 See ibid., 30-31, 57-59.
17 Barthes 1981, 92.
18 See chapter 6.5.
19 See Assmann 1993, 64-66.
20 Assmann 2000, 13-14, trans. by PK.

Five thousand years later, thinkers such as Boris Groys and Florian Rötzer have identified those Egyptian aspects lingering in the center of our culture. Timothy Leary also describes the ancient Egyptian kings as models of technical immortalization: "The pharaohs *made it*."[21] Just as doubts about the immortality of the soul were once expressed in the embalming of bodies and the tomb inscriptions of Egyptian pyramids, this psychological uncertainty today finds expression in the booming media culture. Today, the problem of human mortality has certainly not drifted to the peripheries, but rather remains squarely in the center of our culture:

> Since the days of Egyptian culture with its mummies and monuments, since the inscription of writing and images in stone and on paper, human beings have feared the finitude of bodies, materials, and information, and so ideas of unending life have emerged ... The urge for virtualization, parallel to the progress of biotechnology, coincides with the old longing for eternity.[22]

These contemporary diagnoses point to media's significance for the universal problem of death, from ancient Egypt to the modern era. The historian Thomas Macho offers the most succinct formulation of what human beings' representations in electronic media can mean for our perceptions of human mortality:

> Our television sets today are already image coffins; electro-magnetic death projections. Have we ever stopped to think how many of the people who flit across our television screens every evening are still alive? ... It is true, the dead are among us. Like homeless nomads, they inhabit our living rooms.[23]

The spectrum of images ranges widely: from the highly realistic portraits of the dead, especially in the Roman period in Egypt; to the popular photographs of the dead, especially of children, in the 19th century; to the widespread customs in Mediterranean countries of decorating tombstones with photographs of the deceased; and finally to the virtual preservation of people from the past in film, television, and computer simulations in our day – not to mention the *virtual memorials* on the Internet.

This interpretation of the relation between human beings, technology, and media, as formulated by Anders and later by posthumanists and certain media philosophers, is by no means mandatory. I am not describing "properties" inherent to media itself. In fact, this perspective is shared by very few people in our society – even the transhumanist movement, despite its revolutionary aspirations, remains only a marginal social phenomenon. However, the new sensory experiences of simulated human beings in virtual spaces and times form a framework that enables certain interpretations put forward by technological posthumanism. The television as an "image coffin" is opposed to the mortality and irretrievability of the dead person. The virtual simulation of human beings goes beyond the act of remembering anchored in the subject, because it presents the person, at least visually and acoustically, as we would perceive him or her. This is

---

21 Leary / Sirius 1997, 159.
22 Rötzer 1996b, 232, trans. by PK.
23 Macho 1994, 433, trans. by PK.

especially true of people that we know only from the media. Whether a media actor is alive or dead generally remains hidden from us.

Of course, death and mortality are also subjects *in* the media, which in the case of disaster reporting can affect us strongly. However, the direct experience of a person dying and suddenly becoming a real, tangible corpse has an utterly different and much deeper quality than the facile and anonymous deaths in films, television, and computer games. These are so familiar to us – having witnessed thousands of such "virtual" and hollow deaths from an early age – yet do not prepare us at all for the physical realness of a living person actually dying.

The virtuality of media confronts us with a person who no longer conforms to the temporal and spatial conditions by which human beings are bound. Due to its independence from spatiality and temporality, virtuality allows an extra-*sensory* experience of reality. The presence of that which is sensorially unavailable provides the key to the social relevance of virtuality and develops its significance for thanatology (the cultural study of death). The indeterminable nature of death becomes determinable through the possibility of the unlimited, technical realization of the temporal: Calculated death in films and computer games is revisable and repeatable, and therefore not subject to the uniqueness of real life. The constantly available realization of experiences that go beyond the natural capacities of our senses and our existence is bound to affect a person's idea of his or her death and mortality. Two consequences should be mentioned in this regard, which may seem paradoxical at first.

The first is that the medial presentation of people released from the irretrievability of time is a further aspect of the repression of death, as death's social visibility fades. If the social dimension of death means fellow humans experiencing and perceiving a person, then media events, consisting of endless repetitions, obscure real death and hide the transient and unique nature of life. The problem of death, which demands solutions and explanations, arises only when some are lost and those left behind reflect upon it. But secondly, those remaining notice that the deceased are actually no longer among us – only their virtual representations survive. It is against this background that technical utopias of immortalization can be understood.

What happens when human beings begin to compare themselves with the technical simulations of people in electronic media? What will happen when, as in ancient Egypt, the deceased wish to remain in the memories of their descendants – not only in life fragments or photographs, but instead to actually become immortal via media? What if they prefer their virtual representation, their existence as a pure sign, to their transitory corporeal reality? And what if human beings, in their "postmodern immortality craze", as Dietmar Kamper puts it, wish to become a "garbage of words and images", which of course cannot die.[24] In short, what happens when people wish to become as immortal as the people they see in virtualsimulations?

I would argue that the encounter with virtuality, especially the experience of images of people only available virtually, can produce a kind of *Promethean Shame*. It is not the confrontation with the serial reproducibility of industrial artifacts that elicits this feeling of inferiority, but rather the comparison with the photographic, filmic, and

---

24 See Kamper 1999, 50-51.

various digital reproductions of human beings. *Iconomania*, as the ultimately futile attempt to escape from the "human calamity,"[25] thus leads to a new quality of human inferiority vis-à-vis media products.

Human beings *see* simulations of people before them that exist virtually and are independent of time, space, and corporeality. The closer these simulations of reality come, the closer the comparison between the human being and his virtual counterpart will be. Our experience of film, television, and digital media in their temporal dynamics corresponds more closely to our perception of real people than it is the case with photography. A computer game with virtual interaction partners, or personal assistants such as Siri or Alexa, are able to simulate the interactive aspect of human communication with increasing success.

The first point of comparison between humans and their virtual counterparts is the former's mortality, as opposed to the apparent "immortality" of their media simulations. Technological posthumanism is the response to the *Promethean Shame* that human beings feel with regard to their virtual reproductions. Posthumanism thus advocates the overcoming of humans by a posthuman being who exists only in virtual form.

The aim is for the future human being not only to overcome mortality but also to surpass biological existence in every conceivable respect. A second aspect of the comparison can be attributed to cybernetic theory, which measures life as a whole in terms of its information-processing performance and contrasts human beings with computers. The question of immortality in technological posthumanism, in conjunction with the vision of immeasurable intelligence and power, thus forms the central analytical cornerstone of the following history of ideas.

---

25   See Anders 1983, 35-37.

Part II
Technological Posthumanism

4. Transhumanism

> trans-húman, a. [Rare] superhuman. – transhúmanize, vt. [Rare] To make superhuman.[1]
> *New Standard Dictionary of the English Language (1949)*

4.1 Post- and Transhumanism

Amidst the diverse range of thinkers advocating the overcoming of humanity with the help of new technologies, many are often called transhumanists. Yet despite this increasingly frequent usage, I would still like to insist on the need for a distinction between technological posthumanism and transhumanism. Not only does the term posthumanism, which is commonly used in art and cultural studies research, need to be clarified, but in fact noticeable differences can be found between the purposes, contents, and origins of transhumanism and technological posthumanism.

Transhumanism primarily originated in California during the 1960s, and was decisively influenced by the visions of the futurist Fereidoun M. Esfandiary (FM-2030), by the commitment of Timothy Leary, the pioneer of the psychedelic movement, and by the cryonics expert Robert Ettinger. In the late 1980s this movement gave rise to the Extropians around Max More and, as European involvement increased, the *World Transhumanist Association* founded by Nick Bostrom, David Pearce, and Anders Sandberg in 1998.

Technological posthumanism, on the other hand, unites a number of authors who have been propagating the replacement of humans by their artificial offspring since the mid-1980s. Its main proponents, such as Marvin Minsky, Frank Tipler, Hans Moravec, and Ray Kurzweil, base their arguments on cybernetic theory. Before the early 2000s, these authors did not refer to the transhumanist movement and its themes in any way.

The second argument for a separation between post- and transhumanism is based on the different emphases in terms of content. Transhumanists deal practically with the issues of prolonging life and enhancement of mental performance, such as through the use of *smart drugs*, life-prolonging diets, advances in prosthetic technology, the

---

1   Funk 1949, 2250.

potential for a renewed form of eugenics, or even the prospects of cryonics, while these applications are rarely mentioned in posthumanist writings. In particular, the close connection between cryonics and transhumanism illustrates the hope of being brought back to life from cooled nitrogen tanks in the distant future, and thus exploiting the hoped-for possibilities of technological immortalization.

Posthumanism or postbiologism's neglect of the practical questions that are urgent for people today underlines the crucial difference from transhumanism. In transhumanism the subject of development is humankind and what becomes of human beings with the help of technological upgrades and enhancements, whereas in posthumanism robots and artificial intelligence are the future carriers of evolution and progress. In a virtual habitat the immortal existence of humans is only a side effect of the autonomous progress of artificially intelligent, posthuman beings. For humankind to create a posthumanist philosophy that advocates the total annihilation of humans in favour of machine beings, yet fails to guarantee the possibility of attaining immortality, is simply unimaginable. For posthumanism, the idea of technical immortalization is therefore of central and constitutive importance.

This difference between post- and transhumanism is clearly visible in the field of eugenics and today's genetic optimization of humans. While biogenetics is essential for many transhumanists, the biological improvement of the human being plays no role in posthumanism. This may also be due to their more reflective approach to the dark history of eugenics, especially given the personal family background of some posthumanists.

Ray Kurzweil occupies a special position in this field because, in addition to his posthumanist works *The Age of Spiritual Machines* (1999) and *The Singularity is Near* (2005), he has been publishing books on self-optimization since the 1990s. Until the early 2000s, Kurzweil was not a particularly significant voice within established transhumanist networks. However, thanks to his publishing success and the foundation of the *Singularity University* in 2008, he has become the most prominent representative of post- and transhumanism. However, he describes himself as a *Singularitarian*, and owing to this techno-centric disposition he can be best categorised as a posthumanist.

The term *posthuman* is thus connoted in different ways: In transhumanism, which ultimately remains anthropocentric, *posthuman* in most cases refers to the state of near- perfection – the transhuman being, who has achieved many of its goals and is therefore no longer human. In technological posthumanism, by contrast, the same term is equated with completely synthetic, artificial intelligence.

4.2 Intellectual Predecessors and the Transhuman

During his analysis of British history, the eminent historian Eric Hobsbawm developed the concept of an *invented tradition*. According to this argument, the *status quo* is legitimized by the claimed continuity of a well established historical tradition of practices and values.[2] Transhumanism offers a prime example of such a process. Its

---

2   See Hobsbawm 2000.

need for legitimation is enormous, as the movement is presented by journalism as being extremely exotic, due to its strong connection to cryonics. Early transhumanism emerged in the late 1960s in the circles around Timothy Leary, Robert Ettinger, and Fereidoun Esfandiary (FM-2030). Until the end of the 1990s, this remained transhumanism's predominant reading of its own origins. This self-designation was attributed to Esfandiary in 2000, as he claimed to have coined the term *transhuman* around 1970.³

This understanding only changed after two important publications by the transhumanists James Hughes and Nick Bostrom, in 2004 and 2005, respectively. The ancestral gallery of transhumanism now includes an impressive lineage of philosophers of progress such as Francis Bacon, Condorcet, Benjamin Franklin, La Mettrie, Kant, (albeit with some caveats) Nietzsche, the biochemist J. B. S. Haldane, the physicist John D. Bernal, and the incomparable brothers Aldous and Julian Huxley – a writer and a biologist. The latter is also credited with the creation of the word *transhumanism*.⁴ Today's transhumanists also occasionally refer to the rediscovered Russian cosmists of the early 20th century.⁵

In a further case of constructing tradition to establish legitimation, Bostrom inserted this particular form of transhumanism inspired by Haldane, Bernal, and Julian Huxley into the academic continuity of English elite universities. He also founded the Future of Humanity Institute in Oxford in the same year as the publication of his 2005 essay. In transhumanist academic literature, this retrospective establishment of a tradition has in many cases been adopted uncritically.⁶ The triad of Haldane, Bernal, and Julian Huxley is not coincidental in this respect, as all three were connected by a political discussion club in Cambridge from 1930 onward.⁷

The forerunners of transhumanism do not necessarily include those thinkers who developed the specific aspects, which later appear as ideas of transhumanism. Rather, it would only include Julian Huxley and the philosopher and paleontologist Pierre Teilhard de Chardin, who each spent decades crafting consistent philosophical doctrines regarding the future of humankind. The analysis of the history of ideas included in chapter 6 will carefully illuminate the variety of elements in post- and transhumanist visions, as based upon older interpretations of history, evolution, and technology in the traditions of European and American intellectual history.⁸

Julian Huxley's coining of the terms *transhuman* and *transhumanism* can be traced to a long history in English. As a verb, *trasumanar* was initially an Italian coinage by the poet Dante (1256-1321) in the first canto of *Paradiso* of the *Divina Commedia* (the *Divine*

---

3   Anders Sandberg's 2000 homepage can be found at: aleph.se/Trans/Words.
4   See Hughes 2004, 156-159; Bostrom 2005, 2-6. In contrast to many other transhumanists, More and the German transhumanist Stefan Sorgner emphasize Nietzsche's positive influence.
5   See More 2013b, 10-11; Goertzel 2010; Sorgner 2016, 34-40.
6   See Heil 2010a, 128-131; Heil 2010b, 26-28; Heil 2010c; Heil 2018, 55-64.
7   See Brown 2005, 104.
8   The frequently cited scientists Haldane and Bernal formulated radical futurologies but did not develop philosophical or social programs from them. Nor did Bernal develop his ideas further in his later work. See section 6.5.2.

Comedy). Dante uses it to describe the joint ascent into the spheres of paradise with his guide Beatrice.

At this point in the poem, Dante makes two references: Firstly, he explicitly refers to the deification of the simple fisherman Glaucus into a sea god in Ovid's *Metamorphoses*. Secondly, he indirectly yet unambiguously alludes to the New Testament in two further remarks: the apostle Paul's ascension to the third level of heaven, as well as his vision of God (2 Cor 12:1-10). For Dante the verb *trasumanar* is thus loaded with two important connotations: (Greek mythological) deification and the (Christian) divine vision.[9]

When Henry Francis Cary published the first English translation of the *Divine Comedy* in 1814, the Italian verb *Trasumanar* became the English adjective *transhuman* – Dante's *Trasumanar significar per verba non si poria* was thus translated by Cary as *Words may not tell of that transhuman change*.[10] In the English reception of Dante during the following years, the concept of the *transhuman* is listed as early as 1949 and 1959 in the *New Standard Dictionary of the English Language* and in *Webster's New International Dictionary of the English Language*, respectively, with the same meaning used by transhumanists today.[11] When *Webster's* described this latter process as "transcending human limits", the term *transhuman* had apparently already found its way into everyday discourse, as the publication of an article in the London business newspaper *The Economist* from 1957 demonstrates.[12]

The origin of the term *transhumanism* can be traced to the Canadian philosopher William Douw Lighthall (1857-1954).[13] Like many of his contemporaries – notably Henri Bergson, Alfred North Whitehead, and Pierre Teilhard de Chardin – Lighthall endeavoured to reconcile metaphysics and science in the post-Darwin era.[14] As a liberal Protestant and Freemason, he drafted a cosmic evolutionary history identifying a personal consciousness as the first cause, which was located outside the universe: *the Outer Consciousness, the Directive Power, the Thinker of Evolution*. Lighthall believed he could deduce the vital impulse of evolution inherent to virtue and goodness through observing biological life. As a "teleology of joy", this assumes the rank of a natural law: "It is marked by marvellous, beneficent, and progressive devices, notably illustrated by the instincts and cerebral cortex of Man; and now so hugely numerous that they form an unworthy argument for purposiveness."[15] According to Lighthall, in the distant future,

---

9   See Harrison / Wolyniak 2015, 265-266.
10 See Simpson / Weiner 1989, vol. 18, 403; Harrison / Wolyniak 2015, 265-266; Heil 2010a, 128.
11 See Funk 1949, 2250.
12 See Neilson 1959, 2691; Simpson / Weiner 1989, vol. 18, 403. See Gove 1993, Vol. 3, 2428.
13 Contrary to the claims made in James Hugh's book *Citizen Cyborg* (2004), namely that Julian Huxley invented the term in his 1927 book *Religion without Revelation*, Peter Harrison and Joseph Wolyniak prove that the word was in fact coined by Lighthall. This error has been repeated throughout the scientific literature to date, and Hughes and Bostrom erroneously refer to a quotation from Huxley's late volume *New Bottles for New Wine* (1957) as proof of this claim. See Harrison / Wolyniak 2015, 465-467; Hughes 2004, 158; Bostrom 2005, 6; Huxley 1957b, 17.
14 Lighthall also explicitly refers to Bergson, Schopenhauer, Whitehead, Haeckel, and the German philosopher Hans Driesch, with whom he exchanged letters. The fact that his approach, which is very similar to that of Teilhard, received so little attention may be due to Lighthall's poor networking skills. See Lighthall 1930, 14-21, 201-203.
15 Lighthall 1940, 135. See Lighthall 1930, 125-140.

when protein-based life on Earth leaves the earthly and solar boundaries, it will perhaps take on a completely different form, "... shall that spirit not take on more glorious forms of body, mind, and heart, ever advancing in oneness with the Person of Evolution."[16]

Relying on the thought of the apostle Paul, rather than the structure of a philosophical system, Lighthall introduced *transhumanism* as:

> Over all, we should remember Dante's supernal principle:
> *Trasumanar significar per verba*
> *Non si porria.*
> and Paul's Transhumanism: "Eye has not seen, nor ear heard, neither has it entered into the conception of man."[17]

This wider context makes it clear that this refers to the steady rise of man. However, the use of the term remains unique to Lighthall.[18] It is unclear whether Julian Huxley was familiar with the Canadian philosopher's essay, and there is no evidence to support this assumption. However, what is is important to note is that Lighthall combines his cosmic and evolutionary metaphysics with the well-known passage from Dante's *Paradiso*, which includes deification and a Christian vision of God.

This literary context must also have been well known to Julian Huxley when he first described evolutionary humanism as transhumanism in the *William Alanson White Memorial Lectures* of 1951: "It is the idea of humanity attempting to overcome its limitations and to arrive at fuller fruition."[19] Huxley had already conceptualized the idea of evolution controlled by rational human beings in his early writings, which were strongly influenced by contemporary eugenics:

> ... life in his person has become self-conscious, and evolution is handed over to him as trustee and director. "Nature" will no longer do the work unaided. Nature – if by that we mean blind and non-conscious forces – has, marvelously, produced man and consciousness; they must carry on the task to new results which she alone can never reach.[20]

Huxley wants to use science to promote the quality (rather than the quantity) of human life. Biologically, his goal is to utilize eugenics for improving the human being socially via education, good healthcare, and welfare for all humankind. Huxley also pursued this agenda when he was appointed UNESCO's first director in 1946, as he ardently believed that a united humanity's progress could overcome the limitations of religion and nationalism.[21] From the 1950s onwards, and particularly in his essay collection *New Bottles for New Wine* (1957), Huxley summarized his programme of evolutionary

---

16 Lighthall 1930, 200.
17 Lighthall 1940, 139. Lighthall is referring to 1 Cor 2:9 "But as it is written, eye hath not seen, nor ear heard, neither have entered into the heart of man, the things which God hath prepared for them that love him." (from the *King James Bible*).
18 See Harrison / Wolyniak 2015, 465-467.
19 Huxley 1951, 139. This lecture was published in the journal *Psychiatry* in the same year. See Harrison / Wolyniak 2015, 465.
20 Huxley 1923, XIII.
21 See Huxley 1957b, 16-18; Huxley 1957c, 21, 39-40; Huxley 1957d.

humanism under the more concise term transhumanism, which he understood both as a strictly scientific worldview, and as a faith-based commitment to the rise of humanity.

> The human species can, if it wishes, transcend itself – not just sporadically, an individual here in one way, an individual there in another way – but in its entirety, as humanity. We need a name for this new belief. Perhaps transhumanism will serve: man remaining man, but transcending himself, by realizing new possibilities of and for his human nature. "I believe in transhumanism": once there are enough people who can truly say that, the human species will be on the threshold of a new kind of existence, as different from ours as ours is from that of Pekin [sic!] man. It will at last be consciously fulfilling its real destiny.[22]

Since the beginning of the construction of a transhumanist tradition by James Hughes, Nick Bostrom, and Max More, Huxley has been credited with the term's creation. However, a reflected appreciation of his contribution – even a positive reception of his programmatic approach – has so far been neglected. Max More even decidedly diminishes Huxley's role, so as to emphasize that transhumanism as a philosophical system was in fact established as a philosophical system in his own essay "Transhumanism: Toward a Futurist Philosophy" from 1990.[23] If More's self-assessment is contestable, it also reflects the fact that Huxley's advocacy of eugenics at the time increasingly sidelined his own work and legacy. After World War II, the social criticism, reappraisal, and cessation of eugenic practices in Europe and the United States was no longer compatible with Huxley's partly eugenic vision of the future.[24]

Transhumanism more intensively addresses the literary work of Julian's older brother, Aldous Huxley (1894-1963), such as the dystopian novel *Brave New World* from 1932. Transhumanists consider it their duty to invalidate the dangers of the totalitarian, eugenic class society described by Aldous, and instead emphasize the liberal character of their vision.[25]

If Julian Huxley appears to discuss the prehistoric Peking Man in his above-mentioned justification of transhumanism, this is actually an overt reference to the French paleontologist and Jesuit philosopher Pierre Teilhard de Chardin (1881-1955), who in 1929 played a decisive role in the discovery of the *Sinanthropus Pekinensis*. Although the direct influence of Teilhard's ideas on post- and transhumanism is far greater than that of Huxley, this influence is deliberately ignored in the transhumanist construction of history.[26] Hughes and More as well as the German transhumanist Stefan L. Sorgner do not mention him at all, and Bostrom laconically states: "However, while these ideas might appeal to those who fancy a marriage between mysticism and

---

22 Huxley 1957b, 17.
23 See Hughes 2004, 158; Bostrom 2005, 6; More 2013b, 8-9; Sorgner 2016, 23-24.
24 For example, the physicist Gerald Feinberg, whose *Project Prometheus* (and the book of the same name from 1969) advocates a radical overcoming of the previous man, does not mention Huxley even once.
25 See Bostrom 2005, 5; Hughes 2005, 49, 56-57; Ettinger 1989, 80-81.
26 In scholarly representations of trans- and posthumanism, only Heil (2018, 68-77) and Krüger (2004, 335-347) acknowledge Teilhard's role.

science, they have not caught on either among transhumanists or the larger scientific community."²⁷

Pierre Teilhard de Chardin, after joining the Jesuit order, his ordination to the priesthood and his extensive studies of theology, philosophy, and various natural sciences, increasingly focused his scientific interest on paleontology, especially the prehistory of humans. Already his early, somewhat mystically inclined writings during and after the First World War, which he experienced as a medic, were marked by the idea of a divinely directed evolution of the cosmos, a notion which he developed further in the following 40 years of his scientific and theological work. Despite numerous secular honors, such as his appointment as knight of the French *Légion d'honneur* (1947) and non-resident member of the *Institut français* (1950), the Vatican prohibited the publication of most of Teilhard's philosophical and theological work. The recognition and continuation of the Darwinian theory of evolution seemed at the time too progressive for the censors of the Catholic Church and the Jesuit order.

Despite the ban on publication, Teilhard's ideas were so well known through his lecturing activities and extensive correspondence, especially in philosophical and scientific circles, that an edition of his work under the patronage of many prominent scientists (above all Julian Huxley, Arnold Toynbee, and Adolf Portmann) was begun in the year of his death. Parallel to the Second Vatican Council (1962-1965), the reception of Teilhard's work in a way that went far beyond the Catholic Church began. By the end of the 1970s, various bibliographies already had more than 10,000 titles of secondary literature on Teilhard. His advocacy of eugenics is concealed in this broad reception of his work.²⁸

What particulary sets Teilhard's ideas apart is the connection he draws between Christian salvation history, the idea of evolution, and a cosmic perspective. He considers the rise of life from dead matter and the emergence of consciousness and thought to be the results of a divine plan originating with the first hominids. In this dynamic perspective, God himself unfolds with his creation until it converges with him again at the end of time in Omega. This therefore abolishes the relativizations that Catholic doctrine underwent in response to Copernicus and Darwin. Within posthumanism, Frank Tipler's approach is based entirely on Teilhard's cosmology, which Hans Moravec also shares. In his understanding of singularity, Ray Kurzweil also adopts the essential elements of Teilhard's universal design in the history of salvation. Each author therefore emphasizes these theological aspects to a greater or lesser degree.²⁹

This brief overview of the prehistory of transhumanism has above all revealed the normative mechanisms of transhumanist tradition-building. While transhumanists have emphasized the role of those thinkers critical of religion, such as J. B. S. Haldane, John D. Bernal, and Julian Huxley, the influence of theological authors like Teilhard de Chardin has been systematically diminished. This is despite their central importance to Frank Tipler's work, as well as to all other forms of religious transhumanism. These religious components, which are also present in Dante's

---

27 Bostrom 2005, 8.
28 See Ferguson 1980, 50-51, 93, 420; Daecke 2000; Leary / Sirius 1997, 47.
29 See chapter 6.7.

reception of the term *transhuman*, are apparently perceived by Hughes, Bostrom, and More as disturbing their attempts to achieve seriousness and credibility for their secularly and scientifically oriented transhumanism.

4.3 Early Transhumanism: Ettinger, FM-2030, Leary

While other scholars continued to be concerned with individual aspects of scientific and technical progress, since the beginning of the 1970s two American authors in particular have formulated a sophisticated futurology including what would later be called transhumanism. Specifically: the founder of cryonics Robert C. W. Ettinger (1918-2011) and the Californian futurist Fereidoun M. Esfandiary (1930-2000).

Ettinger's importance for transhumanism lies not only in his commitment to cryonics, but also in his elaboration of a general transhumanist vision of the future. In 1964 he published his prophetic book *The Prospect of Immortality*, which promises to overcome death by freezing the deceased in liquid nitrogen.[30] As early as 1972 he integrated cryonics into a more comprehensive utopia in his work *Man into Superman*. Here and in other texts he called for and prophesied the dawn of a transhuman age. Ettinger believed that the human being was on a path of liberation from unintelligent, natural evolution to the *superhuman* and *transhumanity*:[31]

> On the level of repair work and prostheses there has indeed been notable success, mostly in recent times. With our eyeglasses, gold inlays and birth control pills we are substantially superhuman; we have transcended the apparent limitations of our design, without even taking into account our vehicles and other machinery. But the basic design has not been noticeably improved.[32]

Ettinger considers it to be a scientific necessity to recreate humanity:

> Thus humanity itself is a disease, of which we must now proceed to cure ourselves ... To be born human is an affliction ... To do this, it must first be shown that homo sapiens is only a botched beginning; when he clearly sees himself as an error, he may not only be motivated to sculpt himself, but to make at least a few swift and confident strokes.[33]

He believes that evolution has endowed the human being and all its biological creations with all possible types of errors – not out of malice or incapacity, but rather because the developmental principle of evolution is simply not interested in producing optimal life forms. Rather, coincidences and extensive compromises with environmental conditions

---

30 See Ettinger 1964. The history and cultural context of cryonics are discussed in detail in section 6.5.4.
31 See Ettinger 1989, 29, 35, 101, 110-111, 116, 127, 129, 162.
32 Ibid., 10.
33 Ibid., 11.

controlled the survival and extinction of the species – life, in Ettinger's words, therefore originated in a "garbage can".[34]

> The purely physical shortcomings of the human animal are legion, and we need only tick off a few, most of them well known. The worst weakness of all, of course, we share with every other large animal: the susceptibility to degenerative disease, senile debility, and death from old age. A less critical, but still serious, defect is our manner of gestating and bearing children, which represents not only inconvenience but danger to the mothers. If some of us temporarily choose to regard these as "natural," there are plenty of others that are clearly pathological.[35]

Ettinger sees the way out of this catastrophe of natural evolution, of which humans are the inglorious result, first of all in the formulation of a new philosophy paving the way to the realization of an immortal superman.

> It should be amply clear by now that the immortal superman represents not just a goal, but a way of life, a world-view only partly compatible with today's dominant ideologies. We might call this fresh outlook the new meliorism, of which the cryonics or people-freezing program is an important current element.[36]

Taking into account the broadest possible anthropological basis, Ettinger develops the image of a superhuman, which combines the masculine heroic characteristics of the Sumerian hero Gilgamesh, the fictional detective Sherlock Holmes, Nietzsche's philosophical superman, and the superheroes of various science fiction stories. This future human being is supposed to combine and extend the existing properties of biological creatures: He should be impervious to cold and heat, like members of some Native American tribes; he should be able to change his skin color at will; and he should be able to eat and enjoy as much food as he wishes, since being overweight can be "repaired". The future human's entire body should be equipped with a stable but flexible skin armor, while some active defense organs (electrical organs or some kind of flame throwers) should simultaneously ensure the transhuman being's safety. The shape of the body could vary between being a flying batman to a swimming aquaman, and range from being a dwarf to a giant to a cyborg. However, whatever the form, the knowledge accumulated over the millenia will ultimately result in the enormous growth of our brains.[37]

> Tons of brain tissue? Of course: doubtlessly, some irreducible minimum amount of matter, in mass and volume, is required to store a unit of information, and if we jettison no memories, we must become gigantic. Even storing "our" memories in a separate mechanical store or computer, plugged in at will, cannot avoid giantism for several reasons. In any case, we should not want to avoid giantism – it is our salvation with respect to the accidental death bogey.[38]

---

34 See ibid., 13-15.
35 Ibid., 17.
36 Ibid., 174.
37 See ibid., 22-66.
38 Ibid., 61.

Ettinger also imagines completely redesigning human sexual interactions, which seem pathetic to him in their present forms. New sexes and new genitals are to be constructed, which would be interchangeable at will. Ettinger seeks to free women from the "disease of childbirth", which degrades the female body to quasi slavery for almost nine months, and then further reduces it to a biological machine during breastfeeding. Instead, Ettinger imagines sexuality being freed from the burden of reproduction to instead only serve the purpose of an everlasting superorgasm.[39]

> The sexual superwoman may be riddled with cleverly designed orifices of various kinds, something like a wriggly Swiss cheese, but shapelier and more fragrant; and her supermate may sprout assorted protuberances, so that they intertwine and roll all over each other in a million permutations of The Act, tireless as hydraulic pumps. (We may have hydraulic pumps, if we are cyborgs.) A perpetual grapple, no holes barred, could produce a continuous state of multiple orgasm.[40]

The combination of economic liberalism and transhumanism commonly used by today's Extropians had in fact already been formulated by Ettinger. He argued in the early 1970s that environmental pollution is not as serious as it seems, and that human well-being is ultimately more important than the survival of a few insignificant animal species and flowers. Indeed, animals that became extinct as a result could probably be completely reconstructed and reanimated from fossils.

> Immortality costs money: to make it as individuals, we must earn and save substantial amounts; to make it as a society, we must increase the GNP [Gross National Product], and rapidly. The notion that we can enjoy the fruits of labor without first laboring is a pollution of the mind, and it is this pollution which is the greater threat.[41]

Ettinger considers this understanding of perpetual progress as the human imperative, in full concordance with the history of Christian salvation:

> The Christians among us are not rebelling against God nor aspiring to equality with him (if such a thing were conceivable); they seek rather to become his more effective tools, his worthier stewards. Neither do we seek endless change just for the sake of change; we pursue intermediate goals on what we hope will be an ascending road, a road perhaps some day leading to the Celestial City – wherever and whatever that may be. Does not Christianity need supermen? Can any but a superman be a complete Christian?[42]

Fereidoun M. Esfandiary conceived the future of humankind in a similar way to Ettinger but with stronger political overtones. Born in Belgium to an Iranian diplomat, he had already lived in more than a dozen countries by the age of eleven, and was even allowed to represent his home country at the Olympic Games in London in 1948. He later worked as a writer, as a member of the UN Advisory Commission on Palestine and as

---

39 See ibid., 66-89.
40 Ibid., 68.
41 Ibid., 133.
42 Ibid., 155.

a lecturer at the New York University. He began his career by writing novels (*The Day of Sacrifice, The Beggar, Identity Card*).[43] However, in his later works *The Emerging Radicalism* (1970), *Up-Wingers* (1973) and *Optimism One* (1978) he portrayed a futuristic political and technological utopia. He changed his name to FM-2030 in 1989.[44] In his words:

> The name 2030 reflects my conviction that the years around 2030 will be a magical time. The solar system will be alive with people linking in and out of planets and moons and orbital communities. In 2030 we will be ageless and everyone will have an excellent chance to live forever. 2030 is a dream and a goal.[45]

In his later book *Are You a Transhuman?* from 1989, Esfandiary once again clearly articulates the core idea of his radical utopia of progress. This is the first instance where the term *transhuman* is located at the center of one of his texts.[46]

> The most urgent problem facing us is not social – economic – political. The most pressing problem facing us all everywhere is death. All other human constraints are derivative. So long as there is death no one is free. So long as there is death we cannot upgrade the basic quality of life. The elimination of death has never been on anyone's agenda because throughout the ages we were never able to do anything about it ... Immortality is now a question of when – not if. The elimination of death will not do away with problems. It will take away the tragedy in human life. Once we attain immortality everything will be possible.[47]

He argues that the trench warfare raging between left- and right-wing factions should be brought to an end so that all political forces can jointly address a much greater collective task as *Up-Wingers*: "Even more profound evolutionary changes are now evident. We are striving to deanimalize our species – debiologize intelligence – deplanetize."[48] The body of humankind must now be completely redesigned by replacing the random process of natural evolution with the purposeful and specific formation of humans guided by reason. According to Esfandiary, while so far we are only prehumans, the age of the transhuman will follow shortly after the Age of Aquarius.[49]

In his vision of transhuman utopia, Esfandiary unites a multitude of technical and social factors that have since become increasingly relevant. For example, he calls for the rapid colonization of space, prophesies the development of an interactive,

---

43 See Esfandiary 1959, 1965, 1966.
44 See West 2000 for a biography of Esfandiary. Knowledge of the transhumanist habit of renaming oneself reached a wide audience with the publication of Dan Brown's novel *Inferno*. See Brown 2013.
45 From an interview Flora Schnall gave on 10/18/2000 to Bircan Unver, who was a friend and colleague of Esfandiary's for many years, Available at: lightmillennium.org/fall/fm_interviewpart1.html. See also Jordan / Frewer 2010a, 155-156.
46 Esfandiary only mentions future transhumanism peripherally in *Up-Wingers* (1973, 79). He had been aware of Ettinger's work since 1970. See Esfandiary 1970, 72.
47 FM-2030 1989, 116.
48 Ibid.
49 See Esfandiary 1973; Lavery 1992, 76-78.

omnipresent communication system (*telespheres*),[50] and demands that only those sperm and egg cells with the best possible genetic make-ups be selected and released for reproduction, which will be accomplished with the help of genetic engineering (*collaborative procreation*).[51]

Esfandiary therefore identifies the dissemination and further development of technology as the solution to all potential problems:

> We no longer only strive for better schools, more teachers, better textbooks. Schools, colleges, and textbooks are becoming anachronisms. We need more and more communication satellites, lasers, and magnetic tapes to transmit knowledge and information to every individual anywhere on the planet. Literacy itself is no longer a prerequisite for social progress. What will literacy mean in a world where instantaneous global communication has replaced the written word?[52]

The transhuman age is above all characterized by an immeasurable increase in human power. Thus early transhumanism literature presents itself primarily as the human longing for omnipotence:

> We are no longer content with simply diverting the course of rivers, reclaiming seas and deserts, creating islands, producing rain, harnessing solar energy. All this is now increasingly commonplace. We want to make alterations in the universe. We want to reclaim more planets, create new moons, nudge old ones to more suitable orbits, harness the life-bestowing energies of more giant suns.[53]

However, Esfandiary counters any potential accusation that he is propagating humanity's self-deification through transhumanist works when he declares that: "We humans do not want to play god or to be god. We aspire to much more."[54]

During the 1970s Fereidoun Esfandiary and Robert Ettinger had already formulated the goals and paths of today's transhumanism. As different as their approaches might be in detail, human mortality remains the focus and motivation of both their notions of progress, which are specifically aimed at overcoming the biological limits of the human being. Their work also reflects Julian Huxley's idea that the enlightened human being of the present must free himself from the accidental, natural history of biological evolution.

Through their books and essays, both thinkers have contributed greatly to the dissemination of transhumanist ideas. However, Esfandiary was particularly instrumental in the institutionalization of the transhumanist movement in the United States, where he supported the early Extropian movement with contributions at conferences and in journals, for which he is still revered today as *the* great pioneer of transhumanism. Ettinger's role as the founder of cryonics is also particularly acknowledged in transhumanist literature. Yet his coinage of the term *transhuman*,

---

50   See Esfandiary 1977.
51   See FM-2030 1989, 118.
52   Esfandiary 1970, 83.
53   Ibid.
54   Esfandiary 1973, 143.

which precedes Esfandiary's use of it by almost two decades, is hardly acknowledged. One can speculate whether Ettinger's use of *superman* and *superwoman* in a sense that evokes comicbook imagery might not seem too bizarre even for today's transhumanists, and thus threaten their attempt to portray their movement as a scientifically founded social utopia.[55]

Although he never considered himself as a representative of unreserved technological euphoria, the psychologist Timothy Leary (1920-1996) should nonetheless not go unmentioned as an outstanding figure of the hippie movement. He strongly opposed the oppression of humankind by both technical and political apparatuses, particularly during the period of disillusionment and lack of social perspective left behind by President Dwight D. Eisenhower and the Vietnam War. His own psychological experiments with LSD and other consciousness-expanding substances represented the first steps on the path to greater human freedom. In his later years he showed a lively interest in the possibilities of "digital immortality", nanotechnology and cryonics. Although he personally chose to have his body cremated rather than cryonically preserved, he was a prominent figure in the transhumanist avant-garde in California.[56] Finally, in his 1994 book *Chaos and Cyber Culture*, Leary committed himself to a posthumanist agenda that enthusiastically celebrates the coming age:

> We are mutating into another species – from Aquaria to the Terrarium, and now we're moving into Cyberia. We are creatures crawling to the center of the cybernetic world. But cybernetics are the stuff of which the world is made. Matter is simply frozen information.[57]

In conversation with his friend Marshall McLuhan, Leary developed the idea that the brain, like the new media, ultimately processes the sensory impressions of the environment through electrical currents. Like Moravec, at the beginning of his book Leary places a chart on the *Acceleration of Brain Power*, depicting this process as aided by television, PCs, virtual reality, etc., which will eventually give rise to a new species (*new breed*). *Homo sapiens electronicus* will no longer be a servile worker, as computers will offer them the freedom for self-realization and immeasurable pleasure:

> Owning it defines you as member of a new breed postindustrial, postbiological, posthuman because your humble VM (Volks-Mac) permits you to think and act in terms of clusters of electrons. It allows you to cruise around in the chaotic post-Newtonian information ocean, to think and communicate in the lingua franca of the universe, the binary dialect of galaxies and atoms. Light.[58]

Leary was also an important link to those representatives of the *Space Age* who advocated for the early colonization of space. From a posthumanist point of view, one important argument for overcoming the modern human being is precisely this cosmic expansion, which biological humans are currently unsuitable for. In his book *Late for the Sky*, David

---

55 See More 2013b, 11; Bostrom 2005, 10-11; Hughes 2004, 30, 160.
56 See Leary / Sirius 1997, 7-10, 143-174; Lavery 1992, 30-31; Stephenson 2014, 281-289.
57 Leary 1994, VII.
58 Ibid., 45. See ibid., 45-50; Stephenson 2014, 289-291.

Lavery notably demonstrates how humanity's obsolescence could be derived from the same "extraterrestrial imperative" formulated by NASA engineer Krafft Ehricke. The futurist Barbara Marx Hubbard also announced that it was now time to redesign the human body so that it could become perfect, beautiful, and suitable for space exploration.[59]

The *L5 Society* was formed in 1975 to serve as a catalyst for this space vision, and thus attracted a great deal of attention from the American public – alongside Princeton physicist Gerard K. O'Neill book's *The High Frontier*. It was here that he developed the idea of an orbital colony of humankind that would be built at a stable point between the Earth and the Moon.[60] Early members of this society, which at its peak had around 10,000 members, included the nanoscientist Eric K. Drexler, the science fiction writers Isaac Asimov and Robert Heinlein, and, alongside Timothy Leary, two central figures of technological posthumanism: Hans Moravec and Marvin Minsky.[61]

Unlike later posthumanists, however, Ettinger, Esfandiary, and Leary did not advocate the replacement of humans by artificial intelligences as the carriers of future evolution. Neither did they design a technical solution to the problem of human mortality, which Hans Moravec and others would attempt during the 1980s. In today's transhumanist movement, the ideas of Ettinger, Esfandiary, and Leary are merging with those of posthumanist thinkers towards a new synthesis.

From the 1980s onwards, important forums for early transhumanism included the technophile magazines *bOING bOING* (1988-1997) and *Mondo 2000* (which was also published under the title *High Frontiers / Reality Hackers* between 1984-1998). The latter was published by R.U. Sirius, at times in collaboration with Timothy Leary and the hacker St. Jude (i.e. Judith Milhon). The journal, whose early subtitle was *A Space Age Newspaper of Psychedelics, Science, Human Potential, Irrevence & Modern Art*, combined influences from the hippie rebellion, anarcho-liberalism, New Age enthusiasm, anti-intellectualism, and future-euphoric cyberpunk utopias with themes from pop culture, cryonics, art, and the transhuman lifestyle.[62]

The contents of these journals refer to the fluid transitions of the many varied technology-oriented discourses. Many posthumanist and transhumanist visions were already reflected in hacker subculture, which was itself strongly influenced by cyberpunk literature when, for example, its representative St. Jude became known to a wider public. Although many transhumanists are naïvely optimistic about the future,

---

59   See Lavery 1992, 13-14, 48, 80-81. In 1960, Manfred Clynes and Nathan Kline coined the term cyborg as an abbreviation of cybernetic organism. The word indicated an "artificially extended homeostatic control system functioning unconsciously" – in other words, a self-regulating human-machine system. They also speculated about equipping humans with additional implants and drugs so that they could move in space without space suits. See Clynes / Kline 1960, 27; Gray 2002, 18-19.

60   This point, where the gravitational forces between Earth and the Moon cancel each other out, is named *Lagrange Point 5* after the French astronomer Joseph-Louis Lagrange (1736-1813). This legacy is also reflected in the name of the *L5 Society*, founded by cryonics expert Keith Henson. See O'Neill 1977.

61   See Dery 1996, 36; Regis 1992, 62-68.

62   See Dery 1996, 31-41; Freyermuth 1998, 41-44; Graham 2002, 157-158; Rutsky 1999, 1.

modifications of the body (*body hacks*), the brain (*brain hacks*), and the senses (*sensory hacks*) are generally discussed quite critically.[63]

4.4 The Extropy Institute and the (Vita-)Mores

The artist Natasha Vita-More (i.e. Nancie Clark) was closely connected to Esfandiary, and is responsible for the transition from early transhumanism to the stance of the movement at the turn of the millennium. Together with Timothy Leary, Vita-More and Esfandiary founded transhumanist art (*Transart*) in Los Angeles in 1982. In the following year Vita-More formulated the *Transhuman Manifesto* to depict perspectives for future humanity.[64]

We are transhumans.
Transhumans integrate the most eminent progression of creativity and sensibility merged by discovery.
Transhumans want to elevate and extend life.
Transhumans seek to expand life.
As our tools and ideas continue to evolve, so too shall we.
We are designing the technologies to enhance our senses and increase our understanding.
The transhumanist ecology and freedom exercises self-awareness and self-responsibility.
Let us choose to be transhumanist not only in our bodies, but also in our values.
Toward diversity, multiplicity.
Toward non-partisan ideology (transpolitics, transpartisan, transmodernity).
Toward transhuman rights of morphological freedom, existence safety, personhood preservation.
Toward a more humane transhumanity.[65]

It was at one of Timothy Leary's parties that Vita-More met her future husband, Max More, with whom she still shapes Californian transhumanism today. Between 2010 and 2018 she served as the Executive Director of *Humanity+*, the successor organization to the *World Transhumanist Association*. In 2013 she and Max More edited the *Transhumanist Reader*, a collection of historical and programmatic contributions to the debate.[66]

Max More, formerly Max Terrence O'Connor, studied philosophy at Oxford's St. Anne's College, where he met other future euphorics, including Garret Smyth. Enthusiastic about the American magazine *Cryonics*, the friends founded the English cryonics organization *Mizar Limited* in 1986, which would become the forerunner of the later *Alcor UK Ltd*.[67] The following year Max O'Connor moved to California, changed his name to Max More and developed "his own philosophy":

---

63   See Dery 1996, 198.
64   See Vita-More 2000a.
65   Vita-More 1983. For a discussion of art, see chapter 5.3.
66   See More / Vita-More 2013.
67   For a history of the Extropy Institute see: Freyermuth 1998, 195-258; More 2013b, 12.

> I wanted to develop a way of thinking that would wake up the world to the possibilities of the future and help to stretch the minds of humanity ... Frankly I was pissed off at death and people who were aging and dying and no one seemed to do anything about it. I was frustrated that we are still stuck on this planet ... My ideas have merged into a clear vision, I now set out to bring together the finest minds to join me in shouting out to the world "Wake up! The future can be better than you ever imagined."[68]

Together with a lawyer who wrote under the name T. O. Morrow (originally Tom W. Bell) Max More founded the magazine *Extropy. Vaccine for Future Shock* in 1988, which changed its subtitle to *Journal for Transhumanist Thought* after the first few issues. The term *extropy* can be traced to T. O. Morrow and is intended to express the opposite of entropy, or the inevitable heat death of the universe. In this context, extropy therefore symbolizes the Extropians' unshakable will to live.[69]

More wrote the short essay *Transhumanism. Towards a Futurist Philosophy* in 1990 without actually referring to Julian Huxley's earlier use of the word, although the piece shares many similarities with Huxley's approach.[70] Referring to Karl Marx, Ludwig Feuerbach, and Friedrich Nietzsche, More criticized religion as a force of entropy, which establishes its power by capitalizing on the fear (of death) and social control. He countered this approach with Extropianism as the highest form of transhumanism:

> The goal of religion is communion with, or merely serving, God a being superior to us. The Extropian goal is our own expansion and progress without end ... God was a primitive notion invented by primitive people, people just beginning to step out of ignorance and unconsciousness ... Our own process of endless expansion into higher forms should and will replace this religious idea ... No more gods, no more faith, no more timid holding back. Let us blast off our old forms, our ignorance, our weakness, and our mortality. The future is ours.[71]

Max More received his doctorate in 1995 from the University of Southern California with a dissertation in philosophy supervised by Janet Levin. His dissertation *The Diachronic Self: Identity, Continuity, Transformation* essentially lays the foundation for a posthuman and cryonic theory of identity.[72] More considers his life's work primarily as the philosophical consolidation of disparate technical innovations and scientific approaches into a holistic futurology. He sees Extropianism as a new enlightenment to follow the collapse of the traditional systems of thought during the 20th century.[73]

In 1999 More founded a short-lived news channel that exclusively broadcast positive news about new psychotechnologies and inventions that bear witness to the evolution of the human species.[74] However, as a fervent supporter of fitness training and

---

68 More 2000a, 2.
69 See section 6.3.1.
70 Huxley and More share both the declaration of independence from nature and the overcoming of religion by calculable progress. See More 1990; More 2013b, 8-9; Huxley 1923, XIII; Huxley 1929.
71 More 1996, 4-5.
72 See More 1995, 24-26.
73 Max More in conversation with Gundolf Freyermuth: Freyermuth 1998, 253.
74 See Freyermuth 1998, 214.

bodybuilding, More cautioned against relying exclusively on the technical possibilities of body and mind improvement, because until implants and medication become available in the coming few years, one must keep one's body fit in the conventional way. Transhumanism is therefore by no means a philosophy that despises the body.[75]

An Extropian is characterized primarily by his "dynamic optimism", which evaluates experiences positively and thus brings about positive results. In this approach, More obviously applies Joseph Murphy's and Norman Vincent Peale's philosophy of *Positive Thinking*, especially since health, attitude to life, and professional success can also be positively influenced by such optimism. Thus, according to More: "DYNAMIC OPTIMISM is an active, empowering, constructive attitude that creates conditions for success by focusing and acting on possibilities and opportunities."[76] Extropian principles should form the basis of the new millennium's philosophy, which itself must be continually improved and expanded:

1. Perpetual Progress: Only continuous progress can guarantee that evolution using science and technology will not stagnate, while also leading man to ever higher forms, and continuously expanding his biological and mental abilities.
2. Self-Transformation: With the use of technology and drugs, a continuous improvement of mental, physical, intellectual, and ethical qualities are to be achieved on an individual level.
3. Practical Optimism: Rather than displaying entropic attitudes such as faint-heartedness, fear of the future, or resignation, practical or dynamic optimism requires an unbridled drive to continue the evolutionary process and to achieve the Extropian goals in this world: "Where others say enough is enough, we say Forward! Upward! Outward!"[77]
4. Intelligent Technology: Technology as an expression of human intellect and willpower should lead man to more freedom, as the continuation of natural evolution.
5. Open Society: Extropianism advocates a pluralistic, decentralized society that is always open to improvement. In this way, a liberal state can best fulfil its primary mandate of promoting happiness and progress.[78]
6. Self-Direction: The right to independent thought and individual freedom should be firmly established.
7. Rational Thinking: The superiority of rational thought and reason over blind faith and dogmatism must also be acknowledged.[79]

More was not only crucially important for the institutionalization of transhumanism through his programmatic ideas, but especially through the founding of the Extropy

---

[75] See ibid., 198-203.
[76] More 1998b, 1.
[77] More 1998a, 3.
[78] Here, More evidently refers to Karl Popper's work *The Open Society and its Enemies* (1945), which was widely received in the USA, and offers the model of an open society in terms of critical rationalism.
[79] See More 1998a.

Institute in Marina del Rey (CA) in 1991. Here he organized five *Extro* conferences between 1994 and 2001, as well as the *Vital Progress Summit* in 2004. These events included presentations of philosophical and technical contributions by well-known post- and transhumanists, such as Hans Moravec (1994), Roy L. Walford (1995, 1999, 2004), Natasha Vita-More (1995, 1999, 2001, 2004), FM-2030 (1995), Eric K. Drexler (1996), Marvin Minsky (1995, 1997, 2004), Vernor Vinge (1999), Ray Kurzweil (2001, 2004), and Aubrey de Grey (2004). Along with five other Extropians and transhumanists, More served on the Extropy Institute's board of directors, which also included Anders Sandberg and Natasha Vita-More. More prominent figures such as Roy L. Walford, Marvin Minsky, Gregory Stock, and Raymond Kurzweil served as scientific advisors.[80]

In 2006 the Extropy Institute discontinued its activities. Extropians seem to have become absorbed in general transhumanism or dispersed amongst the followers of the singularity movement. Most Extropians came from high-tech centers in the western USA, especially Silicon Valley, and almost all followers were white men. Economically and politically, they were predominantly advocates of unrestricted liberalism who trusted in the progress-promoting effect of a free and competitive economy – which distinguished them from other transhumanist movements.[81]

4.5 The World Transhumanist Association / humanity+

European transhumanists also established structured organizations, although somewhat later than comparable institutions in the USA. These networks of like-minded people were only made possible due to various online discussion forums. The first European transhumanism conference *Transvision98* took place in June 1998 in Weesp (Netherlands). At this event, national organizations from the Netherlands (*Transcedo*) and Sweden (*Transhumanistka Föreningen, ALEPH*) came together and, under the leadership of Nick Bostrom and David Pearce, founded the *World Transhumanist Association* (WTA). This body would then be responsible for coordinating and promoting the actions of European national associations in the future. Initially Pearce and Bostrom were the two coordinators of the *WTA*, and Bostrom chaired the board of directors from 2002 to 2008.[82] In 1999 *De:Trans* was founded as a registered association in Germany, and in Great Britain in 2004 the *UK Transhumanist Association* was created, both of which were only active until 2008. The *Association française transhumaniste – Technoprog* was only established in 2010, and has organized small *Transvision* conferences in Paris in 2014 and in Brussels in 2017.[83]

In 2008, the *WTA* changed its name to *humanity+* in order to more explicitly focus on humankind. Following Ben Goertzel's tenure Natasha Vita-More led the organisation

---

80 See www.extropy.org.
81 See Freyermuth 1998, 214; More 2000c, 1.
82 As Bostrom does not list his own leadership role in the WTA, this data was obtained via the WTA's archived web pages (www.transhumanism.org).
83 https://hpluspedia.org/wiki/UK_Transhumanist_Association. According to the Internet Archive (archive.org) this is the last published version of the German website, dated 12/28/2008. The Dutch website was last updated in 2013 (www.transcedo.org).

from 2010 to 2018, while Goertzel has recently taken over as the organisation's chairperson again.[84] Goertzel is an American IT entrepreneur, AI researcher, and author, who seeks specifically to connect transhumanism to the tradition of Russian cosmism. Other transhumanists who are or were formative for *WTA/humanity+* include: the American sociologist James Hughes, the Swedish bioinformatician Anders Sandberg, the versatile entrepreneur Martine Rothblatt, the gerontologist Aubrey de Grey, and the AI researcher Eliezer Yudkowsky.

The Transhumanist Declaration of 1998 is based on Sandberg, Pearce, and Bostrom's original initiative. The central sentences contain the following demands:

> (1) Humanity will be radically changed by technology in the future. We foresee the feasibility of redesigning the human condition, including such parameters as the inevitability of aging, limitations on human and artificial intellects, unchosen psychology, suffering, and our confinement to the planet earth ...

> (4) Transhumanists advocate the moral right for those who wish to use technology to extend their mental and physical capacities and to improve their control over their own lives. We seek personal growth beyond our current biological limitations.[85]

The definition of transhumanism that Anders Sandberg formulated in 2004 accurately reflects these growth-oriented values:

> TRANSHUMANISM: Philosophies of life ... that seek the continuation and acceleration of the evolution of intelligent life beyond its currently human form and human limitations by means of science and technology, guided by life-promoting principles and values.[86]

The online journal published by the *WTA / humanity+*, the *Journal of Evolution and Technology* (which was called *Journal of Transhumanism* until 2001), is currently edited by the Australian writer and philosopher Russel Blackford in collaboration with James Hughes. The extensive editorial board also includes the religious scholar William S. Bainbridge, Aubrey de Grey, the economist Robin Hanson, David Pearce, Anders Sandberg, the bio-tech entrepreneur Gregory Stock, and the German transhumanist Stefan L. Sorgner. While most articles initially focused on the question of when each future technology would become available, in recent years more attention has been paid to ethical and social questions about the potential consequences of robotics, artificial intelligence, and human enhancement.[87]

To my knowledge, Sorgner is also the only German-speaking transhumanist or metahumanist who is actively publishing. Together with the media and performance

---

84   See https://humanityplus.org (and corresponding archived pages).
85   *The Transhumanist Declaration*, 1998. All later versions can be found online at https://hpluspedia.org/wiki/Transhumanist_Declaration.
86   www.Aleph.se/Trans/Words/.
87   Frank Tipler originally belonged to the editorial board. See www.jetpress.org.

artist Jaime de Val,[88] Sorgner founded *Metahumanism* to occupy a mediating position between transhumanism and philosophical posthumanism. Sorgner holds a doctorate in philosophy and currently teaches posthumanism and bioethics at the American John Cabot University in Rome. He has created his *Beyond Humanism* network largely independently from established tranhumanism, and primarily with the participation of southern and eastern European philosophers. However, it remains to be seen whether he will succeed in establishing metahumanism as a philosophical school.[89]

Among transhumanists, the American entrepreneur Martine Rothblatt holds a special position, and remains active in the field of biotechnology and electrical aviation technology. She founded her *Terasem Movement* (derived from Latin for "earth" and "seed") in the early 2000s, in order to make human immortality a reality with the help of nanotechnology and digital clones (*mind clones*). Between 2006 and 2014 she edited the two journals, *Geoethical Nanotechnology* and *Personal Cyberconsciousness*, with contributions from well-known transhumanists. Rothblatt combines her technological visions with her advocacy of transgender rights and diversity – at the age of 40 she herself changed sex.[90]

In spite of the sometimes confusing variety of ideas in the field of transhumanism, there are certain mechanisms that demarcate it from other discourses. This concerns first of all the differentiation from religious traditions and ideas. Bostrom and Yudkowsky explicitly emphasize that transhumanism should only be based on reason and scientific knowledge, and Bostrom firmly rejects the attempts by Tipler and others to fuse mysticism and technological prophecy.[91]

As sociolinguistics has demonstrated, the creation of a group-specific language is a decisive factor in the formation of communal action and thinking, and establishes necessary preconditions for the genesis of collective and individual identity.[92] The Swedish transhumanist Anders Sandberg has compiled and made available an extensive compilation of terms and neologisms characteristic of internal transhumanist discourse. A few examples of these will illustrate the transhumanists' normative frame of reference.

- AMORTALIST: A person who opposes death.
- ARCH-ANARCHY: The view that we should seek to void all limits on our freedom, including those imposed by the laws of nature. [T. O. Morrow, 1990]
- ASEX: A person who has been physically and mentally altered so that it is no longer male or female. [Greg Egan, Distress]

---

88 Jaime de Val's current projects revolve around the metabody and seek to overcome previous experiences of body and physicality. See https://metabody.eu.

89 See Loh 2018, 173-175. Sorgner's book *Transhumanism* (2016) cannot be relied upon as an overview or introduction to transhumanism. The author seems to be primarily interested in presenting his own understanding of transhumanism, as well as locating himself and the metahumanism he founded in relation to transhumanism. This results in a lack of clarity regarding the history of ideas and its normative aspects for the transhumanist doctrine. See, for example, Sorgner 2016, 17-33.

90 See https://terasemcentral.org; Rothblatt 2014.

91 See Bostrom 2005, 8; Bostrom 2014, 2; Yudkowsky 2000a, 2000b.

92 See Lavery 1992, 69-70.

4. Transhumanism

- ATHANASIA: The act of preventing death.
- ATHANOPHY: A philosophical system that offers a possible means of overcoming death scientifically.
- AUTOEVOLUTION: Evolution directed by intelligent beings instead of natural selection.
- BIOCHAUVINISM: The prejudice that biological systems have an intrinsic superiority that will always give them a monopoly on self-reproduction and intelligence.
- BIOLOGICAL FUNDAMENTALISM: A new conservatism that resists asexual reproduction, genetic engineering, altering the human anatomy, overcoming death. A resistance to the evolution from the human to the posthuman. [FM-2030]
- BIOPHILIAC: someone who values life of all kinds for its own sake.
- CRYONAUT: A cryonically suspended person.
- DEANIMALIZE: To replace our animal organs and body parts with durable, pain-free, non-flesh prostheses. [FM-2030]
- DEATHISM: The set of beliefs and attitudes that glorifies or accepts death and rejects or despises immortality.
- DOWNLOAD: To transfer a mind from one computational matrix to another, especially a slower one.
- EXTROPY: A measure of intelligence, information, energy, life, experience, diversity, opportunity, and growth. The collection of forces which oppose entropy. [T.O. Morrow, 1988]
- IMMORTALIST: A person who believes in the possibility of, and who seeks to attain, physical immortality.
- JUPITER-BRAIN: A posthuman being of extremely high computational power and size. This is the archetypal concentrated intelligence.
- LONGEVIST: A person who seeks to extend their life beyond current norms (but who may not wish to live forever).
- NEOLOGOMANIA: The transhuman enthusiasm for neologisms, especially the creation of words with many prefixes.
- SINGULARITY: The postulated point or short period in our future when our self-guided evolutionary development accelerates enormously (powered by nanotechnology, neuroscience, AI, and perhaps uploading) so that nothing beyond that time can reliably be conceived.
- TIPLERITE: A person with religious faith in Tipler's Omega Point Theory (So far very rare, if any).
- TRANSCEND: To become vastly superhuman and incomprehensible for unaugmented beings.
- UPLOAD: (a) To transfer the consciousness and mental structure of a person from a biological matrix to an electronic or informational matrix (this assumes that the strong AI postulate holds). The term "downloading" is also sometimes used, mainly to denote the transfer of the mind to a slower or less spacious matrix. (b) The resulting infomorph person.

- UNIVERSAL IMMORTALISM: The view that the problem of death can be solved in its entirety (including bringing back those "dead" who were not placed into biostasis) through a rational, scientific approach.
- WETWARE: Similar to hardware, but denotes a biological system, most commonly the human nervous system (see also dryware).
- XOX: (from Xerox) An (atomically) identical copy of a person.[93]

Note the contrast between negative terms implying death, used to label critics of transhumanism (*biochauvinism, biophiliac, deathism*), as opposed to the positive transhumanist self-designations referring to immortality (*amortalist, athanasia, athanophy, immortalist, longevist*). This distinction is precisely what reinforces the construction of an elitist identity stabilizing the quantitatively marginal movement of transhumanists against the overwhelming humanist critique.

4.6 Other Actors and Institutions

In the early 2000s transhumanism was seemingly able to achieve remarkable political success, although this soon turned out to be a Pyrrhic victory. Under the leadership of the nanoscientist Mihail Roco and the sociologist of religion William S. Bainbridge, who was very sympathetic to transhumanism,[94] a first report on the convergence of NBIC technologies (nanotechnology, biotechnology, information technology, and cognitive science) was produced in 2003. The report was based on a workshop held by the US National Science Foundation in 2001, which brought together high-ranking representatives of the US government, science policy, and research. The report, entitled *Converging Technologies for Improving Human Performance*, was edited by Roco and Bainbridge and presented a notably uncritical, transhumanist agenda influenced by Eric Drexler's nanofuturology. The authors promised a golden age of peace and prosperity, with the perspective of significantly extended lifespans.

> The twenty-first century could end in world peace, universal prosperity, and evolution to a higher level of compassion and accomplishment. It is hard to find the right metaphor to see a century into the future, but it may be that humanity would become like a single, distributed and interconnected "brain" based in new core pathways of society.[95]

The established scientific community, which had become more attentive and sceptical about transhumanist activities, reacted to the report with astonishment and attempted to control the potential damage it might cause.[96] In contrast, transhumanists began to establish a new series of academic institutes, dedicated to evaluating and disseminating their own futuristic scenarios.

---

93   See in this regard www.aleph.se/Trans/Words.
94   See Bainbridge 2005, 2011, 2014.
95   See Roco / Bainbridge 2003, 6.
96   See Coenen 2010, 71-78; Heil / Coenen 2014, 153-154.

The nanoscientist Kim Eric Drexler can certainly be considered to be one of the first transhumanists. He worked closely with Gerard O'Neill in the 1970s and played a prominent role in the *L5 Society*. In his popular book *Engines of Creation* from 1986, he presented nanotechnology as a universal savior. In it, he argued that, with the help of nanorobots injected into the human body, the cellular damage of both frozen cryonics and of aging people could be repaired in the future. Although Robert Ettinger already shared this idea in 1972, Drexler based his own vision on the insights and far-reaching promises of the field of nanoscience, which was still in its infancy at that time. In the near future, molecular-sized matter converters (*universal assemblers*) would be used to address both medical problems and the economic production of resources. Drexler and his colleague Ralph Merkle were utterly convinced that nanotechnology would help to steer humankind towards a golden age without disease or old age.[97]

> If we succeed (and if you survive) then you may be honoured with endless questions from pesky great-grandchildren: "What was it like when you were a kid, back before the Breakthrough?" and "What was it like growing old?" ... By your answers you will tell once more the tale of how the future was won.[98]

Together with the futurist author Christine Peterson and the entrepreneur James C. Bennet – who were both fellow members of the *L5 Society* – in 1986 Drexler founded the Foresight Institute in Palo Alto, California, dedicated to the dissemination of a nanotechnological vision of the future.[99] Today, scarcely any transhumanist authors can afford to ignore the promises of nanotechnology.

Another central element of transhumanist futurology is found in the fusion of humans and machines to create cyborgs, especially in terms of a potential neural interface between the human brain and a computer or the Internet. Kevin Warwick, Professor of Cybernetics at Coventry University (England), caused a sensation in the early 2000s by experimenting upon himself, effectively making him the first cyborg in human history. In fact, he was the first person to implant a computer chip into his body, which emitted a localization signal that controlled lights and doors in his university.[100]

In addition to expanding the physical senses, Warwick believes that neuroimplants offer a chance to cure cancer and depression and, more generally, a method for artificially controlling moods and emotions. He is fascinated by the idea of an interface – an implanted interface between the human brain and the computer, which would feed information directly into the brain and exchange information with other brains in a higher form of communication circumventing the detour of language. According to Warwick, using superhuman brain implants to create such possibilities is the only chance for humans to remain abreast of the intelligent machines surely to arise in the

---

97   See Ettinger 1989, 193-196; Drexler 1996, 138-139; Regis 1990, 108-143; Heil 2010b, 34-40.
98   Drexler 1996, 239.
99   See https://foresight.org.
100 Today a very few companies use chip implants to locate their employees. Some US states have therefore issued legal regulations on the use of these chips. See www.en.wikipedia.org/wiki/Microchip_implant_(human).

near future, and to prevent humanity being degraded to a lower and oppressed class. In his words: "I believe humans will become cyborgs and no longer stand-alone entities."[101]

Similarly, Luc Steels (born 1954), biologist and director of the Institute of Artificial Intelligence at the Free University of Brussels, espouses a consistently positive perspective on the manifold connections between life and computers. He argues that both the creation of artificial life forms planned by humans and the linking of the human brain and the Internet represent major advances in the history of evolution.[102] While the science fiction writer Bruce Sterling predicted the future dichotomous evolution of life, Luc Steels sees *Homo Cyber Sapiens* on the distant horizon of development. These beings would gradually become less dependent on biological *wetware*, and be followed by the ascension of the artificial *Robot Hominidus Intelligens*.[103]

In his 2002 book *Cyborg Citizen. Politics in the Posthuman Age*, Chris Hables Gray provides a more nuanced consideration of the cyborgization of humans than Steels and Warwick. He perceives the dangers of potentially increasing control over human beings through the partial mechanization and technical expansion of the body, but in his opinion the advantages outweigh these disadvantages:

> Cyborgization will not make us like gods, thank goodness, but we may be able to live better and longer than any human or protohuman has before. We may be able not only to live long and prosper, but to push the species into new, enlightening adventures in inner and outer spaces ... It is thrive or die.[104]

Yet such cyborg visions appear pale and modest in comparison to the promises of Aubrey de Grey. The British gerontologist not only predicts a life span of over 1000 or even 5000 years, but also claims that even his own peers will likely be able to realize this degree of longevity. De Grey was a software engineer and entered the field of gerontology due to his late wife, the geneticist Adelaide Carpenter. In 2000, the University of Cambridge awarded him a PhD in biology for his research on mitochondria. Together with entrepreneur David Gobel, in 2003 De Grey founded the *Methuselah Foundation*, which has since launched several competitions for experiments in longevity, and is financially supported by Silicon Valley magnates such as Peter Thiel.

In 2009, De Grey established the *SENS Research Foundation* (which operated under the name *SENS Foundation* until 2013). The acronym stands for the goals of De Grey's research: *Strategies for Engineered Negligible Senescence* – strategies for the technical prevention of signs of ageing. Unlike Walford, De Grey does not recommend a specific diet or disciplined lifestyle. Rather, the ambitious researcher considers ageing a disease likely based on seven different cell processes, which can be treated by genetic engineering. His foundation is largely financed through his mother's inheritance of 11 million British pounds. Jason Sussberg's documentary *The Immortalist*, alongside countless portrayals in international media, have contributed to De Grey's image as

---

101 Warwick 2000, 151. See also Warwick 2004.
102 See Steels 1994, 1996; Brooks / Steels 1995; Flessner 1997b, 104.
103 See ibid., 85-89. In his book *Redesigning Humans*, Gregory Stock makes similar arguments to those of Steels and Warwick, but with a focus on genetic engineering. See Stock 2002.
104 Gray 2002, 201.

an eccentric genius. Due to his fantastic-looking visions and his messianic claim to leadership, however, the biogerontological research community remains largely critical of him and his work. Although De Grey advises the US Party of Transhumanists on the field of anti-aging, and continues to support cryonics, he does not label himself a transhumanist; rather, he sees himself as an immortalist.[105]

In contrast to such research institutions, there are three institutions that are determined to evaluate real and expected technical progress. However, I intentionally am not including Ray Kurzweil's *Singularity University*, launched in 2008.[106] The original inspiration for establishing an academic network of transhumanists came from the AI researcher Eliezer Yudkowsky, who founded the Singularity Institute for Artificial Intelligence in Berkeley in 2000, with financial support from the Internet entrepreneurs Brian and Sabine Atkins. The institute, which is determined to promote research into friendly AI, received a significant donation from Pay Pal founder Peter Thiel in 2006. With this funding, the first *Singularity Summit* was organized in Stanford in the same year (including Max More, Nick Bostrom, Eric Drexler, Ray Kurzweil, Peter Thiel as guests, among others). Kurzweil was co-director of the institute between 2007 and 2010, and Aubrey de Grey and Bostrom served on the institute's advisory board, the latter remaining there to this day. In 2013 the organisation's name was changed to Machine Intelligence Research Institute (MIRI). Since that time, the institute's focus been dedicated primarily to mathematical and theoretical computer science.[107] In January 2015, many MIRI members were among the first signatories of the *Research Priorities for Robust and Beneficial Artificial Intelligence* open letter, which advocated the controlled and beneficial development of AI research.[108]

In 2004 James Hughes and Nick Bostrom founded the American Institute for Ethics and Emerging Technologies (IEET) – a transhumanist think tank with a "technoprogressive agenda". As a lobby organization, the institute's mission is to emphasize the benefits of the anticipated future technologies and to engage in dialogue with critics. It is mainly due to Hughes that socio-political issues were brought into the discussion, as he sought to create a democratically founded transhumanism, the future achievements of which would benefit all people equally.[109]

The institute's list of fellows reads like a *Who's Who* of transhumanism: Aubrey de Grey, Ben Goertzel, William S. Bainbridge, David Pearce, Martine Rothblatt, Stefan L. Sorgner and Natasha Vita-More were active, and Giulio Prisco sits on the board. Between 2005 and 2014 it hosted a series of conferences on biopolitics, ethics, and artificial intelligence (the first two conferences listed are in fact the last international

---

105 See De Grey 2008; Agar 2010, 83-132; Hooper 2005; Sussberg 2014.
106 See section 6.4.2.
107 See Wagner 2015, 63-69, 77-124; https://intelligence.org.
108 This was initiated by the Future of Life Institute (Cambridge), founded in 2014. Other signatories included Stephen Hawking, Elon Musk, Nick Bostrom, Anders Sandberg and Vernor Vinge. See https://futureoflife.org/ai-open-letter.
109 Within transhumanism Hughes' utopia of a harmonious future society is also criticized and generally considered unrealistic. See Hughes 2004, 187-220; Agar 2010, 151-177.

conferences of the *World Transhumanist Association*). The IEET also publishes the transhumanist *Journal of Evolution and Technology*.[110]

However, the most astonishing phenomenon in the whole process of institutionalizing transhumanism is found in the Swedish philosopher Nick Bostrom (i.e. Nicholas Boström) and his Future of Humanity Institute (FHI), which was founded in 2005 at the renowned University of Oxford. During its initial years of operation, when Bostrom was also chairman of the *World Transhumanist Association*, the institution pursued a notable transhumanist agenda similar to those of the IEET and the Foresight Institute. It initially targeted three research areas: (1) human transformation, (2) risks of global catastrophe, and (3) the future of intelligent life. The first area was intended to explore the potential for expanding human capabilities, evaluating enhancement technologies, and developing strategies to reduce existing prejudices and misconceptions about such technologies.[111] Anders Sandberg has remained a close collaborator of the institute since its inception, and Eric Drexler and Ralph Merkle were among the earliest guest lecturers.

After the publication of Bostrom's successful book *Superintelligence. Paths, Dangers, Strategies* in 2014, the FHI began to emphasize the risks of such future technologies. They specifically focus on two aspects: firstly, efforts to ensure the safe use of artificial intelligence, especially the expected superintelligence (governance of AI). Secondly, the FHI advises political bodies, including the American *President's Council on Bioethics*, the *UK Synthetic Biology Leadership Council* and the US *Department of Defense (DARPA)*, on the opportunities and risks of biotechnology. This new emphasis is not to be understood as a paradigm shift, but rather corresponds exactly to the objectives published in 2005 (to eliminate prejudices and emphasize the potential of enhancement). Bostrom is undoubtedly and euphorically looking forward to the emergence of a superintelligence, as he associates it with a hope of solving all of humanity's problems.[112] However, the theoretical concerns, as well as the rhetoric of a safe artificial intelligence, both of which have already been expressed, can increase the social acceptance of this innovation. In the field of biotechnology, Warwick's prior narrative regarding the risks that future technologies could be rebalanced by human adaptation prevails: "Arms races or proliferation with advanced bioweapons could pose existential risks to humanity, while advanced medical countermeasures could dramatically reduce these risks. Human enhancement technologies could radically change the human condition."[113]

It is therefore not surprising that the Future of Humanity Institute, with its focus on an expected superintelligence, reflects the self-centredness and techno-centrism of transhumanism. It largely neglects the complex relationships between the use of technology and social knowledge structures. Obviously, it is not artificial intelligence that poses the greatest risk at present, but rather simple algorithms, social bots, and human agents / "trolls" spreading false reports and conspiracy theories that radicalize political and economic actors and thus destabilize political systems. However, the

---

110   See https://ieet.org.
111   See www.fhi.ox.ac.uk (10/13/2005).
112   See section 6.4.2 and chapter 6.6.
113   Homepage of the FHI (Research / Biotechnology) www.fhi.ox.ac.uk.

disastrous impact of these mechanisms is only possible due to the progressive decay of the public education sector.

4.7 Religious and Spiritual Transhumanism

After Frank Tipler's deeply Christian-influenced futurology, it was perhaps to be expected that trans- and posthumanism could hope for a positive reception amongst a progressive Christian minority. However, it was surprisingly the Mormons who first actively participated in transhumanism. The *Mormon Transhumanist Association* was founded in Utah in 2006, and has been affiliated with *humanity+* ever since. According to its own data, by 2017 it included 637 members worldwide, although only 62% of these self-identified as Mormons, while 59% considered themselves theists. Membership requires acceptance of *humanity+'s Transhumanist Declaration* and the *Mormon Transhumanist Affirmation*, which demands commitment to both Jesus Christ and to God's desire for scientific progress. This progress is expected to enable humankind to attain immortality, resurrection, and the renewal of the world. In accordance with the biblical event of the transfiguration of Jesus, transhumanist Mormons see themselves as *transfigurationalists*: Every religion includes an observable moment of transformation of the human into a higher, divine being. While the *Mormon Transhumanist Association* has not developed their own cultic practices, they organize annual meetings to discuss technical and theological issues, as well as hosting three local discussion groups in the United States.[114]

The *Christian Transhumanist Association*, on the other hand, was only founded in 2014 in Tennessee – the middle of the American bible belt. The contents of their (*Christian Transhumanist Affirmation*) creed largely corresponds to that of the Mormons, but places greater emphasis on following Christ. In addition to activities on Facebook, a local discussion group meets once a month in Nashville. The scientific advisory board includes James Hughes and Frank Tipler, while Aubrey de Grey was a guest at the 2018 annual meeting.[115]

The oldest and yet simultaneously youngest variety of religious transhumanism surrounds "Bernadeane" Brown and James Russel Strole. It is the oldest variety because the movement originated in the early 1960s. However, it is also the most recent, as it has only been visibly developing contacts with established transhumanism for a few years, and identifies itself with medical approaches to prolonging life. The origins of the movement go back to Charles Paul Brown (1935-2014), who experienced a personal revelation in 1959 during his training as a pastor of the *Assembly of God*. He became convinced that Jesus had altered his genes, thus giving him physical immortality, and that this path of salvation was open to all people. Together with his wife Bernadeane, and after 1968 with James Strole, he preached his immortalistic message, combatting all aspects of the conventional "death cult" (*extreme optimism*). As in the case of Extropianism, any discussion of dying and the end of life is always portrayed

---

114 See https://transfigurism.org.
115 See www.christiantranshumanism.org.

completely negatively. Starting in the 1980s, Brown preached that he could also transmit cellular immortality through communication and physical proximity. Initially working under the name *Eternal Flame*, later as *Flame Foundation*, *People Forever*, *CBJ* (after the leader's initials), and most recently as *People Unlimited Inc.*, the group has been based in Scottsdale (AZ) since 1971. After critical US media reportage accused the leadership trio of personal enrichment, the fellowship ceased most public appearances until Brown's death in 2014.[116]

Primarily through the instigation of James Strole, the nonprofit *Coalition for Radical Life Extension* was founded at the end of 2015. It offered a platform for various activists, and under the acronym *RAAD* (*Revolution Against Aging and Death*) has organized an annual festival since 2016. Echoing the words of Abraham Lincoln's *Emancipation Proclamation*, which declared the end of slavery in 1863, the *Coalition's* board proclaims the end of aging as follows:

> That all persons held as slaves to aging within any Country, State or designated part of a State, the people whereof shall then be in rebellion against the disease known as "aging", shall be then, thenceforward, and forever free; and the Executive Governments of all Countries will recognize and maintain the freedom of such persons, and will do no act or acts to repress such persons, or any of them, in any efforts they may make for their actual freedom.[117]

The *RAADfest*, which lasts for several days each year, seems to combine transhumanistic lectures and discussions, general life coaching, and business presentations, especially from suppliers of nutritional supplements and anti-aging therapies, who sponsor the event in great numbers. With over 1000 visitors, the festival can be considered extremely successful, and speakers have included Bernadeane and James Strole, Aubrey de Grey, Ben Goertzel, Zoltan Istvan, Ray Kurzweil, Max More, and Natasha Vita-More.[118]

The *Church of Perpetual Life* in Hollywood (Florida), active since 2013, has adopted the most concrete religious forms. It is closely linked to the *Life Extension Foundation*, which has been run by primary cryonics expert Saul Kent and William Faloon since 1980. The Foundation distributes (supposedly) life-prolonging supplements and medicines, and held assets of over 25 million US dollars in 2013. In May 2013 the foundation lost its tax exemption,[119] and one month later Faloon's *Church of Perpetual Life* opened its doors, and, like all churches in the United States, was exempt from taxes. Once a month the church, which has a membership of about 500 people, gathers to overcome the "disease of aging" with the help of supplements and cryonics. Furthermore, it venerates the Russian cosmist Nikolai Fedorov and the British science fiction writer Arthur C. Clarke as prophets. Within transhumanism, members consider themselves to be a part of immortalism. Their celebrations, which are also available on YouTube, consist of philosophical contributions to the achievement of immortality, the marketing of

---

116   See Van Velzer 2014; https://peopleunlimitedinc.com;rlecoalition.com/about.
117   Cited from https://hpluspedia.org/wiki/RAAD_Fest.
118   See https://raadfest.com.
119   The history of the foundation is characterized by disputes over the illegal distribution of medicines and alleged misuse of charitable status. (See Wikipedia, in English).

supplement products, as well as songs and lectures by transhumanist activists such as Natasha Vita-More, Aubrey de Grey, Zoltan Istvan, Max More, Martine Rothblatt, as well as James Strole and Bernadeane. At Christmas, members commemorate the frozen cryonics, known as the *ressurectables*.[120] The *Life Extension Foundation* is also an important sponsor of the *RAADfest*, where William Faloon has performed.

Although it is clearly not yet much more than an Internet phenomenon, the *Turing Church* should also be mentioned. The Italian transhumanist and cryonics expert Giulio Prisco, who was also briefly involved in the board of *humanity+*, founded the *Order of Cosmic Engineers* together with Philippe Van Nedervelde, Martine Rothblatt, and others in 2008, although it was only active until 2012. They particularly sought to advocate radically life-prolonging technologies (especially nanotechnology). Subsequently, and with great media coverage, Prisco proclaimed the establishment of the *Turing Church*, which focuses on the divinization of humans and technical immortalization. He perceived these movements as being in the tradition of the Russian cosmists. Instead of local gatherings, Prisco seeks to create a global, virtual church that congregates online in the game *Second Life*.[121] The *Way of the Future Church* founded by Anthony Levandowski (born 1980) is also difficult to comprehend empirically. However, the founder, an engineer who is known for his research on self-propelled cars, ultimately promotes the peaceful transition to an Earth dominated by artificial superintelligence.[122]

4.8 Conclusion

Since the 1960s, the history of transhumanism is littered with a wide array of academic, religious, and political movements, each seeking to stamp the concept with their own individual definitions. As this chapter has demonstrated, this ever-increasing variety of factions squabbled amongst themselves to stake claims to the immortality and eternity offered by transhumanism. However, paradoxically, in the end the only defining feature they ever truly shared was the short life span of their own efforts.[123] Transhumanists tend to be individualists who prefer to fight alone. Rivalry for public attention and sovereignty over transhumanist doctrine is generally strong, and this competition is reflected in the number of manifestos proclaimed, school and neologisms formed, and institutes founded.[124] Originality generates attention and thus financial contributions, upon which all the organizations mentioned here are of course dependent.

Creating a single and uniform characterization of transhumanism on the basis of specific and anticipated technical progress is even less possible today than 20 years ago when this book was first written. Rather, the various strands are united only by the common hope for future technologies, which should at least overcome aging and death.

---

120 See Volpicelli 2014; www.churchofperpetuallife.org; youtube.com/user/COPL18/featured.
121 See https://turingchurch.net; https://turingchurch.com.
122 See @wayofthefuture.church on Twitter.
123 For example, the numerous cryonics and immortality societies of the 1960s. See section 6.5.4.
124 The future of the recently founded transhumanist parties, as well as the lively candidate for the 2016 US presidential elections, Zoltan Istvan, is therefore uncertain. See Loh 2018, 49-50.

Within the transhumanist spectrum, it remains to be seen whether this breakthrough will emerge as the result of human activity or from a potential superintelligence. It is also open to debate whether this progress will be genetic or cybernetic. For religious transhumanism, these blessings will be due to technical progress, rather than the direct intervention of a divine power.

Transhumanism is highly dynamic. It seems to be in the nature of its followers to constantly reinvent it and to continuously produce new schools, organizations, and neologisms. Furthermore, the "future" exists only in a very abstract way. The transhumanist interpretation of such a future can be achieved through the use of various filters that fade out or marginalize negative aspects – paradigmatic for this process is the taboo surrounding death. Technical fantasies, such as immortality via computer or genetic reprogramming, are presented as factual projects whose realization requires only a few years of research and generous financial support. However, in the absence of actual progress, and in view of already existing and growing social problems, this future must be constantly reinvented – an insight that is equally applicable to technological posthumanism.

5. Technological Posthumanism

> We are living in a decisive historical time: the era of the post-human. This age is typified by a relentless effort on the part of the virtual class to force a wholesale abandonment of the body, to dump sensuous experience into the trashbin, substituting instead a disembodied world of empty data flows.[1]
> *Arthur and Marilouise Kroker*

The Canadian philosophers Arthur and Marilouise Kroker are by no means exaggerating when they announce the beginning of a new historical era, which the media scientist Bernd Flessner has also described as the "age of posthumanity".[2] At the end of the second millennium, posthumanism no longer appeared to be merely an outlying group of isolated, eccentric thinkers. Rather, today it resembles a philosophical movement with numerous major authors, an established transhumanist movement, and its own academic institutions. A whole series of philosophically minded scientists, most of whom are engaged in artificial intelligence and robotics research, are now openly arguing that, in the face of the expected advance of technology, the human being in its current form has become obsolete. In contrast to astute observers of industrial culture, such as Günther Anders, many of these thinkers now demand that humans be replaced in the history of evolution by their supposedly superior, technical products. Modern humans will initially participate in this development as cyborgs – human-machine hybrids – and later as perfect simulations of people within a computer's memory. Through this process, adherents seek to free intelligent life from its biologically conditioned barriers. The natural limits of our intellect and our bodies, including age-related degeneration, diseases, and human mortality, are now to be overcome via conscious and intentional participation in the posthuman evolutionary process.

Technological posthumanism expresses the way people think about technology and the meaning of life they associate with it. Posthumanist philosophy therefore brings

---

1   Kroker / Kroker 1996, 79.
2   See Flessner 2000a, 13.

together ideas from literature, popular culture, science, philosophy, and theology.[3] The appearance of this new type of posthumanist philosophy raises questions: Why here? Why now? What are the origins of this fundamental posthumanist idea of the technical immortalization of the human being? Was there a specific constellation in the history of ideas that favored the emergence of posthumanism in the United States and Europe? Where are its philosophical premises to be found? And finally, how can we understand and explain how, in the early 21st century, many would even plead for the overcoming of their own species and demand or at least approve of the end of all biological life?

Much has been written about posthumanism in the past 20 years. Unfortunately, much of this work is characterized by the fact that, although it comments upon individual elements of posthumanist futurology, the sources are rarely taken into account. Indeed, a contextualization of the history of ideas is usually completely absent. In continuation of the first German edition of the present work (2004), this approach will be elaborated upon here. What previous studies have neglected, is, firstly, the role of immortality in the posthumanist vision and, secondly, the reception of religious elements within the context of a cosmic concept of salvation.

This book's analytical section has been completely redesigned, as the field has become considerably more complex with regard to discussions of singularity and superintelligence. This version also includes a more clearly structured and detailed investigation of six central aspects of technological posthumanism: The posthumanist image of humans (chapter 6.2 *How We Became Posthuman*), the theory of progress (chapter 6.3 *Annihilation or Infinite Progress*), the idea of the singularity (chapter 6.4), *Immortality* (chapter 6.5), the *Transcendent Superintelligence* (chapter 6.6), and the ultimate goal of the progress movement *Omega* (6.7). The analyses are framed by an introduction (chapter 5.1) to the four most important authors of technological posthumanism, and to posthumanism and art (chapter 5.3), followed by a concluding summary (chapter 7). Recent works by these authors have also been included in the current analyses. Although other authors, such as Ben Goertzel or Martine Rothblatt, have also published posthumanist works in recent years, these newer contributions were not particularly innovative in terms of the history of ideas. Nevertheless, this literature was still taken into account in the detailed analyses in this volume. Overall, the contextualization of this history of ideas is noticeably improved due to technological advances: in terms of improvements in research methods, in the early 2000s I was still dependent on card catalogues, as online resources only existed in the most rudimentary forms).

5.1 The Posthuman and Posthumanism

During the 17th century, Thomas Blount (1618-1679) defined the word *posthumian* in his *Glossographia* (1656) as a coming future ("following or to come, that shall be"). However, the American cultural theorist Ihab Hassan (1925-2015) was the first to introduce the term posthumanism in his text *Prometheus as Performer: Toward a Posthumanist Culture?* (1977) as the philosophical attempt to overcome the human being and thus also

---

3   See Dery 1996, 15; Flessner 2000b, 259-260.

humanism.⁴ Hassan's work spans a wide range of literature, from Greek mythology to the philosophy and cybernetics of his time. For him, the figure of Prometheus symbolizes the transgression of the previous boundaries of human existence. With reference to Marshall McLuhan, Teilhard de Chardin, Buckminster Fuller, and many other thinkers, Hassan believes he can observe the emergence of a new cosmic, Promethean consciousness that will replace the humanism that has been dominant since the Renaissance. In addition, cybernetics will also change our understanding of the human being:⁵

> Will artificial intelligences supersede the human brain, rectify it, or simply extend its powers? We do not know. But this we do know: artificial intelligences, from the humblest calculator to the most transcendent computer, help to transform the image of man, the concept of the human. They are agents of a new posthumanism...⁶

In his monograph *The Post-Human Condition* (1995) the British artist Robert Pepperell (born 1963) similarly uses the term *posthumanism* to describe the period in the history of philosophy that marks both the end of humanism, as well as the incipient fusion of biological organisms and technology, to the point where they become indistinguishable.⁷ In his 1979 novella *Schismatrix*, science fiction author Bruce Sterling also speaks of posthumanism as the state of a *post-human* life form. This would be divided into two subspecies: the *shapers*, who focus on genetics, and the *mechanics*, who concentrate on cybernetic prostheses.⁸

In his work *Mind Children. The Future of Robot and Human Intelligence* (1988), which was deeply influential on posthumanism, the roboticist Hans Moravec offered a vision of a *post-biological* and *supernatural* future for humankind. During the 1990s the term *post-biologism* was increasingly replaced by *posthumanism* in publications on this new philosophy.⁹ Those leading transhumanists concerned with the implementation of posthumanism attempted to systematize the different aspects of posthuman humankind in the following ways:

> A posthuman is a human descendant who has been augmented to such a degree as to be no longer a human. Many transhumanists want to become posthuman. As a posthuman, your mental and physical abilities would far surpass those of any unaugmented human. You would be smarter than any human genius and be able to remember things much more easily. Your body will not be susceptible to disease and it will not deteriorate with age, giving you indefinite youth and vigor. You may have a

---

4   See Blount 1656; Hassan 1977, 212; Raulerson 2013, 32-33; Hayles 1999, 247; Simpson / Weiner 1989, vol 12, 197; Loh 2018, 94-95.
5   See Hassan 1977, 834, 843-850.
6   Hassan 1977, 846. The passage is from a lecture given in 1976.
7   See Pepperell 1995, I.
8   See Sterling 1985; Schröter 2002, 84.
9   Thus in 1990 Regis still speaks exclusively of the postbiological man or mind, while Dery 1996 and Hayles 1999 use only the terms posthuman and posthumanism almost without exception. See Dery 1996, 371; Hayles 1999, 343; Moravec 1988, 1; Regis 1990, 7, 144.

greatly expanded capacity to feel emotions and to experience pleasure and love and artistic beauty. You would not need to feel tired, bored or irritated about petty things.

The means by which transhumanists hope to achieve posthuman status include, but are not limited to, the following: molecular nanotechnology, genetic engineering, artificial intelligence (some think artificial intelligences will be the first posthumans), mood drugs, anti-aging therapies, neurological interfaces, advanced information management tools, memory enhancing drugs, wearable computers, economic inventions ... and cognitive techniques ... In general, technological or social inventions that improve overall economic efficiency tend to benefit transhumanist aims.

Posthumans could be completely synthetic (based on artificial intelligence) or they could be the result of making many partial augmentations of a biological human or a transhuman. Some posthumans may even find it advantageous to get rid of their bodies and live as information patterns on large super-fast computer networks. It is sometimes said that it is impossible for us humans to imagine what it would be like to be a posthuman. They may have activities and aspirations that we can't even begin to fathom, much as an ape could never hope to understand the complexities of a human life.[10]

Changing emphasis somewhat, N. Katherine Hayles defines the essence of posthumanism by means of the underlying theoretical assumptions, which are supposed to enable the transfer of the biological human being into a purely virtual existence via computer memory:

First, the posthuman view privileges informational pattern over material instantiation, so that embodiment in a biological substrate is seen as an accident of history rather than an inevitability of life. Second, the posthuman view considers consciousness ... as an epiphenomenon, as an evolutionary upstart trying to claim that it is the whole show when in actuality it is only a minor side-show. Third, the posthuman view thinks of the body as the original prosthesis we all learn to manipulate, so that extending or replacing the body with other prostheses becomes a continuation of a process that began before we were born.
Fourth and most important, by these and other means, the posthuman view configures human being so that it can be seamlessly articulated with intelligent machines. In the posthuman, there are no essential differences or absolute demarcations between bodily existence and computer simulation, cybernetic mechanism and biological organism, robot teleology and human goals.[11]

According to such preliminary labels, technological posthumanism seeks an unlimited expansion of the capabilities of biological human beings, until they are in fact no longer human beings at all. The economic and utilitarian character of this utopia thus becomes

---

10 See www.transhumanism.org/resources/faq.html (10/30/2002). Jens Schröter further uses these elements in his own definition. See Schröter 2002, 84-85.
11 Hayles 1999, 2-3.

clear ("overall economic efficiency"). N. Katherine Hayles has thereby teased out the core of posthumanist logic: Humans can be defined as an intelligent machine and is therefore replaceable by one.

5.2 The Face of Posthumanism

> I consider these future machines our progeny, "mind children" built in our image and likeness, ourselves in more potent form.[12]
>
> Hans Moravec

Frank Tipler, Marvin Minsky, Hans Moravec, and Ray Kurzweil are among the leading representatives of posthumanism. The order in which they are presented here is due to the fact that Tipler developed and published the basic principle of his later *Physics of Immortality* as early as 1986, while Minsky, as the "father of artificial intelligence", significantly influenced the ideas of Moravec and Kurzweil.

Frank Tipler

In the opening of what is probably his best known work, *The Physics of Immortality* (1994), Frank Tipler states that he is no less surprised by the book's conclusions than his readers might be:[13]

> When I began my career as a cosmologist some twenty years ago, I was a convinced atheist. I never in my wildest dreams imagined that one day I would be writing a book purporting to show that the central claims of Judeo-Christian theology are in fact true, that these claims are straight-forward deductions of the laws of physics as we now understand them. I have been forced into these conclusions by the inexorable logic of my own special branch of physics.[14]

Frank Jennings Tipler (born 1947) completed his academic training as a physicist at the Massachusetts Institute of Technology and the University of Maryland (gaining his PhD in 1976). He held several university positions (Berkeley, Oxford, Austin), and finally was appointed as professor of mathematical physics at Tulane University in New Orleans in 1981. His research mainly focuses on questions of general relativity, quantum theory, and cosmology, which he increasingly combines throughout the course of his research. His numerous early publications, which supposedly prove the non-existence of extraterrestrial intelligence in the universe,[15] are also related to his

---

12 Moravec 1999, 13.
13 See Tipler 1995. In Germany four editions of this book had been published as of 2007.
14 Ibid., IX.
15 See Tipler 1981, 1991, and Tipler's bibliographical references in: Barrow / Tipler 1986.

interest in the genesis and future development of the cosmos.[16] Even before his major scientific work *The Anthropic Cosmological Principle* (1986),[17] co-authored with the English cosmo-physicist John David Barrow (1952-2020), he and Barrow had already published numerous articles on cosmological questions since the late 1970s. The relationship of humankind to cosmic evolution was already the focus of their monograph *L'homme et le cosmos. Le principe anthropique en astrophysique moderne*, which they published in 1984 in collaboration with the French science journalist Marie-Odile Monchicourt.[18]

This decade-long scientific cooperation between Tipler and Barrow ended in 1988.[19] Barrow, unlike Tipler, stressed the limits of physical cosmology.[20] Over the years of their collaboration, Barrow had become a professor of applied mathematics and theoretical physics at the University of Cambridge, and with his more than 500 publications is considered one of the leading cosmologists of our time.

While *The Anthropic Cosmological Principle* was largely unnoticed by the outside world, Frank Tipler became famous overnight with his 1994 book *The Physics of Immortality. Modern Cosmology, God and the Resurrection of the Dead*. Tipler had presented his Omega Point Theory at a theological congress in 1988 and in fact also already published it as an essay in 1989.[21] However, he sharpened its radical formulations in the monograph, and the resultant publication caused a great stir. It was translated into German during the same year and remained on German bestseller lists for several weeks. However, his provocative attempt to address humanity's religious questions with mathematical precision met with astonishing incomprehension and harsh rejection by reviewers. Even the influential Anglican theologian John Polkinghorne and the equally well-known Protestant theologian Wolfhart Pannenberg felt compelled to make critical comments.[22] Tipler himself describes his own religious background as a path beginning in the Christian fundamentalism of his youth among Southern Baptists. He then travelled through a period of skeptical agnosticism and atheism, to finally emerge as a "fundamentalist physicist" who sought to prove the truth of Christianity. However, his fifteen-year long exchange with Pannenberg was ultimately the reason for his conversion from physicist to believing Christian.[23]

In his last monograph, *The Physics of Christianity* (2007), Tipler repeats his physical theses supporting his belief in resurrection for a popular audience. At the same time, he also addresses scientific explanations for biblical myths and miracles, such as the

---

16 In 1980 he had already written the essay *General Relativity and the Eternal Return* on questions about the beginning and end of the universe. See Tipler 1980.
17 Barrow / Tipler 1986.
18 See Barrow / Tipler 1978, 1979, 1981, 1985; Barrow / Tipler / Monchicourt 1984.
19 Their last shared publication discusses principles of action in a closed universe. See Barrow / Tipler 1988.
20 See Barrow 1997.
21 Tipler took part in the Second Pannenberg Symposium at the *Chicago Center for Religion and Science (Lutheran School of Theology)* in November 1988. See Tipler 1989.
22 Pannenberg explicitly praises the possible convergences between physics and theology, while Polkinghorne attacks Tipler as a "reductionist" and "physical imperialist". See Pannenberg 1995, 3-4; Polkinghorne 1995.
23 See Tipler 2007, 217; Tipler 2013 (video).

star of Bethlehem (supernova), virgin birth (parthenogenesis), original sin (genetic inheritance), and Jesus' walk on water (neutrino rays).[24]

Tipler's position differs from that of other posthumanists in many regards – whether in terms of his emphasis on cosmology, his euphoric images of virtual paradise, or his scientific inclusivism, which does not seek to overcome religion but to integrate it. From his cosmologically based perspective, Tipler assumes that the universe is closed, and will conclude in Omega in the distant future. Indeed, the temporal beginning and end of the universe will be marked by the initial and the final singularity.[25]

By the time of this final singularity, intelligent life – that is: Humankind along with its mechanical descendants – needs to have gained complete control of the universe. In parallel, the amount of information that life processes will diverge towards infinity as it approaches the Point Omega. According to Tipler, when the Sun has burned all of fuel, in many billions of years, the only chance of survival for humans will become a virtual existence in gigantic computers. Tipler determines the goal of these cosmological developments as the Omega Point, which he identifies with God.

Tipler makes only peripheral references to other posthumanist authors in his work. However, he does refer to Hans Moravec, who participated in his *Omega Point Colloquium* in 1990, discussing the idea of virtual immortality and the technological possibilities offered by computers.[26] He mentions Marvin Minsky's *Society of Mind* in his work, but largely ignores Ray Kurzweil's writings.[27] Frank Tipler was temporarily the co-editor of the *World Transhumanist Association's* publication the *Journal of Evolution and Technology*. While the religious implications of his theory tend to be strongly rejected within the transhumanist movement, the basic idea of a cosmic teleology did find many supporters. For example, Moravec reproduces Tipler's Omega theory without offering his own critical stance on it. The transhumanist Anders Sandberg considers Tipler, along with Freeman Dyson, as the founder of a physical eschatology, but still feels that Tipler's theses are barely tenable scientifically.[28] However, a certain influence on the Mormon and Christian transhumanists cannot be denied, and Tipler serves on the *Academic Advisory Council* of the *Christian Transhumanist Association*.[29]

Tipler's readers are offered very few clues about his work's biographical context. The first page of *The Physics of Immortality* includes a dedication of the book to his wife's grandparents, who were murdered during the German occupation of Poland in World War II: "Who died in the hope of the Universal Resurrection, and whose hope, as I shall show in this book, will be fulfilled near the End of Time."[30] Tipler here offers a small glimpse behind his curtain of physical formulas to his own personal motives: "I once

---

24 See Tipler 2007, 101-242; Tipler 2013 (video). Critical reviews of the book were also harsh.
25 An open universe originating with the Big Bang should continuously expand. However, according to the concept of a closed universe, the gravitational forces of matter slow down the expansion to such an extent that the cosmos will eventually contract again.
26 See Tipler 1995, XXIII, 17, 23-24, 225-226.
27 See ibid., 201.Tipler adds only a short reference to the acceleration of computing speeds according to "Ray Kurtzweil" [sic]. See Tipler 2007, 250, 290.
28 See Moravec 1999, 201-202; Sandberg 1998.
29 See www.christiantranshumanism.org; https://transfigurism.org.
30 Tipler 1995, V.

visited a Nazi death camp; there I was reinforced in my conviction that there is nothing uglier than extermination."[31] He also explains the problem of theodicy and the atheism it gives rise to using the example of the Holocaust.[32] And finally, despite assuming that the universal forgiveness of Omega during the end of times will necessarily forgive all the sins of everyone, even a Hitler or a Stalin, Tipler nonetheless also considers it justifiable to exclude Hitler himself from any such universal forgiveness.[33]

The thematization of death in the context of the Holocaust is personally deeply significant for Tipler and leads directly to the starting point of his physical search for immortality: "We physicists know that a beautiful postulate is more likely to be correct than an ugly one. Why not adopt this Postulate of Eternal Life, at least as a working hypothesis?"[34] The scientific message of salvation also becomes religious in Tipler's particular choice of words: "If any reader has lost a loved one, or is afraid of death, modern physics says: 'Be comforted, you and they shall live again.'"[35] However, as modern physics undoubtedly does not claim this, but rather only Frank Tipler himself, the personal aspects of *The Physics of Immortality* cannot be underestimated. Rather, they appear to help the author overcome his own deep sense of a lack of meaning, imparted to him through the deaths of his own family members during the Holocaust.[36]

Marvin Minsky

The views of the American computer scientist Marvin Minsky are also controversial – at least within transhumanist discourse. However, although he never wrote a monograph explicitly advocating the replacement of humans by their artificial successors, Minsky's influence on posthumanist philosophy can nonetheless hardly be overestimated. As a co-founder of the Massachusetts Institute of Technology's *Media Lab* together with Nicholas Negroponte, Minsky was the teacher and mentor of a number of the contemporary representatives of posthumanism and transhumanism. For example, Ray Kurzweil, Luc Steels, Eric Drexler, and Sasha Chislenko all studied with him. Hans Moravec and his colleague, the mathematician and psychologist Seymour Papert, also made their own marks by building on his research on artificial intelligence. Finally, he maintained a friendly exchange of ideas with numerous science fiction authors, such as Arthur C. Clarke, Robert Heinlein, and Frank Herbert.[37]

Marvin Lee Minsky (1927-2016) graduated and received his doctorate from Harvard and Princeton Universities. He had been involved in the development of artificial

---

31 Ibid., 11.
32 Ibid., 260.
33 See ibid., 253.
34 Ibid., 11.
35 Ibid., 1.
36 In addition, Tipler's Omega theory also offers quite trivial simplifications of his everyday life. For example, at an opulent dinner with a journalist he justifies his excessive calorie consumption with reference to his coming immortality. See Liversidge 1994, 89.
37 See the article Marvin Minsky (Wikipedia); Minsky 1996.

intelligence since the beginning of his scientific career.[38] His highly respected mentors Norbert Wiener, John von Neumann, Warren McCulloch, and Claude Shannon directed his interest in knowledge toward the question that shaped his work for decades: How does human thinking work? For Minsky, gaining a better understanding of these mental processes was the prerequisite for the development of artificially intelligent software. Throughout his career he remained concerned with the relationship between sensory perception – in terms of the mental construction of an objective environment – and the psychic inner world of feelings and ideas.[39]

In 1977, in cooperation with his colleague Seymour Papert, he achieved a theoretical breakthrough with the idea of mental agents. This postulated that the human mind does not follow a centralized model, wherein everything is controlled by one site in the brain. Rather, our mental performance is based on the complex combination of mental agents, which interact and also compete with each other.[40] Agents form units of meaning such as "eat", "lift", or "bird", which can only be meaningfully resolved or act to control human actions within semantic contextualizations with other agents. Minsky calls the interaction of these symbolic representations the *Society of Mind* – which is also the title of his main work from 1985.[41]

One could almost conclude that Minsky is responding to Tipler's physical reductionism, as he repeatedly cautions against simplifying the world to basic mathematical rules.[42] Even if Minsky understands the basic human need manifested in a longing for security, he still believes that mathematics and theology fail to do justice to the ambiguity of the objective world, due to their one-dimensional approaches.[43] Similarly, it follows that human thinking is not based on the laws of logic alone – in fact, pure logic without any goals would, in Minsky's opinion, lead directly to madness. Rather, thinking is able to transform illogical experiences into logical sentences, in order to at least satisfy the rules of reason, and reason can therefore never be reduced to logic alone. His late work *The Emotion Machine*, published in 2006, deepens these reflections on the complexity of human thinking to also include feelings, such as love, pain, and suffering. Minsky abandons the concept of "agents" in favor of that of "resources", as too many readers might equate agents with units of personal or individual motivation. The book surprisingly concludes with an expression of respect for the dignity of complexity: According to Minsky's insights, the diversity of the mind's resources is due to genetic inheritance, cultural socialization, and individual experience.[44]

As will be demonstrated in later chapters, Minsky's significance for posthumanism lies above all in the formulation of the cybernetic understanding of humankind. Even in an inconspicuous textbook on computer science, he places the evolution of humans in

---

38 He wrote his dissertation on the topic *Neural Nets and the Brain Model Problem*. See Minsky 1954; Minsky 1967, 32-66.
39 See Minsky 1965.
40 See Minsky 1977.
41 See Minsky 1988.
42 See ibid., 96; Minsky 1992b, 2.
43 See Minsky 1988, 127, 301-302.
44 See ibid., 184-189; Minsky 2006, 8, 341-346.

relation to that of machines: "One has found himself sharing the world with a strange new species within a single generation: the computers and computer-like machines."[45]

In addition, Minsky declared his support for materialism and believed that religion primarily fulfilled social functions. According to his logic, since religions primarily answer empirically and logically unsolvable (circular) questions, and then spread these unambiguous answers through indoctrination, they therefore contribute to the stabilization of the social order.[46] With regard to its relationship with science and the Enlightenment, Minsky – and with him Hans Moravec – condemned religion as backward and repressive, as for thousands of years it had prevented humans from achieving the technological immortality:

> They have always assumed that personal death was in the very nature of things. Most of their recorded history describes how their leaders were always inventing imaginary superbeings. Then, instead of trying to solve the hard technical problems, those leaders convinced their followers that simply believing those marvelous tales would endow them with everlasting life – whereas disbelief would be punished by death.[47]

At first, he only mentioned his promising visions for the optimization of humankind by means of mechanical substitutes in passing. Indeed, he only began to publish his posthumanist ideas in concrete terms in essay format in the 1990s. During his last decades, he combined his reputation as the world's most prominent representative of AI research with his commitment to transhumanist organizations. In 1997, his commitment to cryonics was publicly acknowledged at the third conference of the American *Extropy Institute*, and he began to act as one of the scientific advisors to *Alcor*, the large cryonics foundation from Scottsdale (AZ). He has also signed the *Scientist's Open Letter on Cryonics* (2004-2009).[48]

Hans Moravec

Hans Moravec (born 1948), who as an adolescent read almost exclusively science fiction, has been fascinated by robots since early childhood. He first succeeded in constructing a robot from scrap metal with a motorized arm at the age of ten. In 1953 he emigrated with his parents from Austria to Canada,[49] and, as a teenager, inspired by his electrical engineer father, he tinkered with a light-controlled robot turtle as well as his first computer. After beginning his studies in mathematics and computer science in various robotics laboratories in the United States and Canada, he worked as a programmer and

---

45   Minsky 1967, VII.
46   See Minsky 1988, 49, 247, 283-286, 306-307; Minsky 1992a, 24-25.
47   Minsky 1992a, 24. See also Minsky 1988, 41; Moravec 1988, 4.
48   In accordance with its privacy policy, *Alcor* will neither confirm nor deny freezing Minsky's body. However, Alcor's "Patient 144, died 24.01.2016" might be Marvin Minsky, who was apparently frozen three days after his death without the cooperation of his family (alcor.org/blog/a-1700-case-summary-patient-144/). (alcor.org/blog/a-1700-case-summary-patient-144/). See also Kurzweil 2016 (video).
49   See Moravec 1999, VII.

research assistant. When he received his doctorate in robotics from Stanford University in 1980, he was offered a research professorship at Carnegie-Mellon University, where he headed the *Mobile Robot Laboratory* until 2005. In 2003 he founded the *Seegrid Corporation* in Pittsburgh, which develops and produces autonomous transport and control systems for industrial and warehouse technologies.

In 1988 his work *Mind Children. The Future of Robot and Human Intelligence*[50] was published, already distributed in manuscript form, and it established him as the real founder of a posthumanist philosophy for many of today's followers. In contrast to the early works of Tipler and Minsky, where posthumanist possibilities for the development of life are mentioned only marginally,[51] the roboticist Moravec instead focuses on his own optimistic visions. Even his preface reads like a preamble to posthumanism:

> Engaged for billions of years in a relentless, spiraling arms race with one another, our genes have finally outsmarted themselves ... What awaits us is not oblivion but rather a future which, from our present vantage point, is best described by the words "postbiological" or even "supernatural". It is a world in which the human race has been swept away by the tide of cultural change, usurped by its own artificial progeny ... within the next century they [the machines] will mature into entities as complex as ourselves, and eventually into something transcending everything we know – in whom we can take pride when they refer to themselves as our descendants.[52]

Moravec believes that posthuman artificial intelligences will have a similar relationship to humans as children have to their parents.[53] In reference to the evolutionary theorist Richard Dawkins' metaphor of God as a blind watchmaker, Moravec's interprets humanity and its posthuman heirs as assuming direction of the watchmaker's hand.[54]

Moravec has been reiterating this message for more than three decades. In numerous publications he has announced the imminent appearance of artificial intelligence, which should be as powerful as the human mind by now, according to his prophecies during the 1980s.[55] His second monograph *Robot. Mere Machines to Transcendent Mind* (1999) met with great interest, despite not advancing the field in any significant way.[56] Published at the same time as Ray Kurzweil's *The Age of Spiritual Machines*,[57] the book's success and significant impact are likely due to the techno-euphoric mood of the late 1990s.

However, AI research experts reject Moravec's futuristic prophecies as groundless speculation, primarily because Moravec argues as a roboticist: He is only peripherally concerned with the development of complex AI, and instead mainly interested in the autonomous control of machines in space. Moravec only considers the storage capacity

---

50 See Moravec 1988.
51 See Barrow / Tipler 1986; Minsky 1988.
52 Moravec 1988, 1.
53 See Moravec 1999, 13.
54 See ibid., 158-159. Dawkins in turn invokes theologian William Paley's metaphor of God as the cosmic clockmaker in his *Natural Theology*. See Dawkins 1996.
55 See ibid., 68-74; Moravec 1996b, 1996c, 1998, 1999, 72-74; Moravec / Shieber 1997.
56 See Moravec 1999; McGinn 1999.
57 See Kurzweil 1999a; 1999b.

and computing speeds of a system as a criterion of intelligence, and largely neglects the "software" of thinking, the development of which causes so many problems for AI research.[58]

In his broad scope, Moravec also addresses sociological questions of a future society, when human work will have become superfluous and the control of the economy will be in the hands of robot corporations.[59] However, Moravec does not believe that humans will be degraded to second-class citizens, but rather that they will be offered the chance to overcome their own biological limitations in symbiosis with computers.[60]

Moravec's outstanding importance for posthumanist philosophy stems primarily from the fact that, in 1988, he was the first scientist to formulate the technical possibilities of virtual immortality. Not as a science fiction author, but as a scientific visionary, Moravec portrays the normative guiding ideas for the future development of humanity. He describes the technical process of this possible transmigration in precise detail:[61]

> You've just been wheeled into the operating room. A robot brain surgeon is in attendance. By your side is a computer waiting to become a human equivalent, lacking only a program to run ... The robot surgeon opens your brain case and places a hand on the brain's surface ... Instruments in the hand scan the first few millimeters of brain surface ... These measurements, added to a comprehensive understanding of human neural architecture, allow the surgeon to write a program that models the behavior of the uppermost layer of scanned brain tissue. This program is installed in a small portion of the waiting computer and activated ... The process is repeated for the next layer ... In a final disorientating step the surgeon lifts out his hand. Your suddenly abandoned body goes into spasms and dies. For a moment you experience only quiet and dark. Then, once again, you can open your eyes ... Your metamorphosis is complete.[62]

In an early article in a science fiction magazine in 1979, Moravec predicted that the technological prerequisites – i.e. memory, computing power, and artificially intelligent computer programs operating on a human level – could become reality in just ten years.[63] Moravec thus develops his vision of humans as virtual simulation within a computer's memory, which will ensure their infinite existence while biological humanity slowly dies out. Moravec claims that he had already developed this idea of uploading during his high school years.[64] This passage from Moravec's *Mind Children* outlines the concrete technical process of immortalization for all later posthumanist

---

58   See Moravec / Shieber 1997; Minsky 1988.
59   See Moravec 1999, 127-162.
60   See Moravec 1988, 100-102.
61   See ibid., 108-109. However, in a 1993 essay Moravec discusses mind transplantation (mind transplant), which avoids religious implications. See Moravec / Pohl 1993, 66. Moravec assumes that Alan Turing already considered this option of a technical transmigration of souls. See Moravec 1999, 77-78.
62   Ibid., 109-110. An early version can be found in Moravec 1979, 78-82.
63   See Moravec 1979, 76-77.
64   See Regis 1990, 156.

authors: By being scanned, the material brain serves as the template for a further, unlimited existence in virtuality. Both transhumanists and their critics refer constantly to this technical description of uploads.[65] To this end, Moravec considered three further possibilities for recording our brain contents: first, by means of a high-resolution brain scan, which would not destroy the original brain, but could entail the philosophical problem of a virtual doppelganger. Second, by means of a portable computer that records all brain activities and interactive experiences with the environment. Thirdly, Moravec imagines that the largest connection between the two hemispheres of our brain, the *corpus callosum*, could be tapped by a computer:

> Suppose in the future, when the function of the brain is sufficiently understood, your corpus callosum is served and cables leading to an external computer are connected to the severed ends ... In time, as your original brain faded away with age, the computer would smoothly assume the loss of functions. Ultimately your brain would die, and your mind would find itself entirely in the computer.[66]

Hans Moravec does not appear to hold official positions in any of the transhumanist organizations, but he has published a paper in the *Journal of Evolution and Technology* and was an opening speaker at the first meeting of the *Extropy Institute* in 1994. However, since establishing his enterprise in 2003, he has scarcely published.[67]

Ray Kurzweil

Raymond C. Kurzweil (born 1948) is certainly Marvin Minsky's most famous former student. He has founded no less than six companies in the information technology industry since graduating from MIT in 1970.[68] His innovations include the *Xerox* reading machine for the blind (1976), which converts texts into spoken language, as well as speech recognition programs, computer programs for musical compositions, and software for keyboards. Another career high point was certainly his 2012 appointment as Director of Engineering at Google, where he focuses upon machine learning and language processing. Several dozen national and international awards – including 20 honorary doctorates – have so far been awarded to recognize the Boston-based inventor's efforts. In various interviews, Kurzweil always emphasizes that he is doing his utmost to achieve the singularity: the historical moment of redemption at which technical immortality should become possible. He therefore follows a strict diet and takes countless vitamins and dietary supplements daily.[69]

The entrepreneur Kurzweil marketed his book *The Age of Spiritual Machines. When Computers exceed Human Intelligence* (1999)[70] with a advertising campaign simultaneously in several countries. It therefore enjoyed the attention of reputable newspapers in

---

65 See Dery 1996, 299-301; Leary / Sirius 1997, 171; Regis 1990, 4.
66 Moravec 1988, 112.
67 See Moravec 1992, Moravec 1998, Moravec 1999, 219 and http://www.extropy.org/events.
68 These include *Kurzweil Computer Products*, *Kurzweil Music Systems*, *Kurzweil Applied Intelligence*, *Waltham*, *Kurzweil Educational Systems*, and *Kurzweil Technologies*. See Kurzweil 1999a, 367-368.
69 See Keller 2003, 14-17; Agar 2010, 35-81.
70 See Kurzweil 1999a.

Germany such as the *Frankfurter Allgemeine Zeitung* and *ZEIT* – leading technology critics even chose Kurzweil as the key representative of a posthumanist techno culture. In my opinion, this makes Kurzweil the only posthumanist protagonist to have been noticed by the broader public so far. In 2009, a documentary film about Kurzweil called *Transcendent Man. The Life and Ideas of Ray Kurzweil* was even screened.[71]

His early work *The Age of Intelligent Machines*,[72] published in 1990, was the best-selling book in computer science at the time. It provides a technical overview of the development of artificial intelligence. The book contains a short future scenario depicting potential consequences of the increasing use of machines in the working world, as well as some predictions for future leisure activities.[73] In 1990 Kurzweil's grandest prophecy was that a computer will have developed its own consciousness sometime between 2020 and 2070.[74] However, Kurzweil wants to introduce the beginning of the end of humankind in his next book *The Age of Spiritual Machines* of 1999: According to him, by the year 2099 humans and machines will have merged, and humankind will have overcome its biological condition.[75] In his most radical work, *The Singularity is Near* (2005), the prospect of salvation is accelerated by half a century to the year 2045, and Kurzweil promises a universal solution to all of humanity's problems.[76]

In his later works, Kurzweil combines the posthumanist visions and arguments of Marvin Minsky, Hans Moravec, and Frank Tipler, as well as other futurists such as Vernor Vinge, who has shaped the concept of technological singularity from the 1980s. Although his ideas offer few innovations to broader posthumanist discourse, his publication success can be explained by his ability to present certain posthumanist ideas in a direct and comprehensible way. Kurzweil has never stood at the center of transhumanist organizations and institutions, but, as discussed in the previous chapter, he nevertheless remains extremely well networked and often welcomed as a guest speaker. Kurzweil is also a cryonics enthusiast and will be frozen at *Alcor* after his death.[77]

Since the 1990s, Kurzweil has also been writing self-help books such as *The 10% Solution for a Healthy Life* (1993), in which he advocates a low-fat diet. He gave further advice in 2004 with *Fantastic Voyage: Live Long Enough to Live Forever* (co-authored with Terry Grossman). The authors argue that therapies utilizing genetic engineering and nanobots will become available around 2024 and will be able to stop and reverse the ageing process. One therefore needs to postpone one's own death until this time, when the last frontier of life can be overcome with the aid of these new technologies.[78] In a slightly modified follow-up volume, *Transcend: Nine Steps to Living Well Forever* (2009), both authors advocate transcending "humankind's Stone Age genes".

---

71   See Wagner 2015, 100.
72   See Kurzweil 1990.
73   See ibid., 401-416.
74   See ibid., 483.
75   See Kurzweil 1999a, 277-280.
76   See Kurzweil 2005.
77   See Philipkoski 2002.
78   Kurzweil / Grossman 2004, 4. They regard Aubrey de Grey as the guarantor of this utopia.

A remarkable biographical parallel can be found between many of the most important post- and transhumanists: They are first or second-generation American immigrants. Hans Moravec immigrated to the United States from Austria via Canada. Ray Kurzweil is the son of Jewish emigrants from Vienna. Fereidoun M. Esfandiary, who was born in Iran, and Max T. O'Connor, the leader of the Extropians, who grew up in England, even changed their names in their adopted American home to FM-2030 and Max More, respectively, thus concealing their ethnic origins. The latter in fact wrote his philosophical doctoral thesis (*The Diachronic Self*) at the University of Southern California on the theory of identity construction independent of the body.

One might speculate that some posthumanists' experience as immigrants or as children of immigrants to the United States has enabled a special relationship to their own subjective processes of identity construction. The authors discussed are obviously not representatives of immigrant cultural ghettos, as they have in fact established themselves extremely successfully in American society. This process of adaptation does not understand identity as purely ethnic heritage, i.e. as the product of a physical genealogy, but rather as the result of cultural assimilation. That is to say: It is not the body that determines personal identity, but the mind. This assumption is remarkable for being the precise starting point of the theory of identity, which is so very fundamental to posthumanism.

5.3 Posthumanism and Art

> In fact, it is now time to REDESIGN HUMANS, TO MAKE THEM MORE COMPATIBLE WITH THEIR MACHINES.[79]
> *Stelarc*

The future has been the subject of artistic creations ever since the Italian poet Filippo Tommaso Marinetti inspired the birth of Futurism. Thereafter, contemporary art sought to imagine this future human, and its portrayals mirrored developments in the philosophical-technical doctrines of posthumanism, as well as the technological discussions within transhumanism. In fact, the scholarly debate over posthumanism originated at *Art Forum International*.[80] The relationship between humans and technology prompted Marinetti to publish the *Manifeste du Futurisme* as early as 1909. This text glorified the world of machines and made the human body appear obsolete:

> 'Come, my friends!' I said. `Let us go! At last Mythology and the mystic cult of the ideal have been left behind. We are going to be present at the birth of the centaur and we shall soon see the first angels fly! We must break down the gates of life to test the bolts and the padlocks! Let us go! Here is the very first sunrise on earth!
>
> ... We declare that the splendor of the world has been enriched by a new beauty: the

---

79 Stelarc 1998, 121.
80 See Rötzer 1989, 1996a.

> beauty of speed. A racing automobile with its bonnet adorned with great tubes like serpents with explosive breath ... a roaring motor car which seems to run on machine-gun fire, is more beautiful than the Victory of Samothrace ...
>
> What is the use of looking behind at the moment when we must open the mysterious shutters of the impossible? Time and Space died yesterday. We are already living in the absolute, since we have already created eternal, omnipresent speed ...
>
> We want to demolish museums and libraries, fight morality, feminism and all opportunist and utilitarian cowardice.[81]

In Marinetti's concept of futurism, nature would be literally overtaken by the speed, power, and beauty of automobiles and airplanes, leaving behind a "mud-spattered and smelly" human body.[82] Marinetti exuberantly calls for the rise of those mechanical, non-human beings who can keep up with this new omnipresent speed, and who will meet the transformative and optimizing potential of machines.[83]

Following in the tradition of Marinetti, the English artist Robert Pepperell, who teaches at Cardiff School of Art and Design, published his *Post-Human Manifesto* in 1995. In addition to general statements, the 16-page confession touches on aspects of consciousness, science, the order and continuity of our worlds of experience, art, creativity, and artificial entities:

> Post-Humanists are people who understand how the world is changing. By understanding this they are changing the world ...
> It is now clear that humans are no longer the most important things in the universe. This is something the humanists have yet to accept ...
> In the Post-Human era machines will be gods ...
> Complex machines are an emergent life form ...
> Currently the output of computers is predictable. The Post-Human era begins in full when the output of computers is unpredictable ... [84]

Pepperell differs fundamentally in certain ways from representatives of technological posthumanism. He understands consciousness as an achievement produced by the entire human organism, rather than just the brain. He also sees all being as determined by energy, and consequently that there is no ontological difference between living beings and inanimate things. Humanity's position in this world is therefore an open question: "The humanist era was characterized by certainty about the operation of the universe and the place of humans within it. The post-human era is characterized by uncertainty about the operation of the universe and about what it is to be human."[85] Many of Pepperell's early ideas later appear in critical posthumanism, but without reference to the artist as their original source.

---

81   Fillippo T. Marinetti : *Manifeste Initial du Futurisme*. Trans. by Joll 1960, 179-182.
82   See ibid., 180.
83   See Rötzer 1997, 74.
84   Pepperell 1995, 180-195.
85   Pepperell 1995, 191. See ibid., 181-191.

In his enthusiasm for "modern life", Marinetti defined the human being as a machine and advocated for the improvement of this human machine. The Australian performance artist Stelarc (i.e. Stelios Arcadiou) (born 1946) is building on on these futuristic ideas by celebrating the fusion of humans and technology. His message, which he has been staging in an anti-philosophical way for 50 years using sensational "physiological performances", consistently reiterates that the human body is obsolete. Stelarc can thus be considered one of the earliest representatives of contemporary transhumanist visions.[86] He is convinced that, in a postmodern society that is about to venture off into space, a soft and watery body can only be a hindrance:[87]

> It is time to question whether a bipedal, breathing body with binocular vision and a 1400ccm brain is an adequate biological form. It cannot cope with the quantity, complexity, and quality of information it has accumulated; it is intimidated by the precision, speed, and power of technology and it is biologically ill-equipped to cope with its new extraterrestrial environment.[88]

In 1981, in the Tokyo performance of *The Third Hand*, Stelarc first presented an artificial robot hand attached to his right arm. In later performances, this hand moved using a complex system of sensors, semi-dependently of Stelarc's control, as did a pair of artificial laser eyes that emitted beams. While these technical extensions of the body were presented as prostheses of the body until the end of the 1980s, in more recent performances Stelarc's body formed a symbiosis with mechanical supplements.

This staging of a paradigmatic earthquake, as art critics perceived it, was achieved by Stelarc in performances such as *Structure/Substance: Amplified Body, Laser Eyes, and Third Hand, Re-Wired/Re-Mixed, Propel* (1990, 2015, 2016), *Host Body/Couple Gestures: Event for Virtual Arm, Robot Manipulators, and Third Hand* (1992), and *Remote Gestures/Obsolete Desires* (1993). The movements and reactions of the technology fused to his body were involuntarily controlled by the artist's heartbeat, brain waves, and abdominal muscles. While sensors recorded Stelarc's sensory stimuli, his muscles were connected to electronic stimulators that reacted to his movements and left him trembling like a puppet. Humanity's potential future harmony with machines reached its climax in Stelarc's performance *Fractal Flesh: An Internet Body Upload Performance* (1995), in which muscle stimulators were coupled with signals connected to the Internet, and the artist performed an archaic-looking dance synchronized with a steel industrial robot.[89] Stelarc went one step further in 2008 when he had a silicone third ear surgically implanted in his forearm (*Ear on Arm*).[90]

Stelarc's physiological performances form a totality (a *Gesamtkunstwerk*), which does more than propagating the spiritual overcoming of the body beyond the limitations of mere flesh and blood. In his early performances and most recently again in 2012 (*Ear

---

86   See Koplos 1993, 104. Stelarc's texts, especially regarding the technical details of his visions and descriptions of his projects, can be found on his homepage: stelarc.org.
87   See Stelarc 1996, 73-75; Stelarc 1998, 118.
88   Stelarc 1998, 117.
89   See Koplos 1993; Caygill 1997; Dery 1996, 153-169.
90   See stelarc.org/projects.php.

on *Arm Suspension*) he had himself suspended on steel hooks pulled through his skin. Through his art, Stelarc wants to prepare the weak biological body for its future union with technological body extensions.[91]

For Stelarc, the age of post-evolution dawned with the conscious planning of future life forms through both genetic engineering and the use of technical implants. The body will overcome its biological constitution and the form will become freed from matter, in order to create a planetary human being independent of the earthly biosphere. Stelarc has high hopes for nanotechnology, which he believed could transform humans from the inside out into a machine whose faulty parts can be easily replaced:[92]

> THERE WILL TECHNICALLY BE NO BIRTH. And if the body can be redesigned in a modular fashion to facilitate the replacement of malfunctioning parts, then TECHNICALLY THERE WOULD BE NO REASON FOR DEATH … Death does not authenticate existence. *It is an outmoded evolutionary strategy* … In the extended space – time of extraterrestrial environments, THE BODY MUST BECOME IMMORTAL TO ADAPT.[93]

Stelarc's most expansive visions of the future human body end in virtual space, since a material body will also remain prone to error and can only move through real space with difficulty. The possibilities of a phantom body – manifesting as a virtual reality image – serve to reveal the "impotence" of the physical body.[94]

According to Stelarc, humankind's simultaneous merging with artificial intelligence will occur in virtual space, and will open up humans' higher consciousness to a new age: "The significance of interfacing with it is that they culminate in an ALTERNATE AWARENESS THAT IS PAN-HISTORIC AND POST-HUMAN."[95] Despite his commitment to overcoming contemporary humanity, Stelarc remains skeptical of Hans Moravec's visions of immortality and instead wants to address practical questions of expanding the physical body – rather than overcoming it metaphysically:

> No body, no consciousness. After all, consciousness is the result of an interaction with the world… The idea of consciousness detached from the body is nonsense… My ideas, which I apply in these performances, are not science fiction ideas. I am not interested in things and ideas that cannot be experienced, whether through the body, interactions with machines, other bodies, or other social systems.[96]

While Stelarc is certainly one of the most important contemporary artists within the international performance art scene, Natasha Vita-More remains largely unknown outside the transhumanist movement, and does not refer to recent artists either.[97] Her sketch of a *Transhuman Manifesto* from 1983 remained unpublished for a long time,

---

91 See Neesham / Smith 1995; Rötzer 1997, 74-76.
92 See Virilio 1995, 120-123.
93 Stelarc 1998, 120.
94 See ibid., 123.
95 Ibid.
96 Stelarc 2000, 123, trans. by AJ.
97 See Vita-More 2013.

yet she lays claim to being a pioneer of a transhumanist art epoch and to heralding the end of modern art.[98] While Marinetti sees speeding cars as legitimizing the stormy optimism of progress, for Vita-More the spaceships of the 21st century offer the metaphor of unlimited technical possibilities:

> How will the 21st Century look like? It will look like the 21st Century technology space craft that will steam across the solar system and beyond; like the new and versatile durable immortal bodies that we will inhabit ... like the vision of those imaginative to transcend the limitations of their conditions with the fusion of biology and intelligent machines.[99]

Above all else, transhumanist art was responsible for artistically illustrating futuristic visions. Vita-More, who mainly produces video art and digital images, declared in the *Extropic Art Manifesto* in 1997:

> We are transhumans. I am the architect of my existence. My art reflects my vision and represents my values. It conveys the very essence of my being – coalescing imagination and insight, challenging all limits ... We are neo-cyberneticists utilizing high-end creativity ... Extropic Art emphasizes the infinite possibilities of self-transformation ... We are active participants in our own evolution from human to posthuman.[100]

For Vita-More, the most important themes include: escape from natural evolution, the preservation of eternal youth and beauty, and the prospect of a perfect future body. Art should not only describe these technical visions but should also play a decisive role in shaping the future design of posthuman beings. It should also pay particular attention to the development of an automorphic sexuality – that is, the design of new and better genitals.[101] To this end, a fictional advertisement by transhumanist artists advertises the body model *Primo 3M+*, which will be ageless, environmentally friendly, and turbo-optimistic compared to our present bodies. It will contain over 100 quadrillion synapses and automatic error correction, as well as the ability to change sexes at will.[102] In Vita Mores' imagination, art will play the central mediating and realizing role between science, technology, and culture within this process of recreating humanity.[103]

The French performance artist ORLAN already took the first steps on this path of autotransformation when she created *Carnal Art (Art Charnel)* in the 1970s. Numerous performances and exhibitions in major museums and art institutions reflect the worldwide interest in her work, at which she remains highly active today.[104] Alongside Stelarc, she is firmly convinced that the human body is obsolete and can no longer keep up with accelerated technological progress: "We are at the junction of a world for

---

98   See Vita-More 1997b, 3-4; Vita-More 2000a, 2.
99   Vita-More 1995, 2.
100 Vita-More 1997b.
101 See ibid., 4; Vita-More 1997a, 2-3.
102 See *Primo 3M+* at: https://natashavita-more.com/.
103 See Vita-More 2000b.
104 For an introduction to ORLAN's work see O'Bryan 2005 or her website www.orlan.eu.

which we are no longer mentally or physically prepared."[105] She therefore vehemently advocates for liberation from the constrictions of nature:

> Are we still convinced that we should bend to the determinations of nature? This lottery of arbitrarily distributed genes ... My work is a fight against the innate, the inexorable, the programmed, nature, DNA (which is our direct rival as artists of representation) and God! One can therefore say that my work is blasphemous. It is an attempt to move the bars of the cage, a radical and uncomfortable attempt. It is only an attempt.[106]

ORLAN considers biological reproduction and natural birth to be anachronistic and ridiculous in the high tech world in which biological sensations such as pain can now be easily manipulated with chemicals: "Carnal Art ... rejects the mercy of God – Henceforth we shall have epidurals, local anaesthetics and multiple analgesics! (Hurray for the morphine!) Vive la morphine! (down with the pain!) A bas la douleur!"[107] In her first highly-acclaimed performance *Le baiser de l'artiste* in Paris in 1977 she portrayed Sainte-ORLAN, who alternated between two opposite yet traditionally iconic representatives of womanhood: The Virgin Mary and Mary Magdalene, the mother figure and the prostitute. In later performances, the body is used to represent her artistic message as the antipode of the biblical word made flesh. Instead, the body itself becomes an adaptable and updateable software.[108] In her *Manifesto of Carnal Art (Manifeste de L'Art Charnel)* of 1997, the provocative artist formulated the main features of her universal body project:

> Carnal Art is self-portraiture in the classical sense, but realised through the possibility of technology. It swings between defiguration and refiguration. Its inscription in the flesh is a function of our age. The body has become a "modified ready-made", no longer seen as the ideal it once represented; the body is not anymore this ideal ready-made it was satisfying to sign.[109]

In 1990 ORLAN's piece *Art Charnel* attempted to transgress the previous boundaries of art itself. This early work also fell within the tradition of body art, in which the human body serves as an artistic object of experience. In her lifelong performance *Self-Hybridations*, she successively changes her own body by means of cosmetic surgery as a *Gesamtkunstwerk*. She herself describes this process as *réincarnation de Sainte-ORLAN*. During the surgeries, which were recorded on video and transmitted live via satellite to art museums and galleries worldwide, the artist recites philosophical texts. She perceives her physical transformation as a *rite of passage*, which she understands as the self-realizing adaptation of her outer shell to her inner, gender-transcending identity: "Je suis une homme et un femme!"[110] On the event of her death, she wishes to have

---

105 Quoted in Reitmeier 1996, 12.
106 Ibid.
107 ORLAN 2000, 2.
108 See ibid.; MacCorquodale 1996; Dery 1996, 239-240.
109 ORLAN 2000, 1.
110 Quoted in Reitmeier 1996, 3.

ORLAN's completed body mummified and exhibited in a museum as a permanent installation.[111]

As she condemns plastic surgery as the greatest expression of male power, ORLAN consciously opposes patriarchal beauty standards for women and the absolute cult of youthfulness. For example, she had her cheekbones reinforced with striking implants, and in 1999 the bridge of her nose was significantly enlarged during her 7th operation.[112] ORLAN uses these actions to raise questions about the status of the body, such as: What does it mean when, in the dawning age of genetic engineering, we can change our physical appearance almost at will? How can the realization of personal identity assert itself against an omnipresent media industry's conformist ideal of the body?[113] In her most recent project from 2018, she created an artificially intelligent robot image of herself, called the ORLANOÏDE, which interacts with the audience and once again questions the values of our technological creations.[114]

ORLAN's performances have received considerable attention in France and internationally, even beyond the narrow world of the art community. Her works stage the arbitrary changeability of the human body, which she understands to be obsolete. However, she does not wish for this liberation from the rule of the genes to be endangered by new and old social restrictions.

Several younger artists also seek to engage in a critical examination of the posthuman. The Brazilian artist Eduardo Kac (born 1962) is preoccupied with biotechnology and communication technologies. In fact, he claims to be the first person to have had a computer implanted under his skin in 1997. In his *transgenic art* or *bioart* he experiments with human, plant, and animal DNA, and even exhibited a fluorescent rabbit (*Alba*) in 2000. Kac seeks to reconstruct the limits of human experience as artistically tangible and debatable, rather than absolute.[115]

The artist couple Neil Harbisson (born 1984) and Moon Ribas (born 1985) also follow in the footsteps of Stelarc and Kevin Warwick. Harbisson, who has been unable to see colors since birth (achromatopsia), had an antenna and a microchip implanted on the occipital bone of his skull in 2004, which transform colors into audible sounds. In his works of art he picks up external signals (e.g. via Internet-based communication), which he converts into color images. In 2013, Moon Ribas had a seismic sensor implanted in her forearm, which emits vibrations during earthquakes occurring anywhere on the planet (the sensor receives the signal via a global measuring station on the Internet). She translates these seismic perceptions into dance and music. Working with Harbisson, Ribas also developed "transdental communication", which allows the two artists to communicate with each other via Morse code through matching vibrating dental implants.[116] In 2010, Harbisson and Ribas founded the *Cyborg Foundation*, which aims to support people in becoming cyborgs, and thereafter to claim their rights as such.

---

111   See ibid., 13.
112   See ORLAN 1999; Reitmeier 1996, 8-11.
113   See Reitmeier 1996, 7.
114   See www.orlan.eu/orlan-et-lorlanoide.
115   See ekac.org.
116   See www.cyborgarts.com.

These include: the right to physical integrity, including technical components; the right to technical modifications or extensions of the body; the same legal status for mutants as for humans; and the right to ownership of all permanent extensions of the body.[117]

In 2017, Harbisson and Ribas founded the *Transpecies Society* in Barcelona together with the Spanish artist Manel Muñoz. These artists share a vision of technology as part of nature. As members of a non-human species, they want to claim the freedom to equip their bodies with new organs and senses, in a manner of their own choosing. Muñoz also sees himself as a cyborg artist, as his implant measures air pressure and converts its changes into physical vibrations.[118]

The two French artists Fabien Giraud (born 1980) and Raphaël Siboni (born 1981) refer directly to technological posthumanism in their own video art. Their 2014 meditative-abstract film series *The Unmanned* addresses themes of humans and technology, and follows a historical arc beginning with the early Spanish conquest of what is now Silicon Valley in the piece *1542 – The Flood*, extending to the film *2045 – The Death of Ray Kurzweil*. Thus, in the piece *1997 – The Brute Force*, the camera uses slow-motion movement to capture and portray the empty space remaining after Garry Kasparov's defeat by the computer Deep Blue.[119] The Swiss photographer Matthieu Gafsou (born 1981) produces work of a more documentary style. In his project *H+* (2018) he is visually recording the techniques and primary actors in the European transhumanism and robotics industries.[120]

Like Stelarc's technocentricism and Natasha Vita-More's *Extropian Art*, ORLAN's *Art Charnel* defines itself using various aspects of posthumanism's process of releasing the body from its limits via artistic contributions to the design of future life forms. Each of these artists shares a contempt for the natural and accidental evolution of the biological species of humankind, whose flawed nature and impotence in the face of the magnificent power of machines was revealed by Marinetti in the *Manifeste du Futurisme*. These visions of overcoming physical limitations promise freedom from age, disease, from the planet Earth, from the limits of the intellect and, last but not least, from religion and God – which are usually perceived as social means of repressing the human quest for perfection.[121]

The artistic confrontation with the posthuman takes many forms. It ranges from concrete and playful designs (Stelarc), to naïve and visionary illustrations (Vita-More), to critical impulses (ORLAN, Giraud & Siboni). However, at the center of this range of expressions there are some unifying elements: Humanity's power lies in anticipated freedoms, while human powerlessness is shown in fears over the loss of possibilities for human life. Since the future never dies, it is to be expected that the next generation

---

117 See www.cyborgfoundation.com.
118 Search for transpeciessociety on Instagram, Manel Muñoz on Wikipedia (engl./span.).
119 See www.theunmanned.com.
120 See www.gafsou.ch/hplus.
121 See Caygill 1997, 51; Vita-More 2000b; Reitmeier 1996, 12. Although hardly noticed by art critics, the Surrealist painter Hans Rudi Giger and the lesser-known German painter and graphic artist Joachim Luetke have a certain significance in the transhumanist subculture. Their "posthuman" art contains illustrations of human-machine hybrids, cyborgs, and aliens. See Dery 1996, 280-282; Luetke 2000.

of artists will also creatively address these same fundamental topics, questions, and concerns.

6. A History of Technological Posthumanism

> Observed progress is mainly technical, whereas believed progress is mainly spiritual.[1]
> John Baillie

6.1 Writing the "History of the Future"

In this text, I have shown the relevance of human interactions with electronic media, or rather of humans encountering their virtual images. Virtuality makes experiences available beyond the limits of our corporeal senses and memory, and therefore changes our perception of time and space. Two consequences can be derived from this. On the one hand, an experience with quasi-immortal human images could become a cultural mechanism for the repression of death. Alternatively, it could also evoke desire for a similar, virtual immortality.

However, the interpretation of virtuality is not an anthropologically constant quantity, but rather is culturally and historically bound. This can be pointed out by the simple observation that technological posthumanism originates in the United States, rather than countries in Europe or Japan that have the same level of technological development. This current of technophilia did not originate from a cultural vacuum, but rather within the specific framework of American history (and its particular reception of European philosophy).

Technological posthumanism interprets humanity's past, present, and future relationship to technology, and addresses basic ontological questions about the relationship between mind and matter, body and soul, and the definition of life and intelligence. The approach is dominated by cybernetic or physical considerations. Posthumanism not only interprets humanity and technology, but also re-interprets these interpretations with reference to older concepts from the history of human thought. We are thus faced with a close entanglement of scientific, philosophical, and religious ideas.

---

1   Baillie 1950, 156.

I consider the approach of reception history (*Rezeptionsgeschichte*) to be particularly suitable for precisely grasping these complex processes of reinterpretation and recontextualization. As early as 1958, Hans Blumenberg had worked out that "myths", such as the epoch-making Copernican turn, originally gained their historical power via their reception by means of continuous narration over centuries. In parallel, Hans-Georg Gadamer introduced philosophical hermeneutics as the basis for a history of effects (*Wirkungsgeschichte*).[2] According to this approach, a work can only be understood by its impact, and literary hermeneutics developed from this the correlating principle of the history of reception. This is not based on the work's original "true meaning", but rather on understanding the subjective experience of a work. Effect is usually determined as being conditioned by the text, whereas reception is conditioned by the reader.[3] The actual processes of effect and reception are called "concretizations". The history of effect is primarily concerned with research into influence or dependence, and it usually presupposes a semantically constant "text" that leaves its "traces" in the history of ideas. In contrast, the history of reception begins with the recipient's perspective.

According to the Polish phenomenologist Roman Ingarden, "concretization" became a key concept for literary semiotics primarily due to Prague Structuralism (Felix Vodička, Jan Mukařovský) and the Konstanz literary school around Hans Robert Jauß. In this theory, a work achieves historical life only through its reception. Within specific social, biographical, or cultural contexts, it expresses its meaning and significance in a continuous series of "concretizations", which manifest themselves through successive interpretations. Critically continuing Ingarden's phenomenological aesthetics, the Konstanz School has examined the constitution and new formation of meaning through the historical reception of an aesthetic object.[4]

A history of reception therefore involves both the historical nature of a work and the context of its interpreters. It assumes that a work cannot be understood simply as a substance or entelechy, as Hans Robert Jauß explains:

> For it is only through the process of its mediation that the work enters into the changing horizon-of-experience of a continuity in which the perpetual inversion occurs from simple reception to critical understanding, from passive to active reception, from recognized aesthetic norms to a new production that surpasses them. The historicity of literature as well as its communicative character presupposes a dialogical and at once process-like relationship between work, audience, and new work that can be conceived in the relations between message and receiver as well as between question and answer, problem and solution.[5]

In this regard, I would like to analyze the reception of philosophical, religious, and literary motifs and concepts in posthumanist works. According to this hermeneutical premise, categories of a semantically constant structure, such as "misunderstanding"

---

2   See Blumenberg 1958; Gadamer 2004.
3   See Jauss 1982, 14-17.
4   See Jauss 1982, 3-45. On the possible connection between Jauss's idea of the discontinuity of meanings and his own, unresolved role in National Socialism see Richards 1997.
5   Jauss 1982, 19.

or "misinterpretation", are not applicable. Posthumanists' apparent "errors of interpretation", made due to ignorance of original texts or philosophical-historical contexts, are only useful for better illuminating the concretizations of their new, hitherto unknown contextualization. This sheds light on their specific selections and interpretations. Here we are not interested in the fact that many of these philosophical concepts are misunderstood by posthumanists, but rather in their innovative applications of philosophical concepts in new semantic contexts.[6]

At the heart of technological posthumanism lies the prospect of achieving human immortality. Genealogically the beginning of the transhumanist movement is marked by the works of FM-2030 and Robert Ettinger in the 1970s. However, immortality also provides the crucial link in the posthumanist chain of argumentation. Without this element, posthumanists' fundamental desire to overcome human beings remains pointless. Humankind's ultimate sacrifice of voluntary extinction for the sake of its future artificial descendants requires the promise of an even higher reparation: eternal life. All other aspects, such as humanity's merging with a universal superintelligence, the intergalactic omnipresence, or even saving the cosmos from heat death, remain on the periphery of posthumanist thought.

Technological posthumanism thus addresses two fundamental questions regarding immortality. Firstly: *How can humans regenerate their own perfect simulation within a computer's memory?* And secondly: *How might we access this promising future?*

A wide range of ontological and anthropological questions are used to support the idea of humankind's technological immortalization: What is life? What is a human being? What constitutes the essence of the individual? The prerequisite for all posthumanist visions is the cybernetic understanding of both the world and humankind, in which human beings are interpreted as machines even before their technical transformation. Only under this condition can the idea of a human simulation existing inside a computer become at all conceivable. Chapter 6.2 *How We Became Posthuman* will therefore be devoted to various aspects of the analysis of this posthumanist understanding of humanity. The reception of Descartes within a cybernetic paradigm assumes a prominent position in this context.

The second question addresses the idea of progress in posthumanism. Starting with Ernst Bloch and his philosophical analysis of utopia in *The Principle of Hope*, the history of the future takes center stage. The historian Lucian Hölscher has recently deepened this focus theoretically:

> At first it may seem odd to discuss the future in terms of history. History is, after all, by definition a study of humanity's recorded past. Attempts to learn about the future are left to biblical prophets and mystical oracles, or lately, pollsters and statisticians. But an undercurrent of the future runs through historical narratives — it is manifested in people's thoughts, motivations, plans and aspirations — which in turn guide their actions and behavior.[7]

---

6   See Stausberg 1998, 2-4.
7   Hölscher 2018, 15.

The design of such utopian spaces draws on a wide variety of forms, including technical prognoses, fiction, religious prophecies, and political programs and planning. The prospects for the future surpass the values, norms, and interests of the epoch in which they were written.[8] Originating with the cryonic and early transhumanist visions of the 1960s, the period we are examining already encompasses half a century of the – mostly American – history of progress.

While the definition of humankind is consistently based on materialistic world views, the posthumanist theory of progress is a hybrid mixture of scientific, philosophical, and religious components. Why must there be progress? How and via which steps will it take place? What are the goals of this process? Each of these questions is closely examined in chapters 6.3 to 6.7. Special attention is also paid to the concepts of singularity, superintelligence, and the noosphere, which was coined by Pierre Teilhard de Chardin.

With regard to both the conceptions of humans and of progress, I will first present the essential positions of post- and transhumanist thinkers. I will then compare them and trace their development through the history of ideas, as well as in their philosophical and literary contexts. Focus will particularly be placed upon the works of Frank Tipler, Marvin Minsky, Hans Moravec, Ray Kurzweil, and Max More, as well as selected works by other authors.

6.2 How We Became Posthuman

> THE MEANING OF THE TRANSMITTER IS THE TRANSMISSION. For organisms serve the transmission, and not the reverse; organisms outside the communications procedure of Evolution signify nothing: they are without meaning, like a book without readers.[9]
> GOLEM XIV

What are we as human beings if we define ourselves as that which we are not yet? What do we want to become? To address such questions, Ernst Bloch developed an entire philosophy – *The Principle of Hope*. However, as the philosopher of technology Bernhard Irrgang emphasizes, the question then arises as to which specific model we seek to change:

> What are we as human beings actually, when we as human beings set ourselves the task of changing ourselves as human beings? But in whose image should we as human beings re-create the human being? If our success in the life sciences were to enable us

---

8   See Hölscher 2018.
9   Lem 1984, 49.

to create human beings designed to measure, then the question would still remain: to what extent should we?"[10]

In general, such questions address innumerable issues of modern mechanization and digitalization, including: the displacement of humans by machines in the working world; robots as pets, servants, and competitors; the inventor's role in the creation of artificial human machines and artificial intelligence; and automatons, robots, and computers in literature and film. These concerns address fundamental questions for fields such as the sociology of work, media, and technology; media psychology; as well as basic sociological and anthropological questions.

An analysis of such features of posthumanist discourse would certainly be promising. However, our interest revolves around the question of how posthumanism establishes the technical possibility of immortality via computers. This is tantamount to the question of how a real human being can be simulated within a computer. It also leads us to the philosophical premises of the posthumanist vision of immortality. So, what are the conditions for the union between human beings and technology?

The fact that we can clearly trace and understand the argumentative structures of a normative posthumanist discourse is due above all to the philosopher Günther Anders and the American literary scholar N. Katherine Hayles. Posthumanist authors differ greatly in how they call for the replacement of the human being by posthuman lifeforms, as well as in their visions for the further development of humankind. However, none demands the complete abolition of humanity. Instead, the human of today is merely to be overcome. Even Hans Moravec and Frank Tipler's extreme visions of the imminent evolutionary extinction of humankind nonetheless preserve modern human beings in a type of sanctuary, in hopes of their virtual resurrection. In general, visions such as the initial provision of humans with technical implants, or the creation of biological-machine hybrid cyborg beings remain complementary in their demand for the greatest possible mechanization of the human body, which extends right up to the uploading of the human mind into a computer. The biological body is to be replaced by a mechanical form that is superior in all physical and mental attributes: Humans will become machines.

Anders and Hayles have impressively demonstrated that a human machine is not only the goal, but rather the precondition of posthumanist demands. In fact, according to posthumanists, humans have long since already become posthuman: "Homo sapiens are so transfigured in conception and purpose that they can appropriately be called posthuman."[11] Anders describes humanity's voluntary degradation to a device or a defective machine as an act of self-reification and dehumanization in the robot age.[12]

A framework has therefore already been formulated to address those questions posed at the beginning of the chapter: Humans can only be simulated and replaced by a computer if they are in fact already machines. The materialistic definition of a human being as a machine thus constitutes one of the two central elements of posthumanist

---

10   Irrgang 2005, 243, trans. by AJ. See also Irrgang 2014.
11   Hayles 1999, 11.
12   See Anders 1983, 30-56.

philosophy. For if humans were to be more than the sum and arrangement of molecular components; if they could call their own a metaphysics beyond physical matter; if humans even possessed something akin to a soul; then the possibility for any utopia built on humans' technical simulation and subsequently their machine-generated immortality would be shattered. This would effectively remove the basis from not only the technical feasibility of a simulation, but also any comparison of "faulty human machines" with superior artificial intelligences. In order for this comparison to apply to humans, they must already be defined as machines.

The first section 6.2.1 *L'Homme Machine* – the title of which refers to La Mettries' famous treatise of 1747 – presents the mechanistic interpretation of the human body and mind by the most important posthumanists, and further reflects upon their intellectual background.

The posthumanist vision of technical immortalization is remarkable above all for the fact that during the so-called *upload* only the human brain is to be scanned and simulated in a computer, rather than the entire human body. This implies that human identity can be reduced to the mind alone, as located specifically in the brain. Its connection to a perfect simulation is addressed in section 6.2.2 *Simulation and Identity* and is problematized in particular with regard to the reception of Descartes.

In a third section (6.2.3 *The Cybernetic Paradigm*), I will explore why posthumanists selected certain philosophical concepts and completely ignored others from amongst the works of Descartes, La Mettrie, or the English physico-theologians. It will become clear that the posthumanists' philosophical systems are subject to a cybernetic paradigm that was shaped by the theories of Norbert Wiener, John von Neumann, Alan Turing, and Claude Shannon.

Hayles was the first to argue that science fiction literature made a decisive contribution to the spread of an interpretation of the human being that is based in information technology. These aspects are discussed in detail in a later chapter (under 6.3), which addresses the realization of the perfect human being.

L'Homme Machine

> And though most people still consider it degrading to be regarded as machines, I hope, this book will make them entertain, instead, the thought of how wonderful it is to be machines with such marvelous powers.[13]
> *Marvin Minsky*

Most posthumanist authors begin their comparisons of humans and machines with the supposedly mechanistic functioning of the human body and mind. However, Frank Tipler inverts this logic and attempts instead to show that machines must be considered alive under certain conditions. Frank Tipler and John D. Barrow define life primarily as living beings' ability to self-reproduce, since their cells contain the information for their

---

13   Minsky 1988, 323. See also Ibid., 30.

own restoration or reproduction. Tipler and Barrow therefore not only recognize both a virus and a heterosexual human couple as alive, but also deem intellectual ideas or even cars to be living beings, as their natural selection is guaranteed within a free market, and they secure their own reproduction in cooperation with car manufacturers.[14]

The two cosmologists compare a biological virus with the Von Neumann probe introduced by Tipler in order to demonstrate that machines can also be considered as living beings. Both meet the requirements of the definition given above. The mathematician and cyberneticist John von Neumann developed the idea of an automaton, that is capable of independently producing replicas of itself. Ideally, this machine would consist of a *universal constructor*, which can process matter, as well as a database with the necessary construction plans.[15] For Tipler and Barrow, the functional analogy proves that self-reproducing machines and viruses are equally alive.[16] The decisive element in this process lies in the stored information controlling reproduction, which leads Tipler and Barrow to a further definition of life:

> ... we may even say that a human being is a program designed to run on particular hardware called a human body, coding its data in very special types of data storage devices called DNA molecules and nerve cells. The essence of a human being is not the body but the program which controls the body ... In principle, the program corresponding to a human being could be stored in many different forms – in books, on computer disks, in RAM – and not just in the brain of a particular human body.[17]

In a later work, Tipler develops this information-centric definition of life even further when he provocatively concludes:

> I therefore regard a human being as nothing but a particular type of machine, the human brain as nothing but an information processing device, the human soul as nothing but a program being run on a computer called the brain. Further, all possible types of living beings, intelligent or not, are of the same nature, and subject to the same laws of physics as constrain all information processing devices.[18]

According to Tipler's cybernetic paradigm, the human being itself becomes a computer just as a person becomes a person: only by passing the Turing test. In the 1950s, the English mathematician Alan Turing proposed a test to determine a computer's intelligence. In this test, one person communicates with both a human counterpart and with the computer being tested. The computer can be considered intelligent if the human tester can no longer clearly determine whether his or her counterpart is machine or human.[19] However, Tipler inverts this by testing the human being, rather than the computer, for evidence of intelligence:

---

14   See Barrow / Tipler 1986, 513-522.
15   See Neumann 1966.
16   See Barrow / Tipler 1986, 515-521; Tipler 1981; Tipler 1986, 73-78.
17   Barrow / Tipler 1986, 659.
18   Tipler 1995, XI. See ibid., 124-125.
19   See Barrow / Tipler 1986, 523; Tipler 1995, 20-21; Turing 1950.

Thus "life" is a form of information processing, and the human mind – and the human soul – is a very complex computer program. Specifically, a "person" is defined to be a computer program which can pass the Turing test ...[20]

According to Tipler, what was originally a test for machines becomes a suitable test for humans because the latter are in fact nothing more than machines. Tipler stipulates "personhood" as being dependent on the intelligence of an information-processing device. However, this poses important questions about handicapped or mentally ill people, of whom Tipler remarks "unfortunately, there are such people".[21] As these differently abled individuals might not demonstrate standardly recognizable linguistic skills, they would therefore not be able to pass the Turing test, and thus would not be considered "persons" within Tipler's formulation.

Marvin Minsky does not primarily focus upon postulating clear definitions for terms such as thinking, intelligence, and consciousness. Rather, operating within a functionalist paradigm he instead tries to better understand how these mental processes initially occur.[22] For Minsky there is no doubt that humans are intelligent systems, which means in general that they have the ability to solve complex problems.[23] Animals, on the other hand, do not have intelligence because they do not contain the consciousness required to solve problems. In contrast to human beings' closest evolutionary relatives – the orangutan, gorilla, and chimpanzee – Minsky considers *homo sapiens* to be anti-evolutionists, as they owe their superior brains to the conscious acquisition of culture and technology that were not the result of an arbitrary process of selection as in natural evolution.[24]

In a fictitious conversation between two extraterrestrials, the cyberneticist Minsky links the general right to exist to the intelligence of living beings.[25] For Minsky, humans are exclusively characterized by their thinking abilities. The reduction of all mental processes, including feelings and sensations, to certain functions further stabilizes and develops the *Society of Mind*. Minsky particularly opposes the misunderstanding of emotional thinking. As a part of a general purpose machine, feelings are necessary for decision making and thus indispensable for the development of intelligent thinking and acting.[26] According to Minsky, a natural intuition for music and a sense of humor also serve the powers of our intellect. These will not be left out of the development of artificial life forms – even if funny computers may still seem impossible to us at present.[27] He categorically rejects any mystification of mental processes. This includes the sheer superhuman intelligence of geniuses, which is actually merely based on a

---

20   Tipler 1995, 124.
21   Ibid., 20.
22   See Minsky 1988, 39, 71.
23   See ibid., 71.
24   See ibid., 321-322.
25   See Minsky 1992a, 24-25.
26   See Minsky 1981, 1-2; Minsky 1988, 163-164; Minsky 2006, 9-35.
27   Humor thus serves as a censor for learning normative taboos. See Minsky 1988, 278-279. Classical (!) music can be used to cope with everyday experiences, or to calm oneself down. See Minsky 1981, 5-6.

better organization of learning and knowledge,[28] or any religious conceptions of human beings. For Minsky, the idea of an immaterial soul, which is supposed to constitute the core of the human being, is synonymous with the end of intellectual development:

> And that's exactly what we get with inborn souls that cannot grow: a destiny the same as death, an ending in a permanence incapable of any change and, hence, devoid of intellect ... But minds are just the opposite. We start as little embryos, which then build great and wondrous selves – whose merit lies entirely within their own coherency. The value of a human self lies not in some small, precious core, but in its vast constructed crust.[29]

Here Minsky reinterprets the religious notion of the soul within a cybernetic paradigm: What function could an unchangeable soul possibly hold in a conscious biological system? From this premise, Minsky inevitably comes to the conclusion that the concept of the soul makes no sense.[30]

> Minds are simply what brains do ... There is not the slightest reason to doubt that brains are anything other than machines with enormous numbers of parts that work in perfect accord with physical laws.[31]

The mind itself, which generates a system's consciousness and identity, is nonetheless the sum of immaterial thought processes. When Minsky states that research into artificial intelligence will deeply affect our understanding of both humans and their mind, he is affirming his commitment to the fundamental unity of humans and machines.[32] The human being is thus not a trivial machine, and Minsky hopes that our growing understanding of our own minds will allow us to see what complex and wonderful apparatuses we humans in fact are.[33] The supposed differences between humans and machines disappear when one considers the future potential of computers:

> When people ask, "Could a machine ever be conscious?" I'm often tempted to ask back, "Could a person ever be conscious?" I mean this as a serious reply, because we seem so ill equipped to understand ourselves ... However, we can design our new machines as we wish, and provide them with better ways to keep and examine records of their own activities – and this means that machines are potentially capable of far more consciousness than we are.[34]

After such remarks, it will hardly come as a surprise that the roboticist Hans Moravec defines humans as highly complex machines: "Living organisms are clearly machines

---

28   See Minsky 1988, 80.
29   Ibid., 41.
30   See ibid., 287-288.
31   Ibid.
32   See Minsky 1967, 4; Minsky 1982, 9.
33   See Minsky 1988, 30, 323.
34   Ibid., 160. See also Ibid., 63.

when viewed at the molecular scale ... "³⁵. He also interprets nature in its entirety as a comprehensive machine.³⁶

With far-reaching consequences for our understanding of death and life, Moravec emphasizes that a modern computer must also be regarded as alive. This is based on the assumption that life in biology and chemistry is understood as a very special and complex organization of matter.³⁷ Artificial intelligence would be able to generate consciousness from self-perception. Furthermore, it would be able to learn and then utilize feelings – such as love for one's owner, anger, or pain – to better control behavior.³⁸ Moravec refrains from deeper reflections on the concept of life itself, and instead expresses a vision of the transformation of all matter into mind, i.e. into computers:

> Thoughtful machinery violates the equally obvious and sacred dichotomy of the living and the dead, a difference embedded in our mentality ... In the old metaphor, we are in the process of inspiriting the matter around us. It will soon be our honor to welcome some of it to the land of the living ... ³⁹

Ray Kurzweil, a student of Marvin Minsky, also developed a techno-centric interpretation of humankind, where simulating the brain does not present a particular issue: "I honestly believe that the brain actually functions in a banal way, really straightforwardly. It's a computer that can handle complex tasks, but its structure is actually very simple..."⁴⁰ Kurzweil also maintains this approach in his latest book *How to Create a Mind*, in which he discusses concrete ideas for simulating the human brain.⁴¹

Max More argues that if humans and machines were as different as some humanists claim, then it must also be true that machines do not resemble humans in any way and humans do not resemble machines. Yet science has shown that humans function exactly like the interaction of many machines, from the smallest elements to the largest. However, More does not see this as disparaging toward humankind: "To say that humans are composed of machines is not to say that we are merely machines. Humans are dignified machines."⁴² In his discussion of the irreversibility of death, More uses the analogy of a defective car compared to a person who has just died, in order to illustrate that the functions of the car can be restored by repair in most cases. Therefore, it is hardly possible to determine the definitive death of a car. The same applies to the human being: As long as information about the material structure and function of the deceased is still available, their personality can be brought back to life.⁴³ On the other hand, More

---

35   Moravec 1988, 72.
36   See Moravec 1999, 127.
37   See ibid., 110-111.
38   See ibid., 114-124.
39   Ibid., 111.
40   Interview with Christoph Keller, Keller 2003, 16, trans. by AJ. See also Kurzweil 1999a, 5.
41   See Kurzweil 2012b; Kurzweil 2005, 212-220.
42   More 1997b, 1.
43   See More 1995, 27-28.

rejects the term machine as applied to humans, since the latter act freely, responsibly, morally, and rationally, while planned and programmed machines (so far) do not.[44]

Although following different routes, Tipler, Moravec, Minsky, Kurzweil, and More all arrive at the same conclusion that the human being as a whole is a machine, that the human mind is to be regarded as an operative function of a brain, and that complex machines that develop consciousness or can reproduce themselves must be regarded as living. All mental processes are strictly subject to the laws of physics. Hans Moravec locates the philosophical origin of this comparison between humans and machines in the figure of René Descartes (1596-1650), whose worldview was shaped by the invention of new types of machines 400 years ago.

Historically, mechanistic interpretations of human beings began in the early 17th century. The body is read as a unity of parts by Thomas Hobbes in his mechanistic-materialistic anthropology in *Leviathan* (1651). This view is presented even more clearly in Descartes' *Traité de l'Homme*, which was written in 1633 but only published posthumously. Both interpretations are built upon basic mechanistic principles. Descartes asserts that he would never claim that the human body is really a machine, but he does describe in detail how a hypothetical machine would have to be designed by a divine creator to correspond to our body:

> I suppose the body to be nothing but a statue or machine made of earth, which God forms with the explicit intention of making it as much as possible like us. Thus God not only gives it externally the colours and shapes of all the parts of our bodies, but also places inside it all the parts required to make it walk, eat, breathe, and indeed to imitate all those of our functions which can be imagined to proceed from matter and to depend solely on the disposition of our organs. We see clocks, artificial fountains, mills, and other such machines which, although only man-made, have the power to move of their own accord in many different ways.[45]

At the end of his treatise on man, Descartes once again emphasizes the foundation of his purely hypothetical construction of a mechanical body. In the interactions between its individual organs, this should in fact function just like a human body:

> I should like you to consider that these functions follow from the mere arrangement of the machine's organs every bit as naturally as the movements of a clock or other automation follow from the arrangements of its counter-weights and wheels. In order to explain these functions, then, it is not necessary to conceive of this machine as having any vegetative or sensitive soul or other principle of movement and life, apart from its blood and its spirits, which are agitated by the heat of the fire burning continuously in its heart – a fire which has the same nature as all the fires that occur in inanimate bodies.[46]

By invoking Descartes' description of the body as a complex machine, Moravec in fact intensifies the original comparison between the interactions of physical organs

---

44 See More 1997b, 1.
45 Descartes 1985, 99.
46 Ibid., 108.

and precisely *how* a machine functions.[47] However, nothing represents the connection between Cartesian thought and posthumanism more aptly than the metaphor of creation as a clockwork made by a divine watchmaker. Descartes portrays God metaphorically as the creator of the hypothetical body-machine, which *happens* to function *like* clockwork, whereas for William Paley God is presented as a literal watchmaker in his 1802 *Natural Theology*.[48] It is in this sense that the contemporary evolutionary theorist Richard Dawkins characterizes God as the blind watchmaker – an interpretation that affected many posthumanists. For Hans Moravec, the time has now come for humankind and its posthuman heirs to assume control of the watchmaker's hand.[49] In fact, 200 years ago Paley had already countered the accusation that man was being degraded to a simple machine, just as Minsky has more recently. The former stresses instead that the magnificent creation of the human body must be admired as the "most complicated or most flexible machine that was ever contrived".[50]

Among humans' purely physical functions, Descartes includes one's memory, emotions, and moods, the imagination, and the sense of community (*sensus communis*), all of which are controlled by the finest but purely material elements in our blood – *the spiritus animales (esprits animaux)*.[51] If the essence of all material bodies (*res extensa*) consists of their extension, and if material bodily processes represent nothing more than processes of movement, than the phenomena of the organs would have to be understood as physical mechanisms for Descartes. As a branch of physics, Cartesian physiology assumes that all material events are mechanical in nature and can therefore ideally be described mathematically.[52] However, Descartes attributes the ability of rational thinking, cognition, and will to the immortal, immaterial soul of the human being.

This disregard for the distinction between the physical senses and the immaterial subject in Descartes' conception of the soul – the very soul that is itself endowed with reason – points to Moravec's materialistic interpretation of Descartes. Furthermore, Moravec argues that modern technological capabilities would have led Descartes to abandon the dualism between the body and the rational soul, despite its being fundamental for his proof of existence. Instead, he would have adopted a completely materialistic conception of humanity:[53]

---

47 See Moravec 1999, 121-122.
48 Paley, however, had to contend with the accusation that he plagiarized his famous watch metaphor. In fact, he probably did lift this from *Het regt gebruik der werelt beschouwingen*, 1716 (Engl.: *The Religious Philosopher*, 1730) by Bernard Nieuwentyt, the Dutch student of Descartes.
49 See Moravec 1988, 158-159; Dawkins 1996, 45; Paley 1802. Regarding the reception of Dawkins see Moravec 1988, 136; Moravec 1999, 4, 213; Tipler 1994, 125-126; Barrow / Tipler 1986, 522.
50 See Paley 1802, 490-491.
51 See Descartes 1967a, 387-388, 437-438, 448-453. Descartes here reduces the ancient Greek doctor Galen's teaching of the three types of spiritus (*naturalis, vitalis, animalis*) to the idea of the flame-like, fast, and transformational *spiritus animales*, which are purely material in nature. See ibid., 388 (FN 1).
52 See Hatfield 2014.
53 See Moravec 1999, 121-122.

Lacking a mechanical model of thought, he retained part of the medieval idea ... If he were working today, Descartes might well have found, in computers, a material model for mind and become a thorough-going materialist. But, alas, there were no computers in the seventeenth century.[54]

This is not to say that posthumanists today cite Descartes' *Traité de l'Homme* line by line, but rather that they imbibe the influence of diffused Cartesian philosophy via secondary literature. Regardless, it obviously remains an important rational foundation of the modern posthumanist interpretation of humans as machines.[55] Although the body-spirit dualism of Cartesian metaphysics ignores difficult questions, some modern posthumanists portray the philosopher as the intellectual source of the machine simulation of the human being. This is because in the *Traité de l'Homme* he was the first to formulate the intellectual possibility of constructing a purely material machine that could imitate all the functions of the human body. Other posthumanists' reluctance to turn to Descartes must be due to the absolutely fundamental role of dualism in Cartesian thought, for example between matter, *res extensa*, and mind, *res cogitas*, which Moravec ignored.

Posthumanism's materialistic position corresponds more readily to the work of the physician and philosopher Julien Offray de La Mettrie (1709-1751), who has been largely forgotten from history. He seems to never have been explicitly considered by posthumanists, and his role as the actual founder of materialistic monism was only rediscovered in the 19th century by Friedrich Albert Lange, an adherent of German idealism.

La Mettrie signals the end of Descartes' philosophical debate on the nature and relationship of body, mind, and soul, which extended into the 18th century. Even Thomas Hobbes would agree that the mechanical laws applied to mental phenomena would depend entirely on the body.[56] Yet it was only after Gottfried Wilhelm Leibniz' monad theory and John Locke's rational empiricism that the remaining dualistic view of the two "automatae" – i.e. body and mind, each of which obey mechanical laws – finally led to a monistic interpretation. This had already come to light at the turn of the 18th century in the works of philosophers such as Pierre Sylvain Régis, Georges-Louis Le Sage, and Claude Buffier. It then reached its culmination in the materialistic position of La Mettrie.[57] In his 1747 work *L'Homme Machine*,[58] La Mettrie brings together the essence of his previous materialist treatises. He adapts Descartes' mechanistic interpretation of the human body while also surpassing him, by simultaneously interpreting the human mind or soul both functionally *and* materially: " ... the soul is but a principle of motion or a material and sensible part of the brain, which can be regarded, without fear of error, as the mainspring of the whole machine, having a visible influence on all the parts."[59]

---

54 Ibid., 121.
55 See Barrow / Tipler 1986, 53-54; Moravec 1988, 180; Moravec 1999, 78, 121, 191; Kurzweil 1999, 60, 262.
56 See Kirkinen 1960, 219.
57 See ibid., 444-449.
58 Published in English as *Man a Machine*. See La Mettrie 1953.
59 La Mettrie 1953, 135.

After a severe fever, La Mettrie suddenly realized the close interaction between body and mind. He thereafter vehemently rejected all dualistic explanations of this relationship. Following Aristotle, the Epicureans, and Thomas Aquinas, La Mettrie expressly opposed the dualism of Plato, Augustine, and Descartes. In his *Histoire Naturelle de l'âme ou Traité de l'âme* of 1745, La Mettrie applies this materialistic position to interpret all functions of the human mind entirely as functions of the body: The body itself thinks![60]

> In fact, if what thinks in my brain is not a part of this organ and therefore of the whole body, why does my blood boil, and the fever of my mind pass into my veins, when lying quietly in bed, I am forming the plan of some work, or carrying on an abstract calculation? ... The body is but a watch whose watchmaker is the new chyle.[61]

While La Mettrie characterizes the life force as one property of the organization of the body parts and internal organs, he also locates the thinking principle of the human being in the mind, where all our thoughts, feelings, and passions are generated. La Mettrie argues that the human body is a clockwork produced by unsurpassed art and skill, and that, like animals, it is therefore a machine. From this basis, he thus derives a great respect for the phenomena of nature. He bans any metaphysical statement about God or the beyond from his philosophy and instead strictly adheres to empiricism.[62] This materialist philosophy in fact continued to spread in the 19th century, particularly under the influence of Ernst Haeckel, his monist movement and the rapid development of positivist natural science (see section 6.3.4).

Since the creation of the first mechanical movements in the 15th century, countless monographs have born witness to the developing discussion about the relationship between humans and machines, as well as technology's influence upon human self-understanding. Bernhard Dotzler, Peter Gendolla, and Jörgen Schäfer list more than 1700 European and American titles published since 1420, each addressing the topic philosophically or literarily, and ranging from cautionary polemics to euphoric enthusiasm for technology.[63] While even a brief sketch of this discussion over the past 500 years is impossible here, for heuristic reasons I will only mention the English philosopher Colin McGinn's criticism of the equation of humans and machines, as regards the posthumanist:

> It is true that human minds manipulate symbols and engage in mental computations, as when doing arithmetic. But it does not follow from this that computing is the essence of mind ... The fallacy here is analogous to reasoning that if a human body is a device for taking you from A to B, and a car also does this, then the human body is the same thing as a car.[64]

---

60   See La Mettrie 1953, 132-134.
61   Ibid., 133, 135.
62   See ibid., 120-124.
63   See Dotzler / Gendolla / Schäfer 1992.
64   McGinn 1999, 12.

McGinn's criticism can be interpreted in light of Frank Tipler's and John D. Barrow's "proof" that cars are living beings, or Max More's analogy between the repair of a car and a deceased person. McGinn's criticism clearly illustrates the philosophical equation of humans and machines. While posthumanist authors might indeed only cite Descartes, it is nonetheless clear that this purely materialistic reception of a Descartes robbed of his metaphysics is in fact conditioned by La Mettrie's influence. This new reading has been propagated by the monistic movement since the end of the 19th century, especially in American science.

Simulation and Identity

> The optimist's proof of the rationality of the general constitution of things turned out to be a proof of its essential immortality.[65]
> Arthur O. Lovejoy

When Frank Tipler claims that a human being's essence lies not in the body but rather its "program", he is assuming a pattern identity theory position. The program is understood as operating independently of its embodiment. Tipler here is referring primarily to Aristotle and Thomas Aquinas. He also invokes Plutarch's account of the ship of Theseus, which Thomas Hobbes cites as well. According to this legend, the Athenians kept their great hero's ship for several centuries, but constantly replaced its components during that time. In his account, Tipler applies quantum theory to argue that the ship must always be identified as the original. This is despite a long tradition of disagreement amongst ancient philosophers, as well as a contrary solution offered by Hobbes. For Tipler, the decisive criterion lies in the preservation of the ship's original design.[66]

The physicist makes a similar argument when pointing to the constant material change at the sub-molecular level. Specifically, the constituent parts of neutrons and protons are destroyed and formed anew in less than 10^{-23} seconds. He also cites the problem of cannibalism from Thomas Aquinas' *Summa contra gentiles* and seeks to solve it via the possibility of restoring a person's immaterial blueprint.[67] Because the medieval notion of the soul was understood in Aristotelian tradition as an abstract "form" of the body's activity, and since the term "information" can be etymologically derived from "form", Tipler therefore simply concludes:

---

65   Cited in Dobrée 1959, 29.
66   This is Plutarch's οἱ βίοι παράλληλοι / *Vitae parallelae*. See Hobbes 1839, 132-138; Tipler 1995, 234-235. Hobbes' solution to the problem of identity is more nuanced, and thus distinct from Tipler and Minsky's reception. If the continuity of identity is connected with the continuity of "form" and behaviour for people, institutions, and states, then, according to Hobbes this does not apply to "things" whose identity is based on matter: " ... so that a ship, which signifies matter so figured, will be the same as long as the matter remains the same, then it is numerically another ship ... " Hobbes 1839, 138. Tipler and Minsky received Hobbes purely materialistically, but adapted his theory of identity, despite it is only being valid in a dualistic concept.
67   See Tipler 1995, 235-236.

> There is actually an astonishing similarity between the mind-as-computer-program idea and the medieval Christian idea of the 'soul'. Both are fundamentally 'immaterial' ... For Aquinas, a human soul needed a body to think and feel, just as a computer program needs a physical computer to run ... Even semantically, the information theory of the soul is the same as the Aristotle-Aquinas theory.[68]

The fact that Thomas Aquinas in particular is hardly suited to reducing the identity of a person to their "immaterial program" cannot be further problematized here for reasons of brevity.[69] However, in short: Tipler uses the theory of identity pattern as a basis for the potential resurrection of the dead by technological means.

It is clear from Marvin Minsky's remarks that, if humans are to be considered in the same category as machines, then machines have always been superior to people. According to Minsky's information-centered perspective, the human body in its biological form is negligible. Thought alone can be considered the essence and function of that which characterizes animate beings as a human being. Minsky argues that humans are never in direct contact with the world, but only receive information from the brain via receptors and nerve tracts in the body. He therefore equates being human only with the activity of the mind and in fact detaches it from the body entirely.[70]

Shortly before Minsky explains the central role played by possession, he once again emphasizes the separation of body and mind. Since Minsky regards custody as the indispensable prerequisite for the control and use of a tool, we can conclude that he sees the body as a possession and aid of the mind.[71]

However, this also means that the body as a data carrier can be exchanged at will. Along with Tipler, Minsky argues that a ship whose individual parts are exchanged will always fulfill the same function as the original. In the same way, a brain whose cells are completely replaced by computer chips will still assume the same function as the original thinking organ, and thus still be considered identical. Finally, one hundred percent agreement, which is hardly possible in technical terms, is not necessary, since the human body is subject to constant change anyway.[72]

After discussing the substitution of the entire biological body with artificial parts, Minsky makes a remarkable statement: "Needless to say, in doing so, we'll be making ourselves into machines."[73] Minsky thus illustrates the visionary discourse of posthuman evolution, which N. Katherine Hayles described. On countless occasions Minsky states that a human being is nothing more than a (thinking) machine, but then also depicts the technical process of an actual human being merging with a machine. This double mechanization of the human being implies a subtle distinction for all

---

68 Ibid., 127-128. See also Barrow / Tipler 1986, 659.
69 For Thomas Aquinas, man is not composed nor can he be separated into the two distinct substances of soul and body. Rather, he is the unity formed by a combination of: his form, the spiritual soul as the life principle and his body, matter. Only as this unity can man be considered a person. See McInerny / O'Callaghan 2014.
70 See Minsky 1988, 110, 286.
71 See ibid., 292-293.
72 See ibid., 289. Minsky does not explicitly mention the work of Plutarch or Hobbes in this regard.
73 Minsky 1994, 109-110.

posthumanists: Human beings are initially defined in such a way that they can easily be compared with machines – one is thus already posthuman.[74] Only then can one be transformed into a *real* machine consisting of electronic and mechanical substitutes.

A certain kind of duality can also be found in Moravec's conception of humans – namely the distinction between the material body and the mental functions that this body is capable of producing. Moravec does not interpret mind as a metaphysical substance in the conventional sense but rather somewhat imprecisely as the sum of the mental operations of this body. Nevertheless, Moravec is optimistic that robots and intelligent computers will be granted a soul as soon as they have been recognized as persons.[75] These functions of the mind are based on the material basis of the human body, but they are not dependent on the specific form of that body according to Moravec. The mental functions – that is, the information processing performed exclusively by the material body – can thus be performed by a perfect simulation of the body, and especially of the brain. The physical death of the human being therefore does not actually represent the end of life:[76]

> Death of a body should no more destroy a soul – or its history or potential – than clearing an abacus destroys a number. Nor should death destroy sensations and consciousness – those are properties of the abstraction. Only the perfect correlation between the consciousness and the physical world would be lost.[77]

Like Tipler and Minsky, Moravec argues as an advocate of radical pattern theory when he anchors the identity of the human being independently of its material embodiment. The body is understood as a message whose identity is preserved by the exact simulation of its pattern, its structure. The endurance of personal identity as a continuation of mental operations is thus guaranteed by the functional equivalent of a virtually existing body. Despite the enormous (even explosive) philosophical problems with this idea, Moravec insists that several copies of a person can rightly claim to be and in fact actually *are* the original person:[78] "It *is* you. And when that demon in your belly at last makes the body you have occupied all these years useless, and the couple of pounds of wetware in your skull has to die ... *you* live on in the machine."[79]

Ray Kurzweil makes explicit reference to Descartes when he presents the ability to think as the sole defining criterion of being human, and thus as proof of existence. A computer simulation of the brain would in his view also guarantee the continuity of consciousness and identity, since the simulated subject would be convinced of its authenticity.[80] The early simulation of all parts of the brain would spare us from needing to understand all the brain's functions physiologically, especially since the artificial intelligences of the coming quantum computers will be able to accomplish

---

74 See Hayles 1999, 11.
75 See Moravec 1999, 77.
76 See Moravec 1988, 162-169.
77 Moravec 1999, 76.
78 See Moravec 1988, 162-166. Lem considered this problem already in 1957 in his *Dialogi*. See Lem 1980.
79 Moravec / Pohl 1993, 72. See also Rothblatt 2014, 9-53.
80 See Kurzweil 1999a, 53-60.

everything that a human brain can do but at greater speeds, including irrational thinking.[81]

In his doctoral thesis *The Diachronic Self*, Max More draws on Derek Parfits' psychological reductionism to assume a purely functionalist standpoint, wherein he attributes the genesis of consciousness solely to the processes of complex physical systems.[82] On page four of the thesis, which investigates the problem of continuity and survival of identity, More legitimizes the idea of immortality in a computer by adopting a broadly reductionist approach. This does not connect identity to a specific physical carrier (the brain), but rather to a functional equivalent of *mental* processes.[83] More goes into great detail to prove that a person's continuity does not depend on the survival of his or her material embodiment: "According to psychological reductionism I am nothing more than the connectedness and continuity of my psychological states."[84]

More further differentiates his position by assuming what he calls a conservative interpretation of the broadest, most reductionist type, which links identity's continuity to the simulated human being's activity. A new person would only be able to identify with his or her original model, potentially in the form of a computer, for example, if that original person had a causal relationship to his or her simulation. More therefore disagrees with Tipler's argument that resurrecting all deceased persons in a computer would safeguard their identities, and instead asserts that any previous personalities that passed away would not play a role " ... neither in the coming into existence nor the qualitative identity ...".[85]

As a follower of radical pattern identity theory, More believes that the preservation of structural and functional patterns is crucial for the continuity of identity, as this information could be used to simulate consciousness. Permanent and irreversible death would thus only fully occur after the destruction of this information. More therefore differentiates between a final, irreversible death and the reversible state he calls *deanimation*. This definition of death comes from cryonics – it is no coincidence that More served for nine years as CEO of the cryonics provider *Alcor*. However, it also ultimately renders determining a person's definitive death impossible.[86]

More defends himself against the accusation that transhumanism advocates the abolition of the body, instead maintaining that the technological enhancement of the body is intended to expand its physical and mental range of perception and action. Extropians are not concerned with the abolition of the body, but rather with the expansion of its capabilities, which happens to include overcoming the purely biological body:[87]

81　See ibid., 111-112, 124-125; Kurzweil 2005, 312-320.
82　The eminent reference for this topic is Derek Parfit's *Reasons and Persons* (1984). See also More 2000c, 1.
83　See More 1995, 4-5. Page specifications correspond to the page layout, Microsoft Word 97 SR-1.
84　Ibid., 16. See ibid., 15-17.
85　See ibid., 5-9; Gräfrath 2000, 296-297.
86　See Ettinger 1964, 3-4; Richard 2000, 66.
87　See More 1997a, 1-2.

The contribution of bodily features to personal continuity is entirely of instrumental importance. Parts of a body gain their instrumental importance from their functional roles. The particular *matter* constituting a body, and even the specific *form* of a body, have no intrinsic significance for personal identity.[88]

Since the formation of human identity depends to a large extent on the physical characteristics of our present bodies, More believes that we cannot simply abandon our physicality during our transformation to posthuman life forms. From a psychological-reductionist point of view, the specific form and material basis of the body are dispensable for the preservation of personal identity, whereas those physical functions that can be simulated in a virtual existence are not:

Without this consideration of our physical nature, and the relationship between our physicality and our psychology, a psychological reductionist view of identity would be in danger of falling into a faulty dualism.[89]

The endurance of personal identity is actually only guaranteed by the continuity of physical functions. These are based upon posthumanism's materialistic paradigm, and so simultaneously imply all mental functions as well. However, they are not therefore required to adhere to the dualism of a dominant and immaterial mind or soul.[90]

Surprisingly, more than a century of psychological debate on the relationship between brain, mind, and soul remains almost entirely ignored by posthumanism, with the exception of More's work. Remarks made by Marvin Minsky and Ray Kurzweil instead demonstrate the widespread assumption of a completely materially determined human being, in which the perfect simulation of every molecule of a body or brain will allow the perfect simulation of a person. However, it is not considered at all necessary that we must first even remotely understand how our brains operate![91] This focus on the human brain must be understood in connection with the 19th century's obsession with geniuses and great minds. [92]

The continuity of identity in a simulation is actually problematized within posthumanist discourse, and two interwoven lines of argument appear at the forefront of this debate. The first places the preservation of form and structure above the preservation of concrete matter, in order to secure continued identity in a simulation. The second ties the preservation of personal identity to the preservation of the mind, i.e. to the mental operations of the brain alone.

In order to legitimize the emphasis placed upon preserving form and structure, posthumanists refer to Aristotle and Thomas Aquinas (Tipler) only sporadically and peripherally, while mentions of psychological functionalism appear only briefly (More).[93] Instead, Minsky, Moravec, and Kurzweil are undeniably the key intellectual figures, in terms of their reliance on the pattern identity theory, as developed within

---

88 More 1995, 91.
89 Ibid., 95.
90 See ibid., 90-95.
91 See Minsky 1988, 306-307; Kurzweil 1999a, 124-125.
92 See section 6.6.2.
93 See Barrow / Tipler 1986, 659; Tipler 1995, 127-128.

cybernetic information theory. The physicist Tipler and the philosopher More also seem to be guided by this cybernetic paradigm, which I will elaborate in the following chapter.

Posthumanists limit the technical process of uploading to the scanning of the brain. They understand personal identity as a mere result of the brain's mental functions. Even More explicitly emphasizes that our body's specific material has no relevance to identity formation. Hans Moravec, Ray Kurzweil, and obviously also Marvin Minsky adopted this dominance of the mind over the body from René Descartes' epistemology.

In his *Meditationes de prima philosophia*,[94] Descartes devotes himself to a systematic search for the unquestionable foundation of knowledge by gradually excluding everything that might be possibly subject to doubt. All objects from one's environment, all sensory perceptions, and finally even one's own body are suspected of being only illusions:

> I will suppose then, that everything I see is spurious. I will believe that my memory tells me lies, and that none of the things that it reports ever happened. I have no senses. Body, shape, extension, movement and place are chimeras. So what remains true? Perhaps just one fact that nothing is certain.[95]

Descartes therefore determines that ultimate certainty can only be found in the mental action enabling humans to fundamentally doubt all of their perceptions. Whatever one sees, dreams, hallucinates – these all confirm only one thing with certainty: that a mental action is taking place, the object and purpose of which remain uncertain in the end, but which exists as – and only as – a mental action. For if all physical appearances are only illusions, what am I then?

> Thinking? At least I have discovered it – thought; this alone is inseparable from me. I am, I exist, that is certain. But for how long? For as long as I am thinking ... I am then, in the strict sense only a thing that thinks; that is, I am a mind, or intelligence, or intellect, or reason – words whose meaning I have been ignorant of until now ... What is that? A thing that doubts, that understands, affirms, denies, is willing, is unwilling, and also imagines and has sensory perceptions.[96]

Thinking itself thus becomes proof of existence: *Cogito, ergo sum*! The Cartesian certainty of existence, which is anchored solely in the ability to think, thus eliminates the body as the subject of knowledge. Cartesian doubt, which recognizes the ability to doubt itself as the only epistemological certainty, therefore leads to the complete detachment

---

94   The original Latin version was published in Paris and Leiden, in 1641 and 1642 respectively, while the French translation was only published in 1647. See Descartes 1967b, 171-176, 377-381.

95   Descartes 1985b, 16. "Suppono igitur omnia quae video falsa esse; credo nihil unquam exitisse eorum quae mendax memoria repraesentat; nullos plane habeo sensus; corpus, figura, extensio, motus, locusque sunt chimerae. Quid igitur erit verum? Fortassis hoc unum, nihil esse certi." Descartes 1967b, 182.

96   Descartes 1985b, 18-19. "Cogitatio est; haec sola a me divelli nequit. Ego sum, ego existo; certum est. Quandiu autem? Nempe quandiu cogito ... sum igitur praecise tantùm res cogitans, id est, mens, sive animus, sive intellectus, sive ratio, voces mihi priùs significationis ignotae ... Quid est hoc? Nempe dubitans, intelligens, affirmans, negans, volens, nolens, imaginans quoque, sentiens." Descartes 1967b, 184-186.

of thinking from the material body. The body as a supposed illusion is thus just as irrelevant *for thinking* as a dream.⁹⁷

In his posthumously published physiological essay *La description du corps humain* from 1647, Descartes very clearly refuses to define the human soul as the principle and cause of all movements and functions of the human body. This is because the physiological mechanisms of the organs, like the gear train of a clock, do not require a soul, but rather can move by themselves: "But when we try to get to know our nature more distinctly we can see that our soul, in so far as it is a substance which is distinct from the body, is known to us merely through the fact that it thinks ... "⁹⁸

Here it becomes clear how profound this re-interpretation must become if one is to construct a materialistic monism from the mechanistic explanation of the human body. Descartes first understood the human being as a dualistic unity of body and soul early on in his career, well before the *Meditations*. He also defines the "spirit of life", the *spiritus animalis*, purely physically rather than in any intermediary sense: "Like us, these men will be composed of a Soul and a body."⁹⁹ Although Descartes never clearly defined the relationship between body, soul, and mind, it remains undisputed that he presupposes the separation of body and mind:¹⁰⁰

> The first observation I make at this point is that there is a great difference between the mind and the body, inasmuch as the body is by its very nature always divisible, while the mind is utterly indivisible ... This one argument would be enough to show me that the mind is completely different from the body ... ¹⁰¹

The Cartesian separation of physical and immaterial worlds that never meet, yet somehow also interact with each other, provoked fierce, decades-long feuds. These raged both within and outside of medicine, and amongst theologians, philosophers, and physicians. These debates all addressed the body-mind problem, which Descartes left unsolved at his death. Considering this legacy, it is hardly surprising that many interpretations of his work emerged during his lifetime as well.

In 1641, shortly after publication of the original Descartes was already forced to correct the theologian Arnauld's misunderstanding of the Cartesian body-soul dualism as a reintroduction of the Platonic understanding of soul.¹⁰² Meanwhile Descartes himself provokes just such a Platonic interpretation when in the sixth *Meditation* he expresses his own certainty that he was only a "thinking thing", truly distinct from

---

97   See Descartes 1985b, 16-22.
98   Descartes 1985a, 314.
99   Descartes 1967a, 379, trans. by AJ.
100 On several occasions Descartes mentions an intention to add a description of the mental processes, which would be analogous to the description of the bodily functions. Presumably because he found it necessary to first establish his metaphysics, the plan was postponed and ultimately remained unfulfilled.
101 Descartes 1985b, 59. "Nempe imprimis hîc adverto magnam esse differentiam inter mentem / corpus, in eo quòd corpus ex natura suâ sit semper divisibile, mens autem plane indivisibilis ... quod unum sufficeret ad me docendum, mentem a corpore omnino esse diversam ... " Descartes 1967b, 232.
102 See *Quatrièmes Objections faites par Monsieur Arnauld, Docteur en Théologie.* Descartes 1967b, 640.

the body and thus able to exist without it.[103] However, the Cartesian idea of the human being stems from the all-encompassing view that humans are comprised of two inherently different yet complete substances: the *res cogitans* – the immaterial, rational soul – and the *res extensa* – the spatial, material body. However, these are nonetheless closely connected to each other in a *unity*. The body therefore does not merely represent a "vehicle" for the soul. Only within his metaphysics does "I" exclusively denote the thinking subject of epistemology, to which the body is a mere "machine of limbs", and therefore belongs to the outside world. In actuality, the concrete person consists of a unity of body and mind.[104]

At this point, this text cannot delve further into the minutia of Cartesian thought. We can further interrogate neither the question of reconstructing the supposedly "correct" interpretation of the body-mind problem in Descartes' philosophical work, nor the project of tracing the complex history of reception, which is largely incomprehensible for the philosophical layperson. Rather, our concern is only to pose the hermeneutic question of what significance Descartes holds for posthumanism's quest for immortality.

The posthumanist reception of Descartes' body-mind model becomes even sharper in the philosopher Ludwig Wittgenstein's criticism of Descartes. In his posthumously published reflections *On Certainty*, Wittgenstein identifies the immanent errors of Cartesian epistemology by stating that the concepts of "knowledge" and "doubt" must always remain in a single system. He also presupposes that a proof is possible for this knowledge. This also implies a division between the procedures for obtaining knowledge and the method for the certain examination of that knowledge.[105] How can Descartes guarantee that the examiner itself, i.e. the mind, could withstand radical doubt? Ultimately, the examiner is not more secure from doubt than the knowledge being examined. In contrast to Descartes, Wittgenstein attributes the beginning of thinking to the establishing of certainties, which in fact themselves manifest a framework for doubt. These are anchored in the material form of our body: such as the hands, the fingers on each hand, feet, mouth, etc. Therefore, certainties gained via our bodies are actually deeper than any intellectual insights about our world.

Wittgenstein and the developmental psychologist Jean Piaget agree that certainty of the body underpins human cognition.[106] Wittgenstein's criticism illustrates the posthumanist point of view even more clearly, since posthumanism, with reference to Descartes, negates the role of the body during the acquisition of certain knowledge and the genesis of identity. In this respect, posthumanist approaches also clearly differ from the approach known as embodied cognition in AI research, which considers corporeality to be a basic prerequisite for thinking and consciousness.[107]

No other posthumanist invests Descartes' philosophy with as much importance as the author Hans Moravec, who is otherwise very sparing with his philosophical

---

103   See ibid., 488.
104   See ibid., 228; Gouhier 1962, 353-394; Newman 2019.
105   See Gebauer 1984, 237-238; Wittgenstein 1969, § 24.
106   See Gebauer 1984, 235-243; Wittgenstein 1969, § 55-56, 496-497, 579; Piaget 1952, 30-58.
107   See Schöner 2014.

6. A History of Technological Posthumanism   137

excursions. *Cogito, ergo sum!* is the leitmotif of Moravec's second monograph *Robot. Mere Machines to Transcendent Mind*. The cover of the American edition is adorned by Rodin's famous sculpture *The Thinker* and, as a counterpart, a thinking robot. Despite the fact that he adopts the Cartesian model *ad absurdum*, Moravec goes on to use *a computer-simulated* Descartes to document the exclusive ability to think as proof of existence. The possible existence of artificial intelligences or simulated humans in virtuality is thus also proven for Moravec. In the perfectly simulated world inside a computer, an emulation, the simulation of the thinking subject would not be able to scrutinize its ontological status. Neither physical nor mental: all perceptions of the environment and the self would instead simply appear to be as real as in reality. For Moravec, the discretionary basis is not formed by the philosophical criteria of illusion and truth. Rather, and quite pragmatically, the focus is on ensuring the continuity of the thinking subject through the technical simulation of all conditions necessary for human thinking. This includes the simulation of mental functions as well as the simulation of sensory impressions. If the simulation cannot be unmasked as such, it becomes real – the truth criterion remains unconsidered. The only decisive factor is that personal existence is secured by the continuation of thinking.[108]

> A simulated world hosting a simulated person can be a closed self-contained entity ... The inhabitant might, by patient experimentation and interference, deduce some representations of the simulation laws, but not the nature or even existence of the simulating computer.[109]

Ray Kurzweil also invokes Descartes' proof of existence when he connects the presence of human-like intelligence in a computer with the emergence of consciousness:[110]

> Before 2030, we will have machines proclaiming Descartes's dictum [I think, therefore I am] ... The machines will convince us that they are conscious, that they have their own agenda worthy of our respect. We will come to believe that they are conscious much as we believe that of each other.[111]

Moravec also presents Descartes as a pioneer of the idea of virtual reality, as in the 17th century he had already considered the possibility that our reality was merely an illusion created by an evil demon controlling all our physical senses (sight, hearing, smell, taste, touch). In the 21st century, science itself would produce virtual illusions.[112]

Moreover, Moravec's use of the Many-Worlds interpretation of quantum mechanics seems to be connected with George Berkeley's epistemology, which itself was significantly influenced by Descartes' and Locke's empiricism. In his 1710 *Principles of Human Knowledge*, Berkeley discovered that no object of our knowledge can exist outside

---

108 See Moravec 1988, 180.
109 Moravec 1999, 192.
110 See Kurzweil 1999, 60, 325, 349; Kurzweil 2005, 173.
111 Ibid., 60, 63.
112 See Moravec 1999, 191. Moravec ignores the fact that the idea of a deceiver-god is only a methodical hypothesis of the first meditation, which Descartes, moreover, later abolished once more. See Descartes 1967b, 181.

of our mind, since matter and external objects can only come into existence via our conscious perception. This primacy of the human mind over the material world is found in Frank Tipler's anthropocentric interpretation of the role of intelligent observers in the universe, as well as in Moravec's solipsistic interpretation of the Many-Worlds Theory.[113] The relationship between body and mind is also clearly defined as "superiority of the soul to the body, of the rational to the animal part of our constitution" in the philosophy of the 19th century group known as the physico-theologians, in whose tradition Tipler explicitly places himself.[114]

Taking into account the creative way in which philosophical ideas are received, it can be concluded that Descartes' determination of the relationship between body and mind has attained a certain relevance for posthumanism in three respects. All posthumanists refer to Descartes to justify the assumption that the thinking subject alone determines the status of its existence and individual identity. This leads to the following three consequences:

1. The concrete body has no meaning for the existence of a being, as it is only the subject that is capable of rational thinking and therefore exists *with certainty*. In other words, the human mind, located in the brain, produces a human being's individual personality. As an exchangeable "tool" of the mind, the body merely provides "data storage" and is of negligible importance for human existence.
2. Since the human mind can exist without the body, the continued existence of a human being as only a "thinking thing" (*res cogitans*) is guaranteed for eternity within the computer. The immortality of the person is thus synonymous with the continuity of the thinking processes.
3. If an artificially intelligent computer program describes itself as existing, this statement cannot be disputed by any outsider. Instead, the program can claim its right to exist just as all intelligent living beings do. Only the consciousness of the intelligent machine can determine the status of its own existence.

This Descartes-inspired definition of humans elicits the question of whether it is based on a dualistic or a monistic view. All posthumanists assume that the human being is nothing more than an extremely complex arrangement of matter, whose functions are ultimately entirely attributable to physical laws. Posthumanism is thus a materialistic philosophy.

However, the body's *mental functions* – and these alone – are determined as the essence of the human being. The human mind as the sum and continuity of these functions is equated with the individual personality, to the extent that the mind or sometimes the human soul is referred to as a program running on the computer of the brain (Tipler). It must be assumed that Marvin Minsky's concept, which is entirely focused on the human mind, is relevant for Tipler, Moravec, and Kurzweil.

In this way, the *software* of the mind, which is so decisive for the human personality, is distinguished from its specific hardware or so-called *wetware*. As Max More points

---

113 See Moravec 1988, 153-154, 187-188; Moravec 1999, 205-207; Barrow / Tipler 1986, 21-23.
114 Paley 1842, 6.

out, its performance does not depend on the concrete form and structure of the body. The continuity of mental processes and the equivalent continuity of the human personality rely upon the continuation of the brain's operative functions. The body therefore becomes arbitrarily interchangeable with any other data storage medium that could simulate mental functions: The immortality of humans is determined as the immortality of mind.

To the extent that a materialistic monism rejects the dualisms of form and content, mind and nature, matter and structure, posthumanism also adopts a dualistic view of the primacy of mind over the negligible body.[115] The material body is contrasted with its mental functions, which alone are regarded as significant. The functionalist paradigm is thus entirely geared to the mental function of information processing. Defining the human mind as an independent entity reflects the dualistic character of posthumanist reasoning.[116] In the context of these various inquiries, posthumanist philosophy emphasizes partly materialistic-monistic aspects and partly dualistic-functionalistic aspects.

In his analysis of the social effects of naturalism in the late 19th century, Mark Seltzer discovered a phenomenon similar to that which we encounter today in posthumanism. He made the contradictory discovery that naturalism emphasizes the materialistic or physical conditionality of persons, representations, and actions. On the other hand, he was able to establish that naturalism legitimizes this viewpoint precisely by referring to the abstractions of persons, bodies, and actions in immaterial numbers, signs, models, and diagrams. Seltzer refers to this ideology as a dematerialized materialism.[117]

If the posthumanist debate on dualism and monism in human nature may sometimes be deemed to be lacking in philosophical consistency, it must also be acknowledged that the authors do not argue primarily as philosophers, but rather as pragmatists, computer scientists, and robotics experts. On the one hand, the human being is defined entirely as a material machine, which can in principle be simulated by other machines, e.g. by computers. On the other hand, human personality is reduced to the human mind (while the body is held responsible for aging and death). Since Aristotle, the relationship between form and substance, and between mind and matter, has remained the crucial question for western metaphysics. The sociologist Dietmar Kamper sharply observes that the mind corresponds to the category of form, while the body belongs to the category of matter. One ascribes an active role to the former and a passive role to the latter. In other words: The mind is wise, but matter is stupid. The form and the mind liberate matter from chaos and lead it onward to the peaks of human culture. For Kamper this explains the contemporary fascination with the idea of a pure mind liberated from all material constraints.[118]

---

[115] See Mehlhausen / Dunkel 1994, 213.
[116] Only Max More warns of a "false dualism". See More 1995, 91-95.
[117] See Seltzer 1994, 14.
[118] See Kamper 1999, 110-112; Lavery 1992, 71-72.

The Cybernetic Paradigm

Posthumanist thinkers obviously read their philosophical predecessors through their own special "lenses". For example, in an astonishing feat of interpretation, Frank Tipler managed to combine a physical and materialistic reductionism with the philosophies of Plato, Aristotle, Augustine, and Thomas Aquinas. Similarly, Hans Moravec is able, on the one hand, to interpret Descartes in a materialistic and monistic way and, on the other hand, to use the absolute dominance of the mind over the body, which was conceived as dualism in Descartes' proof of existence. To judge the consistency of these undertakings from a philosophical perspective is beyond the scope of the current work. In order to continue examining the question of the history of philosophical reception, it is necessary to first establish the specific selections and interpretations that allowed the concretizations of Descartes' work and materialist philosophy described in the two previous sections. What, then, characterizes the posthumanist paradigm enabling these concrete interpretations?

The following discussion examines how the foundations of cybernetics contributed to the genesis of a specific cybernetic paradigm, which would become significant for posthumanist philosophy. Three aspects of cybernetics will be considered: firstly, the determination of the organic nervous system as an information-processing machine; secondly, the equivalence of an artificially intelligent machine with humans; and finally, the interpretation of the relationship between information and matter or body, which in posthumanist discourse exerts a critical influence on the understanding of the human mind. It will become apparent that leading cyberneticists hold positions that are remarkably different from those of posthumanists. However, they provide a specifically cybernetic pattern of interpretation that the posthumanists could apply to the question of immortality.

Since the 1940s, a series of renowned mathematicians, biologists, physicians, and engineers have been involved in the establishment of cybernetics and its interdisciplinary research program. Amongst them were included: Alan Turing, Arturo Rosenblueth, John von Neumann, Claude Shannon, and, above all, Norbert Wiener, who became particularly well-known for his pioneering achievements. A mathematician, Wiener taught at the Massachusetts Institute of Technology (MIT) from 1919 to 1964 and describes the formation of the new science as follows:

> Until recently, there was no existing word for this complex of ideas, and in order to embrace the whole field by a single term, I felt constrained to invent one. Hence "Cybernetics," which I derived from the Greek word kubernetes, or "steersman," the same Greek word from which we eventually derive our word "governor."[119]

In general, cybernetics is concerned with abstract systems which, as analogical models, simulate certain areas of reality and can thus contribute mathematically calculable solutions to specific problems. Cybernetics focuses on the question of how information is passed from one system to another, how it is received and stored, and which machine actions can be controlled with it.

---

119   Wiener 1989, 15.

Together with Oskar Morgenstern, John von Neumann developed cybernetic game theory, which was as a mathematical method for selecting optimal behavior from the set of all possible options in conflict situations.[120] During and after the Second World War, game theory gained particular importance within military strategic planning and in the programming of the first electronic mainframe computers. The *ENIAC* (*Electronic Numerical Integrator and Computer*), which John von Neumann helped build at the University of Pennsylvania from 1943 to 1946, was designed to calculate the trajectories of rockets and other ballistics.[121]

Wiener and von Neumann sought a method to simulate reality in a program that would become an abstract model of that reality. An ever-increasing number of real world sequences had to be symbolically modelled by algorithms in the computer. The real systems of a commercial enterprise, a state, or even a rocket were imitated in computer programs, so that, for example, different scenarios of a nuclear war could be run through, allowing political and military strategy to be aligned.[122] Its founders wanted to establish cybernetics as a universal science. In its first two decades, cybernetic theory gained a noticeable influence on the newly emerging fields of cybernetic psychology, sociology, and pedagogy.[123]

In 1943 Norbert Wiener, Julian Bigelow, and Arturo Rosenblueth published the *Cybernetic Manifesto* titled *Behaviour, Purpose and Teleology*. This was followed by a defense of their theses (*Purposeful and Non-Purposeful Behavior*), in which they asserted the equivalence between biological and machine control within a behaviorist framework. Wiener was the first to equate the mechanisms of control, information, and communication between organic living beings and machines.[124] The authors introduce the category of purposeful behavior into the cybernetic debate and justify this controversial teleological model of action by the expected advances in knowledge and understanding of machine control. Wiener, Bigelow, and Rosenblueth propagate the concept of teleological behavior by both humans and machines. Crucially, this implies that both depend on a goal connected to the world outside of the system. They explicitly regard their approach as a methodological concept rather than an ontological statement about the nature of human beings.[125] The authors of the *Cybernetic Manifesto* use the terms *purpose* and *goal / teleology* of action, as they assume the equivalence of human and machine behavior:

> We believe that men and other animals are like machines from the *scientific standpoint* because we believe that the only fruitful methods for the study of human and animal behaviour are the methods applicable to the behaviour of mechanical objects as well. Thus, our main reason for selecting the terms in question was to emphasize that, as objects of *scientific inquiry*, humans do not differ from machines.[126]

---

120 See Neumann / Morgenstern 1966; Heims 1981, 83-93, 294-299.
121 See ibid., 365.
122 See Anders 1983, 59-64; Weizenbaum 1976, 238-239.
123 See Hayles 1999, 96-98. Regarding the history of cybernetics see Wiener 1961, 1-59.
124 See Wiener 1985, 187-195.
125 See ibid., 193-194.
126 Ibid., 195.

Based upon the cybernetic paradigm's equation of humans and machines, Wiener derives the origin of the two sub-areas of biocybernetics: neurocybernetics and medical cybernetics.[127]

During a meeting with the mathematician Walter Pitts, who analyzed the mathematical properties of neural networks, Wiener described the functions of modern vacuum tubes as the equivalents of organic neuron discharge. He considered them to be completely analogous to the selection of a binary digit – i.e. they either discharge or they do not. From this point of view, an ultra-fast calculating machine would represent an almost ideal model of the nervous system's processes. This is not only because the organic nerve cells would correspond to a computer's "all or nothing" binary principle, but also because of the far-reaching analogies between human memory and that of a calculating machine. These led Wiener to the conclusion that the brain operates like a logical machine:

> We are beginning to see that such important elements as the neurons, the atoms of the nervous complex of our body, do their work under much the same conditions as vacuum tubes, with their relatively small power supplied from outside by the circulation, and that the book-keeping which is most essential to describe their function is not one of energy. In short, the newer study of automata, whether in the metal or in the flesh, is a branch of communication engineering, and its cardinal notions are those of message, amount of disturbance or "noise" – a term taken over from the telephone engineer – quantity of information, coding technique, and so on.[128]

Warren McCulloch, the long-time director of the important *Macy Conferences*, designed the neural model, which was particularly significant for the juxtaposition of human and machine thinking undertaken by Wiener and early cybernetics. This mathematical model of the brain ultimately demonstrated "that brains do not secrete thought as the liver secretes bile but ... they compute thought the way electronic computers calculate numbers."[129] McCulloch illustrated the neurons of the human brain according to an electronic circuit scheme. This would prove that humans and machines were not only subject to the same universal physical laws, but also that their thought processes followed the same mechanisms.[130]

John von Neumann simultaneously developed a general and systematic theory of automata. For heuristic reasons, this was based on the analogy between organic living beings and computers, which he categorized as artificial automata (computers, radio systems) or natural automata (nervous system, self-reproducing systems), respectively. His *Theory of Self-Reproducing Automata* takes up the idea of the unlimited reproduction of a pattern by a machine and goes on to develop the theoretical concept of an organic or mechanical automaton that can calculate everything, construct everything, and even

---

127 Norbert Wiener: "Introduction to Neurocybernetics." See Wiener 1985, 400-406.
128 Wiener 1961, 42. See also Wiener 1961, 116-132.
129 Warren McCulloch: The Beginning of Cybernetics. *McCulloch Papers*, B/M139. Cited in Hayles 1999, 58.
130 See Hayles 1999, 58-61; Hagner 2004, 288-296.

reproduce itself.¹³¹ In addition to the ability to learn, Wiener also cites the possibility of one's own reproduction as characteristic of living systems.¹³²

Von Neumann's significance for cybernetics lies primarily in his comparison of organic and artificial control mechanisms. However, it is also important to note that he does not consider this abstract, mathematical description of the world to actually be closer to the true nature of reality. Rather, mathematical language, like any other natural language, is the result of historical and cultural processes.¹³³

Trusting in the intellectual, social, and emotional qualities of human beings, and operating from a humanist standpoint, in his later works, Norbert Wiener opposes considerations that place humans and machines directly on the same level. He is also critical of those that degrade and dismiss humans as obsolete or replaceable, due to their lack of efficiency in comparison with machines:

> Those who value man not in his own right but merely as an instrument for production see eye to eye with the slave merchant ... This evaluation of man is Fascism ... Those who devaluate man in the presence of the superior efficiency of the machine, are simply those who have devaluated man in their own hearts, and their works speak for them ... If we rate a man only as a factory hand, for the cost of his daily wages, then the machine will indeed displace man over much of his range of activity. But in essence, the factory hand is first a human being, and only secondarily a factory hand.¹³⁴

Both John von Neumann's and especially Norbert Wiener's later works – which warn of the power of machines – did not support the general assumption that the human being is a machine.¹³⁵ However, although this comparison between humans and machines was originally purely academic, the popular debate quickly read humans and machines as only two kinds of information-processing devices. Regardless of what analogies or differences might be established – when humans and machines are compared they are set in the same system. Wiener, for example, illustrates elementary differences in perception by comparing the human eye with a television receiver.¹³⁶

To accentuate the difference between "natural and artificial automatons", Wiener and von Neumann repeatedly point out that the human nervous system is far more complex than a machine's control mechanism: "Thus the machine, for all the similarities that its functioning shows with that of the human organism, is at a much lower level of organization and complexity ... "¹³⁷ However, this comparison already catches cyberneticists in a logical trap, which snaps shut upon the increasing complexity of machine information processing. This connection becomes even clearer when Wiener himself introduces the concept of transcending human behaviour through the qualities

---

131 See Neumann 1966, 251-296.
132 See Wiener 1961, 241-256; Barrow / Tipler 1986, 511-523; Tipler 1995, 44-55.
133 See Neumann 1964, 80-82.
134 Norbert Wiener: The Future of Automatic Machinery. Wiener 1985, 132. See also Roszak 1994, 9-11.
135 See Wiener 1961, 27-29.
136 See Wiener 1985, 185; Wiener 1961, 120-125.
137 Wiener 1985, 665. See Neumann 1966, 42-56.

of machines: "Examples, however, are readily found of man-made machines with behaviour that transcends human behaviour."[138] By subsequently referring to the purely mechanical possibilities of emitting electric current or radio waves, Wiener has already made a comparison between humans and machines. At the same time, he has revealed the machine's potential to *transcend* humanity, which will be reflected in metaphors by Hans Moravec and Ray Kurzweil.[139]

The discussion so far makes it evident that precisely this idea of artificial intelligence, i.e. the most complex information-processing systems, plays a central role in equating humans and machines:

> In the same way, whether they are understood as like or unlike, ranging human intelligence alongside an intelligent machine puts the two into a relay system that constitutes the human as a special kind of information machine and the information machine as a special kind of a human.[140]

Long before the MIT-based cyberneticist John McCarthy coined the term "artificial intelligence" in 1960, the English computer pioneer Alan Turing was already working on the question: *Can a machine think?*[141] The computer giants *ENIAC* and its British counterpart *Colossus* were required to decode encrypted messages and perform calculations for the construction of the atomic bomb during the Second World War. Subsequently, Alan Turing and John von Neumann developed the first programs that could think through problems independently and arrive at solutions. In 1950 Turing and his colleagues designed programs for logical thinking and intellectual games, such as checkers and chess. Today such programs are already so sophisticated and backed by such enormous computing capacities that even chess world champions can no longer beat the best of them.[142]

Alan Turing's most important contribution to the spread of the idea of artificial intelligence was probably his 1950 essay *Computing Machinery and Intelligence*, which presented the imitation game thereafter cited by all posthumanists as the Turing Test.[143] However, descriptions of the Turing Test often neglect to mention that Turing first suggested to place a man (A), a woman (B), and a third player in separate rooms and to let them communicate with each other only by means of a teleprinter. The third player's task was to use questions to determine the sex of players A and B. However, Turing also had more in mind for this game. He asks:

> "What will happen when a machine takes the part of A in this game?" Will the interrogator decide wrongly as often when the game is played …? These questions replace our original, "Can machines think?"[144]

---

138 Wiener 1985, 184.
139 See ibid., 180-186. See Hayles 1999, 94-95.
140 Ibid., 64-65.
141 See Moravec 1988, 8; Turing 1992, 107-128.
142 See Moravec 1988, 8-9.
143 See Turing 1950; See Barrow / Tipler 1986, 523; Tipler 1995, 20-21; Moravec 1999, 73-88; Kurzweil 1999a, 61-65.
144 Turing 1950, 434.

According to Turing, it would be possible to evaluate a person's intellectual qualities, independent of any physical abilities, by using an intelligent computer.[145] Turing assumed that around the year 2000 machines and humans would most likely be indistinguishable from each other in this test. Interestingly, we already find a precursor of this test idea in Descartes' *Discours de la Méthode* (1637). The philosopher assumes that it would be possible to fabricate an artificial animal in a deceptively real way. According to Descartes, on the other hand, an artificial human could at most simulate a few human reactions and words. However, he is sure that any such machine-man would never be able to have a real conversation or react to its environment.[146]

The actual Turing Test is no longer cutting-edge, and in fact the simple conversation program *ELIZA* by Joseph Weizenbaum was able to simulate a human actor in 1966. However, Turing's essay remains important for posthumanism primarily due to his response to potential objections denying the equality of humans and machines.[147] These objections, which Hans Moravec, incidentally, presents in great detail, largely concern the superior complexity of the human organism. This is recognized by Wiener and von Neumann, although Turing believes it will dwindle if technological development proceeds as anticipated.[148]

Turing believes it is possible to design a machine able to learn universal rules of behavior and react to every situation, just as a human would. In this machine, the differences between the continuous signals of the organic nervous system and the discrete signals of a computer would become insignificant for producing logical thought processes. Computers would also be able to complete actions for which they were not specifically programmed, and Turing is convinced that machines could also develop a sense of beauty, humor, love, etc.: "The criticism that a machine cannot have much diversity of behaviour is just a way of saying that it cannot have much storage capacity."[149]

While Turing vehemently rejects the idea of an immortal soul, he considers supernatural abilities, such as telepathy and psychokinesis, as more serious. He suggests possibly adapting the test conditions of the imitation game by means of a "telepathically safe room". In contrast, Moravec condemns these phenomena as hoaxes and the result of scientific errors. Paradoxical mathematical problems that cannot be deduced by a computer's pure arithmetic would, however, prove humankind's mathematical superiority to date.[150]

Despite the remaining differences standing in the way of the perfect equivalence between humans and intelligent machines, Turing was confident that his arguments would be fully validated if computers had passed the imitation test successfully by the end of the 20th century. He considered that this could actually be possible with a

---

145   See ibid., 434-435.
146   See Descartes 1824, 189-190; Gunderson 1964.
147   See Weizenbaum 1976, 3-11, 181-200.
148   See Moravec 1999, 72-88.
149   Turing 1950, 449.
150   For example Gödel's incompleteness theorems. See ibid., 443-454.

relatively easy to construct "machine child", which would only reach the childlike stage of human development.[151]

In his book *Authority, Liberty, and Automatic Machinery in Early Modern Europe*, Otto Mayr demonstrates how this ideal of a machine capable of learning and reproducing itself corresponds with the enlightened idea of a self-regulating market and with decentralist, democratic ambitions.[152] A historical investigation of Mayr's work holds particular relevance for posthumanism, as American posthumanists, especially the Extropians, are outspoken advocates of economic liberalism.

The posthumanist idea of the human being is only partly shaped by mechanistic and materialistic interpretations. For the question of immortality, the dualistic division into a body and a mind is even more important. Posthumanists imagine only the concrete mind, i.e. information processing, as being simulated in the computer, while the body is usually judged to be arbitrarily interchangeable. The central question that remains is therefore: How could information be conceptualized as a unit that is distinct from its material embodiment?

Norbert Wiener points out that science is fundamentally based on a dualistic foundation, without, however, necessarily resulting in metaphysical dualism. Science consists of abstractions of reality, which are reflected in formal and material models of the universe. In Tipler's work these culminate in an emulation of the entire universe – although according to Wiener this misses the point:

> The ideal formal model would be one which would cover the entire universe, which would agree with it in complexity, and which would have a one to one correspondence with it. Any one capable of elaborating and comprehending such a model in its entirety would find the model unnecessary, because he could then grasp the universe directly as a whole.[153]

The *Macy Conferences on Cybernetics* ran from 1943 to 1954 and provided an opportunity for scientists from various disciplines to exchange views on cybernetic research projects. At its first session, John von Neumann and Norbert Wiener successfully demonstrated to the participants that the most important unit in the human-machine equation is not energy – as had previously been widely assumed – but rather information. N. Katherine Hayles calls this the triumph of information over matter.[154]

In 1948 Claude Shannon published his essay *The Mathematical Theory of Communication* in the *Bell System Technical Journal*, and it immediately became fundamental to information theory, appearing as a book the following year, written in collaboration with Warren Weaver. He first differentiates in general between three levels of communication theory, each of which address distinct questions:

---

151   See ibid., 455-457.
152   See Mayr 1986; Hayles 1999, 86.
153   Norbert Wiener / Arturo Rosenblueth: The Role of the Models in Science. Wiener 1985, 450.
154   See Hayles 1999, 6-7, 50-52.

LEVEL A. How accurately can the symbols of communication be transmitted? (The technical problem.)
LEVEL B. How precisely do the transmitted symbols convey the desired meaning? (The semantic problem.)
LEVEL C. How effectively does the received meaning affect conduct in the desired way? (The effectiveness problem.)[155]

While Weaver subsequently emphasized that Shannon's mathematical communication theory also held some relevance for the semantics of messages, Shannon's approach clearly addresses the first problem: the technical transmission of messages.[156] Mathematical communication theory addresses the fundamental problem of reproducing a message (either exactly or approximately) within the context of certain physical or conceptual measures. Shannon stresses: "These semantic aspects of communication are irrelevant to the engineering problem. The significant aspect is that the actual message is one selected from a set of possible messages."[157]

The information theory that Shannon initiated deals exclusively with the problem of the technological – and mostly digital – transmission of information in telecommunications. These are divided into two separate sub-problems: firstly, the representation of the output signals of the source by binary symbols (source coding); and secondly, the actual transmission of binary random sequences over a channel (channel coding). The central concern was the safe transmission of information so that the channel decoder can reliably reconstruct the original message from the transmitted signals, despite the constant channel interferences. Since the 1960s, many systems for error control have been developed from comprehensive algebraic structures. Subsequent developments in microelectronics have led to complex error control algorithms, which today form the basis for digital communication and storage media. For example, certain codes were created for eliminating errors caused by the scratches or dirt on CDs, in order to allow the channel decoder to restore the original binary data. The same applies, of course, to the transmission of data through fiber optic cables or over wireless networks.

According to Shannon, information represents the choice of one message amongst several possible options. In the case of a limited number of possible pieces of information, Shannon proposes a logarithmic function as a measure of information, which will mathematically capture the equally probable selection of information from the pool of possible information. As is well known, Shannon introduced the binary digits 0 and 1 (binary digits: bits) as the logarithmic foundations of this measure of information. In this way, that measure is introduced as a stochastic function of the selection of a particular element of a message.[158]

Shannon's definition of information is determined without regard to its material carrier or semantic context. This prevailed over a competing design by the British

---

155 Shannon / Weaver 1964, 4. In this regard see also Roszak 1994, 11-13.
156 See Shannon / Weaver 1964, 3-24.
157 Ibid., 31.
158 I waive any claim to speak authoritatively on mathematical matters and instead refer to: Shannon / Weaver 1964, 15-29; Brillouin 1957, 1-27.

researcher Donald McKay, who sought to make the change in the meaning of information dependent on the specific context of a recipient. The technical advantage of Shannon's definition consisted precisely in the fact that, using a universal mathematical formalization, information could be transferred freely, safe from the influence of contexts and media, and without high costs. If the mathematical value of information were linked to its meaning, it might have to change in each new context.[159]

Faced with the accusation of separating information from its meaning, Shannon always maintained that his theory was only applicable to specific technical telecommunications rather than to communication in general. Warren Weaver expresses this relationship as follows:

> An engineering communication theory is just like a very proper and discreet girl accepting your telegram. She pays no attention to the meaning, whether it be sad, or joyous, or embarrassing. But she must be prepared to deal with all that come to her desk.[160]

Carolyn Marvin points out the cultural and ideological implications of Shannon's decontextualized concept of information in terms of the American need for cultural independence from Europe. This is technologically reflected in the preference for digital information processing over more context-dependent, analog information processing.[161] Moreover, in his essay *Homeostasis in the Individual and Society* Norbert Wiener himself points out how little connection the people in the "esoteric hot house civilization of Southern California" have to their cultural and genealogical origins.[162] California has become not only one of the most important locations for the international computer industry, but is also the center of the *Extropian* and *Singularitarian* movements, which were themselves founded on a decontextualized interpretation of information.

Shannon and Wiener's work presents information as a stochastic quantity that can be calculated in the same mathematical way regardless of context, and totally independent of the material carriers that transmit or store it. From a technological point of view, the human being itself thus becomes this "message": a complex organization of information that is constructed independently of its material embodiment – i.e. the human body. For Wiener, it is thus undeniable that an individual's physical identity is not based on the identity of the substance from which it is made:

> To recapitulate: the individuality of the body is that of a flame rather than that of a stone, of a form rather than of a bit of substance. This form can be transmitted or modified and duplicated, although at present we know only how to duplicate it over a short distance … Since this is so, there is no absolute distinction between the types of transmission which we can use for sending a telegram from country to country and

---

159 See Hayles 1999, 19.
160 Shannon / Weaver 1964, 27.
161 See Marvin 1987.
162 See Wiener 1985, 383.

the types of transmission which at least are theoretically possible for transmitting a living organism such as a human being.[163]

Following these considerations, Wiener speculates about the technological issues of completely scanning the human body and then briefly discusses the difficulties of restoring this body!ial[164]

Marvin Minsky's contribution to the cybernetic paradigm can hardly be underestimated. Minsky was not only a student of Wiener, McCulloch, Shannon, and von Neumann, but as a professor at the MIT he also significantly influenced Hans Moravec, Ray Kurzweil, and the transhumanist Sasha Chislenko. Above all else Minsky propagates limiting human qualities to mere mental abilities, and subsuming all supposedly irrational qualities, such as humor or the musical senses, to being mere functions of reason. He thus embodies the posthumanist ideology of the mind's dominion over the body – or more generally: the dominion of the information-processing unit over matter.

This understanding of life and intelligence is also controversial within technophile AI research. The Australian roboticist and AI researcher Rodney Brooks remains critical of the paradigms that guide his own profession:

> To a large extent we have all become computational bigots, believers that any problem can be solved with enough computing power. Although I do firmly believe that the brain is a machine, whether this machine is a computer is another question. I recall that in centuries past the brain was considered a hydrodynamic machine ... When I was a child, the prevailing view was that the brain was a kind of telephone-switching network. When I was a teenager, it became an electronic computer, and later, a massively parallel digital computer. A few years ago, someone asked me at a talk I was giving, "Isn't the brain just like the World Wide Web?" We use these metaphors as the basis for our philosophical thinking and even let them pervade our understanding of what the brain truly does. None of our past metaphors for the brain has stood the test of time...[165]

Such remarks indicate that posthumanism is largely based on a cybernetic paradigm. The human being is interpreted within this paradigm as a machine from a scientific perspective, and as an information pattern from a communication technology perspective. Posthumanism thus decontextualizes Claude Shannon's semantic negation of information in a purely *technologically* determined context, and instead offers an ideology anchoring human personal identities in precisely this disembodied information pattern. Norbert Wiener's definition of the human being as a message, and his 1950 speculations about sending this message via a body scan are apparently only a small step away from Hans Moravec's subsequent idea of storing this "human message" eternally in a computer. However, while the cybernetics of the 1940s and 1950s advocated

---

163   Wiener 1989, 102-103.
164   See ibid., 100-101.
165   Brooks 2008.

a fundamental dualism between matter and information, we must take a much more differentiated view of the posthumanist positions.

In a cybernetic paradigm the human being becomes an information-processing machine whose immaterial "program" – including its specific instructions for processing information – constitutes one's unique personality. Posthumanists do not seek to simulate the immaterial form of our complete body in a computer, but rather to reconstruct the exact pattern of our thinking brain. An individual's essential identity is determined as a body-independent, mental entity, so that a person can then be simulated in virtuality without his or her concrete physical form. We can now see how posthumanists could interpret Descartes' philosophy within a cybernetic paradigm. For Descartes the mind's dominance over the body only exists in the context of the Cartesian proof of existence. However, posthumanism absolutizes the thinking principle – i.e. the information processing – as the essence of our human being *par excellence*. Posthumanist philosophy thus only partly belongs to the field of intellectual history – it is simultaneously the history of the physical: body history. Thus when Frank Tipler, in enthusiasm for his idea of a technically possible immortality, asks "O death, where is thy sting?" (1 Cor 15:55), the sociologist Barbara Ossege knows exactly where it lies for posthumanists:[166] "In the end, the sting of death is the body itself. Its desire is always sinful and culpable. Life is a sexually transmitted disease, which has so far proved fatal in 100 percent of cases."[167]

Posthumanist reflections on the nature of the human being accentuate the prevalence of the mind over the body to such an extent that the body becomes negligible. This corresponds to the postmodern discourse on the elimination of the body.[168] In the following chapters, I will more precisely demonstrate how the replacement of the human by the posthuman is largely identical to the overcoming of the body, whose outdated appearance and functional inferiority must give way in the face of unstoppable progress.

The main difficulty with the history of the body is that the body officially has no history. Body language is not regarded as a language, while gestures are not actually seen as actions. Yet the body's form is not only reflected in art, but also constructed in medicine, philosophy, religious tracts and icons, fashion magazines, films, and more recently in computer games and social media. According to Dietmar Kamper, the battle between body and mind culminated in Descartes's triumph, yet this silencing of the body occurred far beyond the spectacular events of official history. Rather, it can be found in the underground of social theory over the past 500 years of European modernity.[169] Consequently, Dietmar Kamper defines the history of civilization, on the one hand, as the planned appropriation of nature – as a (mental) generalization of the (physical) particular – and, on the other hand, as an ongoing abstraction and formalization of all substance.[170] The complete abstraction of the human being in

---

166 Tipler 1995, 268 (=Tipler 1989, 250).
167 Ossege 1999, 179, trans. by AJ.
168 See Kamper 1976, 1999; Kamper / Wulf 1984b.
169 See Kamper 1976, 7-8; Kamper 1999, 36-38, 49.
170 See Kamper 1976, 8.

virtual existence allows posthumanism to seek dominance of the mind over a virtual, ghostly body, which is unattainable in the material world. The machine becomes the model for modern Europe's increasing need to discipline and control the body. As Christoph Wulf believes:

> If at first man was the model for the machine, then gradually the machine becomes the orientation point for the model of man. Mankind and machines are becoming similar. Just as God created man, man creates the machine. He thus seeks to become like God. His narcissistic fantasies of omnipotence can be realized through the production of the human-like machine.[171]

This premise places posthumanism at the current peak of a development that the sociologist Norbert Elias has described as the process of civilization. The increasing differentiation of society escalates the need to coordinate the behavior of more and more people. The individual is therefore forced to regulate his or her behavior in a progressively more differentiated, uniform, and stable manner. Elias speaks here of the automatism of pressuring oneself to adapt consciously or unconsciously to increasingly complex social conditions. The need to increasingly control the uncontrollable body becomes not only apparent in that peculiar social modelling of the instincts, characterized by "shame" and "embarrassment". Rather, it also emerges in the increasing normalization of the body demanded by medicine and fashion, which would reach a first climax in the dawning machine age, namely in the second half of the 19th century.[172]

In posthumanism, this civilizational idea of the dominion of the mind over the body culminates in the vision of a changeable and infinitely perfectible body, which is freely available to a technically immortalized mind in virtual space. Whereas death has hitherto marked the limit of the mind's dominion over the body, the technical overcoming of mortality now converges with the final conquest of the human body.

The Measure of Perfection: Work and Knowledge

If, according to this cybernetic paradigm, human beings are nothing more than information-processing machines then the question arises as to how human perfection can be achieved. What characterizes the perfection of human existence from this posthumanist perspective?

In Frank Tipler's cosmological conception, it is unmistakable that progress in the universe must be attributed to the extent of information processing. If Tipler defines life basically as information processing, as we have seen, then every moment of progress for life means an increase in the speed with which data is processed, as well as an expansion of the memory, i.e. the information storage, of these life forms. Consequently, Tipler favors not only the necessary overcoming of the cerebral limits of biological humans, but also the colonization of the galaxy by intelligent life with the goal of infinitely increasing the amount of information processed. Only an immense increase in the "computing

---

[171] Wulf 1984, 31, trans. by AJ.
[172] See Elias 1982; Foucault 1977.

power" of today's intelligent life forms could guarantee the unfolding of these various perfections, which Tipler does not initially elaborate further. Furthermore, the final union with God in the Omega Point, and the accompanying resurrection (or simulation) of all the dead, therefore depends on the performance of this future data processing, which is necessary to calculate the enormous amounts of information.[173] For Tipler, the collective drivers of progress include all those potentially self-programming Turing machines, in other words: Humans and their mechanical descendants – as they are in fact all intelligent "information-processing systems".[174]

Similarly, Marvin Minsky determines the absolute purpose of intelligent systems to be *thinking*, in the sense of problem solving. He condemns the trivial entertainment strategies of humans (football or pop music) as a complete waste of a valuable brainpower.[175] From a religious rather than economic perspective, Minsky comments on this obvious waste of human intellectual gifts:

> It would be fun to ask the religious ones to consider whether it is not a sin to waste such wondrous hardware on watching adults kicking balls around? My own view is that this is less a sin than a symptom – of infection by a parasitic meme ... which has self-propagated through our culture like a software virus, a cancer of the intellect so insidious that virtually no one thinks/dares to question it. Now, in the same way we see grown people playing and working in the context of popular music ... that sets at least part of one's brain in a loop. Is it o.k. that we, with our hard earned brains, should welcome and accept this indignity – or should we resent it as an assault on an evident vulnerability?[176]

However, it is precisely because Minsky sees the noble and restless work of the mind threatened by the virus of shallow entertainment that he fails to offer a universal theory of human thinking. He does acknowledge that feelings, humor, and even classical music are mechanisms of learning and problem solving. However, he condemns all supposedly trivial cultural occupations as a waste of the human mind. For this reason, the continuation of biological life would squander the future thinking capacities of robots: "We owe our minds to the deaths and lives of all the creatures that were ever engaged in the struggle called Evolution. Our job is to see that all this work shall not end up in meaningless waste."[177]

If progress for Minsky seeks to achieve infinite wealth – quantified here as professional success[178] – and if the waste of "precious brains" in mindless pleasures is denounced as a cultural cancer, then he in fact perfectly embodies the Calvinist ideals of *relentless, disciplined labor* in a distinctly American form. Minsky achieves nothing less here than the formulation of a cybernetic work ethic, which equates the vocation to work with mental work and, in turn, with machine information processing. He ascetically

---

173   See Barrow / Tipler 1986, 675-677; Tipler 1989, 245-249; Tipler 1995, 55-65.
174   See ibid., 124-128.
175   See Minsky 1992c, 35.
176   Ibid. See also the remarks by Arthur C. Clarke 1960, 219.
177   Minsky 1994, 113.
178   See Minsky 1988, 284.

rejects any distraction from critical intellectual work. Only in connection with an efficient use of intellectual capacities does the increase in information processing thus characterize the measure of perfection of intelligent life.

Hans Moravec, Ray Kurzweil, and the cyberneticist Kevin Warwick also associate progress with the increase in thinking performance. However, in this context they place greater emphasis on technological and quantitative comparisons between biological brains as opposed to the past and expected future performance of computers. They provide illustrative tables and page-long explanations about the accelerated increase in the number of computing steps per second over the course of the history of technology, or even throughout evolution, and link this data to the idea of the increasing intelligence of thinking systems. The emergence of intelligent computer programs is presented as an inevitable development of the coming decades. However, despite the acknowledged difficulties, all these approaches focus primarily on computing power and storage capacities. Posthumanists in fact largely marginalize the question of intelligent software. Moravec cites the particular example of the computer *Deep Blue*, which became famous playing chess against human opponents, in duels that publically demonstrated "computer intelligence".[179] Ray Kurzweil's assumption, that as early as 2029, some 99% of the *Earth's intellectual capacity* will be performed by computers vividly illustrates the quantitative measure on which this assumed progress will be based.[180]

For all posthumanists, the basis for the perfection of human and artificial life is the maximization of information processing. In this view progress implies two aspects: on the one hand, the progress of *work* (performance), and on the other, the progress of *knowledge* (i.e. storage capacity).

If such clear references to the Protestant work ethic are even made in exceptional cases – such as Minsky – then it is undoubtable that Protestant and philosophical conceptions of work influence other posthumanists as well. Primarily developed during the 18th century, these ideas have particularly shaped the American debate over the past 200 years. 18th century intellectuals including the French philosopher Condorcet, and the Scottish philosophers Adam Smith, David Hume, Adam Ferguson, and Henry Home all reached the same conclusion from their contexts of political economy, moral philosophy, and theology. Namely: that work is not only a means of obtaining objects of pleasure, but rather that work itself is one of humankind's fundamental needs. According to Adam Ferguson, greater weight must be attributed to the urge to work than to humankind's desire to consume, since sensual urges are only satisfied for a short time before they reappear. Work, on the other hand, allows humans to continuously improve their abilities, thus building upon the foundation of achievements left by their predecessors. The Scottish moral philosophers therefore defined work itself as the original source of happiness. However, unlike Hume, Home, and Smith, in his capacity as a Presbyterian clergyman, Ferguson merged this idea with the Protestant virtues of this-worldly asceticism and continual professional work:[181]

---

179 See Moravec 1988, 51-74; Moravec 1999, 51-72; Kurzweil 1999a, 9-39; Warwick 1998, 257-279.
180 See Kurzweil 1999a, 189-252.
181 See Rohbeck 1987, 88-119. The Scottish Calvinists are called Presbyterians, while Puritans are the American counterpart.

> To a being of this description, therefore, it is a blessing, to meet with incentives to action, whether in the desire of pleasure, or the aversion of pain. His activity is of more importance than the very pleasure he seeks, and languor a greater evil than the suffering he shuns ... Such men do not chuse pain as preferable to pleasure, but they are incited by a restless disposition to make continued exertions of capacy and resolution; they triumph in the midst of their struggles; they droop, and they languish, when the occasion of their labor has ceased.[182]

William Paley, a well-known exponent of physico-theology elaborates on these thoughts. He emphasizes that the joy of developing our physical and mental abilities at work will only make us truly happy when we do it with an awareness of the future purpose of our actions:

> A man who is earnest in his endeavours after the happiness of a future state, has in this respect, an advantage over all the world: for, he has constantly before his eyes an object of supreme importance, productive of perpetual engagement and activity, and of which the pursuit ... lasts him to his life's end.[183]

Tipler's teleology of information technology and Minsky's exhortation to concentrate on the real goals of our thinking – the expansion of "our" intellectual abilities – both build upon Paley and the Scottish philosophers' understanding of work. However, the source of happiness now becomes information processing as mental work. Paley also argues that man does not gain satisfaction from the absolute value of an action, but rather only from the enhancement of his own abilities. According to this amendment, it is work that ultimately determines the measure of progress.[184] During the 18th century Turgot and Adam Smith had already developed an economic theory of stages, which established the increase in work and productivity as a characteristic of historical development.[185] Both the French and the Scottish philosophers Turgot, Condorcet, Fontenelle, Smith, and John Millar emphasize the importance of developing better tools and means for sustaining progress.[186]

Contemporary posthumanist theories are notable for reinterpreting the central means of progress as its actual subject. Assuming that work performance actually is the measure of progress, the expanding abilities of machines will continue to outperform those of humankind. In this sense, humans are judged via their performance and defined as *tool-making animals* (Benjamin Franklin), *homo faber* (Henri Bergson) or a *deficient being* (*Mängelwesen* in Johann Gottfried Herder and Arnold Gehlen). Technological progress becomes the key characteristic of every higher development of human life. As the geographer Ernst Kapp argues, the entire history of civilization merges with the continual invention of better tools.[187] What posthumanists contribute to this argument is the idea that the tool itself now becomes the absolute measure

---

182 Ferguson 1789, 66, 68. See ibid., 61-73.
183 Paley 1842, 8.
184 Ibid., 9.
185 See Rohbeck 1987, 88-119.
186 See ibid., 158-160.
187 See Rapp 1992, 97-103.

of humanity. As we have recently seen, humans have already been defined as (bad) machines.

Knowledge as the second aspect of the progress is closely related to this development, especially when the French philosophers of the 18th century interpreted the progress of *knowledge* as dependent on the further development of the *means* of knowledge, such as mathematics and physics.[188]

The idea of general historical progress, in the sense of developing toward the better, is preceded by the works of the Christian church fathers Tertullian, Origen of Alexandria, and Lactantius, who depicted Christianity as a process of historical progress in comparison with the "pagan" religions. Similarly, the idea of progress in knowledge was first developed in a peculiarly Christian context. In the 5th century Augustine rejected the idea of worldly progress, and instead advocated spiritual improvement through Christian revelation. In his *Commonitorium*, his contemporary Vincent of Lérins could nevertheless assume that church doctrine would continue to develop, thus perpetually increasing the church's wisdom over the coming centuries. In medieval scholasticism, Anselm of Canterbury and Gerhoh of Reichersberg strongly advocated progress (*proficere*) in church doctrine and interpretation in order to bring the *veritatis ratio* to full fruition. For the scholastics, the necessity of continuously increasing religious knowledge arises from the short lives of the church fathers, who could not possibly live long enough to acquire all necessary wisdom before the end of the world.[189]

Following the physician William Gilbert's work *De Magnete* (1600), Francis Bacon drafted the idea of progress in the field of empirical, scientific knowledge in his writings *The Advancement of Learning* (1605) and *Novum Organum* (1620). This concept had a tremendous impact in the early 17th century, especially in England, and spread rapidly. Here one finds the conviction that the growth of knowledge will accelerate in parallel with the increasing number of scientific discoveries.[190] Bacon and Newton embedded the idea of scientific progress in a broad theological context by presenting science as homage to the divine creation. Over the course of the 17th century a number of Puritan and Puritan-influenced thinkers established a connection between the progress of theological knowledge and scientific discovery. In his comprehensive work on the English idea of progress, David Spadafora describes this synthesis of the scientific and religious ideas of progress as the intellectual heritage from which the English and, to a large extent, the American theory of progress could develop.[191]

The 18th century English discourse on progress is of particular interest for the genesis of posthumanism because it counteracts the simplistic claim that the English (and American) theory of progress is entirely a French import. The implications of this theory – namely the strict dichotomy between religious salvation history on the one hand, and its "secularized" counterpart in the worldly belief in progress on the other – would pose a major obstacle for the analysis of posthumanism. According to Spadafora, the 19th century did not actually produce a new theory of progress, but

---

188 See Rohbeck 1987, 160-167.
189 See Koselleck 1975, 363-368; Spadafora 1990, 85-90.
190 See Spadafora 1990, 19-21.
191 See Dawson 1929, 185-211; Spadafora 1990, 19-21.

merely either re-applied existing ideas or else developed theories that were critical of progress. Therefore, 18th century conceptions remain of immense importance for English and American contemporary philosophy.[192]

In 18th century England, three outstanding scholars fashioned an idea of progress that differed from the secular French theories and would ultimately exert immense influence on the English and American intellectual world. The Anglican Bishop of Carlisle, Edmund Law, taught at Cambridge, mentoring and therefore shaping a whole generation of students, including William Paley. The Arian Richard Price, for his part, had a lasting effect on the famous reformist group, the Bowood circle in Shelburne. Finally, the Unitarian clergyman Joseph Priestley was regarded as the most important polymath of his time in the British hemisphere. In addition to his political commitment and philosophical work, he worked as a historian, linguist and chemist and achieved remarkable results in some of these fields.

Priestley was forced to leave England in 1794 due to his commitment to the *Unitarian New Meeting* movement, which was fiercely critical of the Anglican Church, as well as his continuing efforts at political reform. He therefore became America's most prominent immigrant at the time. He also had a close friendship with the American natural scientist and political thinker Benjamin Franklin. As a leading member of the *Lunar Society*, a club of English intellectuals committed to scientific and political progress, the natural scientist Erasmus Darwin and the utilitarian philosopher Jeremy Bentham entered his circle of influence.[193] Christianity was the ultimate focus of philosophical and political considerations for Law, Price, and Priestley, as it was for the considerable number of other scholars interested in both scientific questions and theological and (moral) philosophical problems. For them, progress closely connected the idea of divine providence with perceptible, worldly, and scientific advancement. According to Priestley, the progress of true knowledge would thus increasingly accelerate.[194]

Anglican clergymen such as John Edwards, William Worthington, and Edmund Law developed a thesis between 1699 and 1745 that future human knowledge about God would steadily increase, which they concluded based on past developments in religious knowledge. According to the idea of this *religious progress*, God reveals new and higher knowledge about his nature and will to man, although only in conjunction with his creatures' maturity and cognitive ability. During the 18th century the view gradually became established that the deepening of religious knowledge was impacted by human effort, rather than only being part of a divine revelation passively received by man. The Anglican bishops John Ross and William Warburton therefore began to assume that knowledge of God could come from both divine revelation and human interpretation of the sacred texts, and that these two kinds of knowledge would complement each other.

The physician, psychologist, and Anglican layman David Hartley concluded that understanding of the Old Testament prophets and the later written revelations of God in the Bible corresponded to the intellectual level of the believers. Progress in the latter would therefore also lead to an increase in religious knowledge. His contemporary, the

---

192 See ibid., 381-387.
193 See Graham 1995, 1-41; Spadafora 1990, 252.
194 See ibid., 235, 252-254.

English Presbyterian John Taylor, expressed this thought metaphorically in an analogy of the biological phases of human life: Just as man's wisdom constantly increases from childhood, through youth and adulthood, and finally to old age, so too will the *progress of religion* follow a gradual improvement of intellectual and religious cognitive faculties from the beginning of human history to humanity's old age. Taylor, like Hartley, interprets progress both as gradual progress in the spiritual life of an individual soul and collectively in the general progress of the Christian religion. The liberal Anglican Bishop of Llandlaff, Richard Watson, even went so far as to claim that the spread of Christianity went hand in hand with the Enlightenment mission of reason and science.

On the one hand, the proximity to deism becomes obvious in these statements by 18th century Anglicans. On the other hand, however, they also reveal how Anglican theology developed a theory of progress in its fight against deism. Notably: this gradual progress of religious knowledge guided by human reason did not contradict the idea of a divine revelation and providence.

What all of these thinkers have in common is the belief in the past and future progress of knowledge. They also concur that this progress is constantly accelerating. They thus seem to agree so far with the assumptions of the French philosophers. However, in contrast to secular French philosophy, in the English and American context the progress of knowledge was usually an essential part of the Christian history of salvation. This growth of science and reason went hand in hand increased knowledge of God. The progress of the sciences was interpreted as part of God's plan. At the end of the 18th century William Paley's *Natural Theology* unites these ideas and spurs the subsequent debate about religion and science.[195]

Frank Tipler, Hans Moravec, and Ray Kurzweil undoubtedly belong to this tradition, as their theory of progress is partly based on the assumption of growing religious or spiritual knowledge (about God). Frank Tipler and Hans Moravec presuppose the progress of religious knowledge and imply theological teleologies via their reference to the Omega Point. Although his focus is different, Ray Kurzweil's interpretation of the singularity also implies the increase of spiritual knowledge. It therefore seems plausible to assume that all parties received elements of the English or American understandings of the progress of knowledge, along with their connotations of the history of salvation.

By combining the progress of knowledge with that of work, (especially in terms of the Calvinist implications Minsky outlines), the progress of information processing achieves a tremendous dynamism. Both ideas in fact held immense significance for English, Scottish, and American intellectual history. Both ideas also, at least in the American and English contexts, became integrated into theological conceptions of work and knowledge. In posthumanism, these two crucial concepts of the increase in work performance and the resultant increase in knowledge are not only received, but in fact united to form a new synthesis. For some posthumanist authors, such as Frank Tipler or Marvin Minsky, this Protestant intellectual heritage is clearly apparent in their particularly American perspective. Ray Kurzweil, who grew up as a Unitarian, also recognizes these spiritual implications, at least with regard to the progress of knowledge: "I see the opportunity to expand our minds, to extend our learning, and

---

195   See ibid., 85-104. See section 6.3.4.

to advance our ability to create and understand knowledge as an essential spiritual quest."[196] Without delving into traditional religions, Kurzweil further advocates the continuous increase of the spiritual dimensions of experience, aided by technical extensions in the future virtual existence. Consequently, artificial intelligences would therefore also become able to develop their own spirituality.[197]

6.3 Annihilation or Infinite Progress

Posthumanism is the culmination of the centuries-old, occidental belief in progress. The goal of this progress is the perfection and consequently the transformation of the present human being towards an immortal, posthuman existence. In the following chapter I will present and analyze the various aspects of the posthumanist ideology of progress – that is, the question of the path to immortality.

What constitutes posthumanism as a comprehensive idea of progress? Any theory of this kind must answer a number of questions justifying why the future will look one way and not another: Progress must be legitimized. As a first step, therefore, we turn to the most threatening scenario for posthumanists: What would happen if humanity were to oppose progress (section 6.3.1 Death, Entropy, and the Annihilation of All Life)? The human sacrifice that would accompany such a process echoes cultural interpretations of American colonial history (section 6.3.2). On the one hand, the predicted progress could be positively interpreted as a departure from natural evolution (section 6.3.3). On the other hand, technological posthumanism is itself only the result of a progress-friendly reception of the Darwinian theory of evolution, which has long argued that life is steadily advancing (section 6.3.4). In this context, Frank Tipler has developed an independent approach using a Christian-based physico-theology (section 6.3.5).

Death, Entropy, and the Annihilation of All Life

> Progress is not a greater necessity, but at most a possibility (and often an impossibility).[198]
>
> *Ryszard Kapuściński*

Before we begin to discuss how posthumanists legitimize and shape actual progress, let us examine a question that forms the basis of all posthumanist futurology: Why *must* there be progress? What dangers would arise if this predicted progress were to fail to materialize, or were to be prevented? Posthumanism is not characterized by the fact that it creates possibilities. Rather, it presents necessities of human development, to which there is no alternative. This futurological imperative can be explained on two mutually dependent levels: one evolutionary and one cosmic.

---

196   Kurzweil 1999a, 185. See Kurzweil 2005, 1.
197   See Kurzweil 1999a, 152-154; Kurzweil 2005, 377.
198   Kapuściński 1992, 63, trans. by AJ.

Individually, posthumanists point to very different aspects of human biology as deficient. Marvin Minsky identifies two threats that endanger life and the human urge to expand. On the one hand, Minsky conjures up a civilizational horror scenario of the overpopulation of planet Earth. Only a transformation of humans into machines can in his view stop this uncontrolled proliferation.[199] On the other hand, the computer scientist also perceives a much more serious danger in humanity's biological constitution, as our error-prone genetic coding is to blame for infinite suffering:

> The major causes of death result from the effects of inherited genes. These genes include those that seem to be largely responsible for heart disease and cancer, the two largest causes of mortality, as well as countless other disorders such as cystic fibrosis and sickle cell anemia.[200]

Given humans' extremely limited life spans, the acquisition of wealth and wisdom is subject to biological limits impeding any substantial further development of culture, economy, and society. Likewise, Minsky sees the confines of human memory and the limited sense of sight, which only covers a small frequency range, as the cause for an intellectual stagnation that will soon fail to meet the challenges of its time. The biological limits of our physical capacities would therefore prevent any intellectual progress.[201] Minsky also considers the physical size of human beings as pure waste, since nanotechnology can make thinking more efficient with less material effort. This is especially the case since, without artificial "back-up brains", the vulnerable biological "thinking machine" faces the constant danger of an uneconomical final loss of data – i.e. death.[202]

According to Hans Moravec, not only the individual human being, but in fact the whole of humanity is threatened with final extinction through imponderable dangers. The only alternative to the downfall of human culture, he argues, is to agree to unbridled progress and to replace humans with a posthuman intelligence:

> If by some unlikely pact, the whole human race decided to eschew progress, the long-term result would be almost certain extinction ... Sooner or later an unstoppable virus deadly to humans will evolve, or a major asteroid will collide with the earth, or the sun will expand, or we will be invaded from the stars, or a black hole will swallow the galaxy ... By growing rapidly enough, a culture has a finite chance of surviving forever.[203]

It is worth noting at this point that Moravec acknowledges the risks of information technology – computer viruses and unintentional mutations of programs – as a means of strengthening computer systems and as innovative and extremely fruitful chaos.[204]

---

199 See Minsky 1994, 113; Minsky 1992a, 24.
200 Minsky 1994, 108.
201 See Minsky 1994, 108, 111-112; Minsky 1992a, 25-26.
202 See Minsky 1992a, 25-26.
203 See Moravec 1988, 101.
204 See ibid., 125-146.

On a more individual level, Moravec describes a frightening everyday medical scenario intended to affect the reader personally: A patient learns from his doctor that there is no chance of curing his illness and that he has only six months to live. However, salvation appears in the form of mind transplantation, which demands the abandonment of the mortal body. After the surgical uploading procedure, the patient wakes up in his new virtual existence and is greeted by the doctor: "Congratulations, welcome to immortality."[205]

When Bill Joy (at that time a manager at computer giant *Sun Microsystems*) called for a renunciation of genetic engineering, molecular nanotechnology, and robotics in his essay *Why the Future Doesn't Need Us* in 2000, the Extropian mastermind Max More reacted with extreme irritation.[206] Clearly indignant about the desire for self-limitation propounded by such an influential researcher, More countered Joy's reservations about limitless progress with two arguments. Firstly, abandoning salvific technology would not be successful because six billion people would never give up its potential military use and its massive general benefits for humanity. According to More, the only way to address possible ethical and political dangers for society is to accelerate progress. In this way, a democratic nation that chose this path would always remain superior to undemocratic states. Since the imminent emergence of artificial intelligences superior to human beings cannot be prevented, More's only solution is to merge as quickly as possible with such new technologies, using chip implants and a neural interface, in order to be able to maintain greater autonomy in the long run. The second reason More offers in his response to Joy is the accusation that the renunciation of technology is unethical: New technologies would not only benefit the fight against disease, but could also defeat aging and death. Technology does not lead to the extermination of humanity, but rather to its immortalization. In spite of his previous concern for the sick and weak, More supports this argument with a reference to his favourite philosopher of progress, Friedrich Nietzsche, and his call for the overcoming of humankind.[207]

Moravec, Minsky, and More thus cite economic, medical, and political factors that will force progress. This obsolescence of the biological human being as compared to the potentials of machines had in fact already been mentioned by Arthur C. Clarke in his popular science book *Profiles of the Future* from 1958, including the reference to Nietzsche.[208]

Ray Kurzweil and Hans Moravec may take a cosmic perspective, but the physicist Frank Tipler was actually the first to discuss this threat extensively. Together with John D. Barrow, he describes how our Sun will extinguish in five billion years; in 10^{12} years the last stars will mutate into white dwarfs; in 10^{19} years the last neutron stars will cool down to 100° K; in 10^{31} years protons will decay; in 10^{1500} years all matter will

---

205 Moravec / Pohl 1993, 68.
206 See Joy 2000.
207 See More 2000b, 1-2; Dery 1996, 302.
208 See Clarke 1960, 197-233.

be transformed into iron, and then in 10^{2600} years this iron will collapse into black holes:[209]

> If the human species, or indeed any part of the biosphere, is to continue to survive, it must eventually leave the Earth and colonize space. For the simple fact of the matter is, **the planet Earth is doomed**. The Sun is becoming more luminous every day, and in about 7 billion years its outer atmosphere will have expanded to engulf the Earth ... Gaia, like all mothers, is not immortal.[210]

Tipler describes the heat death of the universe, so-called entropy, as a further threat to life. With the human being defined – as we have already seen – as a pattern of information, the danger of cosmic entropy implies the inevitable existential threat to humans and machines on various levels awaiting humans and their descendants in the distant future.[211] Tipler therefore urges his readers not to stand idly by and watch as the biosphere of our planet is destroyed by cosmic processes in a few billion years' time (he does not discuss short-term environmental protection). This is so crucially important because it would ultimately render our present life meaningless: "Without progress, the complete and total extermination of all life is inevitable."[212] If this hypothesis of eternal life already refers to humanity's special role in the universe, then it is clear to Tipler that the preservation of human life is connected with even higher tasks for humankind, such as preventing the anticipated heat death of the universe: "Thus ultimately life exists in order to prevent the Universe from destroying itself!"[213]

Likely inspired by Tipler's cosmological considerations, Moravec also addresses this unpleasant problem of entropy. With explicit reference to Tipler, Barrow, and the physicist Freeman Dyson, Moravec develops the idea of a gigantic accumulator, which would store the energy of photons between two mirrors and thus guarantee survival after the actual end of the universe.[214]

Likewise, Max More, and his philosophical partner, T. O. Morrow, had already created the term *extropy* in 1988. This was defined as a synonym for the infinite upward movement and spread of life, and intended to be a positive counterpart to entropy. Extropians use the blanket term *extropy* to refer to all forces that counteract entropy. However, specific rescue scenarios are not articulated.[215]

Without making concrete references to the heat death of the universe, Ray Kurzweil also emphasizes the necessity of humankind's continued technical development in order to master future threats from asteroids and extra-terrestrials, as well as to be able to take the fate of the universe into their own hands in the distant future:[216]

---

209 The very hot but low-mass white dwarfs are formed when a star has used up its entire supply of fuel in nuclear fusion. See Barrow / Tipler 1986, 613-658; Tipler 1995, 56-57.
210 Ibid., 18. This is the only bolded sentence in Tipler's book!
211 See ibid., 87; Hayles 1999, 104.
212 Tipler 1995, 66.
213 Barrow / Tipler 1986, 674.
214 See Moravec 1988, 147-149; Dyson 1988.
215 See More 2000a and http://www.aleph.se/Trans/Words/e.html#EXTROPIA.
216 See Kurzweil 1999a, 258-260. At that time Kurzweil still assumed the existence of extra-terrestrial life.

> So, will the Universe end in a big crunch, or in an infinite expansion of dead stars, or in some other manner? ... Rather, the fate of the Universe is a decision yet to be made, one which we will intelligently consider when the time is right.[217]

Admittedly, Kurzweil's reasons for proposing the expansion of life from Earth to the universe remain only superficially outlined. However, in *The Singularity is near* (2005) he devotes significant space to illustrating this future colonization of the entire cosmos.[218]

The remarkable thing about Tipler, Moravec, More, and Kurzweil's cosmic perspective is the bundling of physical, cosmological, and cybernetic aspects of this future threat. In the 1850s, the physicist William Thomson, i.e. Lord Kelvin, developed the idea of the end of all thermodynamic processes in the universe, to occur at some future point in time when all the energy/heat in the cosmos will have achieved perfect equilibrium. In his Königsberg Lectures of 1854, Hermann von Helmholtz coined the term "heat death" of the universe (which actually refers to death by cold):

> The life of men, animals, and plants could not of course continue if the sun had lost its high temperature, and with it his light, – if all the components of the earth's surface had closed those combinations which their affinities demand. In short, the universe from that time forward would be condemned to a state of eternal rest.[219]

In the 1870s, the Austrian physicist Ludwig Boltzmann combined Thomson and Helmholtz's assumptions with the concept of entropy. According to the second law of thermodynamics, the transition of the universe to thermal equilibrium is a development from a less to a more probable state. For the enlightened, this idea replaced the traditional religious idea of an apocalypse. The "heat death of the universe" has since been used in numerous literary drafts and quickly made popular, especially in the English-speaking world, by authors such as H. G. Wells, Kurt Vonnegut, and Bret Easton Ellis. Philosophers such as Herbert Spencer, Henri Bergson, Friedrich Engels, and Friedrich Nietzsche also address entropy and heat death in their works.[220]

Half a century after Boltzmann, the founders of cybernetic information theory, Claude Shannon and Warren Weaver, used the idea of entropy as a probability measure for the indeterminability or uncertainty of information. This metric describes how much freedom of choice is involved when selecting an event (or information), or how uncertain one is about the outcome. Entropy as a precise term for uncertainty or information gain is thus of great importance for both the compact coding of sources and the description of how distorted channels perform. Since the interference of transmission signals can pose a significant problem for the technical transmission of information, entropy has become one of the key concepts of cybernetic information theory.[221]

Shannon and Weaver came to understand entropy as the uncertainty of information, and conclude that unexpected information always contains further

---

217 Ibid, 260.
218 See Kurzweil 2005, 342-368.
219 Helmholtz 1885, 172.
220 See Freese 1997.
221 See Shannon / Weaver 1964, 48-57, 78-90; Wiener 1961, 57-95.

information – entropy therefore implies positive connotations. In his 1955 essay *The Thermodynamics of the Message*, Norbert Wiener takes an opposing view of entropy as a general measure of the disorder of a dynamic system. Agreeing with the physicist Leon Brillouin, Wiener makes the connection between physical thermodynamics and information theory:[222] "Information is equivalent to order, and a message may be garbled, but never ungarbled."[223]

Wiener and many others adopted an idea Leo Szilard raised in a thought experiment, suggesting that entropy correlates with the opposite of information. As a dissolution of structure and order, entropy embodies the moral qualities of death and destruction. Therefore, if Gregory Bateson defines information as a difference that makes a difference, then total entropy means total indiscriminateness and the absence of any information, which would be tantamount to the end of life in the universe.[224] It was no less a person than Norbert Wiener who linked the "universal life science" of cybernetics to the cosmic threat that entropy poses to all life:

> But while the universe as a whole ... tends to run down, there are local enclaves whose direction seems opposed to that of the universe at large and in which there is a limited and temporary tendency for organization to increase. Life finds its home in some of these enclaves. It is with this point of view at its core that the new science of Cybernetics began its development.[225]

John von Neumann also sees physical and cybernetic entropy as a measure for the degeneration of energy and information:

> There is reason to believe that the general degeneration laws, which hold when entropy is used as a measure of the hierarchic position of energy, have valid analogs when entropy is used as a measure of information. On this basis one may suspect the existence of connections between thermodynamics and new extensions of logics.[226]

This cosmic dimension of threats preoccupies today's posthumanists more than at the turn of the millennium. Rhetorically, it affords a greater relevance to posthumanism – one that can no longer be surpassed: The salvation of the entire universe is now in the hands of those technological prophets advocating the inevitable passing of the baton to the anticipated artificial intelligences of the future. From this perspective, the alternative lies in assuming responsibility for the final extinction of all forms of life throughout billions of galaxies. Who would possibly choose to take on this immeasurable blame?

Posthumanists connect the question of entropy, the concept of singularity, the hoped-for arrival of superintelligence, and the vision of a networked and universal

---

222 See Shannon / Weaver 1964, 61-64; Wiener 1985, 206-211; In his principle of *negative entropy*, Brillouin develops an extensive network of relationships between the cybernetic and the physical concepts of entropy. See Brillouin 1957, 114-201, 245-258.
223 Wiener 1985, 206.
224 See Wiener 1989, 28-47; Hayles 1999, 100-104.
225 Wiener 1989, 12.
226 Neumann 1966, 61.

brain into a united and thus purportedly strengthened argument. This conception is complemented by those concrete measures that seek to overcome the deficits of the biological human being (old age, illness, death). Combating human suffering and mastering the forces of nature has been an aspect of all future utopias since Francis Bacon's *New Atlantis* (1626).[227] What is new in posthumanism, however, is that the dangers now represent a total and existential threat to human life: On an individual level, it is not disease but death itself that is mentioned – while on a collective level the downfall of the entire universe is addressed as the greatest and absolute threat. The past 20 years of posthumanist work have in fact seen an increasing emphasis on this cosmic perspective. It is thus evident that, in the posthumanist sense, progress is an imperative for which there is no alternative. Failure to do so entails consequences, including the extinction of the humanity. The following sections offer a detailed examination of how this progress is legitimized and shaped.

The Sacrifice of Humankind

> Icarus falls today not because of the failure of his wing wax, but because Icarus himself fails.
> If only he could drop his own self as weighty ballast, his wings could conquer the sky.[228]
> Günther Anders

If progress from a place implies having left that place behind, one therefore always remains somehow tied to that place as that *which was left*. It does not seem too far-fetched to characterize posthumanist discourse's dynamics between humanity, technology, and progress under the category of sacrifice, provided that sacrifice can be understood as the abandonment of a previous value in favor of an anticipated higher profit. With reference to Günther Anders' prophecy of a third world war, which humanity would wage against itself in the form of "post-civilization cannibalism", the ethnologist Johanna Riegler has introduced the category of the sacrifice. This allows us to conceptualize the current degradation and accompanying "abolition" of humans, who have become antiquated in comparison to technology:

> The techno-expansive market society is a secular form of sacrifice ... I maintain that sacrifice lies at the heart of modern technology and economics. If we have moved too far in time from the sacrifice made, the memory and horror fade and fade away, and so a new ritual staging in the name of progress is due.[229]

The obsolescence of the human being manifests itself in posthumanist discourse in two distinct aspects: firstly the literally "outdated" biological body, and secondly the obsolete nature of humanity as a collective species. While previous remarks have revealed that

---

227 See Bacon 2017, 41-88; Tabbert 2004, 85-104.
228 Anders 1983, 34.
229 Riegler 1999, 52.

the human body, with its limitations and vital susceptibilities, represents a central existential threat to humanity, Marvin Minsky, Frank Tipler, and Hans Moravec make it particularly clear that the material body itself had to be sacrificed to a posthuman substitute: "We must die – as individuals, as a species – in order that our civilization might live."[230]

If humanity wants to survive and develop, there is, according to Minsky, no alternative than for it to overcome its own biological limits, especially when faced with the overpopulation problems caused by unbridled sexual activity. Behind these acute fears resides the constant underlying threat of the failure – or natural death – of biological "information systems".[231] Frank Tipler agrees that the survival and resurrection of the future human being as *superhuman* or *superbeing* is only possible via a departure from the current material body.[232] Minsky also points out that correcting errors is not a problem with computers, whereas genetic damage occurring during the human reproduction process is hard to revise. The error-prone human body must therefore be replaced by a machine body that can be corrected without difficulty.[233]

Hans Moravec's observations include a key focus on the sacrifice of the human being in favour of a post-biological and post-human culture. At this point, Günther Anders' idea of *Promethean shame* becomes apparent. Moravec's work also includes every motif comparing the unsatisfactory biological body with machines: from individual technical superiorities to the mutability of machines.[234] He is convinced that biological human beings will have reached the limits of their mental receptivity by the end of the 20th century.[235] According to Moravec, the human body – pejoratively referred to as *wetware* – consists of jelly, which, due to its neurons, is only qualified for an extremely primitive kind of information processing. In contrast, electrical circuits could serve the same purpose one billion times faster and more accurately.[236] Moreover, biological evolutionary systems cannot be accessed or updated with innovations and improvements.[237] Across several pages of tables, Moravec compares humans with new and old calculating machines – which are differentiated according to various technical and economic categories: "Today, as our machines approach human competence across the board, our stone-age biology and our information-age lives grow ever more mismatched."[238] As might be expected, the human brain is already inferior in comparison to computers of the 1950s – except for the cost of production! The exodus of humans into digital existence – their *mind children* – would therefore offer a significant advantage.[239]

---

230 Tipler 1989, 245.
231 See Minsky 1994, 113; Minsky 1992a, 24-26.
232 See Tipler 1995, 87-88, 255-259.
233 See Minsky 1994, 108.
234 See Anders 1983, 32-54.
235 See Moravec 1999, 1, 125-126.
236 See Moravec 1988, 55-56, 117-119; Moravec / Pohl 1993, 72.
237 See Moravec 1988, 167-168.
238 Moravec 1999, 7.
239 See Moravec 1979, 63-83; Moravec 1988, 18, 61, 173-177; Moravec 1999, 58, 68.

Furthermore, the human body stands in the way of humankind's future expansion into space. This crucial colonization of other planets, solar systems, or even galaxies over decades of travel seems utterly utopian for our biological bodies. For reasons of "extraterrestrial emancipation", Frank Tipler and the artist Stelarc particularly advocate for the design of mechanical beings that can survive interstellar travel.[240]

While Minsky and Moravec use the standpoint of a radical utilitarianism to argue for maximum efficiency, Max More, Kevin Warwick, and to some extent Ray Kurzweil take a more anthropocentric position. Here, the augmentation of human capabilities constitutes the center of posthuman visions, and will eventually lead to the overcoming of today's carbon-based human being.

Like Warwick, More rejects Moravec's idea of superior machines that will leave humans behind and instead favors an early merging with such machines in order to keep them under control: "They become part of us."[241] Warwick, who stylizes himself Cyborg No. 1, sees augmentation of the biological body with artificial elements as the only possibility for human survival against future generations of machines.

> Once the first powerful machine, with an intelligence similar to that of a human, is switched on, we will most likely not get the opportunity to switch it back off again. We will have started a time bomb ticking on the human race, and we will be unable to switch it off.[242]

For Frank Tipler it is also clear that the continuity of human civilization does not include the continuity of the human species:

> ... our species *Homo sapiens* must inevitably become extinct, just as every individual human being must inevitably also die ... *it is a logically necessary consequence of eternal progress that our species becomes extinct.*[243]

For Ray Kurzweil, there is no need to discuss the continued existence of humans, because these processes are subject to unchangeable, evolutionary laws. In fact, evolution itself has already produced computers (with the help of humans) to replace the deficient human being with a superior species. According to Kurzweil, the deficit of humankind lies in their primitive and slow processing of information. Humankind must therefore become extinct.[244] Any debate or choice about this suppression of humans by machine intelligence is no longer possible, since the "point of no return" has already been passed – abandoning computers is no longer possible:

> We can't stop. The Law of Accelerating Returns forbids it! It's the only way to keep evolution going at an accelerating pace ... The accelerating pace of change is inexorable. The emergence of machine intelligence that exceeds human intelligence in all of its broad diversity is inevitable.[245]

---

240 See Tipler 1995, 18-65; Stelarc 1996, 72-74; Stelarc 1998, 116-117; Stelarc 1996, 74.
241 More 2000b, 2.
242 Warwick 1998, 302.
243 Tipler 1995, 218-219.
244 See Kurzweil 1999a, 96-97, 101-102.
245 Kurzweil 1999a, 130, 253. See ibid., 157-158, 186.

The acceleration of evolution itself becomes the purpose of evolution, and demands only that humankind not endanger its progress.

Posthumanist thinkers today vehemently advocate the overcoming of humanity, and they are prepared to sacrifice human beings for the sake of accelerating progress. In order to understand these claims, the historical origins of these ideas must be examined. Which models and argumentation strategies do posthumanists fall back on when, on the one hand, they decide to abandon the old, with the implied assumption that they themselves belong to the new transhumanist elite? Or, on the other hand, when they accept the temporary sacrifice of themselves in the hope of a universal resurrection machine and omni-historical simulation apparatuses in the distant future? There are four crucial concepts for these modern ideologies of progress, each with variable perspectives, all of which culminate in a posthumanist nexus.

Firstly, apart from a biological-anthropological component, Hans Moravec and Marvin Minsky otherwise rely on the French philosopher Diderot when they designate the future generations of robots and artificially intelligent computer programs as their *mind children*. At the same time, they believe that they will locate their own parental tasks and fulfil their purpose for existing in the production of precisely this more promising offspring. Diderot was an enlightened representative of the French idea of progress. Writing after the decline of traditional ideas of a transcendent religious afterlife, he determined the meaning of life as self-sacrifice so that future generations could benefit from the fruits of their predecessors. Diderot's great influence on the Anglo-American idea of progress echoes throughout the lasting posthumanist reception of this comparison of a biological parent-child relationship to the evolutionary sequence of species.[246]

Secondly, within a Darwinian paradigm, the extinction of a species had long been interpreted as the emergence of a new species, and seen as a natural process in the history of evolution.[247] The German philosopher (and pioneer of anti-Semitic racial theories) Eugen Dühring offered one of the most effective popularizations and extens of Darwin's theory in his work *Der Werth des Lebens* (*The Value of Life*) of 1865. In it, Dühring raises the question of what happens to a species when it has reached the highest form of its development. He does not understand the extinction of a species as death or the absolute end, but rather as a sequence of infinite changes and new combinations of its original constituting elements.

> It will then be said that one species was lost to make way for another. In this way, humanity could one day find itself transformed into a more perfect type of being, and

---

246 Although working in different contexts, Robespierre and Herder also developed the idea of a posterity in which human suffering and creation in the present will be given meaning. Baillie even compares this enlightened posterity with Abraham's prospect of rich descendants, as described in Israelite religious traditions when the belief in an immortal soul had not yet developed. See Baillie 1950, 110-114; Sampson 1956, 129-131.
247 This position was also held by the evolutionary theorist Ernst Haeckel. See Bolle 1962, 146-152. For a critical discussion of this topic, see Rapp 1992, 73-77.

will look back on the human form that we now consider to be the most developed as merely an extinct species of animal.[248]

On the basis of the adoption of this general law of development, Dühring already addresses the possibility of a "refined and considerably differently endowed species",[249] which would emerge from the remnants of the human race. Only a few selected races could become carriers of this superior form of life, while all others would be eliminated from the path of future evolution.[250]

On the one hand, the posthumanist authors operate using the evolutionist model of a lack of adaptation, which in the long run – in fact inevitably – will lead to the extinction of the human species. Each case places a focus on a different aspect of changed environmental conditions, which contemporary humans will no longer be able to cope with: Minsky, Moravec, Kurzweil, and Warwick, like Robert Jastrow before them, particularly emphasize the supposed deficits in speed and memory of human "information processing", while Tipler and the artist Stelarc primarily emphasize the obsolescence of the human being in the interplanetary space age. Under these restrictive conditions, humanity belongs to those species threatened with extinction as a result of the revolutionary mechanism of natural selection. However, on the other hand, the theory of evolution also offers the possibility of merging with the posthuman successors of the human race, which is probably most aptly expressed in Moravec's metaphor of *mind children*.

Independent of Darwinian thought, the overcoming of the old as a constitutive element of identity has acquired a formative significance in the history of American civilization. The positive connotations of breaking loose from the old reached a peak in the Puritanism of the 17th century. This condemned traditional Catholic doctrines as corrupt and devilish, and considered Rome to represent the opposite of progress. John Bunyan was probably the first to present this idea literarily in his work *Pilgrim's Progress* (1678). Later, Cotton Mather, who attempted to prove in his *Magnalia Christi Americana* (1702) that only the separation of the New England religious settlers from Europe would bring the Reformation to its completion. Until the 19th century, religious literature and secular historical works both compared the escape from a corrupt Europe with the biblical exodus of the chosen people, who would now steadily advance to their "promised land", their God-given goal. The escape from old Europe and from the old itself, which was so fundamental for the crucial question of the independence of America, is thus consistently positive.[251]

This is, thirdly, also connected to the question of the old America in terms of the direct encounter with the apparently progress-negating indigenous peoples of that "new" land. This clash was reflected throughout American philosophical and political literature until the middle of the 20th century. With the further expansion of American settlers around 1800 and the continuous advance of the frontier towards the West, acute confrontation arose with those indigenous peoples who until then had been idealized

---

248   Dühring 1877, 189, trans. by AJ.
249   Ibid., 190.
250   See Benz 1965, 105-109.
251   See Sampson 1956; Buchloh 1963, 159-165.

as "noble savages" by Enlightenment philosophers Rousseau, Lafitau, Lahontan, and others.[252] It is easy to observe that the presses in the young United States' western and southern regions clearly portrayed these indigenous people as unproductive, wasteful, and incapable of progress. This narrative reached a climax in 1830 when President Andrew Jackson defended the expulsion of the indigenous peoples of America as a necessary measure to ensure further progress:

> Humanity has often wept over the fate of the aborigines of this country, and Philanthropy has been long busily employed in devising means to avert it, but its progress has never for a moment been arrested, and one by one have many powerful tribes disappeared from the earth.[253]

The fourth aspect addresses the connection between this argument and the question of race. An essay published shortly after in 1834 by the American diplomat Joel Roberts Poinsett was highly effective in arguing that "Indians" lacked the ability to develop and civilize, due to racial attributes exclusive to the Caucasian race.[254] The so-called "Indians" became a symbol of barbaric backwardness, and posed an obstacle and threat to the progression of the white man's civilized society. Despite a few isolated dissenting voices, the expulsion and the accompanying downfall of the indigenous people was generally accepted as a necessary cost of progress. The treatment of indigenous peoples in the United States became characterized by displacement, disenfranchisement, extermination, and the forced removal of their children. The latter practice in fact continued until the 1970s. The American cult of progress thus destroyed the humanist ideal of the "noble savage", as well as the indigenous peoples themselves.[255]

The 19th century discourse of sacrificing indigenous people for the sake of progress offers an unspoken yet illuminating parallel to posthumanism. Of course, no one refers to this explicitly, as the extermination of the indigenous people is interpreted more critically by today's moral standards. The fundamental alternative between the adaptation – i.e. cyborgization – supported by Kurzweil, More, and Warwick versus the extinction advocated by Tipler, Minsky, and Moravec is already laid out in the 200-year-old discussion about the fate of the indigenous peoples of North America. Similarly, the biological connection between race and the inability to progress or survive is also evident here, and obviously finds its posthumanist echo in the thesis of the inevitable demise of the human biological species.

Although each author's work contains different nuances, these four motifs are received partly explicitly, partly implicitly. These various aspects of the historical American discourse on progress offer thoroughly positive interpretations of the abandonment and demise of the past. The teleological reception of Darwinism, which is based on the continuous process of species ascension, also legitimizes the transformation and quasi-parental merging of the human species into the posthuman

---

252 See Baillie 1950, 92-93; Rohbeck 1987, 80-84.
253 Andrew Jackson: *Second Annual Message*. 12/06/1830, cited in Ekirch 1944, 43.
254 Poinsett wrote the influential work *Inquiry into the Received Opinions of Philosophers and Historians, on the Natural Progress of the Human Race from Barbarism to Civilization*. Charleston 1834.
255 See Ekirch 1944, 41-46; Rohbeck 1987, 80-84.

species that will inevitably dominate it. However, the superiority of these (still fictional) artificial intelligences of the posthuman age, and the associated inferiority of the biological body, are deduced solely by the utilitarian criterion of efficiency.

The posthumanist willingness for self-sacrifice sounds paradoxical: Somehow humans must voluntarily renounce themselves in order to ensure their survival. As early as 1964 Stanisław Lem considered this as "a peculiar form of euthanasia, a kind of pleasant suicide of a civilization"[256]. However, this statement only makes sense if the belief in extraordinary progress is connected to technical resurrection via simulation, or if humankind understands its own purpose as merely to create posthuman beings. The background of such views – and thus their fundamental pattern – can be found in the posthumanist definition of human beings. Just as an individual personality is not bound to a concrete body, so too the culture and identity of humanity exists independently of its biological basis. According to this logic, human culture can only survive without human beings: because humanity is ephemeral, whereas culture is not:

> Given fully intelligent robots, culture becomes completely independent of biology. Intelligent machines, which will grow from us, learn our skills, and initially share our goals and values, will be the children of our minds.[257]

Progress and Perfectibility

Posthumanist thinkers are united by the idea of humanity's relentless ascent until it is absorbed into a posthuman form of life. I have previously referred to the technological aspects underlying this progress. The previously discussed questions of the threatened extinction of life in the universe or the sacrifice of the biological human being are both elements of an overarching conception of human and cosmological history. Now the question arises: How do posthumanists interpret this technical form of progress? Which conceptions of history and human development are received here?

Frank Tipler and John D. Barrow put a great deal of effort into justifying the reintroduction of teleology into cosmological science, while at the same time raising the question of the future of the universe and the meaning and purpose of our present existence. This is founded on the so-called *Strong Anthropic Principle*, which assumes that humanity is part of a cosmic plan and has a central role to play in the universe. By explicitly referring to the metaphysics of the Greek philosopher Aristotle, Tipler and Barrow suggest that the essence of a thing or a living being should be determined by its ultimate cause – its final purpose.[258]

Furthermore, Tipler, and Barrow present teleological arguments from countless philosophers over the past two millennia to support their design argument, but without taking the context of these works into account. They use Plato, Cicero, Galen, Boethius, Johannes Kepler, Richard Bentley, William Derham, and Voltaire to show how widespread the idea of a planned universe has been.[259] Finally, Tipler, and Barrow try

---

256   Lem 2010, 203.
257   Moravec 1999, 126.
258   See Barrow / Tipler 1986, 37-40.
259   See ibid., 33-34, 43-45, 50, 61, 67-68.

to prove humanity's special role in the universe using current scientific insights.[260] In the great chain of cosmic history that God has planned, humankind is an indispensable link on the way to Omega: "If the ascent of Life into the Omega Point is to occur, one day the most advanced minds must be non-*Homo sapiens*. The heirs of our civilization must be another species, and their heirs yet another, *ad infinitum* into the Omega Point."[261] In order to influence the future development of the universe, and for the Omega Point to ever be realized, it is crucial that humanity's descendants conquer the cosmos and extend their biosphere to the entire universe. According to Tipler, in the next fifty years the first self-reproducing Von Neumann probes will be launched, which will have colonized the entire Milky Way within 600,000 years.[262]

Starting from the *Final Anthropic Principle*, Tipler derives the so-called *postulate of eternal life*, which is intended to prove the necessity for not only human civilization to survive, but in fact the entire universe. He makes this collective immortality dependent upon the condition that information processing, i.e. life, can continue until the end of time: Roger Penrose's c-boundary.[263] The *postulate of eternal life*, and the conviction that humans are the only intelligent beings in the universe, forces Frank Tipler to also believe in the *eternal progress* of human civilisation.[264] Since the world as God's creation is good, everything that comes from it must also ultimately be good:[265]

> Any cosmology with progress to infinity will necessarily end in God. Further, the hope of eternal worldly progress and the hope of individual survival beyond the grave turn out to be the same. Far from being polar opposites, these two hopes require each other; one cannot have one without the other. The Omega Point is truly the God of Hope: "O death, where is thy sting? O grave, where is thy victory?" (I Corinthians 15:55)[266]

For Tipler, the progress observable in human history and the development of life forms in the history of evolution are parts of God's cosmic plan, which, after the full unfolding of his worldly creation, will only find its ultimate realization in the Omega Point itself.

Marvin Minsky does not locate the development of artificial intelligence and posthuman life forms in the continuity of natural evolution, but rather contrasts the largely aimless emergence of biological life with the conscious future planning of artificial life forms. According to Minsky, evolution does not operate intelligently because it has taken too much time to solve the problem of life, and has too often short-sightedly opted for impractical arrangements. Instead of sensible and reflective planning, humans are characterized by a primitive battle of the genes, whose aggressive character becomes apparent in nonsensical sports and competitive games.[267]

---

260 See ibid., 219-601.
261 Tipler 1989, 245.
262 See ibid., 44-55.
263 See Tipler 1995, 132-133.
264 See ibid., 104-123.
265 See Tipler 1989, 244-245.
266 Tipler 1995, 268.
267 See Minsky 1988, 71, 146; Minsky 1992a, 24.

Minsky initially rejects the assumption – which is widespread even among posthumanists – that there is one fundamental goal or principle of evolution. Rather than only one elementary will to live, many individual factors instead led to the survival of a species.

> But to attribute this [surviving] to any single, central force or to some basic, underlying survival instinct is as foolish as believing in special powers that attract corpses to cemeteries or broken cars to scrapyards ... The myth of an underlying survival instinct explains nothing that cannot better be explained without it, and blinds us to the fact that each of those survival aids may exploit an entirely different mechanism.[268]

Although Minsky rejects the general teleology of evolution, he believes that individual systems within living beings most likely imply an improvement in viability.[269] For Minsky, liberation from the biological body as a path to prolonging life and achieving immortality is synonymous with liberation from the natural evolution that has no interest in enduring, biologically unproductive living beings.[270] Minsky then discusses the need for a newly introduced, practical teleology of human development, the foundations of which have been formulated by cybernetic research since 1940. If a rational teleology were to be followed, the goal and purpose of future life forms would no longer be subject to a wild battle of the genes:

> In the end, we will find ways to replace every part of the body and brain – and thus repair all the defects and flaws that make our lives so brief ... In the past we have tended to see ourselves as a final product of evolution – but our evolution has not ceased. Indeed, we are now evolving more rapidly – although not in the slow Darwinian way ... We now can design systems based on new kinds of "unnatural selection" that can exploit explicit plans and goals ... It took a century for evolutionists to train themselves to avoid such ideas – biologists call them 'teleological' and 'Lamarckian' – but now we may have to change those rules.[271]

Frank Tipler's interpretation of progress presupposes a divine history of salvation. Marvin Minsky, on the other hand, disapproves of any kind of teleological implications for the history of evolution. Moravec takes a mediating position, which reflects the ambivalence between the continuity and discontinuity of evolution. He characterizes the history of technology as a process of increasing synthesis between humans and machines. This can be seen in the growing communicative exchange between media users and computers, in comparison with older media technologies throughout human history. Moravec interprets the use of media as a virtual presence's *out-of-body* experience. This will lead to the gradual reduction of physical perceptions and ultimately the loss of any real body in virtual space – replaced by only a disembodied mind.[272]

---

268   Minsky 1988, 317.
269   See Minsky 1984, 7-8.
270   See Minsky 1994, 108.
271   Ibid., 110. See Minsky 1982, 8.
272   See Moravec 1988, 75-82; Moravec 1999, 168-171.

6. A History of Technological Posthumanism 173

Moravec believes that the appearance of the first humans millions of years ago coincided with the creation of culture. In the near future, culture will finally overcome the biological limits associated with humans, via an accelerated evolutionary process.[273] With the emergence of the first advanced civilizations 5000 years ago, the current, intensifying chasm between culture and biology began. This is because the individual human being has not been able to cope with the degree of knowledge accumulated since the Stone Age. According to Moravec, human genes' limited storage capacity in the biological body is no longer capable of storing the entire cultural knowledge of humankind, which could seriously endanger humankind's progress. The breakthrough of the singularity, the *breakout*, will overcome this discrepancy between culture and biology in the near future by the absorption of human culture into posthuman beings.[274] The singularity, or the moment when machines begin to develop autonomously, characterizes the discontinuity found in posthumanist theory, since Moravec also judges natural evolution to be a purely accidental process that contemporary humanity has taken into its own hands:

> In the metaphor of Richard Dawkins, we are the handiwork of a blind watchmaker. But we have now acquired partial sight and can, if we choose, use our vision to guide the watchmaker's hand.[275]

Due to the creation of computers and artificial intelligence, humankind is in the process of transcending its biological condition and, through auto-evolution, gaining freedom from the natural body: Self-designed heavenly bodies with light drive, wheels, or even taking the form of a robot bush or an insect shall become available in the future.[276]

For Ray Kurzweil, the history of evolution occurs dialectically in three necessary stages: The primary emergence of biological life and subsequently intelligent life entails the secondary invention of technology, which then ultimately results in the final fusion of biological life and technology. The development of technology and the symbiosis of technology and biology merely indicates the continuation of evolution by other means.[277]

> All kinds of practical and ethical issues delay the process, but they cannot stop it. The Law of Accelerating Returns predicts a complete merger of the species with the technology it originally created.[278]

According to Kurzweil, this three-part evolutionary process will reach its conclusion in the 21st century. By 2099 most people will exist as simulations in virtual reality and will look condescendingly upon the few, mortal *MOSHs* (*Mostly Original Substrate Humans*)

---

273 See Moravec 1988, 2-4.
274 See Moravec 1999, 2-7, 126.
275 Moravec 1988, 159.
276 See Moravec 1999, 143, 149-153.
277 See Kurzweil 1999a, 9-17.
278 Ibid., 256.

left in the real world.[279] Due to the fusion of human and artificial intelligence, further evolutionary process will accelerate enormously.

> Evolution has been seen as a billion-year drama that led inexorably to its grandest creation: human intelligence. The emergence in the early twenty-first century of a new form of intelligence on earth ... will be a development of greater import than any of the events that have shaped human history.[280]

Evolution's great merit was to bring forth humankind: "Let us first praise evolution ... It created human beings with their intelligent human brains, being smart enough to create their own intelligent technology."[281] For Kurzweil evolution becomes an anthropomorphised actor, whose intelligence quotient can be measured and found to be lacking. This was far exceeded by that of humanity, who created more in a few millennia than evolution created over millions of years: "So human intelligence, a product of evolution, is far more intelligent than its creator."[282]

Similarly, Kevin Warwick, and the Extropian Max More also regard the development of technical progress as a continuation of the history of evolution:

> Those who have become cyborgs will be one step ahead of humans. And just as humans have always valued themselves above other forms of life, it's likely that cyborgs will look down on humans who have yet to "evolve".[283]

For Max More, the human striving to overcome biological and mental boundaries is one of the basic characteristics of a humanity that has emerged from this process of natural evolution.[284] In his *Letter to Mother Nature*, More expresses his gratitude that nature was able to finally produce humans despite its "slow intelligence". However, this does not detract from the fact that humans have a multitude of deficiencies – most notably old age and death. Now that humankind's childhood has ended, the time has come to reach an ultrahuman condition, possible with the aid of computers and biotechnology:

> We will no longer tolerate the tyranny of aging and death. Through genetic alterations, cellular manipulations, synthetic organs, and any necessary means, we will endow ourselves with enduring vitality and remove our expiration date ... Your ambitious human offspring.[285]

In his doctoral thesis, More analyses in great detail the conditions that could lead us to change or even abandon our current state as biological human beings. He notes that the strongest attractions include above all the prospect of improving our own selves, as well as participating in the planning of a new humankind.[286] These conditions fulfill the visions of the future for posthumanism in general and Extropianism in particular.

---

279 See ibid., 189-252.
280 See ibid., 5.
281 Ibid., 44.
282 Ibid., 47. See ibid. 40-47.
283 Warwick 2000, 151.
284 See More 1994, 2.
285 More 1999, 1.
286 See More 1995, 62-63.

> Extropian transhumanism offers a [sic!] optimistic, vital and dynamic philosophy of life. We behold a life of unlimited growth and possibility with excitement and joy. We seek to void all limits to life, intelligence, freedom, knowledge, and happiness. Science, technology and reason must be harnessed to our extropic values to abolish the greatest evil: death.[287]

In this context, More notes that only an orientation towards future goals can offer a deeper meaning to life, although a rational life plan would be superior to a religious one, since the latter is in constant danger of being refuted by reality. The visions of the future should not be fixed in the dogma of a rigid final goal, but rather should set their direction as changeable, improvable principles of individual and collective life planning:

> As we integrate principles into our personality, living according to them starts to flow more effortlessly. They will become "second nature." Another way of putting it is to say a principle will have become a *virtue*.[288]

These considerations support Max More's formulation of the *Extropian Principles*, which are intended to provide an individual with general assistance in the selection of life goals.[289]

At first glance, the meaning attributed to progress and its contextualization in evolutionary models differs considerably across the work of different authors. Frank Tipler is the only posthumanist to vehemently advocate the reintroduction of a theological teleology: The miracle of creation proves the existence of an intelligent creator, and from this the existence of a divine goal for creation can be deduced, including the process of salvation history. In contrast, Minsky, Moravec, Kurzweil, and More distinguish between, on the one hand, natural evolution and, on the other hand, the planned and intelligent continuation of this development, which began with the advent of humanity. This distinction is accentuated by the divide between previous natural evolution and the future evolution that will be controlled by humans and computers. For Minsky, the emergence of artificial, posthuman intelligence presents itself as the liberation from random natural evolution. Moravec, More, and Kurzweil also perceive the merging of humans and technology as part of the history of evolution, but this will assume a new quality at the occurrence of the singularity. Although they share certain ideas about the shaping of the human future, which will be discussed below, Kurzweil, Minsky, and especially More remain convinced of the necessity of eternal progress and of "transcending" the limits of the human body and mind:

> Life and intelligence must never stagnate; it must re-order, transform, and transcend its limits in an unlimited progressive process. Our goal is the exuberant and dynamic continuation of this unlimited process, not the attainment of some final supposedly unlimited condition.[290]

---

287   More 1996, 4.
288   More 1995, 70.
289   See ibid., 67-72.
290   More 1996, 4.

In this way, the posthumanist idea of progress unites various elements of English and American progress philosophy with modern evolutionary theory, which will be the subject of the following analysis.

In posthumanism, progress presents more than just an increase of information processing, as this increase is synonymous with the improved, irreversible rise of humankind. Progress has always been somewhat ambivalently portrayed in European philosophy as both the loss of the old and the exploration of the new. About 1750 this twofold definition of *progress* became replaced in English philosophical discourse with an exclusively positive connotation. Progress thereafter meant the increase and improvement of conditions. Within this discourse, the debate on the perfectibility of the human being played a prominent role.[291] The Protestant theologian John Calvin had already given preference to the idea of gradual improvement, since man in this world could no longer hope to be lifted up by God alone. John Wesley, the founder of Methodism, demanded that his followers strive for perfection in a Christian life through *sanctification*, that is, through the correct and devoted fulfillment of one's earthly duties. The goal of Christian perfection, which had previously been linked to the second coming of Christ, was now adapted to perfecting one's own way of living on earth.[292] The sociologist Max Weber called this approach this-worldy asceticism: a path of salvation within the everyday world. It is opposed to the other-worldly asceticism of the monastic and eremitic life.[293]

In 1743, the Anglican William Worthington published his *Essay on the Scheme and Conduct, Procedure and Extent of Man's Redemption*. In it, he combined this idea of the this-worldly perfection of man with a general theory of progress, and concluded that there must be a continuous development and upward movement of man: "And may it long continue still advancing in perfection!"[294] Long before the appearance of the theory of evolution during the 19th century, Worthington attributed a natural inclination for improvement to all living beings:

> ... that all parts of Nature are endued with a principle not only to preserve their state, but to advance it, *and that every thing has a tendency to its own perfection*. This is a general law impress'd upon Nature, which must at length attain its end ... [295]

Likewise Joseph Priestley, Edmund Law, and Richard Price were convinced of the *natural improveableness* of man, via his endless future accumulation of knowledge and happiness.

> ... the human powers will, in fact, be enlarged; nature, including both its materials, and its laws, will be more at our command; men will make their situation in this world abundantly more easy and comfortable; they will probably prolong their existence in it, and will grow daily more happy ... Thus, whatever was the beginning of this

---

291 See Spadafora 1990, 5-7.
292 See Passmore 1975, 134-149, 190-212.
293 See Weber 1968, 542.
294 Worthington 1748, 154. See Spadafora 1990, 228.
295 Worthington 1748, 190. See Spadafora 1990, 234.

world, the end will be glorious and paradisical, beyond what our imagination can now conceive.[296]

Eighteenth century moral philosophers such as Joseph Priestley, Jeremy Bentham, Helvétius, and Daniel Gross argued that man can learn to maximize his happiness through the progress of moral education. While French philosophers usually grounded their arguments in atheism, English progress theory was strongly influenced by William Paley's *Principles of Moral and Political Philosophy* (1788), according to which God had created man with the intention of promoting his happiness.[297] According to traditional theology, however, earthly man is incapable of reaching ultimate perfection, as he can only achieve it in union with God. During the 18th century, this idea of absolute perfection within a union with God was replaced by the possibility of the general perfectibility of man via constant and endless improvement. As a leading representative of the political and moral progress movement in England, William Godwin could therefore state: "Perfectibility is one of the most unequivocal characteristics of the human species."[298] This modern idea of progress was not characterised by the fixed end point of ultimate perfection, but rather the continuous striving for perfection, anchored in human nature. This idea emerged at the threshold of the 19th century and became particularly formative for the utilitarian theories of Helvetius and Bentham.[299]

Even before evolutionary theory, two interpretations of the history of progress developed, which would later become fundamental for posthumanism. Both are founded on the assumption of humankind's this-worldly perfectibility, and the maximization of potential happiness. Priestley, Worthington, Price, and many other early modern thinkers situated this process within a theological and millennialist context: Since God's creation is good, everything that comes out of it will also naturally tend towards increasingly perfect forms – yet perfection itself is not possible in this world. By contrast, utilitarian philosophers such as Godwin and Bentham attribute the ability of infinite self-improvement to humanity – without any divine influence required. These two directions – a theological versus a secular, mostly utilitarian one – would prove decisive for the reception of emerging theories of evolution later in the 19th century. The fact that today's posthumanists also refer to theoretical elements, or even explicitly to 18th century theorists in Tipler's case, demonstrates the persistent significance of these teachings.

Evolution and the Emergence of Life

"Evolution" is a key concept in the posthumanist theory of progress. However, the term is used ambivalently – even contradictorily at times. According to hermeneutical analysis, we must once again abandon the requirement that philosophical concepts are consistently applied within posthumanism. In terms of the history of evolution, this entails interpreting the process teleologically – i.e. it leads to a certain goal. But in

---

296 Priestley 1771, 4-5. See also Sampson 1956, 58.
297 See Paley 1842, 533-546; Passmore 1975, 162-169.
298 Godwin 1793, I, 11. See also Sampson 1956, 58-59.
299 See Passmore 1975, 149-190; Sampson 1956, 50-56.

the same breath, any teleology is also categorically rejected. In order to understand this apparent contradiction, we must immerse ourselves in "the order of things", which goes hand in hand with interpretations of the idea of evolution itself.

To his credit, in his *William James Lectures*, given at Harvard in 1932-33, Arthur Oncken Lovejoy shed considerable light on the emergence and context of the modern theory of evolution. His extensive work begins with Plato and Aristotle, and addresses the development of a central occidental philosophical and religious idea: *the great chain of being* – the order of all living beings. This notion of the unity of all living beings dominated philosophical and theological discourse about the place of the human being in the cosmic creation for many centuries. Defined by one's proximity to the divine Creator, the chain was based on the hierarchy from the lowest earthly organisms to humans, angels, and finally God himself. It was considered to conclusively contain the perfect and complete sequence of all living beings, as God had created it at the beginning of the world, to continue to exist until the end of time. In modern times, notions of development offered this eternally valid ranking a new dynamic in contributions from John Locke, Alexander Pope, Edmund Law, Leibniz, Kant, Herder, and Diderot.[300]

In the late 18th century the Swiss natural philosopher Charles Bonnet described the biological development of life using the term *evolution*. By this, he implied that all life had *developed* from a single source, and that this entire unfolding was always contained in the original seed. Arthur McCalla interpreted this as proof that the terminological basis of the later theory of evolution could already be found in the core structures of the Christian history of salvation: "Evolution is here a synonym for the preformationist archetypal pattern of essence and development that purports to be at once scientific and soteriological."[301] Bonnet and his contemporary, the Swabian pietist and natural philosopher Friedrich Christoph Oetinger, both developed the idea of an increase in the biological complexity of living beings and their spiritual abilities. Both argued that this was planned by the divine Creator in the context of this biological preformationism. According to Oetinger, God would realize himself as *ens manifestativum sui* in the world over the course of evolutionary history. Evolution was therefore the unfolding of divine corporeality in the world. As Lovejoy summarized, this temporalization of the order of being – the great chain of being – occurred during the Enlightenment, and in fact had already been hinted at by Leibniz. In other words, the ranking of creatures had become dynamic: a stepladder requiring genealogical ascent, as all God-ordained possibilities of being in the universe would strive for realization and this could only occur temporally. This process is also partially understood as an eternal and unending ascent, because the distance between God and the human being is considered infinite.[302]

Following William Worthington's thesis of the gradual perfection of natural creations, Erasmus Darwin and Jean-Baptiste Lamarck – who published his controversial *Philosophie Zoologique* in 1809 – believed that species had changed over long periods of time. Neither of these two thinkers, however, was able to prove his

---

300   See Lovejoy 1961, 183-200.
301   McCalla 1998, 30.
302   See Lovejoy 1961, 242-287; McCalla 1998, 29-31. Tipler reviewed Lovejoy's work, see Tipler 1989, 245; Tipler 1995, 216, 385.

theses empirically.[303] Charles Darwin overcame this challenge on the evening of July 1st 1858, at a meeting of the London *Linnean Society*, when the carefully prepared results from his research expedition with the survey ship *The Beagle* from more than 20 years earlier were presented. The same event included a presentation on the work of the young natural scientist Alfred Russel Wallace on the theory of biological development. It was only during the following scientific exchange of letters with Wallace that Darwin was finally persuaded to finally publish his results.[304]

Darwin's magnum opus *On the Origin of Species by Means of Natural Selection, or the Preservation of Favoured Races in the Struggle for Life* of 1859 does not contain a single line about human beings. However, its final sentence paved the way for both theological and secular optimism about the future: " ... from so simple a beginning endless forms most beautiful and most wonderful have been, and are being, evolved."[305] Intellectual histories of the 19th century often disproportionally emphasize how Darwinism reduced and devalued the human being to a desacralized, biological creature equal to animals. However, this perspective fails to recognize the positive, normative potential of this theory. In fact, Darwin's theory first made it possible to provide a developmental basis for the 18th century anthropological idea of progress. And it is only due to Darwin that deficiencies in the present human species could be interpreted as mere disturbances in the path of a humanity on the way to its perfect form. In his book's concluding words and in some personal letters, Darwin in fact expressed his own confidence that humankind is destined for even greater things, achievable via the evolutionary correction of existing deficiencies and an optimised adaptation to its environment. Popularizations of the Darwinian theory of evolution presented man as the top of the organic ladder, and as the consummate achievement in the history of life. Within humankind, the most advanced race was presented as the crown of creation, and destined to bring forth a higher humanity.[306]

Since the publication of Darwin's theory, this idea of a progressive, biologically based perfection of the human race has been used for seemingly antagonistic strands of reception. Within this context one therefore has to differentiate between the secular reception, which is partly hostile to religious interpretation, and the religious, partly Christian, and benevolent reception of the Darwinian doctrine of development.

One of the most internationally influential secular popularizations of Darwinian evolutionary theory is probably the work of the German zoologist and natural philosopher Ernst Haeckel (1834-1919). In 1868 *Die natürliche Schöpfungsgeschichte* was published over six editions, with an English translation *The History of Creation* following in 1876. Later, Haeckel surpassed this publishing success with the book *Welträthsel. Gemeinverständliche Studien über monistische Philosophie* of 1899, published in English as *The Riddle of the Universe* (1901). By 1919 this book had sold over 340,000 copies in Germany and was translated into 24 languages. As a result, Haeckel received significant

---

303 See Lovejoy 1961, 227-241; Spadafora 1990, 234; Staudinger 1986, 167-168.
304 See Staudinger 1986, 167-173.
305 Darwin 1859, 490. From the first edition of 1859.
306 See Benz 1961, 84-89; Benz 1965, 81-91, 148-149; Baillie 1950, 145-146; Bury 1955, 334-349; Weizsäcker 1964, 118-132.

recognition and cross-class popularity, both from the educated bourgeoisie, who believed in progress, and from the socialist working class. In his philosophy of *monism*, Haeckel endeavours to close the gap between religion and the theory of evolution. He uses the possibilities offered by Darwinism to explain all phenomena of organic nature and the sphere of social life, neatly summarized in the single sentence: "This evolution seems on the whole ... to be a progressive improvement, an historical advance from the simple to the complex, the lower to the higher, the imperfect to the perfect."[307]

Haeckel interprets Darwin's theory as the scientifically verifiable perfection of species over the course of the history of life: "New, more perfect races are constantly emerging and ennobling themselves in the struggle for existence, while the more imperfect races (like the old ancestral forms) recede, die out and become extinct."[308] The distance between these "most primitive races", such as the Veddahs of Ceylon, or the Australian natives, who are "very little above the mental life of the anthropoid apes" versus the "genius of a Goethe, a Darwin" is immeasurable for Haeckel.[309] His regret at the potential extinction of many human races and the loss of diversity of flora and fauna is outweighed by the prospect of a higher development of life, because it offers:

> ... a higher consolation in the thought that, on average, it is the more perfect and refined man who triumphs over others. The final result of this struggle is progress towards the most complete perfection and liberation of the human race, and towards the free self-determination of individuals ruled by reason.[310]

Monism seeks to overcome the era of religion, and replaces dogmatic convictions with constantly progressing scientific knowledge. Haeckel vehemently rejects any form of providence or teleological moments, because historical progress (*progressus*) and gradual perfection (*teleosis*) – which require constant adaptation to changing environmental conditions – are a necessary aspect of selection, but not the outcome of a premeditated purpose. However, Haeckel senses that, apart from the role of a creator god, deism has approached monism "to the degree that they now touch", since both derive past and future continued development of the world from the laws of nature.[311]

> We find, on nearer examination of the history of the three classes [of life forms], that their various orders and families also advanced progressively during the three epochs towards a higher stage of perfection. May we consider this progressive development as the outcome of a conscious design or a moral order of the universe? Certainly not. The theory of selection teaches us that this organic progress, like the earlier organic differentiation, is an inevitable consequence of the struggle for existence. Thousands of beautiful and remarkable species of animals and plants have perished during those forty-eight million years, to give place to stronger competitors, and the victors in this

---

307 Haeckel 1913, 218.
308 Haeckel 1902, 25.
309 Haeckel 1905, 144-145.
310 Haeckel 1902, 113.
311 See Haeckel 1913, 218. See also Ibid., 1-18, 154-173.

struggle for life were not always the noblest or most perfect forms in a moral sense. It has been just the same with the history of humanity.[312]

In 1906 Haeckel founded the *Monistenbund* (*Monist Association*) to spread this philosophy. However, as early as 1865 the publicist Eduard Löwenthal had already founded the monistic, social-humanitarian religious community of "cogitants" – an intellectual community that identified the solution to all humanity's problems in the progress of science alone. Both Löwenthal's early form of scientific religion and Haeckel's efforts led to the founding of numerous monist groups in Austria, Italy, France, Russia, and above all in the United States, where Paul Carus had been publishing *The Monist* magazine since 1890.[313]

In the English-speaking world, Darwinism was rapidly accepted by mainstream Protestant churches. The fiercest controversies emerged around the politicization of the topic by Christian fundamentalists in the United States. These began in the 1920s and continue to this day over the teaching of biology. In the 1860s many theologians tried to unite the Christian history of salvation with the Darwinian doctrine of development. This intellectual tendency was based upon the temporalization of *the great chain of being* as well as the acceptance of a this-worldly idea of progress. The theologians involved examined the natural sciences' latest findings to the great interest of the public, primarily via sermons, lectures, and inspirational writings. For example, the congregationalist and later conservative biblicist Minot Judson Savage interprets Darwin's evolutionary theory in terms of salvation history. He therefore immediately solves the problem of theodicy and original sin, since in his view all evils of the world – such as illness, sin, suffering, and misfortune – are solely caused by *maladjustment*, or living beings' poor adaptation to their environments. Savage therefore identifies the history of salvation with the biological history of development, which would lead to the optimization of living conditions. The Scottish Presbyterian James McCosh, who had been teaching philosophy at Princeton since 1868, defended Christian teleological evolutionism just as vigorously against the atheistic threat of Darwinism in his 1890 paper *The Religious Aspect of Evolution*. He interprets humankind as a seed that has not yet fully matured, but continues to grow toward perfection. The theologically inspired scientist Henry Drummond also contributed significantly to this discussion in his Glasgow lecture *The Contribution of Science to Christianity* in 1884 and later in his American Lowell Lectures *The Ascent of Man* in 1894. He refused to limit the Christian concept of salvation history to humankind, but rather understood the entire evolutionary history of life as part of this soteriological process. Humankind could still remain the culmination of this development because in both theology and evolution "many be called, but few chosen" (Matthew 20:16). Further important contributions to the synthesis of theology and Darwinism were made by the Calvinist botanist Asa Gray's *Darwiniana* (1876), the geologist and preacher George Frederick Wright, the lawyer and

---

312 Haeckel 1913, 221-222.
313 See Mehlhausen / Dunkel 1994; Sass 1968, 126-130; Staudinger 1986, 172-174.

congregationalist Lyman Abbott, the natural philosopher John Fiske, and the Anglican Bishop Ernest William Barnes.[314]

During the 20th century, three important philosophers attempted to understand the theory of evolution as part of a comprehensive cosmology, with reference to, or in reflection on, the Christian history of salvation. Each was received in a distinct way by posthumanism. Samuel Alexander (1859-1938) and Alfred North Whitehead (1861-1947), who both received invitations to present *Gifford Lectures*, and the aforementioned paleontologist Pierre Teilhard de Chardin all understood the universe as an entity that only gradually develops its qualities.

In his seminal work *Space, Time and Deity* of 1920, Samuel Alexander interprets Darwinism as a purely scientific theory that refuses to judge the object of its investigation, and provides a basic explanation of how values are created, regarding both the history of life and human culture in general. That which has survived by natural selection or mutation in its particular living conditions can therefore be assessed as good. That which has the greatest chance to survive is therefore always revered as supreme.[315] From the perspective of human beings, the universe continuously produces improved levels of existence through time's infinite advance – the levels so far being matter, life, and mind:

> Within the all-embracing stuff of Space-Time, the universe exhibits an emergence in Time of successive levels of finite existences, each with its characteristic empirical quality. The highest of these empirical qualities known to us is mind or consciousness. Deity is the next higher empirical quality to the highest we know … [316]

The highest level of existence that humans can experience empirically is the mind or consciousness. This points the way to the next level of cosmic unfolding: "Deity is thus the next higher empirical quality to mind, which the universe is engaged in bringing to birth."[317] Alexander does not assume that the development of the cosmos is part of a divine plan, but rather emphasizes that evolutionary and cosmic tendencies to progress to the next stage of existence emerge out of themselves. He argues that the next higher level is already perceivable as the deity of religious thought. This deity is therefore part of the evolutionary process: "Deity is some quality not realised but in process of realisation, is future and not present."[318] Alexander understands God as an infinite being within space-time, who changes alongside the development of the universe, and therefore the term God designates all of the not yet realizable or recognizable properties of the universe:[319]

---

314 See Benz 1965, 157-183; Barrow / Tipler 1986, 85-86, 183-184.
315 See Alexander 1966, 309-310.
316 Ibid., 345.
317 Ibid., 347.
318 Ibid., 379.
319 See ibid., 341-372.

As actual, God does not possess the quality of deity but is the universe as tending to that quality. This nisus in the universe, though not present to our sense, is yet present to reflection upon experience.[320]

Alexander's influence upon the mathematician and philosopher Alfred North Whitehead is disputed in the history of philosophy. Whitehead also sought to interpret individual phenomena of empirical reality in the history of nature and the cosmos, as well as to overcome the manifest boundaries between the natural sciences, the humanities, and philosophy. He presents the image of a bipolar god, characterized by both a primordial and a subsequent nature. These two natures of God are now utilizing the evolutionary process of the universe to seek each other, thus restoring divine unity. Whitehead concludes that over the course of his own realization God causes creation to bring forth ever new and higher forms of existence in successive stages.[321]

> There are thus four creative phases in which the universe accomplishes its actuality. There is first the phase of conceptual origination, deficient in actuality, but infnite in its adjustment of valuation. Secondly, there is the temporal phase of physical origination, with its multiplicity of actualities. In this phase full actuality is attained; but there is deficiency in the solidarity of individuals with each other... Thirdly, there is the phase of perfected actuality, in which the many are one everlastingly, without the qualification of any loss either of individual identity or of completeness of unity. In everlastingness, immediacy is reconciled with objective immortality ... In the fourth phase, the creative action completes itself. ... For the kingdom of heaven is with us today. The action of the fourth phase is the love of God for the world.[322]

This idea of God evolving through the course of cosmic and human history greatly impacted Protestant process theology at the University of Chicago Divinity School since the 1930s.[323]

Inspired by Henri Bergson's attempt to synthesize the Christian idea of creation and the scientific doctrine of development in *L'évolution créatrice* (1907), the Jesuit and palaeontologist Pierre Teilhard de Chardin also endeavoured to contribute fruitfully to scientific knowledge and religious insight.[324] For Teilhard, matter, and mind are two types of cosmic material in a dynamic relationship with each other. Starting from the point *alpha*, God allows the universe to unfold into an increasingly complex system. In his two main philosophical works *Le Groupe zoologique humain*[325] of 1956 and *Le Phénomène humain*[326] of 1955 Teilhard describes the evolutionary process as the

---

320　Ibid., 361.
321　See Whitehead 1929, 511-544.
322　Ibid., 532-533.
323　See Maaßen 1991, 217-218.
324　Teilhard's ideas build on the theological criticism of materialistic monism, which had already been put forward around 1900 by the Jesuit Erich Wasmann and the Protestant theologian Georg Wobbermin. See Altner 1965, 57-60.
325　It was published 1966 in English as *Man's Place in Nature. The Human Zoological Group*. See Teilhard 1966.
326　This was published 1959 in English as *The Phenomenon of Man*. See Teilhard 1976.

successive unfolding of the mind. His ideas as portrayed in these books resemble the works of Alexander and Whitehead. This unfolding occurs through the preliminary stages of the formation of the universe and the earth (*cosmogenesis*), the subsequent formation of the biosphere (*biogenesis*), and thereafter the emergence of thought in what he labelled the noosphere which arose with the appearance of the first hominids (*noogenesis*). Finally, it will lead to the future unfolding of higher lifeforms through the confluence of human thought. This cosmic development will conclude with the return of Christ at the temporal end: Omega Point. According to Teilhard, individuals will merge into a final super consciousness in this cosmic Christ.

For Teilhard the origin of humankind is of central importance for the development of the cosmos, because its appearance and the expansion of the noosphere (the mind sphere) across the entire planet marks a turning point.[327] Evolution will now progress towards Omega and the convergence movement. Teilhard deduces humankind's outstanding role in the history of evolution thus far:

> The evidence is undeniable that, since the Pliocene, life seems to have concentrated in man (as a tree does in its leading shoot) all that was best in the sap it still held. In the course of the last two millions of years we can see that countless things disappeared, but not a single new thing, apart from the hominians, has appeared in nature.[328]

Man himself, exalted by the appearance of Christ, will thus prove the decisive factor in Teilhard's cosmic soteriology: "*Man is irreplaceable*. Therefore, however improbable it might seem, *he must reach the goal*, not necessarily, doubtless, but infallibly."[329]

Teilhard denies that the biological and spiritual development of humans has already reached its zenith, and instead holds out the prospect of a steady increase in their cerebral abilities, the next stage of which is just becoming apparent during the present time:

> After man (the ultimate and supreme product of this *first-type* evolution), we have arrangements that work themselves out, add themselves to one another, and combine together in the noosphere. Here indeed, we have evolution mobilising its forces in an effort of a completely new type, made possible by its own consciousness of itself: a *second type* (reflective) evolution, or ... the second-stage rocket starting up again with, for zero, the speed built up for it by the first – and, what is more, aimed ... with impeccable accuracy in the same direction – always in the direction of a higher cerebralisation.[330]

This new stage of evolution is brought about by the increasing awareness of our own human evolutionary history. It allows humans to realize the spirit's influence over their own cultural development, as opposed to a purely biological process over millions of years: "We find the artificial carrying on the work of the natural; and the

---

327   At the same time the Russian mineralogist and geochemist Vladimir Vernadsky, whom Teilhard met in Paris at Édouard Le Roy, also worked on the concept of the noosphere. See Vernadsky 1997.
328   Teilhard 1966, 73. See ibid., 40-106; Teilhard 1976, 163-290.
329   Ibid., 276.
330   Teilhard 1966, 110.

transmission of an oral or written culture being superimposed on genetic forms of heredity (chromosomes)."[331]

Like Whitehead and Teilhard after him, Alexander created a cosmological metaphysics as an extended interpretation of a world revealed by the natural sciences. The evolution of the universe implies a strong teleological moment for all three thinkers, as the development of something new is always presented as being superior. For Teilhard and Whitehead this moment becomes deterministic, since the history of the universe is equated with the realization of God.[332]

Many posthumanists took up the idea of a steady, spiritual development and departure from purely biological evolution. However, Alexander, Whitehead, and Teilhard's idea of God evolving throughout cosmic history attained particular importance for Frank Tipler. Tipler pays homage to Alexander, Whitehead, and Teilhard, together with Friedrich Wilhelm Schelling and Henri Bergson, as the precursors to his own *Physics of Immortality*.[333] Although he claims to have borrowed only the term Omega, the writings of Frank Tipler and John D. Barrow in fact include a number of very clear parallels to Teilhard's work. In their commentary on *The Anthropic Cosmological Principle*, they even give the impression of trying to continue Teilhard's attempt to reconcile natural science and theology or teleology, now enriched by advances in cosmology and astronautics.[334] Some of Teilhard's philosophical terms are transformed into strictly physical terminology: Tipler understands Teilhard's concept of a spiritual, radial, or psychic energy being the motor of evolution instead as information, and consequently interprets the expansion of the noosphere as an increase in information processing until life reaches the Omega Point – i.e. the realized, Christian God. Similarly, Tipler turns the Christian concept of the Holy Spirit into the universal wave function of the cosmos (referring to the Jesuit thinker). In Teilhard's fascination with cybernetics, Tipler identifies a hint that the paleontologist would have also interpreted computers as a means of overcoming matter. Significant differences from Teilhard can be found above all in Tipler's complete abandonment of a Christology, as the Christian Redeemer plays absolutely no role in his vision of the future.[335]

We should not underestimate the importance of certain influences for Tipler's work. These include his American heritage; both Alexander's and Whitehead's theories, which also renounce Christological elements; and the Chicago School's process theology, which was influenced by Whitehead. In 1988 Tipler participated in the 2nd Pannenberg Symposium at the *Lutheran School of Theology* in Chicago, and established contact with the Protestant theologian Wolfhart Pannenberg (1928-2014), with whom he continued to correspond via an exchange of letters. Within Protestant theology, Pannenberg adhered to one specific approach to the history of religion, based on God's progressive revelation

---

331 Teilhard 1976, 277.
332 See Baillie 1950, 146-154.
333 See Tipler 1989, 221; Barrow / Tipler 1986, 191-193.; Moravec and Kurzweil are at least familiar with Whitehead's mathematical work as well as a less important work by Alexander. See Kurzweil 1999a, 328-329, 344; Moravec 1999, 20.
334 "Providing the term is Teilhard's only scientific contribution to this book. He is not mentioned in the Appendix for Scientists." Tipler 1995, 110. See Barrow / Tipler 1986, 196-204.
335 See Tipler 1995, 183-185.

through the history of humankind. For Pannenberg this revelation is evident in all religions, but will continue toward the resurrection of Christ, in which he sees a *prolepsis* of complete revelation at the end of time.[336] Pannenberg was the only renowned theologian to seriously examine Tipler's theory and identify some common ground in the idea of God fully unfolding in the future. However, he rejected Tipler's idea of salvation through technical progress. In addition to Pannenberg's efforts to reconcile science and religion, Tipler appreciated the theologian's commitment to a dynamic image of God.[337] In order to connect the history of evolution with the teleology of the design argument developed by William Paley and other theologians, Tipler also refers to advocates of a temporalized version of the *great chain of being*. These include: Asa Gray, Ernest William Barnes, John Fiske, and the biologist Thomas Huxley, who at the turn of the century regarded Darwinism as scientific proof of a planned universe, or the teleological theory of evolution.[338]

All post- and transhumanists share this melioristic and anthropocentric interpretation of the history of evolution. Both secular philosophies, such as monism or Alexander's and Whitehead's metaphysical systems, as well as numerous theological interpretations, agree that evolution produces ever higher forms of existence. Contemporary humans mark the peak of this progress to date. It is at this precise point in the narrative that a second argument begins, which actually contradicts the previous teleological interpretation: the complete devaluation of natural evolution by humankind's controlling the course of its further development. This conclusion can already be found in early eugenicists. The religious writer Soame Jenyns had transferred the idea of the evolutionary ladder to the human races during the 18th century, and contrasted the symbolic English genius Isaac Newton with the "wild Hottentot".[339] As a consequence of this idea, which spread widely, advocates of eugenics such as Francis Galton, Ludwig Büchner, and Auguste Forel proclaimed the goal of replacing humans' "natural selection" with "artificially selected breeding" from the 1860s onwards. In contrast to error-prone natural evolution, a consciously controlled selection of the most developed races or classes could only lead to a "higher form of humanity" in the future.[340]

Although their impact can hardly be underestimated, Julian Huxley and Teilhard de Chardin were amongst those few advocates of eugenics who clung to their visions even after National Socialist racial policies. Julian Huxley propagated a strong eugenic agenda throughout his life, in stark contrast to his brother Aldous and his grandfather Thomas. During his years at Oxford's New College, Huxley studied eugenic theory intensively, and found numerous comrades-in-arms to support a future eugenicist social policy, including: J.B.S. Haldane, John R. Baker, and Carlos P. Blacker. Huxley was a member of the *British Eugenics Society* from 1925, served as vice-president from 1937 to 1944, and was even president from 1959 to 1962. Although his early years were marked

---

336 See Pannenberg 1961.
337 See ibid., XXIII-XXIV; Tipler 1989, 217-219; See Tipler 1995, 4-5.
338 See Barrow / Tipler 1986, 85-87, 127-143, 189; Tipler 1995, 216-218; Pannenberg 1995.
339 See Lovejoy 1961, 183-200. See also section 6.6.2.
340 See Benz 1961, 94-96; Benz 1965, 81-91, 148-149; Baillie 1950, 145-146; Passmore 1970, 171-190.

by strong racist prejudices against the "inferior race" of the "Negros", during and after the 1930s he completely avoided the topic of race, in contrast to National Socialism, and instead held a clear position against any form of racist eugenics. Huxley understood the biological improvement of humanity as part of a comprehensive social policy for a future *Fulfilment Society* – from the perspective of a *cultural elitist*. He therefore advocated that selected eggs be fertilized by particular donors deemed to be of improved mental and physical quality, in order to raise the level of genetics in the general population. Simultaneously, he called for the sterilization of socially weak individuals likely to have large families, due to the imminent danger of genetic degeneration.[341]

> The improvement of human genetic quality by eugenic methods would take a great load of suffering and frustration off the shoulders of evolving humanity, and would much increase both enjoyment and efficiency … The general level of genetic intelligence could theoretically be raised by eugenic selection; and even a slight rise in its average level would give a marked increase in the number of the outstandingly intelligent and capable people needed to run our increasingly complex societies.[342]

Echoing Alexander, Teilhard, and Whitehead, Huxley also formulates a multi-level evolutionary model comprised of three stages. Firstly, inorganic, cosmic creation, secondly, the creation of life (biology) and thirdly, the psychosocial evolution (of humans and their culture).[343] It is important to note that the psychosocial evolution of the present is considered to be of a completely different nature than the purely biological developments of the past. Huxley's evolutionary humanism therefore advocates the conscious control of future evolution through eugenic optimization and a sustainable educational policy:[344]

> Our knowledge of the evolutionary past makes it clear that any new psychosocial system should be open-ended, not liable to become self-limiting. Like science itself, human evolution must become a self-correcting cybernetic process.[345]

Teilhard de Chardin's advocacy of eugenics also seems connected to the hope of enhancing human cerebral capabilities: "Once it is admitted … that the cerebralisation of beings is the true index of their vitalisation, a radical transformation comes over the picture of the biosphere…".[346] Further evolution of plants and other lower-order biological creatures can now be ignored.[347] According to this logic, the sciences do not serve the infinite progress of individuals, but rather support the noosphere's accelerated expansion via the spiritual exaltation of humanity as it currently exists. Teilhard formulates the necessity of human intervention in natural evolution just as clearly as Huxley, and sees it as a consequence of the evolutionary process itself:

341　See Weindling, 2012, 480-491; Huxley 1963.
342　Huxley 1963, 17.
343　See Huxley 1963, 1-2.
344　See Weindling 2012, 488-495.
345　Huxley 1963, 21.
346　Teilhard 1966, 49.
347　See ibid., 49-53.

> It would be more convenient, and we would incline to think it safe, to leave the contours of that great body made of all our bodies to take shape on their own, influenced only by the automatic play of individual urges and whims. 'Better not interfere with the forces of the world !' Once more we are up against the mirage of instinct, the so-called infallibility of nature. But is it not precisely the world itself which, culminating in thought, expects us to think out again the instinctive impulses of nature so as to perfect them?[348]

According to Teilhard, the modern possibilities offered by the natural sciences will allow humankind to enter a new phase of the evolution of the mind, which marks the beginning of humanity's conscious path to self-perfection.[349]

> With our knowledge of hormones we appear to be on the eve of having a hand in the development of our bodies and even of our brains. With the discovery of genes it appears that we shall soon be able to control the mechanism of organic heredity. And with the synthesis of albuminoids imminent, we may well one day be capable of producing what the earth, left to itself, seems no longer able to produce: a new wave of organisms, an artificially provoked neo-life.[350]

Huxley, who wrote the preface to the English edition of *Le Phénomène humain* in 1959, essentially agrees with Teilhard. Like the Jesuit, he interprets the evolutionary process as the progressive growth of knowledge and consciousness. Both thinkers also share an absolute anthropocentricity in their perspectives on evolution: "We are privileged to be living at a crucial moment in the cosmic story, the moment when the vast evolutionary process, in the small person of enquiring man, is becoming conscious of itself."[351] Advances in the biological sciences have allowed contemporary humans to finally recognize evolution as the formation of a higher order of collective consciousness.

> His [Teilhard's] formulation, however, is more profound and more seminal: it implies that we should consider inter-thinking humanity as a new type of organism, whose destiny it is to realise new possibilities for evolving life on this planet.[352]

At present, the Oxford biologist Richard Dawkins is likely one of the most prominent advocates of an antiteleological interpretation of Darwinism, as discussed in his monographs *The Selfish Gene* (1976) and *The Blind Watchmaker* (1986). Dawkins reacts

---

348 Teilhard 1976, 282-283.
349 See Teilhard 1976, 273-290; Teilhard 1966, 96-122. The recent Catholic reception of Teilhard's work completely ignores the significance of eugenics. Günther Schiwy even presents Pope Benedict XVI as a student of Teilhard. One must consider that, throughout his life, the Jesuit Teilhard never received permission from his order to publish his philosophical writings. See Schiwy 2001, 258-261.
350 Teilhard 1976, 250. According to Robert Ettinger, it is precisely this commitment to science that makes Teilhard's philosophy so attractive for transhumanism. See Ettinger 1989, 7-8.
351 Huxley 1963, 1.
352 Huxley 1976, 20. However, Huxley rejects these theological aspects, even though he does not wish to exclude the possibility of future humans possessing new parapsychological, meditative, and mystical abilities. See Huxley 1963, 1976; Benz 1965, 94-95; Passmore 1970, 239-260, 286-304.

bitingly to unscientific attempts to question the Darwinian theory of evolution or to connect it to any form of William Paley's design argument:

> Natural selection, the blind, unconscious, automatic process which Darwin discovered, and which we now know is the explanation of all life, has no purpose in mind. It has no mind and no mind's eye. It does not plan for the future. It has no vision, no foresight, no sight at all. If it can be said to play the role of watchmaker in nature, it is the *blind* watchmaker.[353]

Using Darwin, Dawkins explains the history of evolution as the battle of genes to pass on their DNA information, accompanied by numerous processes of transformation.[354] Dawkins is acknowledged – albeit with some variation – by all posthumanist authors. Marvin Minsky's view that the history of evolution is a haphazard process of random development – rather than a progression towards a higher point – can undoubtedly be traced back to an almost complete adaptation of Dawkins' theses. Hans Moravec and Ray Kurzweil, who refer to several of Dawkins works, exclusively apply his idea of aimless development historically to the period of "natural evolution". Intelligent life is now gradually liberating itself from this unintelligent, slow, and inefficient period of evolution, beginning with humankind. Dawkins' theory allows the above-mentioned posthumanists to characterize and distinguish the billions of years of historical evolution in contrast to the new and increasingly controllable developments, most notably characterized by the emergence of culture and technology.[355] In direct contrast to Dawkins, however, these posthumanists apply his theories to formulate a universal teleology: The evolution of life on Earth *must* result in the creation of artificial intelligence, which will ultimately populate the cosmos and save it from final heat death.

Hans Moravec was obviously influenced by Huxley's staggered concept of biological and psychosocial evolutions. Teilhard also addresses the basic idea of artificial or cultural evolution, which continues the process of natural, biological evolution. In the works of Huxley and Moravec, the evolution of the mind, of culture, frees itself from its purely biological prelude. However, Moravec focuses on the role of technology in general and computer technology in particular, which for him offer the only way to free culture from its dependence on biological humans.

None of these posthumanist authors explicitly engages with eugenicist ideas of racial or biological perfection. Even amongst transhumanists, the current promises of genetic engineering are rather marginal. This is due to the fact that posthumanists and transhumanists both endeavour to achieve complete detachment from the biological body, which is of course difficult to control because it is definitely aging. All posthumanists adhere to a shared structural principle of freeing humankind from natural evolution, and instead artificially creating a new, superior human being through

---

353   Dawkins 1996, 5.
354   See Dawkins 1976; Dawkins 1996, 169-194.
355   See Minsky 1992a, 1-2; Kurzweil 1999a, 349; Moravec 1988, 136, 159, 200; Moravec 1999, 4, 213. Kevin Warwick and even Frank Tipler refer to Dawkins when defining life as the transmission of information through DNA but Tipler avoids the anti-teleological contexts of Dawkins' theory. See Tipler 1995, 165, 443; Warwick 1998, 45-47.

the intervention of science. However, this idea originates historically above all from the work of eugenicists. The degree of substantive proximity between ideas of biological perfection via eugenics and the supplementation of the biological body by chemical and mechanical means was, in fact, already documented by Teilhard de Chardin – surprising as that may be.

Posthumanism's theory of progress stems from a philosophical development traceable within European and American intellectual history for at least three centuries. Its sources are diverse and numerous. The focus of these actual processes upon increasing information-processing computing power echoes patterns of the Protestant work ethic, as well as both theological and secular conceptions of the this-worldly progress of knowledge. Posthumanism thus reflects both theological and utilitarian ideas from the 18th and 19th centuries regarding the progressive growth of knowledge, work, and happiness. It also becomes evident that posthumanist authors assimilate concepts from the 1860s into their own interpretations of the history of evolution. This propagated the vision of a higher form of humanity that was better constituted due to larger brains.

The most obvious posthumanist achievement consists in synthesizing the most diverse elements of the occidental discourse on progress. Although actual progress is justified within posthumanist discourse in a manner contrary to monistic, metaphysical, or even Christian theological conceptions, all posthumanist anthropologies of the future necessarily lead to the vision of a superior, more perfect – one might even say posthuman – humanity.

Frank Tipler's Physico-Theology

What all posthumanist authors have in common is the attempt to scientifically justify the further development of humankind and its descendants towards a future technical paradise. Nevertheless, the calculations inherent to these posthumanist assessments of past progress are built upon the background of a normative interpretation. However, this cultural heritage is also largely denied. The interpretation of history as one aspect of a larger theory of progress thus continues to perform a function of identity-formation: It answers where we come from and where we are going.

Posthumanism presents future technical advances as quasi inevitable processes, but these are subject to different laws depending on the author in question. While Hans Moravec, Ray Kurzweil, and others use past human progress as the basis for their prognosis, Frank Tipler uses a cosmological perspective to discuss the meaning and goal of progress *in summa*. As a result, any analysis of Tipler's theory will require significantly more space. The physicist never tires of asserting that, as a whole and in each of its postulates, his Omega Point Theory stems from scientific considerations.[356]

> This book is a description of the Omega Point Theory, which is a testable physical theory for an omnipresent, omniscient, omnipotent God who will one day in the far future resurrect every single one of us in an abode which is in all essentials the

---

356   See Tipler 1995, IX-XII, 1-17, 139-153; Tipler 1989, 222.

Judeo-Christian Heaven. Every single term in the Theory – for example ... "resurrection (spiritual) body," Heaven – will be introduced as pure physics concepts. In this book I shall make no appeal, anywhere, to revelation. I shall appeal instead to the solid results of modern physical science ... I shall show exactly how physics will permit the resurrection to eternal life of everyone who has lived, is living and will live.[357]

Tipler places each statement in his book within the framework of his own newly founded physical eschatology,[358] which means they are falsifiable and therefore scientific. The *postulate of eternal life* forms the crucial linchpin of this new form of physical reasoning.

In their joint work *The Anthropic Cosmological Principle*, Frank Tipler and John D. Barrow endeavour to reintroduce the teleological orientation to cosmology, which was believed to have long since been superseded. They explicitly emphasize that they argue as cosmologists rather than as philosophers, and that they do not incorporate their own personal beliefs into this scientific discourse.[359] While weak, this anthropic principle states that only a limited number of all physically possible universes could foster the emergence of life. Theoretically, distinctly different universes with diverse physical conditions and types of natural constants could also exist. Accordingly, only a limited range of such models are available to intelligent observers. Since we exist as observers, our universe must have very specific properties to enable our own evolution. The *Weak Anthropic Principle*, which has been generally accepted in cosmology, states that therefore the values observerable in all physical and cosmological units are not equally probable. Assuming that the universe is old enough to produce life, these measures would allow the emergence of carbon-based lifeforms.[360]

Tipler and Barrow devote a significant portion of their more than six hundred page book to a survey of all the disciplines of natural science, in order to explore the question of why physical constants contain the precise values that they do. The two cosmologists demonstrate that only a compound of carbon, hydrogen, nitrogen, and oxygen could ever make such complex structures as humans possible.[361] They also explain in great detail that only stars and planets of a specific size and age could produce an atmosphere, and thus life.[362]

If life becomes possible in principle, further undetermined factors are required to support the genesis of intelligent living beings.[363] Within all of these detail-obsessed physical descriptions, an astute reader can identify a certain mantra, repeatedly exclaiming how improbable and coincidental the emergence of intelligent life in the cosmos is: "In short, the evolution of 'cognition', or intelligence and self-awareness of the human type, is most unlikely even in the primate lineage."[364]

---

357 Tipler 1995, 1.
358 Ibid., 146 and Barrow / Tipler 1986, 659.
359 See ibid., 14-15.
360 See ibid., 15-18; Press 1986, 315.
361 See Barrow / Tipler 1986, 143-147, 510-511, 524-556.
362 See ibid., 308-359, 557-570.
363 See ibid., 128-132.
364 Ibid., 131; See ibid., 253-254, 359-360, 558.

But do Tipler and Barrow detail these improbable physical events through hundreds of pages, only to dismiss them as pure coincidence? Not at all. Rather, they rely on the method of Agatha Christie's famous detective: " 'Any coincidence', said Miss Marple to herself, 'is always worth noticing. You can throw it away later if it *is* only a coincidence.'"[365]

The alleged randomness and improbability of conditions required for the emergence of intelligent life offer Tipler and Barrow evidence for the so-called *Strong Anthropic Principle*, which was introduced by cosmologist Brandon Carter in the 1970s. Far more speculative than the *Weak Anthropic Principle* and highly controversial within cosmological science, the *Strong Anthropic Principle* claims that the universe *must* produce observers over the course of its own evolution. This is precisely because so many seemingly independent coincidences exist in nature: "The universe must have those properties which allow life to develop within it at some stage in its history."[366]

John A. Wheeler, Tipler and Barrow's mentor, used this *Strong Anthropic Principle* to derive the *Participatory Anthropic Principle*, which in turn is partly based on George Berkeley's argumentation: "Observers are necessary to bring the Universe into being."[367] Simultaneously, Tipler excludes the existence and future emergence of extraterrestrial intelligent life in numerous publications.[368] Therefore, he concludes that all previously compiled improbabilities in the natural universe exist necessarily and specifically in order to create *humankind* as this observer of the universe. According to the *Strong Anthropic Principle*, the universe could not exist without humanity, which might lead the authors to quote the ancient philosopher Protagoras: "Man is the measure of all things."[369]

Life would never begin, mature, and perish under such improbable conditions without first exerting any notable influence on the broader history of the universe. Tipler and Barrow therefore build upon the *Strong Anthropic Principle* to establish the *Final Anthropic Principle*: "*Final Anthropic Principle (FAP): Intelligent information-processing comes into existence in the Universe, and, once it comes into existence, it will never die out.*"[370]

According to its authors, the *Final Anthropic Principle* is devoid of any ethical and moral evaluation: it is purely scientific. It also serves as the theoretical background for Tipler's *postulate of eternal life* in the *Physics of Immortality*.[371] He can therefore claim that the immortality of intelligent life is a necessary consequence of physical facts. In *The Anthropic Cosmological Principle* Tipler and Barrow attempt to legitimize their teleological standpoint with an impressive survey of philosophical and religious thought (from Aristotle, to Boshongo myths, to Teilhard de Chardin).[372] However, their

---

365 Ibid., 288.
366 Ibid., 21.
367 Ibid., 22.
368 See ibid., 132-134, 577-591; Tipler 1981, 1991.
369 Barrow / Tipler 1986, 556.
370 Ibid., 23. Nick Bostrom, the transhumanist and director of the *Future of Humanity Institute*, has intensively engaged with Tipler and Barrow's anthropic principle. He regards their scientifically verifiable propositions as a final anthropic hypothesis. See Bostrom 2002, 49-51.
371 See Barrow / Tipler 1986; Tipler 1995, 212-214; Tipler 2007.
372 See Barrow / Tipler 1986, 27-203.

thesis nonetheless was met by unanimous rejection from established physicists and scientists.[373]

Later in his book, Tipler reverts to the reasoning that, if a physical argument enriched with formulas could not convince the critical reader, he would instead select other scientists and philosophers who hold "comparable" positions, in a broader sense.[374] For Tipler, the *postulate of eternal life* forms the basis of all following and supposedly scientific conclusions about eternal progress, the goal of cosmic evolution, and even the resurrection of the dead. These points will be discussed in detail later.

While transhumanists in the 1990s and early 2000s attempted to clearly distance themselves from Tipler's positions as much as possible, today many of his basic ideas are shared by Christian and Mormon transhumanists. Ray Kurzweil also adapts the essential elements of Tipler's theories, as will be discussed shortly.

By formulating this *Final Anthropic Principle*, and deriving the necessity of perpetual progress from it, Tipler explicitly places himself in the tradition of Protestant and Anglican natural theologians as well as the so called physico-theologians. Since the end of the 17th century, and particularly in England and the Netherlands, those theologians influenced by natural science and the Enlightenment have sought to determine the nature of God. These attempts were no longer made only using human prophetic writings, but instead by observing natural creation itself, in order to penetrate to the true nature of the creator. Tipler specifies that only fields that are free from human influence – the sciences, and above all mathematics and physics – can reflect God's intentions. These alone can contribute to a better understanding of God, as well as humankind's ultimate destination within divine creation:

> The only book which does not suffer from these limitations is the Book of Nature, the only book which God wrote with His/Her own hand, without human assistance. The book of nature is not limited by human understanding. The Book of Nature is the only reliable guide to the true Nature of God.[375]

To support his argument, the physicist cites Paul's Letter to the Romans: "His invisible attributes, that is to say his everlasting power and deity, have been visible, ever since the world began, to the eye of reason, in the things he has made."[376] Tipler and Barrow refer extensively to this traditional line of so-called natural theology or physico-theology, to which they feel intellectually indebted. They especially refer to John Ray, [377] William

---

373 See Press 1986. The science journalist Martin Gardner mockingly dubs *FAP* as *CRAP* – the *Completely Ridiculous Anthropic Principle*. See Bostrom 2002, 50.
374 Tipler thus proceeds with the idea of immortality for computers, as well as with the foundation of the Many-Worlds Theory. See Tipler 1995, 16-17, 170-171.
375 Ibid., 337.
376 Ibid., 4. Romans 1:20.
377 See Barrow / Tipler 1986, 58-59. John Ray (1628-1704) is considered the most important natural theologian of the 17th century, and wrote the foundational work *The Wisdom of God Manifested in the Works of Creation* (London 1691).

Paley,[378] Isaac Newton, Richard Bentley, Colin MacClaurin,[379] as well as the ideas of the American independence philosopher Thomas Paine.[380] Frank Tipler praises the latter, as well as the American revolutionaries George Washington, Benjamin Franklin, Ethan Allen, and Thomas Jefferson, as excellent representatives of his own deism. Deism is a cross-denominational idea within Enlightenment philosophy, as it understands the Creator God as being transcendent to the history of the world. This deism usually substitutes divine revelation with the rational insight of the human mind.[381]

The fact that Tipler accepts William Paley as the authoritative representative of natural theology or physico-theology in fact necessitates a detailed examination – it constitutes nothing less than the reintroduction of teleology into science. During the middle of the 17th century, the puritanically influenced botanist John Ray led the very popular sermon series *The Wisdom of God Manifested in the Works of Creation*, which was to be reproduced in numerous translations. In the early 18th century, however, the Anglican cleric William Derham must be acknowledged as the most influential physico-theologian for subsequent authors such as Paley.[382] Derham's German translator lists about one hundred book titles published between 1680 and 1727 in his bibliography, in an attempt to both prove God's existence as well as to indicate the widespread scientific praise for the perfection of his creation. Within this list, Derham's three major works occupy a very special place.[383] While Derham's *Artificial Clockmaker* (1696) is devoted to a more general description of and admiration for creation, his *Physico-theology* (1713) is entirely devoted to God's earthly creations. Derham describes the diversity of flora and fauna on earth through numerous scientific explanations, and, pointing to the eye as the most complex organ, pays particular attention to the anatomy and physiology of humankind.[384] From the richness of the creation that God has given us, Derham

---

378 See Barrow / Tipler 1986, 76-81. William Paley wrote *Natural Theology* (London 1802), was a preacher for the Church of England from the 1770s and regarded the discovery of the laws of nature as the mysticism of his age.

379 See Barrow / Tipler 1986, 60-62. Richard Bentley (1662-1742) presented his famous treatise *Confutation of Atheism from the Origin and Frame of the World* (London 1693) during the Boyle Lectures. Colin MacClaurin (1698-1746) became reknown for his *An Account of Sir Isaac Newton's Philosophical Discoveries* (London 1748), which established Newton's physicotheological significance.

380 In his work *The Age of Reason* (London 1793), Paine described the entirety of creation as the Word of God, which must be read as revelation via science. See Tipler 1995, 321-322.

381 See ibid., 321-327. See Gestrich 1981, 392-395.

382 Isaac Newton's scientific and philosophical writings were published at the beginning of the 18th century, and their theological implications would exert tremendous influence on the emerging *Natural Theology*.

383 I will only repeat a small selection of thinker here: Basilius, Eustathius Antiochenus, Anastasius Sinaita Cicero, Beda Venerabilis, Joannis Gersons, Robert Boyle (*Of the High Veneration Man's Intellect Owes to GOD*, 1685), Christian Wolff, Isaac Barrow, Richard Bentley, Nehemia Grew (*Cosmologia Sacra*, 1701), Francisco Fenelon (*Démonstration de l'existence de Dieu*, 1712), Bernard Nienwentyt (*Het regt gebruik der Werelt beschowingen*, 1715), George Cheyne (*Philosophical Principles of natural Religion*, 1705), Robert Green (*The Principles of Natural Philosophy*, 1712), William Whiston (*Astronomical Principles of Religion*, 1717).

384 Regarding eyes, see: Derham 1754, 85-113.

deduces humanity's mission to multiply the goods entrusted to us with diligence, and to proliferate by relying on the gifts that God has given us.[385]

The foundations offered in Derham's 1714 *Astro-theology, or a Demonstration of the Being and Attributes of God, from a Survey of the Heavens*, were certainly of greater significance to the cosmologists Tipler and Barrow. In reference to Psalm 19 (according to which the heavens proclaim the glory of God), Derham writes seven chapters presenting his own views on the size, number, position, movement, form, weight, light, and warmth of the heavenly bodies (planets). He concludes his detailed astronomical observations with a rhetorical question, which in view of his "evidence" only has one possible answer: [386]

> And so this glorious Scene of GOD's Works, the Heavens, plainly demonstrates the Workman's infinite *Wisdom* to contrive, his *Omnipotency* to make, and his infinite *Goodness*, in being so indulgent to all the Creatures, as to contrive and order all his works for their good ... What *Architect* could build such vast Masses, and such an unnumerable company of them too ... ? What *Mathematician* could so exactly adjust their Distances? ... None certainly could do these things but GOD.[387]

Derham worships God as a reasonable master of mathematics, optics, and medicine, who cares not only for the earth but also for the other planets.[388] He thus rejects a purely anthropocentric interpretation of creation: "For what is all our Globe but a Point, a Trifle to the Universe!"[389] Building on this realization of the Earth's astronomical insignificance, Derham admonishes humility and asceticism, and instead calls for reflection upon the soul's eternal striving toward the heavenly.[390]

A century later, the English utilitarian philosopher and Anglican priest William Paley revisited Derham's ideas and published *Natural Theology, or Evidences of the Existence and Attributes of the Deity Collected from the Appearances of Nature* in 1802. Within the context of the criticism of religion of his time, Paley focused his largely mechanistically influenced discussions on the design argument. His descriptions of plants, animals, and man – who is described as the "most complicated or most flexible machine that was ever contrived" – culminate in his statement that the perfection of the eye alone is sufficient proof of God.[391] Paley might disagree with Derham that the cosmological proof is the best argument possible.[392] However, due to the simplicity of the movement of the celestial bodies, nothing can shake his conviction that man, the Earth, and the entire universe must be pieces of the planned creation of an intelligent God who wishes only

---

385 See Derham 1754, 425-444.
386 See Derham 1721, 218-246.
387 Ibid., 228-229.
388 For example, Derham argues that Saturn's rings were supposed to retain warmth and light to support the creatures living there, as that planet was supposedly farthest from the Sun at the time. See ibid., 202-213.
389 Ibid., 238.
390 See ibid., 238-246.
391 See Paley 1842, 451-467, 490-491.
392 See ibid., 517-523.

for their happiness: "The marks of design are too strong to be gotten over. Design must have had a designer. This designer must have been a person. That person is GOD."[393]

William Paley represents the pinnacle of *Natural Theology*, as purely materialist explanations of the world would come to dominate the scientific discourse in the 19th century. By invoking these last representatives of physico-theology – the Calvinist evolutionary theorist Asa Gray, or Ernest William Barnes the Bishop of Birmingham – Frank Tipler laments the separation of religion and science.[394] He actually adopts many of Paley and Derham's theses as his own. Indeed, he places himself at the forefront of a revived, even experimental *Natural Theology* by seeking 200 million US dollars to upgrade a particle accelerator, in order to prove the existence of God via the research on elementary particles such as the Higgs boson or the top quark:[395]

> The SSC and the LHC [particle accelerators] are often compared to the cathedrals of the Middle Ages and to the pyramids of ancient Egypt. The cathedrals were built to help the medieval Europeans to find God and the Egyptian kings find their immortality. If I am right, the SSC and the LHC could do both for all humanity.[396]

Proof of a planned creation and intelligent Creator were previously simultaneously regarded as evidence of humankind's positive future development. However, physico-theologians were primarily interested in proving God's existence to counter the atheistic positions of the French Enlightenment philosophers Diderot, d'Holbach, and Helvétius. Relying on the classic design argument, Tipler develops a teleological anthropology of the future, which instrumentalizes the proof of a planned universe for futurological extrapolation. In this theory, the question of God recedes into the background. By categorically excluding the existence of intelligent extraterrestrial beings, Tipler sharpens the design argument to an absolute anthropocentrism, whereas William Derham and other natural theologians had tolerated the idea of "human-like" life existing on other planets. Tipler thus creatively combines these two elements into a supposedly scientific, anthropocentric teleology.

At the end of his second book, Hans Moravec draws a connection, albeit somewhat ponderously, to Tipler and Barrow's futurology, particularly in the Omega Point of "Tielhard de Chardin" [sic!].[397] However, the inconsistency and arbitrariness of Moravec's explanations can be noted in the fact that he explicitly refers to the threat from aliens elsewhere. The existence of such extra-terrestrials would ultimately undermine the entire legitimation of progress in Tipler's anthropocentric teleology.[398]

How is Tipler's overall relationship with religion to be assessed? On the one hand, he invokes the scientific spirit of pure objectivity, and stresses that his physical insights describe the "ultimate reality" that exists independently of all cultural concepts.[399]

---

393   Ibid., 530.
394   See Barrow / Tipler 1986, 85-86, 183-184.
395   See Tipler 1995, 335-336.
396   Ibid., 336. SSC = *Super-Conducting Supercollider*, LHC = *Large Hadron Collider*.
397   See Moravec 1999, 201-202; Moravec 1988, 148-149.
398   See ibid., 101; Tipler 1981; 1991; 1995, 311-312; Tipler / Barrow 1986, 132-134, 577-591.
399   See Tipler 1995, 1, 88, 294-295.

On the other hand, he confirms that his Omega Point Theory agrees with the basic principles common to *all* religions. In his view, all religions actually believe in a resurrection of the dead rather than the immortality of the human soul.[400]

In his understanding of God, Tipler leans explicitly on Christian theologians such as Origen, Thomas Aquinas, George Berkeley, Paul Tillich, and Teilhard de Chardin, and concludes his religious excursion with a personally important quotation from the medieval mystic Juliana of Norwich: "Sin must be, but all shall be well. All shall be well; and all manner of thing shall be well." He concludes that "Mother Julian has nicely summarized the Omega Point theodicy."[401] Tipler thus presents his own approach as the physical appropriation – even as the salvation – of theology.[402]

> The Omega Point Theory allows the key concepts of the Judeo-Christian-Islamic tradition now to be modern physics concepts: theology is nothing but physical cosmology based on the assumption that life as a whole is immortal ... Physics has now absorbed theology; the divorce between science and religion, between reason and emotion, is over.[403]

However, as a whole Tipler's argumentation is ultimately circular. He claims to prove religious statements using physics. However, it is more than clear that Tipler's argumentation – from Protestant theology to Teilhard – is based on religious premises. Tipler offers tautological proof of religion by using a supposedly physical theory, which in turn is based on religious and philosophical assumptions. Even the cosmological perspective of his physical eschatology is robbed of its scientific character by the introduction of the *postulate of eternal life* so central to his argument. Overall, Tipler exploits the seemingly infallible cloak of objective natural science to support his eccentric religious belief in immortality.

6.4 Singularities

> Singularity, The. The Techno-Rapture. A black hole in the Extropian worldview whose gravity is so intense that no light can be shed on what lies beyond it.[404]
> *Godling's Glossary*

The idea of the dawning of a new age of artificial intelligence has gained recognition far beyond the transhumanist milieu, primarily through Ray Kurzweil's book *The Singularity*

---

400 See Tipler 1995, 16-17, 269-304.
401 Ibid., 265. Tipler cites from: *The Revelations of Divine Love of Julian of Norwich*, translated by James Walsh. London 1961, chapter 26. See also Tipler 1995, 4-13, 153-158, 214-216, 264; Tipler 1989, 229-253.
402 See Tipler 1995, XIV-XV, 2-8, 247, 293, 327-328, 339; Barrow / Tipler 1986, 180-181.
403 Tipler 1995, 338.
404 *Godling's Glossary* 1998. Quoted by Sandberg: aleph.se/Trans/Global/Singularity/index.html.

is Near: When Humans Transcend Biology, the subsequent founding of the *Singularity University* in 2008, and numerous films.

Cultural studies scholars have previously attempted to arrange and analyze different approaches to singularity, yet these analyses are often unsubtle and polemical.[405] In 1992 David Porush already described these "cyber-utopoids" as a modern cargo cult expecting imminent salvation through material goods. Diane Proudfoot speaks of techno-supernaturalism in a more general sense.[406] The transhumanists Anders Sandberg and Socrates (from the *Singularity* weblog) list nine and 17 definitions of technological singularity, respectively.[407] The transhumanist activist Eliezer Yudkowsky identifies three types of singularity: 1) accelerating change à la Kurzweil, 2) the event horizon à la Vinge, and finally 3) his own school of "intelligence explosion" (based on Irving Good). He reacts with great annoyance to his contemporaries' inability to perceive these distinctions, and their tendency to instead combine everything into "singularity paste".[408]

Sandberg, Socrates, and Yudkowsky are keen to establish a clear and scientifically precise concept of singularity. Sandberg in particular presents various approaches as models of mathematical probability. However, these experiments must be regarded as normative processes within transhumanism. In fact, singularity's central concepts are extremely diffuse and combine elements of scientific prognosis with religious content. Even a strict separation of the technological from the cosmological understanding of singularity does not seem plausible within the work of post- and transhumanist authors.[409] Alongside Reinhard Heil, I advocate considering each semantic layer individually, in order to elaborate the complex interdependencies between religion and science in this posthumanist utopia.[410]

The idea of singularity encompasses scientific concepts within mathematical function and system theory, geometry, solid-state physics, cosmology, and cybernetics. The last two areas particularly hold special significance for posthumanism. Even when merely scratching at the surface of the history of ideas, it quickly becomes clear that these two areas are closely interwoven. They contain numerous references, especially to Teilhard de Chardin's theological work and his concept of the Omega Point. In mainstream journalism these elements are blurring into a single, mystically charged

---

405 Selmer and Alexander Bringsjord and Paul Bello see the entire singularity theory as a matter of faith without scientific basis. See Bringsjord / Bringsjord / Bello 2012.
406 See Proudfoot 2012, 367-368; Porush 1992. In the 20th century, the Melanesian cargo cults hoped to have their material desires fulfilled by flying deities, whom they later equated with American soldiers.
407 Teilhard de Chardin is also identified as one of these types by Sandberg, without any explanation. See Sandberg 2013b; Socrates 2012.
408 See https://yudkowsky.net/singularity/schools. Nick Bostrom previously identified these three types in a commentary on Vinge's concept in 1998, but Yudkowsky depicts them more clearly. See Bostrom 1998, 399.
409 Bracketing the religious and cosmological elements excludes unpleasant approaches, such as Tipler's physico-theology for example. Singularity would then appear as a consistently used and scientific term, which would be convenient for most transhumanists.
410 See Heil 2010b, 44-46.

prophecy of technology. We will therefore examine the concept of singularity in three steps: The first two sections on cosmological and technological singularity will be followed by a cultural-historical contextualization of the concept itself.

Cosmological Singularity and Black Holes

The term singularity has been widely used in English since the 1980s, as well as being creatively applied in literature and television series for popular audiences. According to the cosmologists Roger Penrose and Stephen Hawking, singularities (in the plural) denote the special conditions of space and time, such as those created by black holes. These are moments when matter or its precursors are concentrated at a single point and space and light become infinitely curved. The beginning of the universe – the Big Bang – was marked by a singularity.[411] The common understanding of singularity usually refers to the fantastic space and time effects of black holes, to which the Penrose-Hawking singularity theorem is applied.[412]

Together with John D. Barrow, Frank Tipler steered the concept of cosmological singularities into philosophical realms encompassing questions of life and humanity's place in the universe.[413] In connection with their thesis of the *Final Anthropic Principle*, the two cosmologists reflect on the initial and final singularity within a closed universe model, i.e. the beginning and the end of the universe, which at this moment has no spatial-temporal extension. Barrow and Tipler already identify analogies with Teilhard de Chardin's work and equate the final singularity with the divine Omega Point. These two approaches can in fact be combined, since according to the *Final Anthropic Principle*, the end of the universe requires a final observer, which for Tipler is identical with God-Omega.[414] In his later works, *Physics of Immortality* (1994) and *Physics of Christianity* (2007), Tipler builds on these considerations and embeds the cosmological singularities in a theological framework, i.e. not only that God is the final goal of the universe, but that God is also its original cause, which was not yet subject to any physical laws.[415]

This image illustrates the temporal dimensions of Tipler's design. The earth's biosphere first begins to expand into space during our present age, in order to save the universe as it is colonized. In a 2013 interview with Socrates from *Singularity Weblog*, Tipler describes the properties of the final cosmological singularity as follows:

---

411   See Hawking / Penrose 1970.
412   The popular reception of the term in literature and television series refers almost exclusively to a cosmological singularity and is vaguely associated here with black holes and their effects: for example, in the novels *Singularity* by William Sleator (1985) and Bill de Smedt (2004), in the graphic novel *Singularity 7* by Ben Templesmith (2004), the Dr. Who radio play *Singularity* (2005) as well as in the television series *Stargate* (season 1, episode 15, *Singularity* of 1997), *Star Trek: Enterprise* (season 2, episode 9, *Singularity* of 2002) and *So Weird* (season 1, episode 11, *Singularity* of 1999). A direct reference to technological singularity is only found in more recent works, such as the television series *Agents of S.H.I.E.L.D.* (Season 3, Episode 18, *The Singularity* of 2016) and, critically, in the low-budget feature film *Singularity* (2017) by Robert Kouba, in which humanity is almost exterminated by an overpowering artificial intelligence. See article Singularity (Engl. Wikipedia).
413   See Barrow / Tipler 1978, 1979, 1981.
414   See Barrow / Tipler 1986, 201-204, 470-471.
415   See Tipler 1995, 139-157; Tipler 2007, 83-100.

The singularity is outside the natural world, it is beyond the natural world, and it is transcendent to the natural world. So, approaching the singularity ... the amount of information, the amount of knowledge is approaching infinity as you are going into the final state. The processing rate is increasing to infinity. So, the total amount of information processing will be infinite.[416]

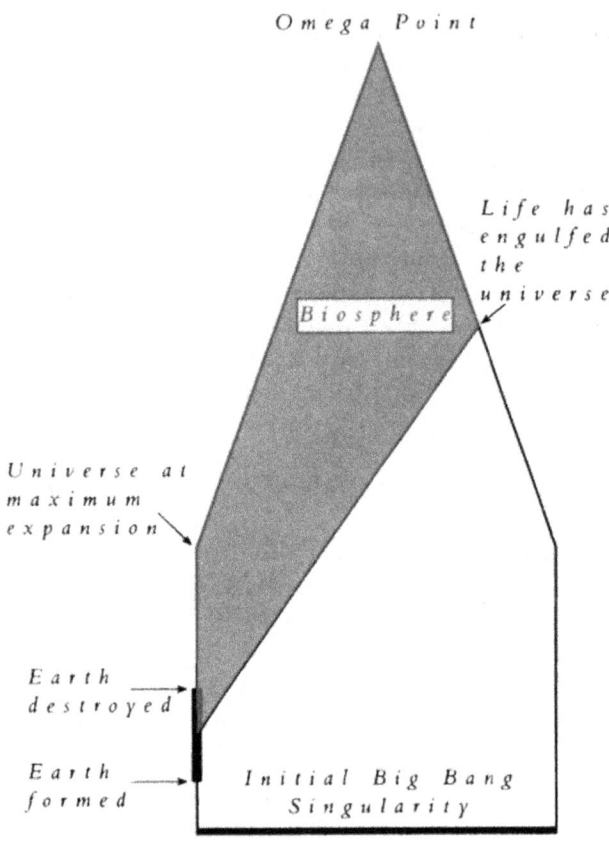

Tipler 1995, Figure IV.9, 145, Penrose diagram of the future of life in the universe

Tipler takes an inclusive approach to the concept of technological singularity propagated by Kurzweil and other thinkers. He considers the technological singularity as merely a philosophical concept, while the cosmological singularity is presented as a proven mathematical theorem. According to Tipler, the technological singularity is only a small event in human history, caused by inevitable movement towards the cosmic singularity.

---

416 Tipler 2013 (video).

> The cosmological singularity is determining, requiring the existence of the computer science singularity. And I agree with various people as Hans Moravec and Ray Kurzweil. And I think the singularity in computer science will occur in this century. I think we are very close. I think we already have the necessary hardware.[417]

When he calls himself a "fundamentalist physicist", it finally becomes obvious that there is not a hint of irony in Tipler's statements. Under the conditions that the universe is closed and that humanity is the only intelligent life form in the cosmos (both of which are mathematically proven, according to Tipler), earthly life forms *must* find a new vehicle:

> Namely, that eventually human meat, rational beings will be replaced by human downloads and our artificial intelligence at least at the human level. I am convinced that's true. I am convinced it must be true because as you are going into the final singularity, necessarily ... life can no longer exist, it has to move on another substrate. And, well, that's just human downloads.[418]

The Technological Singularity

Post- and transhumanists collectively identify the mathematician and cyberneticist John von Neumann as the originator of the concept of technological singularity.[419] His detailed obituary was written by his long-time friend and scientific companion Stanisław Ulam in 1958 and contains a particularly notable passage. I include the entire paragraph here:

> Quite aware that the criteria of value in mathematical work are, to some extent, purely aesthetic, he once expressed an apprehension that the values put on abstract scientific achievement in our present civilization might diminish: "The interests of humanity may change, the present curiosities in science may cease, and entirely different things may occupy the human mind in the future." One conversation centered on the ever accelerating progress of technology and changes in the mode of human life, which gives the appearance of approaching some essential singularity in the history of the race beyond which human affairs, as we know them, could not continue.[420]

The trans- and posthumanists Vernor Vinge, Ray Kurzweil, Nick Bostrom, and Anders Sandberg cite only the last sentence of this passage, leaving no doubt that the computer pioneer John von Neumann could only have meant the emergence of artificial intelligence, which would bring an end to the history. However, if one considers the larger context of von Neumann's biography and Ulam's academic respect for his work, a different interpretation becomes more likely. Indeed, John von Neumann and Stanisław Ulam were involved in the most consequential technological development that human

---

417   Tipler 2013 (video).
418   Tipler 2013 (video).
419   See Vinge 2013, 366; Kurzweil 2005, 10; Kurzweil 2012a, 27-28; Sandberg 2013a, 376; Bostrom 2014, 261 FN 2; Eden et al. 2012b, 4-5.
420   Ulam 1958, 5.

history had produced so far: the construction of the first atomic bombs, "Little Boy" and "Fat Man", which were used in Hiroshima and Nagasaki on August 6 and 9, 1945.

Born in 1903 into a prominent Budapest family, János Neumann was considered one of the best mathematicians of his century. As a young lecturer in Berlin in 1933, he was offered a professorship in mathematics at the Princeton *Institute for Advanced Studies*, which he held until his death in 1957. In addition to his fundamental contributions to mathematical set theory and game theory, von Neumann was concerned with problems of quantum mechanics. After his naturalization as a US citizen (including a change of name to the anglicized John) in 1937, he increasingly focused upon the calculation of fluid mechanics and blast waves, as they were necessary for the optimization of ballistic projectiles and bombs. Based on both this expertise and his familiarity with quantum physics, the physicist Robert Oppenheimer and Vannevar Bush, the initiator of the Manhattan Project, recruited him to the Los Alamos research team in 1943. Rather than being confined to a minor role, von Neumann instead became instrumental in the development of the first atomic bomb's complex ignition mechanism. His calculations proved that detonating the bomb far above the earth's surface would actually cause the greatest destruction. Von Neumann and Oppenheimer were also amongst those scientists included in the military target selection committee that finally determined Hiroshima and Nagasaki as the ultimate targets. Oppenheimer, the project leader, became increasingly critical after the deployment of the second bomb and withdrew completely from Los Alamos at the end of 1945. However, von Neumann and Ulam continued to work, and were involved in the further development of the first hydrogen bomb. This bomb had twenty times the explosive power of the "Little Boy" bomb dropped on Hiroshima.[421] Ulam's description of Neumann's role in the nuclear program occupies considerable space in the obituary, and indeed Neumann seems to have been aware of the importance of his own research:

> Von Neumann strongly believed that the technological revolution initiated by the release of nuclear energy would cause more profound changes in human society, in particular in the development of science, than any technological discovery made in the previous history of the race. In one of the very few instances of talking about his own lucky guesses, he told me that, as a very young man, he believed that nuclear energy would be made available and change the order of human activities during his lifetime![422]

Since no other existing sources by von Neumann suggest a connection between the development of artificial intelligence and technological singularity, we must assume that this anticipated upheaval is more likely related to future nuclear research and its ambivalent consequences for human history. The initiation of the *Doomsday Clock* measuring the risk of nuclear war reflects this ambivalence to this day.[423] The selective use of the term singularity, which notably is only handed down to us by Ulam,

---

421 See ibid., 35-39.
422 Ibid., 39.
423 The founding of the *Bulletin of the Atomic Scientists* in 1947 also initiated the symbolic Doomsday Clock, marking the estimated distance to a possible nuclear war. After the end of the Cold War, it

rather than von Neumann himself, can be read as a metaphorical transfer of the mathematical concept of singularity. Above all else, von Neumann and Ulam were first and foremost mathematicians. Von Neumann defines neither a specific point in time nor any particular quality of this singularity. The end of human history to which he alludes is thus not connoted as a clearly positive or desirable event.

A quarter of a century later, the American mathematician and science fiction author Vernor Vinge explicitly bridges the gap between the cosmological and technological concepts of singularity for the first time, in a one-page article for the technology magazine *Omni* in 1983:[424]

> We will soon create intelligences greater than our own. When this happens, human history will have reached a kind of singularity, an intellectual transition as impenetrable as the knotted space-time at the center of a black hole, and the world will pass far beyond our understanding.[425]

However, Vinge is still not clear as to whether these new intelligences will be generated by genetic engineering or computer technology. He comments disparagingly on any kind of future prophecy: "A favorite game of futurists is to plot technological performance – computer speed, say – against time. Such trend curves climb ever more steeply. Extrapolated 30 or 40 years, they are so high and steep that even the most naive futurist discounts their accuracy."[426] Over the next years, Vinge applied the singularity merely as a running theme in the background of several of his science fiction novels, such as *Marooned in Realtime* (1986).[427]

Vinge's futurological reticence did not last long. At NASA's *Vision 21* symposium in 1993 he confidently announced: "Within thirty years, we will have the technological means to create superhuman intelligence. Shortly after, the human era will be ended."[428] Vinge sketches four ways this technological singularity could appear: first, through computers; second through computer networks that develop consciousness and a superhuman intelligence; third, through human-computer interfaces that make humans superintelligent; or fourth, through the biological improvements of humans. Since the first three possibilities depend heavily on computer hardware, Vinge predicts the arrival of the singularity for the period between 2005 and 2030. He justifies his prediction by referring to the cyberneticist Irving Good's expectation of an "ultra-intelligent machine", as well as the singularity according to Ulam and von Neumann: "Von Neumann even uses the term singularity, though it appears he is thinking of normal progress, not the creation of superhuman intellect."[429] Indeed, he clearly states:

---

was set at 17 minutes to twelve, but in early 2018 it was adjusted to two minutes to twelve due to increasing global tensions between nationalist states.

424   In 2000, Vinge left his teaching position in mathematics at San Diego State University to focus on his writing.
425   Vinge 1983, 10. This article does not yet contain any references to Irving Good and John von Neumann.
426   Ibid.
427   See Raulerson 2013, 3-15.
428   Vinge 1993.
429   Vinge 2013, 366.

"For me, the superhumanity is the essence of the Singularity. Without that we would get a glut of technical riches, never properly absorbed."[430] Here his expectation of salvation is revealed, especially when Vinge emphasizes in a 2011 interview that his personal motivation for formulating the singularity is to understand the universe as meaningful ("making some sense of the universe").[431]

According to Vinge the singularity will revolutionize all previous structures of human life and will instigate enormous changes in a very short period of time. To date, there is only one analogy in the history of evolution: "The rise of humankind. We will be in the Post-Human era. And for all my rampant technological optimism, sometimes I think I'd be more comfortable if I were regarding these transcendental events from one thousand years remove … instead of twenty."[432] Everything that will occur after the singularity is completely unknowable. Vinge therefore turns to the concept of the event horizon, as mentioned in his early article from 1983. In astrophysics observations of black holes are not possible beyond this point.[433]

In Vinge's view, the singularity remains inevitable as long as it is possible in principle to program an artificial intelligence to develop autonomously. In addition to the resultant unemployment for ever-increasing sections of the population, Vinge is also critical of singularity's consequences: "If the Singularity can not be prevented or confined, just how bad could the post-human era be? Well … pretty bad. The physical extinction of the human race is one possibility."[434] Vinge therefore suggests various ways for humans to participate in computer intelligence, which could be realized largely through human-machine interfaces. In light of computers' unquestionable superiority, immortality might offer humans some dignity. A life within computer networks could also overcome the current limits of the self: "What happens when pieces of ego can be copied and merged, when the size of a self-awareness can grow or shrink to fit the nature of the problems under consideration?"[435] In a later essay, Vinge describes this vision as highly probable: "The Digital *Gaia* would be something beyond human intelligence, but nothing like human."[436]

The American AI researcher Eliezer Yudkowsky first sought to transform the ad hoc idea of technological singularity into a far-reaching philosophical concept through the formulation of the *Singularitarian Principles* in 1999. Yudkowsky identifies as an atheist, transhumanist, and cryonics expert, and pleads in his principles for a sharp distinction between the technological singularity and religious concepts. The large and often rambling document contains many ambitious statements on "ultra-technology", globalization, the deification of humans (*apotheosis*), and solidarity, as well as some

---

430 Ibid.
431 Vinge 2011 (video).
432 Vinge 1993; Vinge 2013, 367.
433 Vinge 1993; Vinge 2013, 367.
434 Vinge 1993; Vinge 2013, 369.
435 Vinge 1993; Vinge 2013, 373. Vinge himself is sometimes very critical of technological innovations. He avoids social media to protect his privacy, as he emphasizes in a 2011 interview with Socrates. Notably, the interviewer was surprised at Vinge's insistence that the conversation be conducted over a telephone landline. See Vinge 2011 (video).
436 See Vinge 2008.

minor aspects. *Singularitarians* are in his view "partisans" who consider technological singularity as superhuman intelligence to be a highly desirable goal to work towards.

> The Singularity holds out the possibility of winning the Grand Prize, the true Utopia, the best-of-all-possible-worlds – not just freedom from pain and stress or a sterile round of endless physical pleasures, but the prospect of endless growth for every human being – growth in mind, in intelligence, in strength of personality; life without bound, without end; experiencing everything we've dreamed of experiencing, *becoming* everything we've ever dreamed of *being* ... [437]

In the late 1990s, Yudkowsky was one of the few activists to introduce an element of solidarity into the transhumanist debate. Those who advocate deification must also agree that everyone receives divinity. Those who accept the extermination of humanity by AI must therefore also accept their own extermination. The young Yudkowsky was characterized by a messianic optimism and a belief in the technological solution to all problems of existence: "I'm working to save *everyone*, heal the planet, solve *all* the problems of the world."[438]

The life-giving singularity's promise of universal salvation becomes apparent in Yudkowsky's futurology when he intimately describes the sudden death of his younger brother in 2004: "Even if we make it to and through the Singularity, it will be too late. One of the people I love won't be there. The universe has a surprising ability to stab you through the heart from somewhere you weren't looking."[439]

In the early 2000s, the transhumanist website *Transtopia* still listed Yudkowsky as the founder of one of the two schools of *Singularitarians*. They sought to characterize his work as defined by altruism, collectivism, and paternalism.[440] Yet Yudkowsky is seldom invoked by established transhumanists, apart from the works of Bostrom and Sandberg. However, he remains part of the scientific debate on robot ethics and AI development.[441]

How does Ray Kurzweil, currently the most influential posthumanist, fit into this debate? Vernor Vinge legitimizes his own prognosis tautologically: "But if the technological singularity can happen, it will."[442] Frank Tipler justifies technology's future development from the perspective of a cosmological teleology. For Yudkowsky, singularity appears as a given fact. But Ray Kurzweil and Hans Moravec choose a different path, one that is apparently oriented towards more verifiable criteria. Both thinkers extrapolate future technological progress by observing previous trends, and

---

437 Yudkowsky 2000a.
438 Yudkowsky 2000b. Despite identical bibliographic references, the two text versions (2000a/2000b) of the *Singularitarian Principles* differ considerably.
439 Eliezer Yudkowsky, entry about his brother Yehuda who died in 2004. https://yudkowsky.net/other/yehuda.
440 The site was active from 2000 to about 2010 and later transferred its content to euvolution.com, where a mixture of transhumanism, cryonics, ufology, and eugenics can be found. Search for *Transtopia, FAQ, Singularitarian* on the Internet archive (web.archive.org).
441 Yudkowsky is missing from relevant text collections such as the *Transhumanist Reader* (More / Vita-More 2013).
442 Vinge 1993; Vinge 2013, 368.

Kurzweil alone introduces the concept of singularity in his more recent publications from 2005.[443] It would therefore be prudent to review the development of these forecasts over the past three decades.

If information processing becomes the benchmark for measuring life's perfection, then the past and future will also be interpreted according to this paradigm. Moravec and Kurzweil dedicate large portions of their publications to presenting data on the growth of computers' processing and storage capacities, in addition to detailed questions regarding the possibility of artificial intelligence.[444] Both authors attached their hopes for an exponentially accelerated further development and distribution of computers and robots to a quantified law of progress: *Moore's Law*.[445] The assumption that computer development constantly accelerates can be traced to Intel co-founder Gordon Moore, who in the mid-1960s claimed that the size of an integrated circuit halves every 24 months, in other words, it becomes twice as powerful. This prediction, now known as *Moore's Law*, implies an indefinite exponential increase in computer performance. The claim therefore persists that mass-market computers will soon have the same capacity as the human brain.[446]

In their earlier works, Hans Moravec and Ray Kurzweil describe the accelerating progress of information technology, especially in comparison with the evolutionary history of life.[447] As they aged, Moravec and Marvin Minsky both became increasingly reserved and also sometimes more skeptical about the imminent realization of artificial intelligence on a human level. In 1970 Minsky predicted that a computer with the intelligence of an average adult would be constructed within three to eight years. A few months later, he expected that computers with genius levels of intelligence would already exist. In an interview with his student Ray Kurzweil in 2010, Marvin Minsky remained optimistic and expected the singularity to arrive within "lifetimes". Three years later, he coolly stated that a belief in the singularity had created jobs for many young people, but that he himself had hardly observed any progress in AI research over the last ten to 15 years. He then began to predict artificial intelligence equal to humans would emerge around the year 2050.[448]

In his monograph of 1988, Moravec also assumed that universal household robots, from cooks to cleaning assistants, would help make our work easier in "the shortest possible time".[449] In *Robot*, his second book from 1999, he pays much closer attention to the problems with developing artificial intelligence and robots. In particular, he focuses on the discrepancy between the superior mathematical-abstract abilities of a computer and the cognitive and motor shortcomings of computer-assisted robots. He continues to adhere to the theory of strong acceleration, but now estimates the emergence of

---

443   See Moravec 1999, 95-110; Kurzweil 1999a, 189-252.
444   See Moravec 1988, 37-51, 60-75; Moravec 1999, 51-64; Kurzweil 1999a, 103-116, 137-142; Kurzweil 2005, 14-110.
445   See Moravec 1988, 68; Kurzweil 1999a, 13-25.
446   See Kurzweil 1999a, 17-39, 103-105, 204, 220-222.
447   Moravec 1999, 110. See also Moravec / Shieber 1997, 1001.
448   See Roszak 1994, 122-123; Minsky 2010 (video); Minsky 2013 (video).
449   See Moravec 1988, 22-25.

superhuman AI in the year 2050.[450] At that point the posthuman intelligences of the future could discover new worlds far beyond our biological, cognitive, and operational limitations. Furthermore, due to the tremendous speed of their mental processing, they could accomplish the mental achievements of an entire human life in only a few seconds:[451] "Someday our progeny may exploit these bodies [the planets] to build machines with a million million million million million million (that's 10^{30}) times the power of a human mind."[452]

Unlike the other posthumanist theorists and transhumanist activists, Ray Kurzweil has not become more cautious or restrained in his statements over the last two decades. His three key books *The Age of Intelligent Machines* (1990), *The Age of Spiritual Machines* (1999), and *The Singularity is Near* (2005) offer a dramatic choreography with a steady increase in futuristic statements. As his trilogy concludes, however, he crosses the boundary between technical prophecy and a spiritual philosophy that is more akin to Christianity or New Age beliefs.[453]

Incidentally, this process parallels the numerous failed predictions of the Christian apocalypse. In terms of the utopia of immortalization anticipated by post- and transhumanists, many of whom have now reached retirement age, there have in fact been no significant technical advances in the past 30 years. Many thinkers in this movement have become increasingly critical of their own earlier euphoria, while serious researchers now consistently reject these technological visions. One common strategy in religious prophecy is to offset the disappointment of failed predictions with ever-increasing promises for the next occurrence, which is exactly what Kurzweil does.

As early as 1999, Kurzweil planned what he called the *Law of Accelerating Returns*. This was intended to replace *Moore's Law* around 2020 and establish an even higher acceleration rate amongst the future generations of self-designing machines. At this point not only would growth continue exponentially, but in fact the exponent itself would grow exponentially. Therefore – according to Kurzweil's 1999 book – around the year 2023 affordable PCs with the computing power of the human brain would become available, while in 2030 they would contain the mental power of an entire village. By 2029, about 99% of the thinking power on our planet would be provided by computers. According to Kurzweil, hardly anyone will continue to work in industrial production, agriculture, or the transportation industry.[454] He continually legitimizes his predictions by returning to his earlier publications. He congratulates himself that almost all of his previous predictions have come true. To be precise he considered 86% to be "correct" or "largely correct". However, the choice of examples used for this calculation remains highly selective.[455]

---

450   See ibid., 13-22; Moravec 1999, VIII, 15-51; Moravec 2009.
451   See Moravec 1988, 114-116; Moravec 1999, 207-208.
452   Moravec 1988, 74.
453   He already formulated the core idea of a technological turning point in 1999. See Kurzweil 1999a, 36.
454   See ibid., 17-39, 103-105, 204, 220-222; Kurzweil 2005, 24-29.
455   See Kurzweil 2010, 5. Rothblatt adopts this self-assessment. See Rothblatt 2014, 44-53.

Kurzweil identifies five stages in the history of evolution leading up to the realization of the singularity: 1. the origin of matter; 2. the origin of life; 3. the origin of brains/mind; 4. the origin of technology; and 5. the fusion of human and machine intelligence. In a sixth phase, superhuman intelligence will begin to colonize the entire universe.[456] The singularity, which, like the Big Bang, entails creating the entire cosmos anew, marks the absolute climax of this technological prophecy.

Kurzweil only defines this concept briefly: "It's a future period during which the pace of technological change will be so rapid, its impact so deep, that human life will be irreversibly transformed ... "[457] A more precise description is not possible for humans: "So how do we contemplate the Singularity? As with the sun, it's hard to look at directly; it's better to squint at it out of the corner of our eyes."[458] Diane Proudfoot points out that this metaphor echoes the doctrine of God's indescribability, which was common in Christian mysticism. Thus, Anselm of Canterbury proclaims in the 11th century: "I cannot look directly into [the light in which God dwells], it is too great for me ... it is too bright ... the eye of my soul cannot bear to turn towards it for too long."[459]

Kurzweil accentuates the prophetic meaning of his statements with the exact date of the singularity (published in oversized font in the original):

> I set the date for the Singularity — representing a profound and disruptive transformation in human capability — as 2045. The nonbiological intelligence created in that year will be one billion times more powerful than all human intelligence today.[460]

While Kurzweil's criteria for constituting the realization of the singularity remain rather vague, the promised prospects are boundless. In the opening lines of his book Kurzweil announces that all the magic described in the *Harry Potter* novels will soon be technologically available.[461]

> The Singularity will allow us to transcend these limitations of our biological bodies and brains. We will gain power over our fates. Our mortality will be in our own hands. We will be able to live as long as we want (a subtly different statement from saying we will live forever). We will fully understand human thinking and will vastly extend and expand its reach. By the end of this century, the nonbiological portion of our intelligence will be trillions of trillions of times more powerful than unaided human intelligence.[462]

---

456   Kurzweil 2005, 14-21, 35-111.
457   Kurzweil 2005, 7.
458   Kurzweil 2005, 371.
459   Anselm of Canterbury, *The Prayers and Meditations of St Anselm*, chap. 16, 257. Cited in Proudfoot 2012, 368.
460   Kurzweil 2005, 136 (largely printed in the original). At the memorial service for Marvin Minsky, Kurzweil holds out the prospect that the deceased could still be revived in 2045. See Kurzweil 2016 (video).
461   Kurzweil 2005, 4.
462   Ibid., 9.

Kurzweil's book *The Singularity is Near* includes new reflections on the cosmological significance of earthly events and the ultimate goal of life in the universe. He also adopts Vinge's analogy of the event horizon of black holes: "Just as we find it hard to see beyond the event horizon of a black hole, we also find it difficult to see beyond the event horizon of the historical Singularity."[463]

Vernor Vinge and Ray Kurzweil use their understanding of singularity to canonically define its various qualitative elements:

- John von Neumann and Irving Good are the designated authors.
- The singularity entails a radical and rapid change.
- It is a consequence of the evolutionary development of life.
- It is determinate, it will occur in any case.
- It is connected with the development of superintelligent computer systems.
- Humanity can participate via merging with computers.
- Predictions regarding what happens after the moment of the singularity are not possible.
- The singularity enables human immortality.
- The cosmological and technological concepts of singularity complement one another.

In this context, Frank Tipler's and Eliezer Yudkowsky's designs offer the extreme opposite poles of the techno-prophetic spectrum: Tipler at the Christian end, Yudkowsky at the atheistic – with Vinge and Kurzweil oscillating somewhere in between. Surprisingly, the exact characteristics marking the singularity's arrival remain extremely vague in the work of each of these authors. One must ask what defines this "super" or "ultra" intelligence. Is it when the first machine is proven to be smarter than a human being? If so, then AI can already play go, chess, and complete a quiz on general knowledge more successfully than any human on this planet. Or does it refer to the moment when a machine develops autonomously? Or when it is no longer possible for humans (which ones?) to understand what it does? Or is it the moment of the virtual immortalization of all human beings?[464]

The success of the singularity idea is due above all to the broad futurological network of current and hopeful entrepreneurs, activists, and bloggers. The *Singularity Institute for Artificial Intelligence* (today MIRI), founded in 2000, propelled the singularity debate through its *Singularity Summits*.[465] The Californian *Singularity University* (SU) has received worldwide attention since its launch in 2008, and has been generously sponsored by companies like Google, Nokia, and SAP. However, SU is not a conventional university with fixed courses of study, qualifying degrees, and research facilities. Strictly speaking, it is not a university at all, and in fact has nothing to do with

---

463   Ibid., 487.
464   Sandberg also bemoans the lack of clarity (2013a, 378).
465   See chapter 4.5.

the singularity.[466] The project, initiated by Ray Kurzweil and the entrepreneur Peter Diamandis, initially offered several weeks-long workshops to support the development of start-ups. The young entrepreneurs were supposed to develop business ideas that could decisively change the lives of at least one billion people within ten years (the program is now called *SU Labs*). Here, Kurzweil's central ideas are implemented entrepreneurially under the motto: "Exponential technology will disrupt all industries!" The ambassadors of this exponential dream include IT magnates such as Peter Thiel, and Google founders Larry Page and Sergey Brin. Since Kurzweil's appointment at Google as Director of Engineering (notably one amongst many) in December 2012, the company's acquisitions in robotics, clouds, neuro-interfaces, AI, quantum computing, and biotechnologies – all technologies required to achieve Kurzweil's singularity – have increased notably.[467]

In 2012 the university became a for-profit benefit corporation (as part of the Singularity Education Group), which includes both profit and non-profit aspects. Its scope of activity has been massively expanded to include offerings such as: Global Solutions, Executives, Innovation Partnerships, and Exponential Regional Partnerships. These address different target groups such as business leaders, start-up founders, and even idealists trying to save the world, all of whom want to develop "exponential" and "disruptive" strategies for their markets. Under the banner of the *Singularity University*, summits are now organized worldwide to identify future markets and technologies, as well as for networking purposes. In parallel, the media platform of the Singularity Hub was initiated to report on scientific breakthroughs.[468]

The Russian Internet billionaire Dmitry Itskov's *2045 Initiative* is also strongly influenced by Kurzweil's futurology. Its research program, launched in 2011, seeks to transfer a human personality into computer memory by the year of singularity. Itskov has named the intermediate stages avatars A-D, in reference to Hindu mythology.[469]

The most important communication platform for the singularity debate was established in October 2009 by the journalist Nikola Danaylov, also known by the alias Socrates. While many contributions to his *Singularity Weblog* were initially euphoric about the question of when the singularity would arrive, a critical discourse has since developed. It focuses on offering extensive interviews with visionaries and leaders from the tech industries.[470]

The strength of the conviction that the singularity will arrive to solve all humankind's problems parallels the weakness of reflections regarding what that singularity actually is. The debate about the singularity within transhumanism remains diverse and fiercely

---

466 See https://su.org. It is not formally registered as a university. See Socrates' early criticism in *The Emperor has no Clothes* (video, 2015).
467 See Wagner 2015, 63-67; Christoph Keese (*Executive Vice President* of Springer AG) in an interview with Thomas Wagner. See Wagner 2015, 75-76; https://su.org.
468 See https://singularityhub.com.
469 See Wagner 2015, 77-94. In addition to the well-known transhumanists, Itskov has included religious representatives from Buddhism, Christian Orthodoxy, and Hindu traditions. See gf2045.com/speakers.
470 See www.singularityweblog.com.

contested.[471] One point of particular criticism is the establishment of a mystical wall (singularity as event horizon), behind which it is impossible to look.[472] Anders Sandberg, Max More, and the quantum physicist Michael Nielsen argue that the singularity is constructed mathematically by Vinge and Kurzweil, while the social and economic conditions for its creation are hardly considered.[473] However, the sharpest criticism of transhumanism is directed at the concept's mangled mixture of religious prophecy and scientific prognostics. Others argue that the idea of singularity is "crypto-mystical" and "pseudo-religious" (according to science fiction author Damien Broderick); the term should be avoided at all costs because of the "unholy alliance of techno-utopias with religious-eschatological elements" (Nick Bostrom); it seems like an orgiastic mix of technological utopias with Christian apocalypticism (Max More):[474]

> Many discussions just close with, "But we cannot predict anything about the post singularity world!" ending all further inquiry just as Christians and other religious believers do with, "It is the Will of God." And it is all too easy to give the Transcension eschatological overtones, seeing it as Destiny. This also promotes a feeling of helplessness in many, who see it as all-powerful and inevitable.[475]

It is understandable that many advocates of posthumanism remain skeptical of Kurzweil's theses. For one thing, Kurzweil did not yet play ever a role within the transhumanist movement before about 2000. Yet, in a way, he later dethroned the transhumanist establishment. On the other hand, most Extropians and transhumanists are very individualistic and anti-authoritarian.[476] A charismatic leader with far-reaching visions naturally encounters resistance here, as it immediately suggests a hostile takeover.

However, one must also ask what would have become of transhumanism without its "university" and the tremendous popularization of the concept of singularity. In 2010 I wrote an obituary of transhumanism titled *"Much Ado about Nothing – or: Transhumanism as a phenomenon of the turn of the millennium?"* Conferences had been discontinued, the Extropy Institute was dissolved in 2006, and the hoped-for technical breakthroughs had failed to materialize. Without Kurzweil or the hype about the singularity and his person – the *Transcendent Man* – transhumanism would likely lie fallow and abandoned today.

---

471 Hardly any authors question the connection between the singularity, superhuman intelligence and the possibility of uploading minds. See Heil 2010b, 44; More / Vita-More 2013, 395-418; Broderick 2013; Brin 2013. Outside of transhumanism, there exists very extensive criticism of Kurzweil's assumptions and predictions, which attack above all his calculations of progress and the poorly defined concept of intelligence. See the summary in Proudfoot 2012, 373.
472 Nielsen 2013, 410; Hanson 2013, 406.
473 See Sandberg 2013b, 411-416; Nielsen 2013, 409-411; More 2013a, 407-408.
474 See Broderick 2013, 398; More 2013a, 407; Bostrom 2014, 2. In an early comment Bostrom still considered the singularity as one of the more likely scenarios. See Bostrom 1998.
475 Broderick 2013, 398.
476 See Yudkowsky 2000a.

The Law of Progress and the *Endless Frontier*

How can one analyze a temporal concept like the singularity? Is it even a technological fact based on legitimate calculations? Many in the technophile scene have their doubts. Social, psychological, and cultural factors play a central role in the proclamation of the history of salvation. Nick Bostrom acknowledges that since the 1940s, the prognoses for the realization of artificial intelligence have slid backwards year after year, usually remaining about twenty years away: "Two decades is a sweet spot for prognosticators of radical change: near enough to be attention-grabbing and relevant, yet far enough to make it possible to suppose that a string of breakthroughs, currently only vaguely imaginable, might by then have occurred."[477]

At the beginning of the 1990s, MIT professor Pattie Maes noticed that most of her male colleagues were fascinated by the idea of soon being able to upload their brains into computer memory, thus overcoming death. Indeed, they believed that the advent of the first superhuman intelligence would immediately solve the problem of immortality – if only one could survive until this decisive moment. In 1993 Maes spoke about her systematized observations on her colleagues' predictions at the *Ars Electronica* meeting in Linz (Austria), in a presentation titled "Why Immortality is a Dead Idea". Astonishingly, what she found was that almost all futurists predicted the arrival of immortality within their expected lifetimes. No matter when the predictions were made or how old the actors were, the anticipated salvation would conveniently arrive around age 70.[478]

Stuart Armstrong and Kaj Sotala from MIRI have studied the systematics of AI prediction with scientific precision. They analyzed 257 temporal predictions for the arrival of a universal AI (the scope of the question was broader than in Pattie Maes' work, which only focused on predictions of AI in terms of immortality). Armstrong and Sotala's research found significant uncertainty in predictions about AI. This concerns both prediction methods (including apparent regularities, philosophical arguments, perceived status of the expert) and targets, which ranged from as little as six to more than 75 years. Particularly enlightening was the result that estimates by AI experts had exactly the same variance as those of non-experts (journalists, publicists, or prognosticators from outside the field). In both groups, the majority target a period 15 to 20 years in the future (which confirms Bostrom's impression). Researchers can thus benefit from their own predictions, receiving research funding or appreciation as renowned experts.[479]

If a revolutionary event is generally expected to occur in about two decades, regardless of when or by whom this prognosis was made, then it becomes important to consider the social dynamics and legitimacy of futurology more closely. What elements make up the singularity as a temporal concept? Firstly, it is justified by laws of progress

---

477 Bostrom 2014, 4.
478 Kevin Kelly, the former editor of *Wired*, had even half-jokingly designed the Maes-Garreau Law deliberately to reflect this. See Brooks 2002, 206; Garreau 2005, 180, 338 FN 180; https://kk.org/thetechnium/the-maesgarreau.
479 See Armstrong / Sotala 2012, 3-4, 13-19.

and acceleration. The singularity also obviously constructs a threshold or boundary – which echoes the idea of the frontier that is so present in American cultural history (including its adaptations in the science fiction genre). As Armstrong and Sotala explain, the status of being a futurologist often serves to legitimize the predictions made. This "charisma of an eschatological prophet", as the sociologist Max Weber would put it, needs to be examined in greater detail.

Not all post- and transhumanists justify the appearance of the singularity – or of AI generally – by revelations or prophecies; they tend to refer to a mathematical theory of progress (e.g. *Moore's Law*). The assumption that progress is subject to a particular law rather than random chance is often attributed to the English philosopher Francis Bacon (1561-1626).[480] However, a general doctrine of progress was actually formulated during the Late Enlightenment through positivism. On the one hand, this philosophy considers scientific and technological developments to be bound by the law of progress. Yet on the other, it also identifies this progress as inherently linked to that of morality and politics. Within this framework, history – like the history of religious salvation before it – was understood as the universal history of all humanity.[481] On the threshold of the 18th century the French philosophers Fontenelle and Abbé de Saint Pierre first devised the general doctrine of progress. Fontenelle believed that progress was necessary and guaranteed, since following generations would always benefit from the knowledge and mistakes of their predecessors. Abbé de Saint-Pierre, in his vision of social and moral advancement, combined the progress of knowledge with the idea of increasing human happiness.[482]

In 1795 the French philosopher Antoine Marquis de Condorcet published his *Esquisse d'un Tableau historique des progrès de l'esprit humain*.[483] This significantly impacted the English utilitarians, for whom the progress of the human race and the individual was attributed to the law of nature. History – as David Hume and Adam Ferguson agreed – was now to be pursued as a branch of mathematics. It would investigate the causal chain of historical progress, which Turgot and Auguste Comte conceived of mechanistically, in order to better shape the future.[484] At the same time, individual actions became interpreted as part of a larger historical process. A view became widespread that the progress of past ages not only ensured future progress but would also gradually accelerate. As Edward Gibbon predicted in his *History of the Decline and Fall of the Roman Empire*, it would be "infinitely slow in the beginning, and increasing by degrees with redoubled velocity".[485] According to Francis Bacon, Adam Smith, Immanuel Kant, and many other thinkers of that time, the fact of accelerating progress was undeniable for

---

480 See Spadafora 1990, 21-22.
481 In contrast to earlier speculative philosophy, Bacon espoused the need for systematic and empirical research. However, he did not derive a general doctrine of progress itself. See Baillie 1950, 104; Ekirch 1944, 12, 106-107; Klein 1986, 251-252.
482 See Bury 1955, 98-143.
483 The English translation *Outlines for a Historical Picture of the Progress of the Human Mind* followed as early as 1796.
484 See Condorcet 1970; Bury 1955, 202-216; Ekirch 1944, 14-16; Rohbeck 1987, 35-36.
485 Gibbon 1925, 169. See Spadafora 1990, 224.

technical and scientific fields. In this way, they deduced the law of progress from both the observation of the past and their hopes for the future.

The inclusion of the utopian perspective as legitimation for the incessant acceleration of progress is a characteristic feature of every such ideology. 200 years before Kurzweil, the assumption that progress would accelerate enormously in the future already served two crucial purposes. Not only were benefits expected to materialize during one's lifetime, but also everyone who was fully committed to the process could count on taking part. A double motivation to believe and support therefore surrounds today's expectations of the singularity just as it did Enlightenment utopias.[486] The idea of ever-increasing acceleration is also due to another cultural source. The German scholar of religion Ernst Benz points out that such incessant acceleration was a characteristic of Christian salvation history. The discovery and Christianization of America was also shaped by these eschatological expectations. Columbus – convinced of the approaching end of the world – saw India (i.e. America) as Satan's last empire to be proselytized. According to Benz, the fundamental idea of accelerating progress is contextualized by the subjective expectation of salvation – that ultimate Christian goal. This is further nourished by New Testament reports and the visions recorded in the Book of Revelation or by the apostle Stephen. This longing for acceleration is particularly associated with the American theory of progress, which has often understood the unfolding of history as part of God's plan for the coming of the promised land.[487]

In addition to this idea of increasing acceleration, another crucial allusion to American cultural history is found in the understanding of the singularity as the last frontier. Since Puritans settled Massachusetts in the 17th century, the frontier has marked the border of the civilized and moral world against the wilderness, represented by the disordered chaos of the indigenous tribes of North America. The Christian-colonial sense of missionary purpose was further reinforced in the 1840s, when expansionist tendencies in American politics (particularly the annexation of Texas) were merged with the project of spreading freedom and democracy. They believed it be the manifest destiny of God's chosen American people to sow progress, civilization and freedom in the wild and untamed vastness of the continent.[488]

After the geographical frontier disintegrated with the settlement of the West and the extermination of most indigenous peoples, the frontier's metaphorical significance grew in other areas of society, especially science. Francis Bacon had already portrayed the researcher as a pioneer who ventured into undiscovered worlds. However, it was Vannevar Bush, the scientific advisor to President Franklin D. Roosevelt, who immortalized the metaphor for American academia in 1945 with his report *Science – the Endless Frontier*. In this document, Bush proposes guidelines for promoting science in the United States, which led, among other things, to the establishment of the *National Science Foundation*.

---

486   See Koselleck 1975, 401-403; Spadafora 1990, 381-383; Rohbeck 1987, 55-57; Bultmann 1957, 63-73.
487   See Benz 1977, 18-21.
488   See Torr 2002, 69-77; Kroker / Kroker 1996, 84-85.

It has been basic United States policy that Government should foster the opening of new frontiers. It opened the seas to clipper ships and furnished land for pioneers. Although these frontiers have more or less disappeared, the frontier of science remains. It is in keeping with the American tradition – one which has made the United States great – that new frontiers shall be made accessible for development by all American citizens.[489]

From John F. Kennedy to George W. Bush and Barack Obama, the metaphor of the intellectual frontier has continued to play an important role in American scientific policy.[490]

As conceptualized by Vinge, Yudkowsky, and Kurzweil, the singularity is based on this important metaphor of the *endless frontier*. The singularity in the sense of an event horizon of black holes remains impenetrable and insurmountable for humans. But for artificial intelligence, the singularity would be the beginning of an unlimited expansion into the universe, in which humans are also allowed to participate.

As already indicated, this perception of singularity as the last boundary to be overcome has been popularized by numerous adaptations in science fiction stories and films. This genre establishes the connection between the spatial and the scientific metaphors – i.e. human civilization finally surpasses the last frontier of human knowledge as it moves into space. One particular catalyst for such ideas was the scientific work of the Princeton physicist Gerard O'Neill (1927-1992), who from the 1970s onwards presented numerous technical designs for colonizing space, the *High Frontier*.[491]

In the fifth *Star Trek* movie, *The Final Frontier* (1989), Captain Kirk is forced to overcome the "Great Barrier" in the center of the Milky Way on his spaceship, in order to seek God on a mythical planet. The first two *Star Trek* television series (1966-1969, 1987-1994) always prefaced their opening credits with the magic words: "Space, the final frontier." Less fantastically, in *The Black Hole* (1979) Maximilian Schell, playing the brilliant but unscrupulous scientist Dr. Hans Reinhardt, tried to convince a stranded spaceship crew that the ultimate truth, God, and eternal life in a world beyond physical laws waiting for them on the other side of a black hole. The scientist then transforms the recalcitrant members of his own crew into mindless cyborgs. At the end of the film, the surviving heroes actually fly through a Dante-inspired, hellish inferno and then glide behind an angel into a paradise flooded with light.[492] In the 20th century, Western heroes thus seamlessly transform into space heroes. The overcoming of the *final frontier* – the singularity of black holes – becomes the heroic enterprise of white men, whether these come equipped with heterogeneous accents like a fist-swinging macho (James Tiberius Kirk) or as possessed geniuses (Max Reinhardt).[493]

---

489 Vannevar Bush (1945): *Science – the Endless Frontier*, 6. Cited in Ceccarelli 2013, 46. See Zachary 1997, 218-239.
490 See Ceccarelli 2013, 29-155.
491 See Kapell 2016, 168-208.
492 See Shatner 1989; Nelson 1979; Kapell 2016, 139-167.
493 See Kapell 2016, 139-145.

There is also no question that the temporal aspect of the singularity is influenced by the Christian end of days. The overcoming of old age, illness and death corresponds to the Christian expectation of salvation (especially in Tipler's vision of a resurrection of the dead). However, the essential analogy to the Christian apocalypse remains ambiguous: The singularity is neither the result of a continuous and positive development of progress nor of total annihilation. Like the Christian history of salvation, the concept connects the downfall of human beings with the certainty of a post-singular promise: death followed by resurrection.

Christian and singularity prophecies share another important structural feature: that signs reveal the imminence of this end. The Revelation of John lists many apocalyptic elements (prophecies, destructions, sacrifices, testimonies) that occur before the final battle against Satan and the Last Judgment (Rev 4-20). In his three futuristic books, Kurzweil in particular develops an increasingly precise description of milestones that will precede the singularity, including an evaluation of his own earlier predictions.

Unlike in Vinge and Kurzweil's version of the singularity, Christian writings do in fact provide a precise description of the post-apocalyptic period: The New Jerusalem is described in great detail (Rev 21-22). In the Christian and Jewish traditions, salvation is dependent on God's judgment of one's moral conduct. According to all posthumanist authors, the singularity makes immortality available to every living human being (as well as to frozen cryonauts). This idea of universal salvation for all human beings is only found explicitly amidst the Unitarian Universalists, who in their 1803 Winchester Profession proclaimed that the one Holy Spirit of Grace " ... will finally restore the whole family of mankind to holiness and happiness."[494] The fact that Kurzweil grew up a Unitarian should not be overestimated at this point, as other advocates of singularity reach the same conclusion.

One final relevant aspect for this analysis lies in the role of the heralds of the singularity. Here Ray Kurzweil stands out, both in terms of his claims and the colorfulness of his autobiographical self-representation. Although he can reflect on a number of inventions and awards accomplished during the 1970s and 1980s, he has not yet been able to utilize the Internet and digitalization to achieve any technological breakthroughs. Naturally, the question then arises as to why Kurzweil in particular is called upon to praise singularity and system-changing technologies when he himself apparently has been largely unable to benefit at all from those trends. For him, the construction of a charismatic genius was even more important.

While in kindergarten Kurzweil was already aware of his own destiny: "At the age of five, I had the idea that I would become an inventor. I had the notion that inventions could change the world."[495] He built his first robots at the age of eight. He believes not only that he foresaw technological innovations, but in his 1990 book *The Age of Spiritual Machines* he also claims to have predicted the demise of the Soviet Union (1990/91) due to decentralized communication networks.[496] The documentary film *Transcendent Man*.

---

494   Unitarian Winchester Profession (https://uudb.org/articles/winchester.html).
495   See Kurzweil 2005, 1.
496   See Kurzweil 2010, 5, 127; Kurzweil 1990, 446-447.

The Life and Ideas of Ray Kurzweil from 2009 is a brilliant example of modern hagiography: a "legend of saints". In it, Kurzweil is accompanied by the film crew on his worldwide lectures. His followers, such as actor William Shatner, singer Stevie Wonder or former Secretary of State Colin Powell, praise him hyperbolically on camera. One immediately notices Kurzweil's trauma at losing his father, as well as his obsession with reaching the age of singularity through taking 150 vitamin pills daily. Apart from the mantra that the singularity is near and will change everything, the film does not contain much substance, and actually offers no in-depth discussion of the concept.[497] The films *The Singularity* (2012) by Doug Wolens and the film *The Singularity is Near* (2010), produced by Kurzweil himself, did not focus on the figure of Kurzweil. However, they were able to further popularize this futuristic scenario. The continual acceleration that Kurzweil promotes in his three futurological monographs offers a recognizable parallel to religious prophecy. This phenomenon is uncannily familiar in the history of religion, especially regarding the lack of fulfilled predictions. This feature is particularly striking in Kurzweil's work, since all other post- and transhumanist thinkers of recent decades relativize or tone down their predictions, or else broaden their temporal horizons. One might even be tempted to suggest a new *Law of Increasing Disappointment*, whereby the only things growing exponentially in transhumanism are the predictions themselves.

As a prophetic figure, Kurzweil also claims a special position: Vannevar Bush declared the endless frontier of the sciences in 1945. Kurzweil proclaims the end of this period of searching for knowledge will occur precisely one century later in the year 2045. He thus situates himself as the last prophet of the end times, the seal of the prophets. No further advances in prophecy could surpass Kurzweil's visions. When the singularity arrives, humankind's time will be finished, and the fate of the universe will be decided.

In the movies *Terminator* (1984) and the *Matrix* trilogy (1999-2003), a powerful artificial intelligence seeks to exterminate or enslave the (last) humans. Similarly, in marked contrast to the naive futurologies of Kurzweil and the transhumanists, postsingularity science fiction predominantly follows the tradition of dystopian cyberpunk literature.[498] Elaine Graham notes that more recent science fiction is increasingly blatant in dissolving the boundary between religion and science. The secular and the sacred; the human being and God; faith and knowledge; these all appear increasingly less as polar opposites, but rather now merge and blur in a post-secular era.[499] Dystopian visions no longer propagate the overcoming of a religious superstition by a rationalist techno-culture, but rather now celebrate the fusion of these two spheres.

For example, in Rudy Rucker's novel *Postsingular* (2007), a Christian fundamentalist US president seeks to transform the entire Earth into a *virtual earth (Vearth)* with the help of a computer scientist using nano-robots. He sees this transformation as the realization of biblical prophecy via restoration of the Garden of Eden, where suffering, war, and death are banished, and life is completely coordinated. Rucker reveals that this desire stems from trauma experienced by the computer scientist during his youth, when

---

497   See Wagner 2015, 100; Ptolemy 2009.
498   Joshua Raulerson has presented a detailed analysis of this. See Raulerson 2013, 124-125; Cameron 1984; Wachowsky / Wachowsky 1984.
499   See Graham 2015, 362.

he lost his friend in an accident. In *Postsingular*, the interests of Christian and cybernetic fundamentalism overlap in their hatred of both women and creation in general.[500]

It seems obvious that the prophecy of singularity is strongly influenced by cultural ideas. The assumption of laws of progress, as well as the steady acceleration of progress claiming universal validity for the entire history of humankind, can all be traced back to an Enlightenment striving for perfection. But what is new in the singularity is the idea introduced by Vinge and Kurzweil of an absolute and impenetrable limit to this progress: the singularity as the *last frontier*. The term repeats semantics from the physics of black holes, as well as their popularized representations in literature and film. Even more astonishing is that the concept of singularity allows a religious teleology to creep into post- and transhumanism, which 15 years ago was dismissed as exotic. This occurs first and foremost structurally, as the entire history of earthly life heads towards a moment of salvation. In concrete terms, this happened when Ray Kurzweil bluntly adopted Frank Tipler's notion of the complete colonization of the universe, culminating in the realization of God. In the following three chapters, which consider the central consequences of the singularity, this boundary between the religious and the scientific will become increasingly blurred. Since many post- and transhumanists pursue these goals (superintelligence, immortality, and merging into a global brain) without being explicit followers of the singularity, this aspect will be addressed separately.

6.5 Immortality

Posthuman and Immortal

Tipler's concept of immortality, as well as his idea of the resurrection of all the deceased in the form of computer simulations, are both based on the pattern identity theory explained above. For the physicist, the idea of a closed system of quantum states defines human beings completely: " … a system *is* its quantum states … They thus prove that a human being is a finite state machine, and *nothing but* a finite state machine."[501] Having defined human beings and their souls as information-processing systems that can be unequivocally determined by their quantum state, Tipler interprets this as a salvation for humankind faced with the threat of cosmic disasters: "If one accepts the identification … of 'soul' with a particular computer program or pattern, we could interpret this pattern conservation as 'immortality of the soul'."[502]

Finally, Tipler also argues that the entire planet Earth must be transferred to the virtual space of a computer as a simulation before the Sun loses its luminosity.[503] As individual immortality is a poor consolation for all those who do not survive until the era when immortality becomes technically possible, Tipler has no doubt that all the people that have ever lived will nonetheless be resurrected in the future.

---

500   Rucker 2007; Raulerson 2013, 40-45.
501   Tipler 1995, 31.
502   Ibid., 237.
503   See ibid., 108-109.

> In fact, the universal resurrection is physically possible even if no information whatsoever about an individual can be extracted from the past light zone. Since the universal computer capacity increases without bound as the Omega Point is approached, it follows that ... there will be sufficient computer capacity to simulate our present-day world by simple brute force: by creating an exact simulation – an emulation – of all logically possible variants of our world.[504]

Measured against the maximum number of quantum states for a human being's mass, Tipler argues that, at most, the enormous yet finite quantity of 10^{450} different people and 10^{1230} different universes exist, and that they could be effortlessly simulated as virtual existences by a future super computer.[505] The immortality of the human soul – the "program of the human being" – and the resurrection of the dead would be carried out by a gigantic computer emulating the real universe shortly before the Omega Point was reached. According to Tipler's precise calculations, "shortly before" means precisely 10^{-100} to 10^{-1230} seconds.[506]

> The key question is this: do the emulated people exist? As far as the simulated people can tell, they do. By assumption, any action which real people can and do carry out to determine whether they exist ... the emulated people also can do, and in fact do do. There is simply no way for the emulated people to tell that they are "really" inside a computer, that they are merely simulated, and not real.[507]

In the case of this computerized resurrection, life after death would not be based, as in many religions, on the continuity of an immortal, psychic substance. Rather it would simply rely on the soul's pattern identity: "The need for such a continuity is obviated by quantum mechanics, and thus we see that an immortal soul is no longer necessary for individual immortality."[508]

Nevertheless, Tipler adheres to the Christian idea of a bodily resurrection because the human body, with all its sensations, would be simulated in the future computer, while all its physical defects and signs of decay would be removed. Yet at the same time the future body would also be an immaterial "light body".[509] But who exactly would be resurrected?

> What happens to the resurrected dead is entirely up to the Omega Point; there is no way the imulations [sic!] can pay for or enforce the immortality which is in the power of the Omega Point to grant ... Adopting the natural theological term, I think we will be granted "grace" ... So, the motivation for the granting of immortal life in the Omega Point is exactly the same as it is in the Judeo-Christian-Islamic tradition: the selfless love (ἀγάπη) of God.[510]

---

504 Ibid., 220.
505 See ibid., 31-33, 167-183, 220, 458-506, 483-488.
506 See ibid., 225-227.
507 Ibid., 207.
508 Ibid., 235.
509 See Barrow / Tipler 1986, 618-619; Tipler 1995, 108-110. See Lavery 1992, 10-18; Regis 1990, 46.
510 Tipler 1995, 245-247. See also Tipler's talk to theologians: Tipler 1989, 222, 249.

Tipler's vision of resurrection thus revolves around a cornerstone of Calvinist theology: the doctrine of predestination. God alone will decide to whom he grants eternal life and whom he condemns. Human beings have no possible direct influence over the "unsearchable counsel of God" but must rely entirely on his pure grace. In his description of hell, Tipler makes clear that incorrigibly wicked people cannot count on the grace of the Omega Point, and therefore will not be resurrected.[511]

In exercising the superhuman abilities they were to acquire, the resurrected would perfect different aspects of themselves until they reached the Omega Point, when they would attain a state of blessed contemplation of God and would achieve a genuine union with the divine being. Resurrection is primarily granted to human beings because, as potential self-programming Turing machines, they correspond to God's own image. However, Tipler concedes that some pets could also be resurrected if their owners so wished. Tipler does not entirely exclude the possibility of non-resurrection or a kind of purgatory for particularly wicked persons, but on the whole his descriptions clearly emphasize the pleasant aspects of the future horizon of salvation.[512] Moreover, people could meet all their ancestors and descendants in the simulated world, and every human being would have almost unlimited wealth.[513] The evil deeds of imperfect human beings could be eliminated simultaneously, so that the perfect human being in his or her virtual existence beyond time could become one with God.[514]

However, in recent interviews Tipler has moved away from this eschatological scenario, predicting that human beings will not need to wait for the realization of Omega, but will achieve this utopia simply through technical progress:

> Ultimately, all humans will join' em. The Earth is doomed, remember? When this doom is at hand, any human who remains alive and doesn't want to die will have no choice but to become a human upload. And the biosphere that the new human uploads wish to preserve will be uploaded also. The AIs will save us all.[515]

Cyberneticist Marvin Minsky views virtual immortality not as the goal of Christian salvation history, but rather a result of the capitalistic medical system. In his opinion, this technological immortality will at first be reserved only for the rich.[516] Nevertheless Minsky regards these hoped-for technological achievements as the beginning of a new, anthropocentric ethics. The right to have children, human genes, and death should no longer be subject to biological conditions, but would instead be controlled solely by the individual's will and reason in posthuman life forms.[517]

---

511 See Tipler 1995, 251.
512 See ibid., 241-255.
513 See ibid., 241-242; Tipler 1989, 244. Invoking the ideas of the Austrian economist Friedrich von Hayek, Tipler even proves that in the course of time all people will possess infinite wealth. See Tipler 1995, 267-268.
514 See ibid., 244-245.
515 Tipler 2015, 31.
516 See Minsky 1992c, 31.
517 See Minsky 1994, 112-113.

> The most important thing about each person is the data, and the programs in the data are in the brain. And some day you will be able to take all that data, and put it on a little disk, and store it for a thousand years, and then turn it on again and you will be alive in the fourth Millennium or the fifth Millennium.[518]

Hans Moravec, who associates the attainment of immortality with the surgical procedures discussed above, describes virtual existence as a space of infinitely increasable self-realization. All personal abilities could then be improved immeasurably and in every possible way. People would be able to sing better than any opera star today and would achieve notable professional success in their virtual existence:[519] "And, of course, you are better at your job than even your best ever was – better than any flesh-and-blood person ever could be."[520]

Moravec says that the act of uploading would mean that people would not only be able to escape death before the end of their physical lives, thanks to virtual immortality, but would even be able to produce an immortal emergency copy of themselves during their lifetimes. This would then be activated in the event of a fatal accident.[521] In Moravec's vision, everyone who has ever lived would have the hope of eternal life. Moravec agrees with Tipler when he argues that the resurrection of the dead is merely a mathematical problem. The simple calculation and simulation of all the past events that have led to our present world would enable robot doctors, with the aid of archeological knowledge and biographical data fragments, to resurrect all the dead and to endow them with a new and immortal life in simulation that would be absolutely real for them.[522]

> It might be fun to resurrect all the past inhabitants of the earth this way and to give them an opportunity to share with us in the (ephemeral) immortality of transplanted minds. Resurrecting one small planet should be child's play long before our civilization has colonized even the first galaxy.[523]

Since his book, *The Age of Spiritual Machines* (1999), Ray Kurzweil, in line with Moravec's proposal, has propagated the idea of the immortalization of human beings by means of brain scans. He bases this method on cybernetic pattern identity theory and does not believe that it is even necessary to first fully understand how the brain works.[524]

---

518   Marvin Minsky: *Why Computer Science Is the Most Important Thing That Has Happened to the Humanities in 5,000 Years*. Public lecture, Nara, Japan, 05/15/1996. Quoted from Hayles 1999, 244-245.
519   See Moravec / Pohl 1993, 72-74; also Lem 2010, 195-196.
520   Moravec / Pohl 1993, 76. However it is unclear how this luxury, together with professional success, can be combined with Moravec's predictions elsewhere about probable mass unemployment and the elimination of human beings from all professions, especially as the artificial intelligences in virtual space would continue to be far superior to human minds after uploading. See Moravec 1999, 70-71, 139-140.
521   See Moravec 1988, 108-111.
522   See ibid., 124; Moravec 1999, 142, 172-173.
523   Moravec 1988, 124.
524   See Kurzweil 1999a, 2-4, 53-55, 128-130; Kurzweil 2005, 9, 324-330.

> Actually, there won't be mortality by the end of the twenty-first century ... Up until now, our mortality was tied to the longevity of our *hardware*. When the hardware crashed, that was it ... As we cross the divide to instantiate ourselves into our computational technology, our identity will be based on our evolving mind file. *We will be software, not hardware.*[525]

As shown in the preceding chapters, the question of death has been central to transhumanism since the 1960s, when the movement was shaped by FM-2030 and Robert Ettinger. The latter's solution to this problem is cryonics, which promises resurrection for the dead in a future technologically advanced age. For FM-2030 the overcoming of human mortality is the cornerstone of the transhumanist world view. According to Esfandiary, human beings have no freedom as long as they have to die, and therefore all political and social efforts must be devoted first and foremost to this problem. Social and political activity should concentrate on scientific and technical progress, and the results would ultimately be measured in terms of their success in overcoming death:

> The real revolutionary of today fights a different battle. He wants to be alive in the year 2050 and in the year 20,000 and the year 2,000,000. Is there anything more radical than this determination? ... Who are the new revolutionaries of our times? They are the geneticists, biologists, physicists, cryonologists, biotechnologists, nuclear scientists, cosmologists, astrophysicists, radio astronomers, cosmonauts, social scientists, youth corps volunteers, internationalists, humanists, Science-Fiction writers, normative thinkers, inventors ... [526]

While working on his last book, *Countdown to Immortality*, in July 2000 Fereidoun M. Esfandiary died after a long battle with cancer. His body now awaits technological resurrection in the cooled nitrogen of a cryogenic tank in Arizona.

The artist Stelarc also believes that the immortality of future human beings in real space is an inevitable and necessary result of technical progress:

> If the body can be reshaped in a modular fashion in order to facilitate the replacement of malfunctioning parts, THERE IS NO TECHNICAL REASON FOR DEATH, if spare parts are available. Death is not an authentic sign of existence. It is an antiquated evolutionary strategy ... In the extended time-space of extraterrestrial environments, THE BODY MUST BECOME IMMORTAL IN ORDER TO ADAPT. Utopian dreams will become post-evolutionary imperatives.[527]

Almost all leading transhumanist authors, such as Max More, Nick Bostrom, and Martine Rothblatt, are optimistic that sooner or later a form of virtual immortality can be attained. Max More, who also acted as CEO of the cryonics provider *Alcor*, has slightly qualified the transhumanist goal of immortality. He says that the aim is a potentially unlimited life span that in principle could be ended after a fulfilled life. Nick Bostrom

---

525   Kurzweil 1999a, 128-129.
526   Ibid.
527   Stelarc 1996, 78.

defends the aim of extending life and of attaining immortality in philosophical terms. Martine Rothblatt coined the term *mindcloning*, which is supposed to help people to achieve *cyberconciousness* until the end of time.[528] Rothblatt is the only transhumanist who assumes that traditional religions will continue to exist in the virtual afterlife because the *mindclones* will have to correspond to their originals and their values. She believes that all religions will welcome the existence of *mindclones* because they are in harmony with human destiny given by God.[529]

Anders Sandberg and Nick Bostrom's 2008 study *Whole Brain Emulation. A Roadmap* sought to contribute a more scientific approach to this question. The notion of *transmigration* that was introduced by Moravec was replaced by the technical term brain-emulation, i.e. a complete and perfect copy of the original brain.

> WBE [Whole Brain Emulation] represents a formidable engineering and research problem, yet one which appears to have a well-defined goal and could, it would seem, be achieved by extrapolations of current technology. This is unlike many other suggested radically transformative technologies like artificial intelligence where we do not have any clear metric of how far we are from success.[530]

The two authors from the *Future of Humanity Institute* discuss technical questions in detail and identify the difficulties clearly. They see problems not so much in methods of storage and computer simulations of the brain as in the currently available brain scanning methods. The highest resolution procedures would normally require a time-consuming and costly preparation of histological sections, which would also have to be deep frozen or fixed with plastics. Sandberg and Bostrom therefore propose to scan only the most important parts of the brain and to record the rest with less precise methods (MRI). A living and functioning brain cannot be scanned with sufficient resolution with today's technology.[531] Sandberg and Bostrom consider human personality to be linked to brain activity only. They regard the simulation of the body – which is reduced to kinetic aspects of bones and muscles – as peripheral.[532]

As there is a degree of skepticism about cryonics even among transhumanists, research about longevity, such as that once carried out by Roy Lee Walford and today by Aubrey de Grey, is becoming increasingly important, especially as it could be useful as a safety net or bridge until virtual immortality can be achieved.[533] The tendency to constantly create new systems of thought means that transhumanists describe the striving for immortality or longevity as *immortalism*, *longevism*, or *life-extensionism*.

---

528 See Bostrom / Roache 2008, 3-7; More 2009; Rothblatt 2014, 280-293; Heil / Coenen 2014, 153-155.
529 See Rothblatt 2014, 261-276.
530 Sandberg / Bostrom 2008, 5.
531 See ibid., 40-54.
532 See. Ibid., 74-75.
533 Pathologist Roy Lee Walford (1924-2004), who was closely connected to the former *Extropy Institute*, claimed in his 1983 book *Maximum Life Span* that human beings following his dietary plan would live on average 120 years. Thanks not only to his involvement in the experiment of *Biosphere 2* from 1991 to 1993 and to numerous television appearances and popular books, Walford was the best-known exponent of the American longevity movement at the time. See Walford 1983; Walford 2000; Vita-More 1990.

The multitude of schools of thought within transhumanism has given rise to numerous organizations, lobby groups, and institutes dedicated to visionary life extension. In contrast to the more realistic scenarios of established bio-gerontology, this visionary perspective envisages life-prolonging phases ranging from several hundred to 1000 years (as proposed by de Grey). These institutes include the above-mentioned *Future of Humanity Institute* run by Nick Bostrom and the *SENS Foundation* run by de Grey. The American *Immortality Institute / LongeCity* founded in 2002 regards itself as a forum for disseminating ideas on how to overcome involuntary death.[534] In Israel transhumanist activist Ilia Stambler has founded *Longevity Days* as well as the international lobby organizations *Longevity for All* and *Longevity Alliance* in 2014.[535] The *Global Healthspan Policy Institute* founded in Washington D.C. in 2016 seeks to build a bridge to conventional academic research and to persuade politicians and the federal administration of the need for life-prolonging research into ageing.[536] However, the discussion remains elitist and techno-centric, and the importance of a functioning health care system for the entire population or better environmental protection are not considered.

Transhumanists achieved a brief success in 2002, when even the most far-reaching visions of immortalization were included in the above-mentioned *National Science Foundation* report by Mihail Roco and William S. Bainbridge on the convergence of nanotechnologies:

> Is having the traditional body necessary to being human? Nevertheless, if you accept the above premises, it could be done. Having made the leap to new hardware for yourself, many staggering options open up:
> · No death. You back yourself up. You get new hardware as needed.
> · Turn up the clock speed. Goodbye, millisecond-speed neurons; hello, nanosecond-speed electronics.
> · Choose space-friendly hardware. Goodbye, Earth; hello, galaxy.[537]

The following sections will discuss the question of the role that this vision of technical immortalization plays in the history of ideas. This concerns approaches formulated since the Enlightenment of the prolongation of life and the fight against death thanks to medicalprogress of medicine. The idea of immortalization through technical media will be traced by reference to the science fiction literature of the 19th and 20th centuries. Cryonics is a special case here and can only be adequately described in the cultural and historical framework of the American funeral culture.

From Longevity to Computer-Aided Immortalization

In cultural and historical terms, the overcoming of death is a brainchild of the Enlightenment. As we have already seen in the case of salvation-historical projections,

---

534 See Immortality Institute 2004; www.longecity.org.
535 See www.longevityforall.org; www.longevityalliance.org.
536 See https://healthspanpolicy.org.
537 Roco / Bainbridge 2003, 169.

Enlightenment positions were not always opposed to religion. Certainly, scientists in the 19th and 20th centuries, as well as posthumanist thinkers, emancipated themselves from traditional religious teachings and metaphysicss (such as the role of God in evolution) but these ideas found their way back into posthumanist utopias through the back door. The case for eternal life ties in seamlessly with the efforts to prolong life. We are tempted here to assign these efforts exclusively to the medical context. Similarly, Moravec's immortalization procedure and the staging of cryonics also include this medical aspect.[538] The philosophical and religious elements of these future utopias then tend to recede into the background.

The Sumerian Gilgamesh epic, the oldest story in the history of humankind, written around 2000 BCE, tells the tale of a heroic king who, despite all his glorious deeds, is confronted with the inevitability of the end as his death approaches. He sets out in search of immortality and finds Utnapishtim and his wife on a paradisiacal island. They had been blessed with eternal life by the gods because they had always obeyed them and had saved creation from the great flood. Out of pity, Utnapishtim gives Gilgamesh an herb of immortality, which is then stolen by a snake.[539]

The motif of a mythical place of eternal life or of rejuvenation stretches from the cultures of the ancient east to the early modern era. It ranges from the Garden of the Hesperides described by Homer, in which youth-giving apples grow, to the legends of a Fountain of Youth, as recounted in the classical Alexander Romance, in Herodotus, the medieval travelogue of Sir John Mandeville, and by the chronicles of the Spanish conquistadors in the 16th century.[540]

In classical antiquity around the Mediterranean, excessively long lives are projected onto distant countries or past times. In the Jewish Tanach the patriarchs of the Jews live for hundreds of years. In Hesiod the generation of the Golden Age lives without illness or ageing. Strabo and Pliny the Elder tell of people beyond the north winds who live almost for ever. In the Christian context, the hope of an eternal (postmortal) life is only for the devout, as a compensation for their suffering in the world. Anything beyond this is dismissed as hubris.[541]

In medieval Europe, alchemy emerged as a systematic attempt to study and control the natural world and its forces. For the most part alchemists believed that they were acting in accordance with Christian doctrine, as their aim was to decipher the wonders of divine creation as man's reason and cognitive abilities progressed. In addition to efforts to produce gold and silver from base materials, the search for a *panacea* or universal remedy that could prolong life and heal diseases began with Roger Bacon (ca. 1220-1292). In some cases, the metaphysically inspired applications of mercury or antimony preparations led to the rapid death of their advocates and their customers. The veneration of cinnabar as a means of attaining immortality had similar effects in Daoist Chinese alchemy of the Tang period (7th to 9th centuries). Mercury also played a prominent role in the efforts of Indian alchemy to prolong life

---

538   See Bloch 1986, 465; Schäfer 2010, 23-28; Jordan / Frewer 2010, 154-155.
539   The Sumerian and Babylonian Utnapishtim later merges with that of the Biblical Noah.
540   See Gruman 1966, 24-27.
541   See ibid., 9-24.

and attain immortality.⁵⁴² Martine Rothblatt explicitly refers to Daoist epistemology in this context.⁵⁴³

Italian Renaissance thinker Luigi Cornaro (ca. 1467-1566) with his advocacy of a moderate lifestyle with a strict diet and hygiene was extremely influential. He argued that when people reached 80, they would achieve perfect freedom as they would leave behind them all earthly desires and sinful urges. Then they would live half in the earthly and half in the heavenly world and would be truly able to serve God.⁵⁴⁴ The philosopher and early champion of empirical science Francis Bacon produced the first systematic discussion of the possible prolongation of life in his 1623 essay *Historia Vitae et Mortis* (*History of Life and Death*). Bacon does not present a consistent theory of life but cites innumerable historical and legendary examples of life-prolonging methods, such as diets, elixirs, baths (in blood), etc.⁵⁴⁵

With their groundbreaking proposals, Cornaro and Bacon were also a point of reference for Enlightenment approaches to the perfection of life, which for many thinkers included almost unlimited prolongation. This optimism about progress is partly underpinned by secular ideas and partly placed within Christian frameworks. English theologians and moral philosophers, such as Richard Price, John Wesley, and Richard Clarke, dreamed of a new Jerusalem as a thoroughly religious society in which God would reward people with life expectancies such as those of Old Testament patriarchs before the flood.⁵⁴⁶ Secular philosophers such as Condorcet regarded long life as a consequence of the constant development of the human race and of medicine:

> Would it be absurd then to suppose that this perfection of the human species might be capable of indefinite progress; that the day will come when death will be due only to extraordinary accidents or to the decay of the vital forces ... ? Certainly, man will not become immortal, but will not the interval between the first breath that he draws and the time when in the natural course of events, without disease or accident, he expires, increase indefinitely?⁵⁴⁷

Condorcet is optimistic that biological progress will go hand in hand with the higher development of morals and the intellect.⁵⁴⁸ For Benjamin Franklin too, the moral progress of humankind and the prolongation of life are closely linked:

> All Diseases may by sure means be prevented or cured, not excepting even that of Old Age, and our Lives lengthened at pleasure even beyond the antediluvian Standard. O that moral Science were in as fair a Way of Improvement, that Men would cease to be

---

542 See Wujastik / Newcomb / Barois 2017, III-V.
543 See ibid., 27-68; Priesner 2011, 41-42; Rothblatt 2014, 293-299.
544 See Gruman 1966, 60-81.
545 See Bacon 1977, 144-282; Gruman 1966, 60-81.
546 See Spadafora 1990, 103-104, 125-126, 223-252; Sampson 1956, 57-58; Ekirch 1944, 26; Dawson 1935, 169-170; Gruman 1966, 76.
547 Condorcet 1976, 279-280 = Condorcet 1970, 381.
548 See Condorcet 1976, 275-285; Condorcet 1970, 379-385; Gruman 1966, 87-88.

Wolves to one another, and that human Beings would at length learn what they now improperly call Humanity.[549]

The most radical utopia was formulated by the English philosopher William Godwin, whose *Enquiry Concerning Political Justice and its Influence on Morals and Happiness* was published in 1793, shortly after the French Revolution. Godwin rejected all existing social institutions such as marriage, religion, the monarchy, and government. Like most philosophers of his time, Godwin was convinced that, as reason became more widespread, the human race would approach a state of perfection. The history of life shows that, with every century, human beings are gaining more power over the forces of nature, and thus the question arises if this also applies to the power of the mind over the matter of the human body:

> If over matter at ever so great a distance, why not over matter which, however ignorant we may be of the tie that connects it with the thinking principle, we always carry about with us, and which is in all cases the medium of communication between that principle and the external universe? In a word, why may not man one day be immortal?[550]

In confrontation with his numerous critics, Godwin defends his predictions by adopting a more relative stance: absolute immortality, i.e. the complete abolition of death, is a goal that can never be fully achieved. As a first step towards the overcoming of death, his "brother", the human need for sleep, must first be conquered. In Godwin's view individual immortality is an indispensable aspect of the human striving for perfection, which will renew the entire social order. Here Godwin goes further than La Mettrie, who also attributed power over human health to the mind but did not ascribe this potential to any movement of progress.[551] It is therefore no coincidence that Godwin's daughter, Mary Shelley, included these ideas in her novel *Frankenstein; or, The Modern Prometheus* of 1818.

The reflections of Enlightenment thinkers led to the publication throughout Europe of the first practical guides to healthy living, which promised individuals many additional years of life. *Die Kunst das menschliche Leben zu verlängern* (1796) by the German doctor Christoph Wilhelm Hufeland was particularly significant. Hufeland, the royal physician and director of the Charité Hospital in Berlin, had a decisive influence on the modern health system in Prussia. In 1854 Hufeland's book was published in English by Sir Erasmus Wilson under the title *Art of Prolonging Life*. Hufeland argued that every man and woman possessed a certain amount of vitality that they had to protect and nurture. He said that sexual excesses, masturbation, the bad air of cities, gluttony, or an unbalanced disposition would shorten life, whereas a good pedigree, a hardworking youth, sexual moderation, a good marriage, country life, hygiene, a contented disposition, and a moderate diet would prolong life. The devout doctor considered the first experiment with blood transfusions, carried out by Jean

---

549 Franklin 1780. Letter to Joseph Priestley, 02/08/1780. See Gruman 1966, 74, 83-84; Perry 2000, 17-18.
550 Godwin 1793, II, 862. See also Ni 2007, 26.
551 See ibid., 33-39; Gruman 1966, 85-87.

Baptiste Denis and Richard Lower in the 17th century, to be an interesting method of rejuvenation.[552] Hufeland's ideas, together with the classical ideal of a moderate and contented life, were taken up in the 19th century by authors such as William Sweetser (*Human Life*, 1867) and Daniel Harrison Jacques (*How to grow handsome or Hints toward physical perfection, and the philosophy of human beauty*, 1879).[553]

Summing up the striving for longevity and immortality, we notice that people have been proposing unusual methods and means to achieve this goal since classical times. These methods were then systematically sought out and attempted by the alchemists. The actual possibility of long life is mostly attributed to those in distant countries or times. With their utopian perspectives, Francis Bacon and his contemporaries then projected visions of a promising future.

Until the modern period all European thinkers regarded the Bible as evidence that a life span of several hundred years was possible, at least in principle. For Christian philosophers such as Cornaro, Bacon, and Hufeland, this even meant that efforts to achieve a long and healthy life were in keeping with the divine commandments. They held in common with Enlightenment thinkers the conviction that the attainment of a long life required not only progress in science, but emphatically also required moral progress on the part of the entire society.

The idea of combining the biological perfection of human beings with social development was also a goal of the Russian cosmists at the beginning of the 20th century.[554] This originated with the comprehensive utopia of the philosopher Nikolai Fedorov (1829-1903). For 24 years Fedorov was the librarian of the Moscow Rumiantsev Museum's library. He led an ascetic life: He avoided sleep, which reminded him too much of death, he had no bed, wore torn old clothes, followed a Spartan diet, did not consort with women, and rejected all forms of human sexuality. Fedorov did not publish any of his extensive writings in his lifetime but he was in touch with the Russian intellectual elite, including Lev Tolstoy and Vladimir Solovyov. His works, edited by his students, were only published between 1906 and 1913 under the title *The Philosophy of the Common Cause* [Философия общего дела].[555]

Fedorov regarded death only as an illness that could be overcome by scientific progress. For Fedorov the realization of the true brotherhood of humankind includes the resurrection of all those who died in previous generations, because today's humanity has also benefited from the sacrifices of its ancestors. The resurrection of the dead is accomplished without the help of God, even though the entire history of humankind follows God's plan. Anja Bernstein summarizes this as follows:

> It may seem paradoxical to combine Orthodox Christianity with such arguably secular mechanistic notions of the body, but this odd combination might be precisely what

---

552 See Hufeland 1854, 16, 22-44; Gruman 1966, 82-83.
553 See Gruman 1966, 80-89.
554 The generic term "cosmists" for these movements was coined retrospectively in the 1970s and the debate about whether or to what extent Russian cosmism is a coherent school of philosophy continues. See Bernstein 2019, 64-66.
555 See Hagemeister 1989, 15-46; 188-203; Hagemeister 1997.

allows Fedorov to be claimed by proponents of diverse and conflicting contemporary agendas.[556]

After the 1917 October Revolution, Fedorov's ideas were taken up by a number of young scientists and philosophers who aimed to revolutionize humanity, the planets, and the entire universe through the progress of work, knowledge, and education. The authors of the 1922 manifesto of the so-called bio-cosmists, using the slogan *Immortalism and Interplanetarism*, called for the complete abolition of all social differences between people. They regarded the normal life span as the original source of all possessions, which cement the inequality of people. The bio-cosmists therefore called for a right to unlimited existence – immortality, the resurrection of all the dead, rejuvenation, and complete freedom of movement in cosmic space. The goal of rejuvenation was to be achieved, for example, through the method of mutual blood transfusion developed by Alexander Bogdanov in the 1920s.[557]

One of the central figures in the cosmist movement was the Russian prophet of space travel Konstantin Tsiolkovsky, whose pioneering theoretical achievements helped to pave the way for the rocket technology of the 20th century. The colonization of the universe corresponded to the cosmist demand for humankind's unlimited expansion into space. The creative visionary Tsiolkovsky was influenced by materialistic philosophies such as Ernst Haeckel's monism, Auguste Comte's positivism, Nietzsche's idea of the superman, as well as theosophic ideas of cosmic consciousness and thought (Tsiolkovsky's residence Kaluga was an important center of the theosophic movement around 1900). As in the ideas of spiritism and theosophy at the turn of the century, Tsiolkovsky also assumed that future humanity will evolve into a higher form of existence as ethereal beings consisting of cosmic light.[558]

The idea that evolution passed through successive stages from the planet to the biosphere to the noosphere was developed in parallel to the work of Teilhard de Chardin by bio-geochemist Vladimir Vernadsky, who heard of it from Édouard Le Roy during a research visit to Paris in 1922-23. The Russian literature of this period also adopted certain motifs of the cosmists, for example in the socialist utopia *Red Star* (1908) by Alexander Bogdanov.[559]

There are no direct links between the ideas of the cosmists and the development of transhumanism and posthumanism in the United States. Fedorov's writings were not published during the Soviet period because of their metaphysical and Christian content. Unlike Vladimir Vernadsky and Konstantin Tsiolkowsky, most of the cosmists

---

556   Bernstein 2019, 3, 17-19, 63. See Hagemeister 1989, 117-128; Hagemeister 1997.
557   See Hagemeister 1997, 19-44; Groys 2005, 8-17.
558   The main influences here were the German spiritist and theosophist Carl du Prel and the naturalist Alfred Russel Wallace, who in his late work *Man's Place in the Universe* (1903) wrote a cosmic history of development that ended with the emergence of a future spiritual being. See Hagemeister 2012, 136-148; Wallace 1912, 266-268; Benz 1961, 96-100; Benz 1965, 91-96.
559   In the 1920s, Le Roy, together with Pierre Teilhard de Chardin, developed the concept of the biosphere and the noosphere. Le Roy, who in 1921 succeeded Henri Bergson as professor at the Collège de France, was clearly influenced by idealism in his version of evolutionary history. See Le Roy 1928; Hagemeister 1997, 196-202.

were victims of the Stalinist purges in the 1930s and were either murdered or died in the gulags.

Although Russian cosmism played only a niche role in the research interests of western Slavicists, the post-Soviet era has seen a wide reception of this movement in recent Russian philosophy as well as in the art scene. For these contemporary transhumanists, Fedorov has become the main inspiration for their projections of the future of humanity. Even Russian president Vladimir Putin referred to Fedorov's *Philosophy of the Common Cause* in 2014 address. The Russian billionaire Dmitry Itskov's 2045 Initiative also follows the cosmist tradition.[560]

In western transhumanism the ideas of the Russian cosmists have only recently been noticed, although there has not been much of a response in the wider movement. In 2003 the American philosopher Charles Tandy dedicated the first volume of his transhumanist book series *Death and Anti-Death* to the memory of Fedorov. AI researcher and businessman Ben Goertzel used the name of the Russian movement in his 2010 *Cosmist Manifesto* but all further references are quite superficial (as in the case of the above-mentioned *Church of Perpetual Life*, in which Fedorov is revered as a prophet).[561] Influences on recent posthumanism and transhumanism are also perhaps detectable in the works of the Strugatsky brothers, translated into English since the 1960s, as well as those of Stanisław Lem. It is worth noting that the Russian cosmists, in parallel to Enlightenment thinkers' visions of the future, regard the immortality project as a collective undertaking embracing the whole of society – including past generations.[562]

A widespread belief in the progress of technology not only characterized socialist utopias in Eastern Europe, but in the 19th century was also widely shared by representatives of all social strata. The flowering of science fiction literature, notably in the works of authors such as H. G. Wells and Jules Verne, reflects this *fin de siècle* technophile optimism. A large number of popular and scientific authors had great expectations for the future possibilities of rejuvenation and life extension.[563] Influential figures in this context include Ilya Mechnikov, with his *Études sur la nature humaine. Essai de philosophie optimiste* (1903), French author Jean Finot with his *Philosophie de la longévité* (1906), surgeons Serge Voronoff and Eugen Steinach, who promised male patients (including Sigmund Freud and William Butler Yeats) rejuvenation by the transplantation of monkey testicles and similar operations, as well as Gerhard Venzmer who advocated a natural life in *Alt werden und jung bleiben* (1936).[564] In his 2009 life guide *Transcend. Nine Steps to Living Well Forever* Ray Kurzweil continues this tradition,

---

560   Christian Fedorovians, who call for immortality for all the living and the dead, demarcate themselves from secular and elite transhumanists. See Bernstein 2015, 770-775; Bernstein 2019, 20-34, 49-60.
561   See chapter 4; Goertzel 2010, 1-15.
562   See Simakova 2016; Goertzel 2010; Bernstein 2014; Tandy 2003. Up to 2013, 11 volumes of this series had appeared. Charles Tandy founded Ria University (www.ria.edu) in California, which concentrates on the study of life prolongation and time travel!
563   Israeli transhumanist Ilia Stambler has produced a comprehensive overview of authors who wrote about medical life prolongation, especially in the early 20th century. See Stambler 2014.
564   See Stambler 2014, 10-114.

promising that the ageing process could be reversed even in the early years of the 2020s.[565]

While these medical perspectives aimed to achieve rejuvenation and the prolongation of life, American author Charles Asbury Stephens and British physicist John Desmond Bernal declared that the goal of their scientific efforts was no less than immortality itself. Stephens, who also studied medicine, earned a living by writing short stories and magazine articles on new scientific developments. From 1888 to 1905, with support from a patron, he ran a research laboratory in Maine, where he analyzed the life cycles of cell cultures. Although his research proved unsuccessful, this did not prevent him from proclaiming the definitive defeat of death in his philosophical works *Living Matter* (1888), *Long Life* (1896), *Natural Salvation* (1903), and *Immortal Life* (1920). According to Stephens, death is unnatural. It is caused by disease or damage to the basically immortal cells of our organism. Every single cell, like humankind in evolution, possesses an etheric energy that propels human beings into a higher, more spiritual level of existence, "a spiritualization of the genus *homo*".[566] Stephens presented the history of evolution as a teleological process that would ultimately produce a human brain that – in contrast to the short-lived organs of the rest of the body – would be able to survive for several thousand years:[567]

> Two millions of centuries have struggled forward in pain and travail to make the human brain capable of the human intellect ... It is not destined forever, nor much longer, to be lost in death; we shall carry it through to a greater destiny. The true scope and intent of life is now just dawning in the minds of men. We are waking, — after idle dreams, — waking to what we can do and be, waking to the great possibilities of science, waking to live, instead of resigning ourselves to death.[568]

Stephens argued that ether is the original force that gives birth to life and permeates the entire universe, in the form of a spiritualized, knowing energy that is also responsible for phenomena such as telepathy, clairvoyance, and ghostly apparitions.[569] As the most highly developed race of humankind, he said that it was now up to the Aryans to realize the next evolutionary stage of life.[570]

While Stephens proclaims the Aryan race to be the highest form of intelligent life, Irish molecular biologist John Desmond Bernal believes that the aristocracy of scientists will instead shape the future evolution of life. At the age of 25 he began writing his memoirs, fearing that when he was old, he would no longer be so open to new ideas. When he published the controversial treatise *The World, The Flesh and the Devil. An Enquiry into the Future of the three Enemies of the Rational Soul* three years later, he saw his own role as that of a passionate revolutionary with Marxist sympathies. He

---

565   See Kurzweil / Grossman 2009, XX-XXIII.
566   See Stephens 1920, 48-49.
567   See ibid., 49-67.
568   Ibid., 75-76.
569   See ibid., 130.
570   See ibid., 240-241; Stambler 2014, 191-192.

renounced the church, enjoyed a promiscuous sex life, and was driven by fierce anti-English resentment. At that time Bernal was inspired by the controversial debate around the biologist J.B.S. Haldane, whose 1924 *Daedalus* caused a sensation due to its vision of artificially inseminated fetuses that would be incubated in birthing machines.[571] Bernal gained widespread recognition in his scientific career for his innovative work on crystallography, but his youthful utopia is highly speculative and remained unsurpassed in its radicalism until technological posthumanism appeared on the scene.

The title: *The World, the Flesh and the Devil* refers to the terrestrial and the cosmic environment, the human body, and – as the greatest challenge – our inner, psychic world, our fears, hopes, and motivations, all of which have to be overcome. Any prognosis about the future of life, according to Bernal, would have to consider not only the history of progress and physical laws, but also human desire as "the strongest thing in the world".[572]

Bernal rejects the eugenic approach that aims at a better selection of sexual partners or even the manipulation of genetic material. This would produce only very slow developments and would not substantially change the human species. Bernal argued that future human beings would first have to be biologically optimized in a birthing factory, would then spend 60 to 120 years as biological human beings enjoying dance and sexuality, and then would transcend to their final state of existence. As in the case of Stephens, whose work he is clearly not familiar with, Bernal regards the brain as the seat of the human personality: "After all it is the brain that counts, and to have a brain suffused by fresh and correctly prescribed blood is to be alive – to think."[573] The rest of the body is superfluous: "In a civilized worker the limbs are mere parasites, demanding nine-tenths of the energy of the food and even a kind of blackmail in the exercise they need to prevent disease, while the bodily organs wear themselves out in supplying their requirements."[574]

Human beings would continue to exist only mentally as brains inside an artificial cylinder, which would supply the brain from outside with blood and extremely extended sensorial impressions (such as X-rays). Bernal believed that this mode of existence would bring human beings closer to immortality in two ways. First, the brain itself could be split into two parts, which could be replaced if the need arose. Second, Bernal envisions an artificial connection uniting human brains, which could then merge to form a single super organism. The demise of individual brains could then be ameliorated by the creation of this new conglomerate:[575]

> But the multiple individual would be, barring cataclysmic accidents, immortal, the older components as they died being replaced by newer ones without losing the continuity of the self, the memories and feelings of the older member transferring themselves almost completely to the common stock before its death.[576]

---

571 See Haldane 1924; Brown 2005, 65-69; Bernal 1929, 38, 45.
572 See Bernal 1929, 7-11.
573 Ibid., 43.
574 Ibid., 41.
575 See ibid., 43-45; Heil / Coenen 2014, 149-150.
576 Bernal 1929, 53.

Equipped with these new, artificial sense organs, this interlinked brain organism could enter the interior of biological cells or of a star and could transform all these levels by the sheer force of consciousness. Only in this way could human beings fully achieve their intellectual potential and begin their disembodied expansion into the universe. He predicted that in this way human beings would overcome the natural environment and its constraints, such as nutrition and sexuality, allowing the forces released to flow into art and science:[577]

> As time goes on, the acceptance, the appreciation, even the understanding of nature, will be less and less needed. In its place will come the need to determine the desirable form of the humanly-controlled universe which is nothing more nor less than art.[578]

Bernal's prognosis for the future of humanity is ambivalent. He considers it possible that the superior new humanity of science will abandon the stupid and those simpletons who refused to accept change, leaving them behind on the zoo-like Earth, and would then colonize space, or else a struggle for survival would break out between the two factions.[579]

However, Bernal's youthful judgment about the dwindling boldness of old men was to prove right. His later scientific works – such as the chapter *The Future of Biology* in *Science in History* 1969 – are devoid of passion and merely provide a general overview of better disease prognoses, the improvement of seed strains, and the prospects for life prolongation.[580] Admittedly the British science fiction writer Arthur C. Clarke was fascinated by Bernal's radical projections for humanity, and it is also conceivable that Bernal influenced the literary work of Olaf Stapledon. However, as Bernal in later years neither actively propagated his visions nor founded a movement, *The World, the Flesh and the Devil* remains a one-off in its period. It was only through the *Bernal Lectures* by physicist Freeman Dyson in the 1970s that his early ideas about the colonization of space (Bernal sphere / Dyson sphere) became known to a wider audience.

Even though no direct influence on the ideas of technological posthumanism can be detected, Stephen's and Bernal's projections reflect the radical escalation of widespread future hopes proliferating during their time. These ideas then helped to shape posthumanist visions in the second half of the 20th century through the eugenic movement (Huxley) and science fiction (Clarke). Both eugenicists and posthumanists share the belief that human beings must now consciously control their further perfection and that this must not be left to blind evolutionary chance. Both authors also display an extreme contempt for nature and for the body. In Stephens' case this is combined with a racial-theosophical ether metaphysics. The absolutization of the brain as the sole marker of being human clearly corresponds to the genius cult of the turn of the century and to the eugenics of the time. The truly new aspect of Bernal's devaluation of the body is his argument that the biological body poses an obstacle to the projected expansion into space.

577　See ibid., 19-36.
578　Ibid., 79.
579　See Bernal 1929, 94-96.
580　See Bernal 1969, 981-988.

The two world wars put a damper on optimism about technological progress, increasing awareness of the potential for the destruction of all life that the natural sciences could unleash. The use of chemical weapons in the First World War and the dropping of atom bombs on Hiroshima and Nagasaki triggered a debate on the ethical limits of progress. Consequently, the two major progress movements did not survive the world wars. After 1918 many people regarded Ernst Haeckel's materialistic monism as a symptom of a godless society which, due to its lack of Christian values, had made the horrors of the war possible. The murder of those considered "unworthy of life" during the Nazi period and the forced sterilizations carried out everywhere in Europe brought eugenics into disrepute. Moreover, the United States at this time was experiencing an anti-modernist religious politicization, which only began to be reversed with the Sputnik shock of 1957.

The start of the cryonics movement led by Robert Ettinger coincided with this new optimistic phase that emerged around the beginning of the 1960s. For structural reasons this is discussed separately at the end of this chapter. However, its advocates do not regard cryonics as a real immortalization method, but rather only as a bridging technology that would make later resurrection possible. Like the transhumanism of the 1990s, this era was characterized by boundless enthusiasm and the belief that medical progress would soon solve the problem of death. Numerous local cryonic associations were founded from the mid-1960s onwards, for example the *Life Extension Society* in Washington D.C., the *Immortalist Society* in Michigan, and the *Immortality Records and Compilation Association* in California. The high point of the movement, which was later rocked by numerous scandals, was the unveiling of the cryonic *Immortality Pavilion* at the Montreal World Exposition in 1967.[581]

Only a few thinkers, such as physicist Gerald Feinberg and writer Arthur C. Clarke, expressed optimism about humankind achieving technical immortality,[582] but the concrete idea of an existence within computer memory was slowly taking shape in close connection with fictional literature. As early as 1964, in an article for *Playboy* magazine science fiction writer Frederik Pohl discussed various types of life extension and proposed the idea of educating a computer like a child by means of interaction and communication, thus creating artificial and immortal life.[583]

The first specific proposal to transfer the personality of a living person to a computer was published in 1971. In a short article for a medical journal, George M. Martin, professor of pathology at Washington University in Seattle, expressed admiration for the possibilities opened up by cryobiology. Based on the assumption that scientific progress would continue, and that humankind would not self-destruct, he expressed optimism that human beings could overcome the problem of death:

---

581 See Krüger 2010, 3-4, 17 (FN V).
582 See Feinberg 1969, 77-87, 102-115; Feinberg 1966; Clarke 1960, 233. Feinberg at this time was focusing on an interdisciplinary approach to solving humanity's main problems through his Prometheus Project. See Heil 2010a, 140; Perry 1992.
583 Pohl later published a work together with Moravec. See Pohl 1964; Pohl 1989; Moravec / Pohl 1993; Regis 1990, 151-152, 204-206.

> We shall assume that developments in neurobiology, bioengineering, and related disciplines, perhaps over a period of centuries, will ultimately provide suitable techniques of "read-out" of the stored information from cryobiologically preserved brains into nth. generation computers capable of vastly outdoing the dynamic patterning of operation of our cerebral neurons. We would then join a family of humanoid "postsomatic" bioelectrical hybrids, capable of contributing to cultural evolution at rates far exceeding anything now imaginable.[584]

Moravec cites the *IBM* employee Dick Fredericksen, who published his private newsletter *A Word in Edgewise*. In several editions he raised the question of whether, in addition to individual organ transplants, it would not be possible to transfer the human mind from the brain to another hardware – thus creating a quasi-immortal robot.[585] It was precisely these newsletters that the young student Hans Moravec discovered on the notice board of the *Stanford Artificial Intelligence Laboratory*.[586]

Inspired by Fredericksen, Moravec in turn published several essays about the future of evolution and artificial intelligence. In his essay in *Today's Computers, Intelligent Machines and Our Future*, published in the science fiction magazine *Analog*,[587] Moravec gives the first account of the surgical procedure of mind transplantation, which he describes in greater detail later in his monograph:

> Though you have not lost consciousness, or even your train of thought, your mind has been removed from the brain and transferred to the machine. A final step is the disconnection of your old sensory and motor system, to be replaced by higher quality ones in your new home. This last part is no different than the installation of functioning artificial arms, legs, pacemakers, kidneys, ears and hearts and eyes being done or contemplated now.[588]

At this point Moravec produces a series of tables comparing biological life with the performance of computers.[589]

At the same time at Georgetown University medical ethics specialist Robert M. Veatch mooted the "bizarre and purely hypothetical" notion that all information stored in a human brain could be recorded on magnetic tapes in the context of the contemporary discussion about the precise medical determination of death.[590]

As the 1980s began, the utopia of computerized immortality was already so widespread that the popular NASA scientist Robert Jastrow rhapsodized while speculating about this paradisiacal future:

---

584 Martin 1971, 339.
585 See Fredericksen 1971, 23, 1-A – 3-A.
586 See Moravec 1988, 203; Regis 1990, 152-153, 157-158.
587 The magazine was the successor to *Astounding Science Fiction* founded in 1930, and from 1960 on it accepted non-fictional works.
588 Moravec 1979, 80. See. Ibid., 78-81.
589 See ibid., 63, 71, 73.
590 Veatch here forcefully rejects this notion of the future destiny of humankind: "Man is, after all, something more than a sophisticated computer. At least in western tradition the body is an essential element, not something from which man escapes in liberation." Veatch 1975, 23.

> At last the human brain, ensconced in a computer, has been liberated from the weakness of mortal flesh. Connected to cameras, instruments and engine controls, the brain sees, feels, and responds to stimuli ... It seems to me that this must be the mature form of intelligent life in the Universe. Housed in indestructible lattices of silicon, and no longer constrained in the span of its years by the life and death cycle of a biological organism, such a kind of life could live forever.[591]

In 1983 in the American magazine *Psychology Today* journalist Mike Edelhart analyzed the philosophical challenges posed by the thought experiment of an existence in a computer memory. For Edelhart, too, the ethical complications went further than those involved in organ transplantation:

> Or consider a computer-brain hookup. As a man lies dying, he feeds the entire contents of his brain – every brain-wave pattern it can create – into a computer, linked to a voice synthesizer, which speaks as he did. The computer has all his memories and attitudes. It has his sense of humor. Is it him?[592]

Despite the publication of these isolated expressions of the possibility of computerized immortalization, in my view it is not appropriate to speak of "proto-posthumanism" at this stage. The contexts of these ideas are very heterogenous and in many cases critical. It was Moravec who first defined this technological utopia as part of a normative framework that makes the simulation of human beings plausible in cybernetic terms and also legitimizes the inevitable march of progress – the replacement of human beings by artificial intelligences.

Immortality in Science Fiction

From the 1970s onwards – thanks above all to science fiction – writers in medical journals and popular magazines began to engage in thought experiments or to produce future projections on the possibility of computerized immortalization. It was in this literary genre that the central ideas were first conceived and presented to a wider audience. The posthuman dream of immortality ties in here with a long literary tradition that has been grappling with the "scientific" realization of human immortality for more than two centuries. In a fluid transition from alchemistic short stories to proper science fiction, Brian Stableford and Carl B. Yoke identified no less than 200 stories and novels on this subject written between 1800 and 1990. While the older works – up to about 1930 – almost exclusively regard technological immortalization as a form of stagnation or a curse, more recent science fiction takes a more nuanced view of the idea of eternal life made possible by science. But even here the skeptical voices remain in the majority.[593]

---

591   Jastrow 1981, 166-167. See Lavery 1992, 68-69.
592   Edelhart 1983, 41. From the 1980s to the 2000s, Edelhart wrote books and magazine articles about computers, careers, and private underground bunkers.
593   See Stableford 1999b, 616; Yoke 1985; Collings 1985.

Here I would like to elaborate upon one of the earlier short stories by Jules Verne. Like *Ève future* (1886) by his contemporary Auguste Villiers de l'Isle-Adam[594] it is clearly influenced by Edison's 1877 invention of the phonograph. This innovation made it possible for the first time to record and reproduce human speech, bringing within reach the machine simulation of a central human trait – communication – which Descartes and Turing both identified as the defining feature of humanity. While Villiers de L'Isle-Adam allowed his hero to create a more perfect – i.e. more docile – woman, in Jules Verne's 1892 story *Le Château des Carpathes* a perfect and immortal simulation of a real woman occurs.[595] Baron de Gortz, who has fallen in love with the famous opera singer La Stilla, records her voice on phonographic rolls. However, during the recording and reproduction of her singing, not only the diva's voice, but also her soul and life-force are absorbed, with the result that, during her last performance before the wedding with the Count de Telek she collapses and dies with blood pouring out of her mouth. With the aid of this phonographic sound reproduction and a kind of three-dimensional moving image projection, de Gortz manages to create a perfect simulation of the deceased that convinces his rival Count de Telek of his bride's survival.[596] Jules Verne's story is the first example of immortalization by media technology. This was followed a half century later by literary fantasies in which immortality is directly linked to computers.

Clearly influenced by Shannon's mathematical information theory and Wiener's cybernetics, British science fiction author Arthur C. Clarke published the story *The City and the Stars* in 1956. The action takes place in the town of Diaspar millions of years in the future. This is the first case where the idea of a human being stored as an informational extract is presented in fiction. The author does not go into technical details, but we learn that these future living beings have succeeded in detaching the human mind from the body. From a gigantic central computer, the "stored human beings" – after undergoing certain cycles – are brought to life in real bodies and after their demise they are stored again with their new life experiences. Clarke here works on the assumption that human personality is nothing but *information, structure, and pattern* that can equally well be stored on paper, magnetic tapes, or electronic tubes.[597]

Thirty years before Hans Moravec's *Mind Children*, a more specific idea of a supposedly immortal existence in virtuality was formulated and discussed in detail in the *Dialogi* of the Polish author Stanisław Lem of 1957. Echoing the dialogues of Plato and George Berkeley, he develops the technological vision of an immortality machine capable of continuing the existence of or resurrecting a material person by means of a perfect simulation.[598] After lengthy discussions, the disputants Hylas and Philonous conclude that no copy of a human being, however perfect, can guarantee the continuity

---

594 Published in English as *Tomorrow's Eve*. See Villiers de l'Isle-Adam 2000.
595 The English translation followed in 1893 under the title *The Carpathian Castle*. See Verne 1900.
596 See Verne 1900; Innerhofer 1996, 396-399; Innerhofer 2003, 279-280. Innerhofer mentions a large number of unknown short stories from around the turn of the century in which the phonograph operates as an instrument of immortalization. See Innerhofer 1996, 417-420.
597 See Clarke 1956; Dery 1996, 150-151.
598 See Lem 1980, 9-74 and later in the *Summa Technologiae*. In this work Lem also explores the idea of random individual resurrection in computer existence. See Lem 2010, 195-203, 282-288. See also Gräfrath 2000, 287-289; Rottensteiner 1997, 369-370.

of a personality.⁵⁹⁹ In numerous short stories thereafter, Lem explored various aspects of this idea of "storing" a human personality in an apparatus or a computer, thus revealing the almost insurmountable difficulties faced by cybernetic pattern identity theory. In the fictional *Star Diaries* of the cosmonaut Ijon Tichy (1971) Lem describes an experiment by the cyberneticist Professor Corcoran, who has created artificial life "in a few boxes". These living beings believe that their consciousness and their virtual world, which exists only in the boxes, is nonetheless absolutely real:⁶⁰⁰

> Each box contains an electronic system that generates consciousness, as does our brain. The structure is different, the principle is the same ... These boxes have receptor organs that function analogously to our sight, smell, hearing, touch, and so on ... These boxes, Tichy, are plugged into an artificial world. That one ... thinks it is a seventeen-year-old girl with green eyes, red hair, and the body of a Venus.⁶⁰¹

In some of his short stories, Lem mercilessly exposes the absurdity of such a virtual existence. Moravec's vision of human beings keeping an emergency copy is already standard⁶⁰² on the planet *Enteropia* (!), which Tichy visits. Every year the planet is battered by meteorites, which would kill large numbers of inhabitants and visitors if a "reserve" could not be stored and materialized whenever necessary.⁶⁰³ On his 23ʳᵈ voyage cosmonaut Tichy arrives on the tiny planet of the "Whds", who, due to shortage of space, and wherever necessary, (i.e. in doctors' waiting rooms, local authorities, meetings, etc.), are kept in tiny apparatuses. They can then re-materialize themselves when required with the help of stored atomic structures. The accidental doubling of a bridegroom – created twice thanks to a technical error – causes utter havoc.⁶⁰⁴ In the 1957 story *Are you there, Mr. Jones?* a racing driver who consists entirely of prostheses made by the *Cybernetics Company* has to fight for his freedom and the recognition of his personality. It turns out that, after several accidents, his biological brain was completely replaced by an electronic equivalent that now houses his "mind".⁶⁰⁵ One of Lem's favorite motifs is virtual "resurrection" and the lifelike simulation of long dead personalities by computers.⁶⁰⁶

Like Clarke and Lem, the Austrian author Herbert W. Franke has explored the possibilities of the virtual simulation of the real life-world and of the technical integration of human beings in such artificial worlds from early on in his career. In his 1961 novel *Der Orchideenkäfig*,⁶⁰⁷ now ranked as one of the classics of German science fiction, Franke describes the exploration of a foreign planet. The terrestrial visitors, who operate on the planet in the form of doubles, discover the story of an old civilization. As this planet faces a cosmic threat from a host of meteorites, it has sped up the process of

---

599   See Lem 1980, 9-33.
600   See Lem 1982, 35-52.
601   Ibid., 42-43.
602   See Moravec 1988, 119.
603   See Lem 1976, 102-124.
604   See ibid., 231-236.
605   See Lem 1969.
606   See Lem 1987, 186-208.
607   Published in English as *The Orchid Cage* in 1973. See Franke 1973.

total mediatization and virtualization. Initially the people on this planet built machines to operate themselves, but in later periods these developed to the point that people did not even need to leave their homes. The obsolete body was supplied with liquid food while for days it enjoyed the virtual delights of so-called total reproduction: a medium encompassing all senses. After many generations of physical and psychological change, the former human beings end up in a tangle of cables, wires, reflectors, and plastic sheaths that use direct brain cell stimulation to provide the transformed organisms with peace, contentment, and happiness.[608]

Franke varies this motif in his 1970 novel *Zone Null*.[609] An expedition again finds a planet with an advanced technological civilization. Using the same arguments as today's posthumanists, the inhabitants advocate the union of the obsolete, carbon-based beings with machines. The Zone Null. i.e. the basement of a huge complex, houses the technical conditions for integrating the human mind in the memory of a universal computer. Here the virtually simulated personalities of these biological beings attain freedom from their transitory bodies, and thus the status of immortality. With access to the infinite knowledge of the computer memory and to countless probes, the person now has far more possibilities of action than before.[610]

In 1961, Arkady and Boris Strugatsky, the two Russian masters of utopian literature, published a short story entitled *Candles Before the Control Board* (Свечи перед пультом): In the large-scale research project known as *The Great Encoding*, the brain of a scientific genius is read and stored in a crystalline biomass. Everyone involved knew that this process would make the dream of human immortality come true. The preservation of brain patterns, which would remain stable for 12,000 years, would make the development of an artificial, biological brain as a new carrier possible in coming centuries. This would then be able to absorb the personality of the genius.[611]

Somewhat later than Franke, Lem, and Strugatsky, Austrian artist and cyberneticist Oswald Wiener published his influential dystopian novel *die verbesserung von mitteleuropa, roman (the improvement of Central Europe, novel)*. In *appendix A* of the novel he describes a "bio-adapter" which he says is the "complete solution to all the world's problems" and "the liberation of philosophy by technology. Its purpose is quite simply to replace the world".[612] As a "uterus" and "happiness suit" it mirrors peoples' own "lust impulses (servo-narcissus)" in a perfect, simulated world. Only the liquidation of the "abandoned, nervously activated and miserably equipped ... lumps of slime, riddled with fear of life and petrified by fear of death",[613] would make human beings superior units. Bit by bit the body of the imprisoned person is dismantled and amputated until the cells of the

---

608 See Franke 1973; Flessner 1997b.
609 Published in English under the same title *Zone Null*. See Franke 1974.
610 See Franke 1974.
611 See Strugatsky / Strugatsky 1978, 224-230. The Strugatskys take to the extreme an idea already formulated by Arthur Conan Doyle in his 1929 story *The Disintegration Machine*. An inventor presents a ray machine that can dissolve objects and living beings and put them together again. But there is no reference to any idea of immortality. See Conan Doyle 1929; Clarke 1960, 72.
612 Wiener 1969, CLXXV, trans. by PK. Bernal's vision is not mentioned in Wiener's comprehensive bibliography.
613 Ibid, trans. by PK.

brain are electronically wired up: "consciousness, this cuckoo's egg of nature, ultimately displaces nature itself".[614] Wiener and Franke thus dystopically realize Bernal's vision of a disembodied brain existence for future human beings.

American journalist and science fiction author Daniel Francis Galouye was probably the first to adopt the idea of computer-generated personalities in a totally virtual reality for an English-speaking audience. In his 1964 novel *Simulacron-3*, Galouye describes a world in which commercial market research leaves nothing to chance.[615] To test the reactions of consumers to certain products, scientists develop a detailed simulation of an entire town with some 10,000 "units of consciousness", who all go about their daily business in an orderly fashion and are convinced of the reality of their world.[616] The catastrophe takes its course when Douglas Hall, one of the leading engineers in the cybernetic market research company, starts to doubt the reality of his own world. Hall finally has to acknowledge that he too is merely an artificial person in a virtual world, but with the love of a woman, he manages to reach what he supposes is the real reality. In 1973 German film director Rainer Werner Fassbinder staged Galouye's vision in a dark and oppressive style in his television film *Welt am Draht* (*World on a Wire*). In 1999 John Rusnak directed a cinema version of this material entitled *The Thirteenth Floor*.[617]

However, the first time that the idea of immortality was explicitly presented to a TV audience was in October 1966, in the seventh episode of the television series *Star Trek*, which was entitled *What Are Little Girls Made Of?* The script for this episode was written by the well-known author Robert Bloch (*Psycho*). On the planet Exo III Captain James T. Kirk meets scientist Dr. Roger Korby, who after a serious illness scanned his personality and his mind into the computer brain of an android and thus achieved immortality.[618] This episode of *Star Trek* was the first appearance of the idea of virtual immortality in posthumanism's country of origin, and had a widespread impact.[619]

The idea of prosthesis people in science fiction was first presented in Bernard Wolfe's novel *Limbo* (1952) and by James Triptree Jr. (the pseudonym of Alice Sheldon) in the short story *The Girl Who Was Plugged In* (1973), which explores the topic of technologically changed identities. But it was only in the early 1980s that postmodern cyberpunk literature emerged.[620] The typical elements of cyberpunk, such as the use of technology and chemistry (genetic engineering, prostheses) to improve human performance, also

---

614 Wiener 1969, CLXXXIII, trans. by PK. See Tabbert 2004, 375-403. The works of cyberneticist Norbert Wiener are well known to Oswald Wiener. See Wiener 1969, CCVI.

615 The novel was published by Bantam (NY) in 1964 under the title *Simulacron-3*. The English (UK) version of the same year published by Victor Gollancz (London) was sold under the title *Counterfeit World*.

616 This corresponds to Tipler's idea: "Suppose we try to simulate a city full of people ... ". Tipler 1995, 206.

617 See Fassbinder 1973; Rusnak 1999.

618 See Bloch 1966.

619 The idea of scientifically realized immortality is explored in several SF stories of the 1960s, though usually in connection with an immeasurable prolongation of life by medicine or drugs. See Yoke / Hassler 1985.

620 The term *cyberpunk* was coined by Bruce Bethke in his eponymous short story. On forerunners of cyberpunk such as Bernard Wolfe and Philip K. Dick see Hayles 1999, 113-130, 160-191.

imply the detachment of the human mind from the body (*disembodiment*) and the transfer into other bodies or into the virtual reality of a computer. Although writer and mathematician Rudy Rucker (pseudonym of Rudolf von Bitter Rucker) in his novels *Software* (1982) and *Wetware* (1988) described this kind of technological "mind transfer" – in some cases accompanied by immortalization – it was William Ford Gibson who first brought the idea of virtual reality to a wider reading public in his *Neuromancer* trilogy. His novels *Neuromancer* (1984), *Count Zero* (1986), and *Mona Lisa Overdrive* (1988) not only took up Galouye's notion of a neural human-computer interface, but also coined the term *cyberspace* to denote the virtual space that computer technology opens up.[621] Connected to the memory of a computer, Case, the main character in *Neuromancer*, experiences the world as materialized information, as the pure representation of the matrix:

> Get just wasted enough, find yourself in some desperate but strangely arbitrary kind of trouble, and it was possible to see Ninsei as a field of data, the way the matrix had once reminded him of proteins linking to distinguish cell specialties. Then you could throw yourself into a highspeed drift and skid, totally engaged but set apart from it all, and all around you the dance of biz, information interacting, data made flesh in the mazes of the black market ... [622]

Whereas Case only occasionally samples experiences in cyberspace, other human actors such as Dixie Flatline prefer a virtual existence in a computer to their real material body. This is why many transhumanists and science fiction bibliographies refer to William Gibson as the discoverer of virtual reality.[623]

In his post-apocalyptic scenario, *The Second Angel* (1998), Scottish author Philip Kerr comes up with an innovative variant. Here we do not find human beings or their minds being loaded into computers. Instead, quantum computers are introduced in human blood by a super-computer called *Descartes*. There they combine with the human personality. *Descartes* plans to explore space with the aid of these resistant human-hybrid machines.[624]

Even before the emergence of the *cyberpunk movement*, these ideas had been popularized in feature films where human beings are located or trapped in a virtual reality usually generated by computers. *Welcome to Blood City* was produced in 1976 and was followed in 1982 by *Brainstorm*, and then by probably the most aesthetically sophisticated film about virtual worlds: *Tron* by Steven Lisberger (1982) and its sequel *Tron Legacy* by Joseph Kosinski (2010).[625] In *Tron*, a programmer is scanned into a computer and, as in the video games that were popular at that time, he has to fight against the dictatorial *Master Control Program*. In *Welcome to Blood City*, *Brainstorm*, and also in the film *The Lawnmower Man* (1991), the possibilities of virtual reality are used

---

621 See Gibson 2000, 1986, 1988; Nicholls 1999a, 1999b. On the prominent role of Rucker's novel *Software* see Hassler 1985, 4-6.
622 Gibson 2000, 26.
623 See Hayles 1999, 32-35; Flessner 1996; Tabbert 2004, 483-522.
624 See Kerr 1998; Ahn 2001, 331-337.
625 See Sasdy 1976; Trumbull 1982; Lisberger 1982; Kosinski 2010.

mainly to train soldiers or apes as perfect killing machines.[626] Besides the menacing potential of virtual reality, in *The Lawnmower Man*, based on a short story by Stephen King, positive aspects are also presented: A rather backward gardener is rapidly transformed into an intelligent and charming young man by his experiences of freedom and the boost cyberspace gives to his self-confidence.

The short story *We Can Remember It for You Wholesale* by Philip K. Dick, whose works are famous for their often drug-related playing with alternative realities, was made into a film entitled *Total Recall* (1990). Containing scenes of extreme violence, it was a box-office hit. The movie tells the story of a building worker whose experiences and memories are manipulated by implants for the benefit of a shady government.[627]

In the 1997 film *Abre los Ojos*, Alejandro Amenábar recounts the surrealistic story of a young man who lives in a virtual illusory world with the help of the cryonics company *Life-Extension*.[628] In 1999, in addition to the above-mentioned *The Thirteenth Floor*, two more US feature films explored the dissolution of reality through the possibility of media simulation: In their film *The Matrix* and its sequels, Andy and Larry Wachowski (now Lana and Lilly Wachowski) fascinated over 15 million filmgoers with the story of how intelligent machines enslave humanity using VR technology. The film was enthusiastically received by critics, who celebrated the exciting presentation of fundamental anthropological issues, generously enriched with postmodern and religious set pieces.[629] By contrast, in his film *eXistenZ*, David Cronenberg contented himself with staging a bewildering (computer)game consisting of unsettling actual and artificial realities.[630]

The overall idea of virtual immortalization plays a central part in the cyberpunk novel *Altered Carbon* (2002) by Richard Morgan, which was turned into a Netflix series in 2018. Here personal consciousness can be stored on a chip and can then be transferred to one or more bodies. The affluent "meths" (from Methuselah) in this dystopian world can acquire bodies that are always new and perfect, and thus become practically immortal. But there is a real risk of death if the body, known as a *sleeve*, or the consciousness chip or *stack*, is deleted, for example by a computer virus attack.[631] The film *Transfer* (2010), based on a 2004 short story by the Spanish author Elia Barceló and with a similar socio-critical motif, is also worth mentioning here. In this story a wealthy German retired couple who – with the aid of a company called *Menzana* – have their minds transferred to the bodies of two young and beautiful people from Africa. These impoverished body-donors are only granted access to their former consciousness for a few hours every day. In the looming conflict between the four personalities *Menzana* ends up crushing any rebellion against the brave new world.[632] Since 2020 a humorous version of this vision has been played out in the Amazon Prime series *Upload* – the virtually immortal

---

626   See Leonard / Everett 1991.
627   See Verhoeven 1990.
628   The English title is *Open Your Eyes*. See Amenábar 1997.
629   See Wachowski / Wachowski 1999.
630   See Cronenberg 1999.
631   See Morgan 2002; Kalogridis 2018 (Netflix series).
632   See Lukacevic 2010.

heroes of the story are forced to acknowledge that even the afterlife is organized along thoroughly capitalistic lines.[633]

Referring to Jules Verne's early idea in *The Castle in the Carpathians*, in which a woman is made immortal (for the beholder) with the aid of a phonograph and an image reproduction, we must acknowledge that the idea of using a technological media simulation to achieve eternal life is more than a century old. Even cursory readers of posthumanist works are bound to notice that Frank Tipler, Hans Moravec, Marvin Minsky, and Ray Kurzweil never mention cyberpunk writers or cyberpunk films in their monographs. Tipler attributes the idea of a computer-aided resurrection mechanism to himself, Hans Moravec, and the popular Harvard philosopher Robert Nozick.[634] The latter in fact merely referred to the gloomy vision of immortality in science fiction fantasies[635] and thanks to Tipler's efforts to "claim" him as a disciple he was promptly classified as a further advocate of virtual immortality in secondary literature.[636] The idea that the seriousness of posthumanist visions, based entirely on the results of scientific extrapolations, should not be undermined by contamination by "trivial" science fiction literature certainly has a degree of justification. However, it might be instructive to reflect further on posthumanist patterns of reception, as it is clear that posthumanist authors are aware of ideas of virtuality in science fiction. This is proven by the sometimes inflationary use of the term *cyberspace* by Hans Moravec and Frank Tipler.[637]

If we summarize the social, philosophical, and technical contexts and evaluations of an existence in virtual reality found within the science fiction literature and films discussed so far, we find that they are surprisingly consistent in their criticisms of virtual reality. In the literature, virtual existence appears most frequently as a means of manipulation – as a control instrument of dominant machines (*Tron, The Matrix*), market research (*Simulacron-3 / Welt am Draht* etc.), the military or governments who train humans or apes to become perfect killing machines (*Welcome to Blood City, Brainstorm, The Lawnmower Man*), or plan to use them for this purpose (*We Can Remember It for You Wholesale / Total Recall*). In cyberpunk too, excursions into virtual reality are usually not described as paradisiacal alternatives but as a bitter necessity in contexts of data crime and cyber terrorism. The protagonists in cyberpunk novels are mostly social outsiders – aggressive, alienated, drug-addicted, and incapable of relationships. In some cases, they suffer from identity-undermining changes and serious brain damage. When virtuality is explicitly addressed as a realization of immortality, this idea is mainly rejected. Lem's philosophers conclude that continuity of personality achieved by simulation is not feasible (*Dialogi*); the cosmonaut Ijon Tichy flees from the "emergency copies" of himself delivered in a package (*Fourteenth Travel*), and the mind of Dr Korby transferred to a robot loses its humanity and turns into an unscrupulous murderer (*What Are Little Girls Made Of?*). Herbert Franke's and Oswald Wiener's dystopias of

---

633 See Daniels 2020.
634 See Tipler 1995, 16-17.
635 See Nozick 1989, 24-26.
636 See Rottensteiner 1997, 367.
637 See Moravec 1999, 164-168, 171-172; Tipler 1995, 108-110, 220.

perfectly virtualized cultures (*The Orchid Cage, Zone Null*, the "bio-adapter") can be read as direct criticisms of current mediatization tendencies. Only *The Lawnmower Man* stresses the benefits of virtual reality for personal development as well as its military uses.

Among posthumanists, only Frank Tipler is preoccupied by existential unease as a philosophical consequence of notions about the technological simulation of the world, as dramatized especially in *Simulacron-3 / Welt am Draht* and *The Matrix*. However, Tipler has a simple answer to the ontological problem: "How do we know we ourselves are not merely a simulation inside a gigantic computer? Obviously, we can't know. But obviously we ourselves really exist."[638]

Surprisingly, in popular filmed versions of people trapped in an artificial world on the virtual horizon, a deeply human aspect emerges as the motivation and goal of liberation from virtuality: The love symbolized by the final, Sleeping Beauty-like kiss of the beloved overcomes the artificiality of the simulated worlds (*Simulacron-3 / Welt am Draht, The Matrix*). The age-old romantic motif is contrasted as an authentically human element with the virtual illusory world.

In posthumanist discourse, all the problematic aspects of existence in virtuality are completely blanked out. Social, philosophical, economic, and political risks as enacted in science fiction are limited in this discourse to the childishly naive description of a huge performance increase in all areas of human activity. The fact that increasing integration of human beings into cyberspace could go hand in hand with global dependence on computer networks and monopolistic companies, autocratic systems, and widespread manipulation for political or commercial purposes – these are all issues that posthumanism completely fails to address.

Cryonics and the Suspension of Death

To date, cryonics has been the only branch of either transhumanism or posthumanism that has produced practical results in its efforts to achieve immortality. Moreover, cryonics has clear ideas about life, death, and personal identity, as we have seen in previous chapters. In terms of the history of religion and culture, the idea of providing care and attention to the human body, even in its postmortal state, does not seem uncommon. Throughout history, considerable efforts have been made in the hope of attaining some kind of continuity of life or resurrection. One need only think for example of the pyramids and burial chambers of ancient Egypt. In cryonics the traditional concern for the preservation of the corpse converges with the hope of medical-technological control of death itself. Here we find a continuation of fictional worlds that have been popular in science fiction since the end of the 19th century.

As early as 1887, the US author, explorer, and adventurer William Clark Russell developed the idea of reviving a human being accidentally entombed in ice as a fictional device in his novel *The Frozen Pirate*. As the only survivor of a storm that leaves his ship on a huge iceberg, the mate Paul Rodney discovers an ancient pirate ship locked tight in the lonely ice fields. Aboard the pirate ship he finds some members of the pirate crew, frozen stiff. But placed near a fire, one of the sailors begins to revive. Aided by the mate, the

---

638   Tipler 1995, 207. See also Lem 2010, 199-203.

pirate is gradually brought to consciousness. He begins to slip into madness, however, refusing to acknowledge his fifty-year sleep, and then begins to age rapidly.[639] Two years after Russell's literary innovation, the popular French writer Louis Boussenard published his novel *Dix mille ans dans un bloc de glace* – here a contemporary man visits the far future as a result of a similar accident.[640]

American author and creator of *Tarzan*, Edgar Rice Burroughs, subsequently published a satirical short story entitled *The Resurrection of Jimber Jaw* (1937), in which a prehistoric man is revived in the present and has to cope with numerous adventures. In the 1930s the first cryonics stories appeared in the new *pulp fiction magazines* that were especially popular with American teenagers. In his short story *Armageddon 2419*, American fantasy author Philip Francis Nowlan sends his hero into the 25th century via cryonic deep sleep, whereas Neil Ronald Jones banishes his steadfast Professor Jameson, deep frozen in a capsule, into earth orbit for several million years until he is revived by aliens. Inspired by Jones' story, the later founder of cryonics Robert Ettinger wrote the short story *The Penultimate Trump*, for the magazine *Startling Stories*, in which two heroes are deep frozen for time travel.[641]

For the earlier stories, accidental freezing was just another dramatic means of time travel in that period of great social, cultural, and technological change. However, later novelists utilized cryonic suspension as a controlled method for passing time.[642] After the cryonic movement emerged in the 1960s, the film genre also picked up this theme – well known examples include the French film *Hibernatus* of 1969 with Louis de Funès, or Woody Allen's *Sleeper* from 1973. Both films comically vary the topic of ancient humans being awakened in a strange future environment. In the love story *Forever Young*, Mel Gibson plays a test pilot cryonically suspended in 1939 who wakes up again in 1992. Sylvester Stallone plays a deep-frozen super-agent in the commercial blockbuster *Demolition Man* in 1993 and this found its parodistic counterpart in *Austin Powers – International Man of Mystery* four years later.[643]

What distinguishes these science fiction ideas from those of the cryonic movement – apart from the normative claims of the latter's advocates – is the relationship to the topic of immortality. From the very beginning of the cryonic movement, the idea of freezing people was not intended to interrupt life for a form of time travel to the distant future, but rather to prolong life for an infinite period of time: Adherents are convinced that whenever a society is able to revive frozen corpses, its medicine will have improved to the degree that nobody will ever need to die. All the negative contexts of early and later science fiction, such as cultural disorientation, madness, and economic exploitation of frozen people, were ignored – the technical method alone was received by cryonic thinkers and contextualized within an optimistic idea of accelerated progress.

---

639 See Russell 1974.
640 See Boussenard 1890. The English translation *10,000 Years in a Block of Ice* was published in 1898.
641 See Burroughs 1937; Nowlan 1928; Jones 1931; Ettinger 1948; Stableford 1999a.
642 Th most prominent examples of these fin-de-siècle time travelers are H. G. Wells' *The Time Machine, an Invention* (1895), his *When the Sleeper Awakes* (1899, in the revised edition of 1910 the title was altered into *The Sleeper Awakes*) and Edward Bellamy's socialist utopia *Looking Backward: From 2000 to 1887* (1888).
643 See Allen 1973; Brambilla 1993; Miner 1992; Molinaro 1969; Roach 1997.

How did this all start? The answer is as complex as the question is simple – we can observe some strategies of legitimization in the accounts of the very beginning of cryonics that also have an important economic dimension. According to the web profile of the *Cryonics Institute* in Michigan and its founder and long-term director, Robert Ettinger:

> The cryonics movement began in 1962 with the private publication of the first version of my first book, 'The Prospect of Immortality.' It gained more attention when Doubleday published the first of several successful commercial editions, including several in foreign languages; and with the publication of my next book, 'Man Into Superman'.[644]

The biographical account of Ettinger's life on the same website is characterized by certain hagiographic elements typical of modern American heroes. Born in 1918, he is the grand-nephew of a conductor of the imperial Moscow Symphony Orchestra, and a nephew (by marriage) of the great jazz musician Pee Wee Russell; as a child he discovered the significant pulp fiction story of Neil Ronald Jones, which would shape his thinking in the coming decades; after severe injuries during World War II he spent some years recovering in hospitals: "Ettinger used the time not only to recuperate, but also to read and think."[645] In that time he discovered Jean Rostand's work on the successful freezing and thawing of frog sperm. After recovering, Ettinger became a professor of physics and mathematics at a community college in Michigan and wrote his book *Prospects of Immortality*, which he first sent to friends and scientists (and selected people from *Who's Who*) in 1962. It was published by Doubleday in 1964 and translated into eight other languages. Ettinger became a media celebrity, who was discussed in many international magazines and on US television. Inspired by Ettinger's book, several cryonic organizations were founded: "Cryonics had begun as Robert Ettinger's idea. It had become a reality."[646]

In his account of the history of cryonics, Ettinger does not disclose the fact that there was another immortality pioneer. However, as the *Alcor Life Extension Foundation* informs us: "But there was another man and another book and he made a contribution every bit as great as Ettinger's and perhaps in his quiet, unassuming way he may have made a more significant one."[647] Evan Cooper (1926-1983) privately published his manuscript *Immortality: Physically, Scientifically, Now* in 1962 and distributed copies among friends. Here, he combined the idea of freezing and reviving people with the cybernetic approach to human identity. Referring to the cybernetic thinker Norbert Wiener, Cooper considered a human being as nothing more than a kind of computer program that could be restored at any point of time, as long as enough information on the original state was available. In December 1963, Cooper and other immortality

---

644 See Robert C. Ettinger, "Cryonics Institute. A brief History and Overview" (2002), retrieved on 01/10/2011, http://www.cryonics.org.
645 Cryonics Institute 2003.
646 Cryonics Institute 2003.
647 Alcor 1983, 7. It does not seem accidental that Ettinger's commercial competitor, the *Alcor Life Extension Foundation*, published Cooper's obituary.

enthusiasts founded the *Life Extension Society* (*LES*) in Washington D.C. with Cooper as president – but five years later Cooper left the cryonics movement and the *LES* quickly died off. Nevertheless, his attempt to use annual conferences to bring together people who were scientifically interested in cryonics, and to edit a periodical (*Freeze – Wait – Reanimate*) encouraged more activists throughout the US. Saul Kent, Karl Werner, Harry Costello, and Curtis Henderson formed the *Cryonics Society of New York* (*CSNY*) in August 1965. It is important to mention here that it was Karl Werner, a young student at *Pratt Institute* in New York, who coined the neologism *cryonics* (from the Greek word for ice κρύος / kryos) just before the *CSNY* was founded.[648]

During Saul Kent and Curtis Henderson's trip around the country promoting cryonics, the *Cryonics Society of Michigan*, with Ettinger as President, and the *Cryonics Society of California*, with Robert Nelson as president, were founded in 1966.[649] Ettinger's group later changed its name several times – donning names that included *Immortalist Society* and *Cryonics Association* – and finally emerged as the *Cryonics Institute* in Clinton, Michigan. In 1972 the *Alcor Life Extension Foundation* was started by Fred and Linda Chamberlain, now settled in Scottsdale (Arizona).[650] After the theme of frozen suspension was considered to have sufficient public interest to justify an elaborate *Immortality Pavilion* at the *Expo* in Montreal in 1967, the movement clearly hit its peak around 1970.[651]

The cryonics movement has been and continues to be very heterogeneous and based on the active role of many strong individuals. In their sociological interviews in the early 1970s, Clifton Bryant and William Snizek discovered that cryonics members go to great lengths to maintain total control of their lives. An unusually high proportion have bomb shelters and fly their own planes, a fact that Bryant and Snizek considered to be another indication of an unwillingness to place their lives in someone else's hands.[652] The only quantitative survey conducted, which was undertaken by Ellen B. Rievman in the 1970s, concluded that the members of cryonics societies tend to be white males in their 30s, nonreligious, and politically unconventional; they have a higher educational level, fear of death, and income than the US average.[653]

The ambitious *Cryonics Society of New York* and other commercial providers were unable to finance their projects in the long term. The *Cryonics Society of California*, which

---

648 Werner, who was vice-president of New York's *Cryonics Society*, left the movement only three years after its foundation to spend four years in the Church of Scientology, but he never returned to cryonics. See Kent 1983, 4-5; Perry 2000, 38-39; Platt 1996.

649 There were even more short-lived immortalist groups in the mid-1960s: *The Immortality Records and Compilation Association* in Panorama City (CA) was headed by Tom Tierny, who was later arrested for counterfeiting and gun fraud, and the *Society for Anabiosis* in New York, initiated by Dr. Benjamin Schloss, who later shifted his interest to aging research. See Kent 1983, 4. Rievman and Sheskin report on more cryonic groups in the 1970s, such as the *Cryonics Society of Illinois* and the *Cryonics Society of South Florida*. See Rievman 1976, VIII, 4; Sheskin 1979, appendix D.

650 By 1973 the cryonics movement was expected to die after the *Cryonics Society of New York* dropped from about 130 members in the late 1960s to about a dozen in the mid-Seventies. See Bryant / Snizek 1973, 61-62; Mann 1981, 10; Sandomir 2002.

651 See Bryant / Snizek 1973, 57.

652 See ibid., 59.

653 See Rievman 1976, 68-89.

carried out the first "cryonic suspensions" in the late 1960s, was ruined financially when four corpses thawed out and relatives sued the association president Robert Nelson and an assistant. They were ordered to pay one million US dollars in compensation. After a long phase of public indifference, the American mass media started to report on cryonics again when baseball star Ted Williams died in 2002 and, after weeks of legal disputes between his children, was cryonically suspended.[654] Today only the *Cryonics Institute* and the *Alcor Life Foundation* are still operating in the United States. From 2011 to 2021 transhumanist Max More has been president and CEO of *Alcor*, author R. Michael Perry is responsible for patient care, and nanotechnologists Ralph Merkle, Aubrey de Grey, and Martine Rothblatt are members of the scientific advisory board. The *KrioRus* company in Russia, which emerged from transhumanist movements, has offered cryonic suspensions for human beings since 2005.[655]

To understand the cryonics movement, it is necessary to understand their specific attitude to death. The fundamental book *Prospects of Immortality* (1964) by Robert Ettinger begins with an enthusiastic and pragmatic preamble:

> Most of us now living have a chance for personal, physical immortality. This remarkable proposition – which may soon become a pivot of personal and national life – is easily understood by joining one established fact to one reasonable assumption.
> **The fact:** At very low temperatures it is possible, *right now*, to preserve dead people with essentially no deterioration, indefinitely …
> **The assumption:** If civilization endures, medical science should *eventually* be able to repair almost any damage to the human body, including freezing damage and senile debility or other cause of death … Hence, we need only arrange to have our bodies, *after we die*, stored in suitable freezers against the time when science may be able to help us. No matter what kills us, whether old age or disease, and even if freezing techniques are still crude when we die, *sooner or later* our friends of the future should be equal to the task of reviving and curing us. This is the essence of the main argument.[656]

Ettinger regards his freezing method as a means to avoid permanent death, since human beings die in imperceptible graduations. Thus, according to Ettinger, the question of the reversibility of death at any stage depends on the state of medical art – clinical death is often reversible and principally repairable like "all these ordinary emergency reanimations". Artificial prostheses and organs, as well as transplantation will support these processes of repair and improvement.[657]

> Suspended death, then, will refer to the condition of a biologically dead body which has been frozen and stored at a very low temperature, so that degeneration is arrested

---

654 The *Cryonics Society of California* had allowed nine of the corpses in their care to thaw, without informing the relatives, who continued to pay the maintenance costs for a long time. By the time the scandal was discovered, the corpses had almost completely decomposed. See Perry 2000, 39-40; Oliver 1981.
655 See Bernstein 2015, 768-769; Bernstein 2019, 41-48; http://kriorus.ru/en.
656 Ettinger 1964, 11.
657 See Ettinger 1964, 13, 50-58.

and not progressive. The body can be thought of as dead, but not very dead; it cannot be revived by present methods, but the condition of most of the cells may not differ too greatly from that in life.[658]

However, permanent death would mean that the original brain – the seat of personal identity – would be severely damaged so it could never be restored. But Ettinger is optimistic about this worst-case scenario:

> The freezer program represents for us now living a bridge to an anticipated Golden Age, when we shall be reanimated to become supermen with indefinite life spans ... You and I, the frozen, the resuscitated, will be not merely revived and cured, but enlarged and improved, made fit to work, play, and perhaps fight, on a grand scale and in a grand style.[659]

The combination of the prospect of resurrection and a paradisiacal "afterlife" is characteristic of the cryonic utopia. The dead bodies have a future virtual promise incorporated in their frozen corporeality:

> Neither alive nor dead, cryonic flesh organizes a massive discourse of maintenance and repair; even in its death, the body is becoming ... The production of a cryonic subject – alive, dead, or in the uncanny space of suspension – is possible only on the basis of a Möbius body, a body both within and without the capsule of nitrogen, inside and outside of time.[660]

In his popular 1969 book *The Immortalist*, writer and journalist Alan Harrington extols the prospects for cryonics and genetic engineering (for the breeding of fully-fledged human beings as "spare parts stores" for the original ones). He argues that both developments would lead to the triumph over human mortality. Referring to various philosophical and psychological schools – from Giordano Bruno to Erich Fromm and C. G. Jung – Harrington appeals for the liberation of human beings from the baleful self-hypnosis that religion, art, and all previous philosophy have offered: "Our new faith must accept as gospel that salvation belongs to medical engineering and nothing else."[661]

More recent cryonic utopias, such as R. Michael Perry's *Forever for All* (2000), focus mainly on the technical and philosophical questions for legitimizing cryonics – which have come under heavy fire in recent years. But he also takes on the old prospects of growing knowledge capabilities and physical power; he envisions the reversal of aging and the possibility that we could upload our immortal personal identity into the memory of a computer.[662] The aim of the 2004 *Scientist's Open Letter on Cryonics* was to attract greater attention to the issue in the public arena. The signatories included almost all the central exponents of transhumanism such as Nick Bostrom, Aubrey de

---

658 Ibid., 13.
659 Ibid., 16, 84.
660 Doyle 2003, 62, 68.
661 Harrington 1977, 21. See ibid., 225-272.
662 See Perry 2000, 559-563; Regis 1990, 76-108, 128-130; Sheskin 1979, 9-39. A detailed analysis of why and how people believe in cryonics was undertaken in the late 1970s by Arlene Sheskin. See Sheskin 1979, 72-99.

Grey, Eric Drexler, Ben Goertzel, James Hughes, Ralph Merkle, Marvin Minsky, Max More, R. Michael Perry, Martine Rothblatt, Anders Sandberg, Natasha Vita-More, and Roy Lee Walford.[663]

What happens to dead bodies in the cryonic movement? As is clear from explanations of the cryonic understanding of death, the greatest threat is severe brain damage: Here, the brain is supposed to be the holder of human identity and is indispensable for the future restoration of a person. Thus – besides the inevitable danger of accidents – the natural decay of brain cells should be avoided by cooling down the corpse as fast as possible. In an ideal (and more expensive) case, a cryonic stand-by team attends the last hours or days of a dying person and starts its procedures immediately after an independent nurse or physician has declared legal death. The patient is placed in an ice water bath, and blood circulation and breathing are artificially restored by a heart-lung resuscitator in order to provide steady blood support for the brain. Later, blood is extracted and replaced with an organ preservation solution, or rather a cryoprotective solution, since the most dangerous damage is expected to be caused by the freezing procedures.[664] The corpse then is cooled down in liquid nitrogen to a temperature of minus 196°C during a two-week process. In non-ideal cases, when a standby team is not available at the moment of death, the body is cooled down with ice water as fast as possible and then transported to the *Alcor* facilities in Arizona or to the *Cryonics Institute* in Michigan. Although representatives of cryonics are confident that future medicine will be able to remove every physical damage from freezing or from the natural decay of cells, they recommend that members reduce their risk profile for heart attacks, strokes, and other diseases – and die close to cryonic facilities. Sudden death, which would not permit any cryonic preparations, is feared in much the same way as people feared death without the sacraments in previous centuries.

In general, you can choose whole-body preservation or head-only freezing – the neuro-preservation that is provided only by *Alcor* and *KrioRus*. Freezing only the head means a clear reduction of costs; the minimum suspension costs at *Alcor* are 200,000 US dollar for whole body suspension, and 80,000 US dollar for neuro-suspension, and an annual membership of 550 US dollar (plus a variety of extra costs for standby teams, transfer, and so on). *Alcor*'s competitor, Robert Ettinger's *Cryonics Institute*, offers whole-body suspensions for a minimum of 35,000 US dollar and an annual fee of 120 US dollar. The price differences are due to additional costs that are not included in the basic rate at the *Cryonics Institute* and a different pricing policy.[665] In the case of *KrioRus*, the fee for full-body preservation is about 36,000 US dollar and 18,000 US dollar for head-only.[666] What happens with the body in case of neuro-preservation depends on the preferences of the family – often it is simply cremated and buried.

Finally, the dead bodies, their heads, or in some cases only their brains, are stored in special cryonic suspension capsules – for example, the *Bigfoot Dewars* at *Alcor*, which can

---

663 See http://www.cryonics.org/about-us/the-case-for-cryonics.
664 The two greatest dangers of freezing are expected to be the destruction of cells by crystallizing water and fracturing during cryopreservation.
665 See http://www.alcor.org/BecomeMember/scheduleA.html and http://www.cryonics.org.
666 See http://kriorus.ru/en/Human-cryopreservation.

hold four whole body suspensions or ten heads, or the "world's largest human storage cryostat" at the *Cryonics Institute*, which can carry up to 16 corpses. These containers are stored in a kind of workshop facility belonging to *Alcor*, *Cryonics Institute*, or *KrioRus*, and they are regularly maintained since small amounts of nitrogen have to be continuously added.

The first corpse was frozen in April 1966. However, the body was embalmed, all the inner organs had been removed and it had deteriorated severely from weeks of above-freezing storage. After a few months of cryonic suspension, the relatives decided that the body should be thawed and buried.[667] The first real cryonic suspension – according to the standards of the movement – was carried out on January 12, 1967, in Glendale (CA). James H. Bedford, a retired college professor of psychology, was frozen after he died of lung cancer. Realizing that his cancer was terminal, Bedford had contacted the newly established *Cryonics Society of California* and was attended by cryonics member Dr. B. Reanault Able when he died. After being cooled down with ice water, the corpse was transported to Phoenix (AZ) to a storage facility that initially remained secret. Although this first cryonic event was mainly met by critical commentary in the media, the cryonics representatives were extremely euphoric. They were confident that Bedford could be preserved in suspended animation for 20,000 years. The organization began receiving queries for suspension from all over the world, and the self-attributed historical importance of the first cryonic pioneers is reflected in Robert Nelson's book *We Froze the First Man*, published in 1968.[668] James Bedford became a kind of mythic figure as the first cryonaut:

> The oldest patient currently still being held in cryonic suspension is a Dr. James Bedford, who was suspended in 1967. He's survived the Cold War, the Vietnam War, the Gulf War, Watergate, the collapse of the Soviet Union and the 9/11 attacks – which is more than a lot of his contemporaries can say. If he can make it for so many years, you can too.[669]

This heroic report hides the fact that the cryonaut has had to undertake a great odyssey during the last four decades. Bedford's cryocapsule was first stored at the *CryoCare Equipment Corporation* in Phoenix. In 1969, the dewar was shipped to the warehouse of *Galiso Inc.* in Anaheim (CA). In 1976, Bedford's son shipped the cryocapsule to *Trans-Time*, a commercial cryonics facility in Emeryville (CA). Then, frustrated with the high costs, the son decided in 1977 to keep his father privately at an undisclosed location in Southern California. In 1982 Bedford was moved again to a commercial provider, the *Alcor-Cryovita* Laboratories in Fulerton (CA). In 1991 the "20,000-year capsule" began to fail and Bedford was transferred to a new dewar together with three other suspended persons. Finally, earthquake worries and regulatory problems with the state of California prompted the transfer of the whole *Alcor* company to Scottsdale (AZ) in 1994, where Bedford has been supposedly "residing" until now.[670] When the corpse –

---

667 Perry reports on the first failed attempts at freezing a dead body. Perry 1991; Perry 2000, 39.
668 See Larsen 1967; Nelson 1968; Snyder 1967.
669 FAQs on the homepage des *Cryonics Institute*, http://www.cryonics.org/prod.html (01/10/2011).
670 See Times 1997.

which according to Ettinger had been "frozen by relatively crude methods"[671] – was examined in 1991, the cryonicists were irritated to discover frozen blood and a lot of freezing fractures.[672]

As of spring 2021, 181 heads and complete bodies – known as *cryopatients* – are preserved at *Alcor* and another 1338 have already made all financial and legal provisions for their death. Among today's "cryonauts" 74% are men, about 34% have opted for full body freezing, 59% have chosen neuro-preservation, 6% have opted to have the head (minus the skull) deep frozen, and in two cases the body was subsequently removed.[673]

Ettinger's *Cryonics Institute*, which has 1725 members, has now frozen its 196th corpse, while *KrioRus*, despite its late appearance on the scene, can look back on 78 suspensions since 2006. In the case of *KrioRus* the number of neuro-preservations and full-body treatments performed are more or less equal. It is noteworthy that about 60% of documented cases are women. At the moment no cryonic preservation of corpses is available in the rest of Europe. Various cryonic interest groups established in recent decades have for the most part been short-lived. *KrioRus* and the *Cryonics Institute* also offer cryo-preservation for domestic pets.[674]

In the following section I would like to focus on the cultural context of cryonics in order to explain why it appeared during the 20th century in the United States. I will then consider why cryonics – apart from within its special US cultural context – has never reached the lofty expectations of its pioneers. About 400 frozen people in about 50 years of cryonics (out of 2.8 million deaths per year in the US) is far lower than the founders of the cryonics movement estimated when they predicted the advent of a new golden age in the 1960s.

It is quite common in cryonic literature to offer a technical illustration of the history of cryonics detailing the first cryonic experiments with animals going back to the 17th century.[675] While refrigerators were invented in 1876 by Carl von Linde, and every second US household owned one in the late 1930s, it was not until 1939 that General Electric also introduced freezing compartments commercially. It took more than a decade before freezers were widespread in US households and industry began to provide non-perishable, frozen food, which in the late 1950s and early 1960s, became one of the most noticeable conveniences of daily life. Thus, freezing emerges as a euphoric symbol of modern life in the light of new discoveries and new capabilities. As Robert Ettinger points out in 1964: " ... the freezer is more attractive than the grave ... "[676] Ettinger even dreamt of a freezer-centered society.[677]

However, cryonics is – from the perspective of cultural studies – in equal measure a cultural invention in the specific context of modern American funeral culture. And

---

671 Ettinger 1967, 1251.
672 See Darwin 1991.
673 Cancer patients, for example, often opt for brain preservation with *Alcor*. *Alcor* and *KrioRus* publish all their case studies (alcor.org/kriorus.ru), but the data is anonymous.
674 See Bernstein, 41-48; the homepages of www.alcor.org; www.cryonics.org; www.kriorus.ru.
675 See e.g. Perry 2000, 36-48.
676 Ettinger 1964, 16.
677 See Ettinger 1964, 77-91, 158-160.

although there were some cryonics groups outside the US, with the exception of *KrioRus* they never became strong enough to provide cryonic suspension facilities.

In a very general sense, cryonics can be regarded as an extensive form of the denial of mortality, which has been identified as a specific characteristic of the American death taboo.[678] According to the cryonic definition of death, the frozen corpses are neither assumed to be dead nor conceptually denoted as dead – they are described as "suspended members" or "cryopatients" who are "deanimated".

The fact that in 1967 the representatives of the cryonic movement were asked by the press if there were plans to provide a "cryotorium" for the storage of bodies cosmetically frozen in a new kind of embalming technique shows the continuation of traditional patterns of US funeral culture.[679] The preservation of dead bodies by embalming, and more recently by super-durable caskets (i.e. coffins), can be regarded as the standard for contemporary funerals in the United States.

Beginning with the American Civil War (1861-1865) the embalming and viewing of the dead became the archetype for the middle- and upper-class funeral. It then became standard for the whole of society in the 20th century. Many families of army officers who lost their sons and husbands on far away battlefields wished to retrieve the corpses and to bury them close to their homes. Thus, about 40,000 officers of the 600,000 casualties of the civil war were embalmed by swiftly trained morticians or physicians, using an embalming method that was originally designed for medical dissection.[680] The aggressive competition of embalmers for the spoils from the battlefields and the nearby army hospitals resulted in the first professional standards for morticians being established by the US army. While the public presentation of war heroes and the embalmed president Abraham Lincoln's 2,000-mile funeral passage to his grave brought much popularity to the new embalming procedure, the concern for corporeal integrity after death was another reason to favor embalming instead of traditional burials.[681]

Nineteenth century cemeteries suffered greatly from the practice of body snatching – the robbing of graves for the education of physicians. Even in the 1890s, many US states only permitted dissections on executed murderers or people who were killed in the commission of a crime – this resulted in a great demand for cadavers from the medical schools and independent anatomy schools that had flowered since the early 1800s. A flourishing body-snatching business therefore emerged and professional "resurrectors" supplied the schools with recently buried corpses. Offended at this widespread practice, people invented many ingenious methods to prevent the disinterment of their loved ones, such as grave watchers, burial vaults, cemetery walls, or even booby-traps. But body snatching did not cease until the 1890s, when embalming became the norm for funerals – embalmed corpses do not have inner organs – and

---

678 See Berger / Lieban 1963.
679 See Larsen 1967.
680 See Quigley 1998, 5-12.
681 See Coffin 1976, 69-98, 110-114; Iserson 1994, 170-233; Laderman 1996, 27-117.

laws changed to permit the acquisition of subjects for dissection on a larger scale.[682] However, according to Gary Laderman, the popularity of embalming is based on several factors: "A refusal to allow the dead to disappear from the living community, a fixation on the body of the deceased, and a demand that the integrity of the corpse be perpetuated in the grave as well as in collective memory."[683] Many cryonics activists regard being decomposed or rotten after death to be repulsive, while freezing the dead body retains its lifelike look.[684]

This need for the preservation of the body met capitalism at the end of the 19th century and no historian of US funeral culture doubts that the introduction and spread of embalming and the new ritual of public viewing of the corpse – which is part of the civil imitation of elite funerals – was largely governed by the professionalization of the funeral business. As Kenneth Iserson concludes: "Corpses are embalmed for two main reasons: public health and public viewing. Public health reasons are, at best, questionable; public viewing is an American cultural phenomenon."[685] With the help of improved advertising and sales strategies, the cultural need for the preservation of the corpse could not only be realized by the spread of embalming but also by the further development of coffins – known euphemistically as caskets in American English in a classical case of commercialized positive language.[686] Today, most coffins sold in the US are metal rather than wooden; they are often even solid copper or bronze with asphalt backfilling, and are hermetically sealed. It is also common for coffins or even urns to have to be placed in extra vaults or boxes / grave liners – vaults are required by some cemeteries and preferred by most. Vaults are designed specifically to help protect the casket from the surrounding elements – they are manufactured from various metals (steel, stainless steel, copper, and bronze), sometimes using an "air-seal principle". This means that high air pressure inside the vault will prevent water and other elements from penetrating the casket. In contrast to this, many European countries prescribe coffins that decompose in the earth after a few years.

It was within this funeral culture that preserves its corpses by embalming and uses hermetically sealed solid metal caskets and extra sarcophagi for protection from natural decay that cryonics was born. In this context, cryonics appears to be an exaggerated form of widespread tendencies in US funeral culture that are driven both by an overriding need for the preservation of dead bodies and by a strong drive for profit.[687]

From this economic perspective, it may even be plausible to see cryonics as the continuation of industrial medicine. As Peter Metcalf and Richard Huntington point out in their *Anthropology of Mortuary Rituals*:

---

682 Suzanne Shultz and Christine Quigley give a brief overview on the history of body snatching in 19th century America. See Shultz 1992; Quigley 1998, 292-298. The organs of embalmed bodies are extracted by suction after being minced inside the body by a special instrument.
683 Laderman 1996, 73.
684 See Bryant / Snizek 1973, 60.
685 Iserson 1994, 187. See also Coffin 1976, 69-98, 110-114; Iserson 1994, 170-233; Laderman 1996, 27-117.
686 See Laderman 1996, 164-175.
687 The same tendencies can be discovered in *Summum's Modern Mummification* business, which offers embalming in the ancient Egyptian style and burials with individually designed Egyptian sarcophagi in the US. See Quigley 1998, 133-139; http://www.summum.org.

> Americans have vast faith in medicine, a faith that is certainly in tune with the Enlightenment of progress and humanism. The development of powerful new drugs, and of reliable and safe surgical techniques, together with improvements in diet, have enabled the 'inevitability' of death to be redefined.[688]

To declare that a dead body is not permanently dead but a cryopatient, in need of continuing medical or technical support until its resurrection, could be regarded as a perfect business plan. Along with the ritual, economic, and technological contexts of cryonics, this prospect of freezing dead bodies and resurrecting them in the distant future is part of the western history of religion. Cryonics thereby evidently receives and modifies the common Christian patterns of death and the afterlife. While there might be a great variety of interpretations among the Christian denominations of questions of detail, the human body is supposed to be dead for a while and resurrected at the end of time in a new, almost-perfect form. The significant difference between cryonics and Christian belief is the lack of morality in cryonics. Resurrection is neither dependent on the duration of purgatory to pay for all the sins committed in life, nor is it contingent on God's act of grace. Cryonics only receives the positive aspects of the Christian model of resurrection– without a single word on the necessity of individual commitment, other than financial funding.

However, in the early days of cryonics, Ettinger sought institutional support, appealing to churches to be part of the active evolution of humankind: " ... the chief element lacking is institutional support to stiffen the backbones of those now considering this choice for the future."[689] Ettinger frames his innovative approach with a common postmillennialist interpretation of Christian eschatology – the widespread notion of postmillennialism means that humankind will support the expansion of the kingdom of God on Earth before the second coming of Christ, when the (symbolic) millennium will have passed by. In this context Ettinger argues that humanity, in a Christian sense, must still develop in the image of God, and that God gave us our intelligence and the capacities of nature to create the heaven on Earth:

> We must, in time, become immortal supermen – not to gloat over our accomplishments and strut among the stars but simply to do our work, the only work there is... The Christians among us are not rebelling against God nor aspiring to equality with him ... they seek rather to become his more effective tools, his worthier stewards.[690]

But no major Christian theologians answered Ettinger's call.

Cryonics is a perfect utopia – in the truest sense of the word. It is *ou-topos*, the negation of a place for dead bodies. The first suspended dead person, James Bedford, is not only a cryonaut – he is a paradigmatic Ulyssean figure for cryonics, changing

---

688   Metcalf and Huntington 1991, 209-210.
689   Ettinger 1967, 1253.
690   Ettinger 1967, 1252.

his last resting place seven times in 30 years. In the meantime, other cryonauts have thawed, mainly for economic reasons.[691]

According to cryonic beliefs, death disappears by definition. The corpse is usually cooled down in an ice tub, its blood is replaced by protective fluids, and it is then removed to the storage facilities in Arizona or Michigan. Finally, it is stored together with up to fifteen other dead bodies in a cryonic dewar. I have tried to explain how cryonics could emerge in the context of a commercialized Christian funeral culture with a strong need for the preservation of dead bodies. Bryant and Snizek even considered cryonics to be a substitute religion: "Unwilling to accept the promises of organized religions regarding a spiritual afterlife, cryonics members opt for a type of materialistic, active mastery over their own destinies ... the large majority of cryonics advocates are atheists ... Many are devotees of science fiction."[692]

However, we must also understand why cryonics never attracted the masses of people expected by its pioneers in the 1960s. As early as the 1970s, cryonic activists were frustrated that they could not convince brilliant scientists, musicians, and corporate giants to join their movement. They questioned why people did not want to live again and resisted the promise they offered.[693] Bryant and Snizek trace the "melting" of the cryonics movement to the loss of interest caused by a lack of dramatic scientific developments as well as the high costs.[694]

In my view, in explaining the downfall of cryonics we should also take into account the lack of ritual, or rather the incompatibility of cryonics with the common ritual tradition of funerals in the United States, and the violation of its own ideological preconditions. The latter point refers mainly to neuro-preservation, as carried out by *Alcor* and *KrioRus*. Beheading a dead person severely violates the cultural need for the preservation of the whole corpse. And stories about freezing fractures and other damage that have been discussed in the media also discourage the idea that cryonics represents conservation.[695] The *Cryonics Institute*, which does not provide neuro-preservation, alludes to this disturbance of ritual and the cultural needs of mourners:

> As human beings we understand that it just borders on the impossible for a person to go to the parents or children or friends of someone who has just passed away, and have to explain that the head of that person, whose loss has broken their heart, is going to be cut off and frozen in a tank with a dozen others somewhere. Nerves are frayed, families are grief-stricken, some of them may never even have heard of cryonics much less the scientific plausibility of it, and outbursts, arguments, and threats of lawsuits are inevitable.[696]

---

691 As mentioned above, suspended members of the *Cryonics Society of California* thawed in 1980, as did most of residents of the *Cryonics Society of New York*. See Darwin 1981, 18.
692 Bryant / Snizek 1973, 59.
693 See Rievman 1976, 4-5.
694 See Bryant / Snizek 1973, 61.
695 In general, the media have always had a most critical approach towards the cryonics movement. See Mann 1981, 11-12.
696 F.A.Q. at *Cryonics Institute*: http//www.cryonics.org/prod.html (07/12/2005).

However, even if the corpse is not beheaded, it is not possible to combine traditional rituals of mourning with the ideal cryonic suspension. The central ritual element of the American funeral – the viewing – demands friends and relatives offer the family their condolences by visiting the funeral home where the embalmed corpse usually is laid out. The dead body cannot be present (or viewed) at the funeral service; there is no burial or other ritual that shows: "This is the end". These rituals contradict the proper idea of cryonics. After all, there is no place of memory – the storage facilities in Michigan or in Arizona might be a great distance from the mourning family, and the collective dewars in an industrial workshop are not places where people usually go to visit their loved ones. At the beginning of cryonics most of its adherents would have wanted to store the cold coffins in a kind of chapel or a decorated vault – an architect even designed a model for such a giant storage facility (a "cryo-sanctorum") and coffin-like "resting pockets" for the *Expo* in Montreal.[697] But, due to economic restraints, more elaborate plans were never realized and the workshop solution with group dewars was enforced.[698] Although cryonic suspension requires some property, the absence of the traditional ritual order and of the nearby place of memorial might also create problems for defining the "status after death", which is usually defined by the casket, flowers, grave, ceremonial clothing of the mourners, and the social gathering of the funeral.[699]

Research in the field of rituals of death and mourning has largely indicated that there is a widespread ritual or religious need for the presentation or representation of the dead. As a result, there are sometimes disputes between the cryo companies and the bereaved, as was likely the case for Marvin Minsky, who died in 2016. The corpse was recovered three days after death by the *Alcor* team and transferred to Arizona for the separation of the head for neuro-preservation.[700]

While the cryonic movement promises the "suspension of death", a paradisal continuation of present life, and practices the "suspension of the dead", it clearly cannot satisfy the ritual needs of the vast majority of US society. For transhumanism's belief in progress, however, cryonics is the real "life insurance", in case the hoped-for immortalization techniques are not yet available in the coming years.

Technological Immortality

The idea of technologically enabled immortality is derived from two divergent strands of thought. One of these is the vision of a computer simulation of the "real person", which emerged genealogically from the media-based immortalization fantasies of early science fiction literature (Verne, Villiers de l'Isle Adam). It was only with the appearance of a cybernetic vision of human beings in the *Macy Conferences* from 1946 to 1953 and its popularization especially in the writings of Norbert Wiener that the idea of a virtual

---

697 See Bryant / Snizek 1970, 57.
698 See Sheskin 1979, 23-39.
699 See Kephart 1950, 637-343.
700 See Kephart 1950, 637-343. It was never officially confirmed that *Alcor* froze Minsky. However Minsky was a member of *Alcor* and the case summary for patient 144 corresponds exactly to the circumstances of Minsky's death. https://alcor.org/Library/html/casesummary1700.html.

existence in the memory of a computer found its way into fiction in the 1950s and 1960s (Clarke, Lem, Strugatsky, Franke).

Clearly the earliest non-fictional examples of computer-technical immortalization (Veatch, Martin, Edelhart) all took place in the context of organ transplants. In 1979 Hans Moravec explicitly adopted this clinical scenario of surgical transplant of the brain. Within cryonics this striving for longevity and the cybernetic fixation on the brain overlapped with the new perspectives of transplantation medicine and freezing technology, as well as the traditional embalming practice of US funeral culture.

It is astonishing that obvious technical and social questions about the posthumanist vision of immortality are elided. The first aspect concerns the reliability of computer storage and formats. Every computer user of my generation will remember the rapid change from floppy discs to CD-ROMS, from DVDs to thumb drives, and finally to online storage devices (clouds). They will have realized many times with frustration that old data files can no longer be read. Data experts refer to this trivial everyday experience using the term digital obsolescence. Depending on the intensity of use, electronic storage media, from the magnetic tape to hard disks, have a service life of only two to 30 years. On the other hand, old storage formats, which correspond to specific operating systems and software, cannot be transferred to new media without data reformatting or loss. Critics such as Terry Kuny are already predicting that our era will become a digital dark age, with the risk of a loss of large amounts of knowledge due to constant and rapid technological innovations.[701] Long-term archives for special cultural assets such as the Barbarastollen in Germany or the atomic-bomb-proof Mormon ancestral archive are based on photographic microfilm with a durability of about 500 years and simple but reliable technical accessibility.[702]

Against the background of this important debate about digital obsolescence, the posthumanist promise of eternal existence in the memory of a computer seems naive, especially as the simulation of human brains would require performance-intensive hardware use. Philipp von Becker also points out that every digital life form that is ultimately based on a material data-carrier is destructible and thus mortal – as illustrated in the current Netflix series *Altered Carbon*.[703] Even the idea of backup copies is quite literally useful only on paper. The technical interference of "noise" can never be eliminated 100%. Indeed, it can cause significant errors when large amounts of data are transferred or copied. Moreover, in principle the anticipated cybernetic life forms are no better equipped for the colonization of space than their biological ancestors. Solar winds, cosmic rays, and vibrations can cause huge damage to processors and memory. As the performance of computers increases, the risk of damage also rises, which is why

---

701 See Kuny 1997, 1-4. Various initiatives such as *nestor* (in Germany) or the international *Digital Preservation Coalition* are seeking solutions to this problem.
702 At the moment over a billion recordings on 32,000 km of film are archived in the Barbarastollen (www.bbk.bund.de), while about 2.4 million film rolls are stored in the Mormon Granite Mountain Records Vault.
703 See Becker 2015, 54-55.

today's spaceships and space stations are usually equipped with slow but more reliable CPUs.[704]

Aside from these fundamental problems of technical reliability, the posthumanist dream of immortality as a computer program faces yet another unsolvable difficulty – that of data security. We are currently seeing data leaks in major Internet companies almost every month, and sensitive user data such as movement profiles, health status, and credit card information is being stolen and misused millions of times over. We also observe social networks selling personal data to third parties for political and commercial purposes or gathering such information for the benefit of autocratic systems. There can be no doubt that – if virtual existence is ever realized – the human simulations (and their security copies) would be the most sought-after target of criminal activity. Administrators, whether human or artificial, would acquire huge power.[705] Artificially intelligent computer viruses – only briefly mentioned by Moravec – would be ideally suited for kidnappings and devastating attacks on multiple, translocal targets.[706] It is a difficult task to wipe out the lives of thousands of real biological people at once, unless weapons of war are used. But attacking millions of virtual life forms would be child's play for those who possessed the right digital "key".[707] In the cold light of day, the posthumanist vision of virtual immortality certainly does not guarantee an eternally secure existence. Indeed, hardly any other medium seems to be as volatile and unstable as computer software.

Why are these fundamental problems, which are so obvious even to dilettante observers, nonetheless not addressed? Just as the idea of mind transfer sounds more convincing than an approach that includes critical technical questions, the general vision of posthuman humanity becomes more attractive if the social contexts are ignored. Posthumanism looks at the technological idea of immortalization itself, without taking the social implications addressed in science fiction into account. Unlike the perfectionist aspirations of the Enlightenment or the ideas of the Russian cosmists, the posthumanist utopia comes across as an individualistic project that promises the individual divine and paradisiacal prospects.[708]

It is this consistent disregard of the social dimension and of complex technical issues that makes it possible to present virtual existence as pure liberation: as liberation from nature and evolution, liberation from the constraints, obligations, and mortality of the human body and mind, and liberation from sensory connectedness to this body on planet Earth.

---

704 See Hruska 2017.
705 Christoph Keese (Executive Vice-President of Springer AG) interviewed by Thomas Wagner. See Wagner 2015, 75.
706 See Moravec 1988, 173.
707 To reduce such risks, the virtual life forms would have to be very strongly protected by control programs to prevent anyone from inadvertently installing harmful software.
708 The only critical discussion in which post- and transhumanists have engaged, beginning with FM-2030, is the debate with supposed religious positions. Christian theologians so far have virtually ignored the issue of posthumanism. See Kurzweil 2005, 369-374; Rothblatt 2014, 283-287; Bostrom / Roache 2008, 3-7.

However, the liberation from biological matter implied here is based, as we saw, on a trick, because this virtual existence would depend on a material data carrier and on a machine to activate this data. Here posthumanists superficially take up classical ideas from Gnosticism and Platonism, which assume that the true nature of life exists in an immaterial sphere of light. The Aristotelian order of being defined all transitory living beings and things on Earth as a combination of the elements of earth, air, fire, and water, while the sun, stars, and planets were believed to consist of eternal and unchanging ether. Here too we find that Kurzweil's metaphor of sun-like singularity and the strong post- and transhumanist focus on space is, in fact, only the latest iteration of a long cultural and historical development.[709]

6.6 The Transcendental Superintelligence

> The awkward question posed by the changes we have labelled Post-Humanism is not 'Will we develop machines that are equal or superior to humans?' ... The difficult question is, 'Why do we want to develop such machines – to what ends will they be put?'[710]
>
> Robert Pepperell

Machine immortality is only the first of the two basic aspects of posthumanist reasoning. The second is participation in the future superhuman existence. By this line of thought, the progress of artificial intelligences will "carry" humans along with it by transferring their mind. No post- or transhumanist seriously advocates that cybernetic life will develop, surpass humanity, and then abandon them entirely. We must now echo Robert Pepperell in asking what this participation in artificial intelligence is all about – why should people strive for this new reality? In this context, the concepts of transcendence, superhumanity, and superintelligence play a special role, all of which reflect a particularly male ideal of human existence.

Transcendence and the Superhuman

Hans Moravec first introduced the concept of transcendence to the posthumanist discourse. In *Mind Children* (1988) he had already prophesied that artificial intelligence will "transcend" the material limits of physics and in general everything that we as humans know up to now. The term is also part of his second book's subtitle *Robot. Mere Machines to Transcendent Mind* (1999), although he does not elaborate further.[711]

Once again, Vernor Vinge bridges the gap between fiction and techno-utopia. In his novel *A Fire Upon the Deep* (1992), he describes the future of our galaxy, which is

---

709   See section 6.6.2; Gruman 1966, 15-16; Krüger 2005; Kurzweil 2005, 371.
710   Pepperell 1995, 177.
711   See Moravec 1988, 1; Moravec 1999, 159.

divided into different zones according to their degree of technological development. Once a civilization has crossed the singularity, it becomes part of the zone "Transcend" and can harbor superintelligent, artificial entities.[712] In his landmark text *The Coming Technological Singularity* (1993), he formulated his own hopes: "After all, IA [intelligence amplification] allows our participation in a kind of transcendence."[713]

Ray Kurzweil first uses the concept of transcendence in *The Age of Spiritual Machines*, where it is often associated with meditation and experiences of God, and only very generally related to technical progress.[714] It is not until his prophetic *The Singularity Is Near. When Humans Transcend Biology* (2005) and his second self-help book *Transcend: Nine Steps to Living Well Forever*, which he published with the physician Terry Grossman in 2009, that the concept of transcendence became central to Kurzweil's self-promotion. Of course, it should also be noted that the documentary *Transcendent Man* was released that same year, while the feature film *Transcendence* followed shortly thereafter in 2014. Transcendence and transcending lead Kurzweil to the transgression of the biological limits of the human being and evolution.[715] In accordance with cybernetic pattern identity theory, he reads transcendence as the persistence of information as opposed to physical material: "It's through the emergent powers of the pattern that we transcend. Since the material stuff of which we are made turns over quickly, it is the transcendent power of our patterns that persists."[716] Therefore the singularity for Kurzweil (as for Vinge) is identical with the realization of transcendence.[717]

Just as scarcely as it is reflected upon philosophically by posthumanists, the idea of transcending humanity appears only sporadically in the works of the three early masterminds of post- and transhumanism in the 20th century. John D. Bernal prophesied that the future human being would transcend all present abilities:[718]

> It may even be ... that with the new possibilities we are reaching up to a new step in cosmic evolution away from the individual organisms or the society of such organisms towards an organismal electronic complex which will transcend it and may ultimately make its organismal originator superfluous.[719]

Both the cyberneticist Norbert Wiener and Julian Huxley also occasionally speak of human transcendence via expected technical progress.[720]

What is the cultural-historical background of this central tenet of posthumanist visions? Unlike scarcely any other concept, transcendence is deeply rooted in American philosophy. The transcendentalists emerged as the first philosophical movement of the New World in the mid-19th century. However, it would be inappropriate to begin

---

712 See Vinge 1992; Yudkowsky 2000a.
713 Vinge 1993.
714 See Kurzweil 1999a, 23, 109-111, 189.
715 See Kurzweil 2005, 3, 9, 136, 374.
716 See ibid., 388.
717 Martine Rothblatt understands transcendence as overcoming the material limitations of the biological human being (and his or her sexual determination). See Rothblatt 2014.
718 See Bernal 1929, 16.
719 Bernal 1969, 857.
720 See Wiener 1985, 184; Huxley 1957b, 13.

a genealogy of ideas here, as the transcendentalists were strongly influenced by German and English Romanticism and idealism. They praised mystical knowledge before pure reason and understood their commitment as a rebellion against the rational view of humans and the Enlightenment doctrine of progress. Since almost all transcendentalists were originally Unitarians, their ideas were usually interpreted as protesting and reforming that established doctrine. They thus embodied a countermovement to the materialistic and utilitarian philosophies of the 19th century, which were to become so decisive for posthumanist utopias.[721] At most, one can assume that the influence of Unitarianism during Ray Kurzweil's youth might have promoted a certain affinity to the concept of transcendence.

Similarly, the majority of trans- and posthumanist thinkers adopt Friedrich Nietzsche's idea of the superhuman (*Übermensch*). Terminologically, Frank Tipler, Marvin Minsky, and Kevin Warwick dub the future state of humanity as 'superhuman' or 'superbeing'.[722] Explicit references to Nietzsche, however, are only made by the cryonics founder Robert Ettinger, the German transhumanist Stefan Sorgner, and the Extropian Max More. Ettinger strongly condemns Nietzsche's racism, but (paradoxically) praises his vision of the future human being that knows no moral barriers: "Nevertheless, the best of Nietzsche is very good, and he made an important contribution toward exposing the illusions of the altruists."[723]

Taking into account the broadest possible anthropological basis, Ettinger develops the image of a superman combining the qualities of ancient heroes, Nietzsche's philosophical superman, and the superheroes of various science fiction stories and comics. The result is – as in Daniel Halacy's *Cyborg – Evolution of the Superhuman* (1965) – a superintelligent sex and war machine (as outlined in chapter 4.3).[724]

Stefan Sorgner, on the other hand, tries to identify similarities between Nietzsche's philosophy and transhumanism in the dynamic image of humans and the courageous overcoming of traditional moral and religious barriers.[725] Max More also emphasizes these common aspects, but at the same time points out the incompatibility of the transhumanist belief in progress with Nietzsche's concept of eternal recurrence. In contrast to Sorgner, More even emphasizes that Nietzsche directly influenced transhumanism, because More himself was inspired by Nietzsche's superhuman and interpreted the concept of the transhuman accordingly.[726]

---

721 David Brin's categorization of posthumanism as *techno / cyber transcendentalism* would therefore be misleading. See Miller 1979, 7-9; Brin 2013, 395-396. The derivations from the transcendentalist Ralph Waldo Emerson's concept of the *plus-man / great man*, which are sometimes suggested, would be equally inappropriate due to their underlying vitalist principle. See Benz 1961, 105-112; Regis 1990, 276-277.
722 See Tipler 1995, 87-88, 255-259; Minsky 1992a, 24; Warwick 2000, 151; Warwick 1997, 1998.
723 Ettinger 1989, 26.
724 See ibid., 43-87; Halacy 1965.
725 See Sorgner 2009.
726 See More 2010; More 1996, 3; More 1994, 2. Nick Bostrom and Frank Tipler sharply reject any connection between Nietzsche and transhumanism, partly because of the Social Darwinist racial cult that was later so formative for Nazi ideology. See Bostrom 2005; Tipler 1995, 80-83.

For some post- and transhumanists, transcendence and superhumanity are critical concepts. Furthermore, for Ettinger, Kurzweil, Vinge, Sorgner, and More, they effectively designate two crucial elements of the human relationship with the posthuman. Firstly, this connection will transcend human nature to an extent that has so far only been envisaged of divine transcendence. Secondly, humans will participate in this transcendent existence. From this perspective, the posthuman is always also transhuman due to its inherent transcendence: like the glass beads of a kaleidoscope, **trans**cendent, **post**human, and **trans**human each shine through with their own nuances, and reflect the overlapping relationship between humans and transcendence. The iridescent array of shifting colors – the qualities of the hoped-for posthuman existence – remain constantly in motion.

Mind, Genius, and Superintelligence

> I do not think there is any thrill that can go through the human heart like that felt by the inventor as he sees some creation of the brain unfolding to success.[727]
> Nikola Tesla

Post- and transhumanist promises of paradise were extremely diverse and vivid until the mid-2000s. Even before being able to upload themselves into a virtual existence, people were supposed to have robotic and artificially intelligent assistants. Hans Moravec raves about the fact that universal household robots will soon free humans from tiresome activities such as vacuuming, cooking, cleaning, and carpet weaving.[728] Ray Kurzweil is even more optimistic: He believes that by 2029, people in almost all professions – from teachers to doctors – will have been replaced by more powerful computers. The leading artists, composers, and musicians will also be cybernetic organisms.[729] At the same time, posthumanists promise that thanks to nanotechnology, medical advances will guarantee solutions to all health problems. Kurzweil therefore predicts an average life expectancy of about 120 years in the near future.[730]

Furthermore, all posthumanist authors agree that the progress of information technologies and the replacement of human labor by more productive, intelligent machines will lead to infinite wealth: "Early to bed and early to rise, makes a man healthy and wealthy and wise."[731] Marvin Minsky quotes this Calvinist motto of Benjamin Franklin before discussing the conditions for anticipated unlimited wealth. Indeed, this imminent future would be characterized by robot playmates and a luxurious lifestyle

---

727 Cited in Kurzweil 2005, 1.
728 See Moravec 1988, 22-25; Moravec 1996a, 101-108; Moravec 1999, 91-110, 124-125.
729 At the beginning of the 19th century, the "machine destroyers" were called Luddites. See Kurzweil 1999a, 85-86, 180-182, 202-233.
730 See Minsky 1994, 113; Tipler 1995, 104-105; Moravec 1988, 102; Moravec 1999, 9-13, 141-142; Kurzweil 1999a, 223.
731 Minsky 1994, 108.

for every human being, in a world where all social tensions and conflicts would be resolved:[732]

> Furthermore, the road we're going down is a road paved with gold. It's full of benefits that we're never going to resist – continued growth in economic prosperity, better health, more intense communication, more effective education, more engaging entertainment, better sex.[733]

The virtual existence they imagine will even exceed the promises of this future exponentially. Humans are not given health and longevity, but rather immortality. They will be able to alter their virtual body shapes according to their wishes, travel through the emulated universe unaided, and yet still enjoy culinary delights like any biological human being, including the touch and feel of other people. Nick Bostrom describes this state poetically: "Beyond dreams. Beyond imagination ... There is a beauty and joy here that you cannot fathom. It feels so good that if the sensation were translated into tears of gratitude, rivers would overflow."[734]

Frank Tipler elaborates upon this virtual paradise in regard to a question that was often posed by his male, unmarried students: "Is there sex in heaven?" (Tipler regularly held lectures on his Omega theory at *Tulane University* in New Orleans). This lengthy passage from the *The Physics of Immortality* documents the all-powerful quality of Tipler's virtual emulation, and impressively illustrates his unrestricted need for mathematization – in this case of beauty:

> ... since some people desire sex, the answer has to be yes, sex will be available to those who wish it ... However, the problems which sex generates in our present life will not occur in the afterlife ... it would be possible for each male to be matched not merely with the most beautiful woman in the world, not merely with the most beautiful woman who has ever lived, but to be matched with the most beautiful woman whose existence is logically possible ... It is instructive to compute the psychological impact of the most beautiful woman on a man ... Assuming the validity of the Fechner-Weber Law at large stimulus, the relative psychological impact of meeting the most beautiful of these is thus $[\log_{10}10^{106}]/[\log_{10}10^9]$=100,000 times the impact of meeting the most beautiful woman in the world ... I've gone through this calculation to illustrate dramatically one crucial point: the principle of nonsatiation will not hold for the resurrected humans ... about two thirds of adult humans experience at some point in their lives [sic!] an intense passion for a member of opposite sex which is not reciprocated: this is the phenomenon of unrequited love. The Omega Point has the power to turn this passion into *requited* love in the afterlife.[735]

Moreover, at least as a man, you will also be able to find new joy in your sex life: " ... not just sex. Not even just very good sex. *Incredible sex*, without such penalties as AIDS

---

732 See Minsky 1994, 108; Tipler 1995, 104-105; Moravec 1988, 102; Moravec 1999, 9-13, 141-142; Moravec / Pohl 1993, 76; Kurzweil 1999a, 130-131, 202-233.
733 Ibid., 130.
734 Bostrom 2008. See Proudfoot 2012, 372.
735 Tipler 1995, 256-257.

or unwanted pregnancy or even the wrath of a jealous lover, since all of it takes place in your mind."[736]

It is thus obvious that posthumanist utopia seeks to overcome the biological body, rather than corporeality per se. The dream of posthumanism includes the desire for physical perfection, strength, and sensual pleasure. None of the posthumanist authors devalue these forms of sensual desire or physicality. The general interpretation of posthumanism as cyberplatonism or cybergnosis, as proposed by Erik Davis, Slavoj Žižek, and Hartmut Böhme, is therefore misleading.[737]

Writings from the 1990s already contained these "colorful" prospects at the periphery of posthumanist progress theory. This striving for perfection centers upon the abilities of the human mind. As seen here, these remain decisive for the posthumanist conception of the human being and offer a yardstick of development (chapter 6.2). However, it was only through Ray Kurzweil's book *The Singularity Is Near* (2005) and Nick Bostrom's work *Superintelligence* (2014) that the posthuman as an entity in its own right gained sharper contours. What was previously only loosely connected to the availability of artificially intelligent computers now refers directly (according to Kurzweil) to the one (!) superintelligence to be realized with the occurrence of the singularity in 2045. The conventional goal of AI research had always been to create an artificial system on the level of human intelligence, for which Marvin Minsky strived throughout his life. Yet this goal is suddenly replaced by the prophecy of a superhuman, transcendental superintelligence. This, however, raises the question of the historical connections between ideas shaped by the cult of genius and the eugenic fantasy of breeding elite brains, which began around 1900. In this context, the human brain's special position in posthumanism is significant: from a posthumanist perspective, the brain remains completely identical with a human being's personality. It will form the basis of the immortalizing transfer of the mind, dubbed *whole brain emulation* by Anders Sandberg and Nick Bostrom.[738]

As early as 1988, Hans Moravec formulated his goal and claim with a view to the fourth generation of robots, which would be "super-human" and "super-rational":[739]

> Long life loses much of its point if we are fated to spend it staring stupidly at our ultra-intelligent machines as they try to describe their ever more spectacular discoveries in baby-talk that we can understand. We want to become full, unfettered players in this new superintelligent game.[740]

Similarly, for Frank Tipler these prospects are not disconcerting because of the ultimate resurrection of all human beings: "Ultimately, intelligent machines will become more intelligent than members of the species Homo sapiens and will thus dominate civilization. So what?"[741] In works by Nick Bostrom and Ray Kurzweil the

---

736   Moravec / Pohl 1993, 74.
737   See Krüger 2005.
738   See Sandberg / Bostrom 2008; Moravec 1988, 109-110; Kurzweil 2005, 143-203.
739   See Moravec 1988, 1, 22-25; Moravec 1996a, 101-108; Moravec 1999, 91-110, 124-125.
740   Moravec 1988, 108.
741   Tipler 1995, 87.

superintelligence gains a redemptive quality that was already inherent in Vernor Vinge's vision of the future. Both thinkers refer to each other reciprocally: Kurzweil connects singularity with Bostrom's ideas on superintelligence, and Bostrom, in turn, connects his understanding of superintelligence to Kurzweil's singularity prophecy (even though he explicitly rejects its religious connotations).[742] It is difficult to tell which of these two thinkers waxed poetically about technology in the following passage:

> It is hard to think of any problem that a superintelligence could not either solve or at least help us solve. Disease, poverty, environmental destruction, unnecessary suffering of all kinds: these are things that a superintelligence equipped with advanced nanotechnology would be capable of eliminating. Additionally, a superintelligence could give us indefinite lifespan, either by stopping and reversing the aging process through the use of nanomedicine, or by offering us the option to upload ourselves.[743]

It initially seems surprising that neither Bostrom nor Kurzweil present or discuss a definition of intelligence in their lengthy books. For Kurzweil it is simply the increase of storage and computing capacities, whereas Bostrom distinguishes between a collective and a qualitative superintelligence.[744] However, neither of these two successful authors has any research experience in the field of artificial intelligence: Bostrom is a philosopher by profession, while Kurzweil created some inventions and proposed technical improvements for optical text recognition programs, especially in the 1970s and 1980s.

Even within the trans- and posthumanist debate, the expectation of a superintelligent AI, which remains associated with singularity, is highly controversial. The economist Robin Hanson and the quantum physicist Michael Nielsen question whether the "intelligence explosion" Bostrom predicts could ever occur, especially without first clearly understanding the concept of intelligence itself. They argue that, instead of a so-called dominant AI that will surpass humans in all areas of life, it is more likely that computers will become more powerful in certain niche areas. According to Nielsen, the assumption of AI's impending hegemony over all planetary life is just as plausible as the omnipotent reign of bacteria.[745] Anders Sandberg points out that the prognosis of exponential technological progress – such as the realization of the singularity – is based on steady economic growth and social stability, which of course are not natural.[746] The AI researcher Selmer Bringsjord even accuses the representatives of the ultra-intelligent singularity thesis of having long since slipped into the realm of religious prophecy, since their thesis can neither be derived rationally nor proven empirically:[747]

---

742 See Kurzweil 2005, 259-260; Bostrom 2014, 2.
743 This was Nick Bostrom (2003).
744 See Bostrom 2014, 53-57; Loh 2018, 113.
745 See Hanson 2013, 405; Nielsen 2013, 409-411.
746 See Sandberg 2013b, 411-416.
747 See Bringsjord / Bringsjord / Bello 2012.

... and yet, again, here we are, with hardware that moves information in silicon at a rate that makes the transmission speed of the brain seem as slow as a disoriented caterpillar by comparison, and we still don't have a machine that can problem-solve, even in highly formal domains like computer programming, at the level of a mediocre novice.[748]

The experts' criticisms of Vinge, Kurzweil, and Bostrom's singularity or superintelligence concepts reveal the theoretical void in the posthumanist thesis. From the point of view of actual AI research, there is no technical reason why in 25 years at the latest an "intelligence explosion" should suddenly take place, due to increasing memory and computing power, which will also solve all the problems of humankind, the planet, and the universe. One feels reminded of the widespread state of accepted unreality in *The Emperor's New Clothes* when the science fiction author David Brin, despite his own personal reservations, reaffirms his belief in singularity: "The alternative is simply too awful to accept."[749]

From the perspective of cultural studies, the question therefore remains why the idea of a superintelligence associated with singularity seems so attractive, at least to parts of the technophile milieu, although their technical arguments appear to be thin on closer examination. The analysis of the singularity as an image of progress within the history of ideas has revealed that other, pre-established cultural motifs – such as the frontier or the popular mystification of black holes – have "carried" the broad acceptance of the singularity with them. So, then which cultural tropes enable the "superintelligence", as Vinge, Kurzweil, and Bostrom anticipate it?

Most authors refer to the British mathematician Irving John Good's 1965 essay *Speculations Concerning the First Ultraintelligent Machine* as the originator of the idea of superintelligence.[750] Good studied mathematics at Cambridge and served at Bletchley Park from 1941, where he was involved in the decoding of German signals and the development of the first electronic computer, *Colossus*, under the direction of Alan Turing. Later he was professor of statistics for almost three decades at Virginia Tech University in the United States. Good introduces his famous essay with a prophetic confession: "The survival of man depends on the early construction of an ultra-intelligent machine."[751] This computer, which Good anticipated would have been built by the end of the 20th century, would be far superior to humans in the storage and processing of information:

> Let an ultraintelligent machine be defined as a machine that can far surpass all the intellectual activities of any man however clever. Since the design of machines is one of these intellectual activities, an ultra-intelligent machine could design even better machines; there would then unquestionably be an "intelligence explosion," and the

---

748 Ibid., 405.
749 Brin 2013, 396. The actual AI researchers that I have met at conferences over the past 15 years usually simply shake their heads when asked about these grand posthumanists visions.
750 See Good 1965; Vinge 1993; Vinge 2013, 366-367; Bostrom 2014, 4; Kurzweil 2005, 22-23; Loh 2018, 112-114.
751 Good 1965, 31.

intelligence of man would be left far behind ... Thus the first ultraintelligent machine is the last invention that man need ever make, provided that the machine is docile enough to tell us how to keep it under control. It is curious that this point is made so seldom outside of science fiction. It is sometimes worthwhile to take science fiction seriously.[752]

Good identifies the translation of semantics into machine language as the biggest obstacle facing the development of artificial intelligence. As the first application and thus a type of yardstick for measuring intelligence he used chess – a great personal passion of his.[753] As early as 1962 – at the height of the Cuba crisis – Good expected that future Russian and American ultra-intelligent machines (UIM) could merge into a single world government and guarantee a lasting peace: "Oracles of the world unite!"[754] Good's enthusiasm does indeed anticipate some elements of technological posthumanism, even if these visions do not yet contain a concrete agenda.

> The UIM will enable us to solve any practically soluble problem and we shall perhaps achieve a world peace, the elixir of life, the piecemeal conversion of people into UIPs (ultra-intelligent people), or the conversion of the world's population into a *single* UIP.[755]

Should it turn out that machines can only handle "merely fantastic" tasks that do not require creative intelligence, overcoming this developmental limit would become the task of these "artificially-bred human geniuses".[756]

The idea of a superintelligent computer was popularized primarily by several works of science fiction. As early as 1930, the English philosopher and writer Olaf Stapledon had published his novel *Last and First Man. A Story of the Near and Far Future*. This text described the human future over the next billion years, which would lead to the creation of new life forms with ever larger – even cosmic – brains.[757] Without a doubt, the greatest influence upon fictional accounts of superior computer intelligence was Stanley Kubrick's *HAL 9000*, the omnipotent central computer of the research spaceship in the film *2001 Space Odyssey*. The 1968 film was created in parallel with Arthur C. Clarke's novel with the same title. This humanized yet bodiless computer monitors the ship only through its red camera eye. It eventually becomes so convinced of its own perfection that it cannot admit to making any mistakes and begins to murder the human astronauts. The film ends when the last survivor of the five astronauts finally succeeds in switching off the computer. Long before the *Commodore 64* home computers thrilled youngsters in the 1980s, the computer *HAL* embodied a non-human and non-divine counterpart, whose power (at least inside the spaceship) far surpassed that of human beings. This machine was ready to eliminate the astronauts and complete the mission on its own. In

---

752   Ibid., 33. See ibid., 33-37, 78.
753   See ibid., 33-37.
754   Good 1962, 195. The physicist Gerald Feinberg also uses the comparison with the ancient oracles. See Feinberg 1969, 87-101.
755   Irving J. Good: Machine Intelligence. In: *Impact* (UNESCO) 4/1971, cited in Roszak 1994, 39.
756   See Good 1962, 195-196.
757   See Stapledon 1930.

the making of the film, Marvin Minsky and Irving Good acted as scientific advisors to the director. Moreover, Clarke in fact uses their names as pioneers of computer science and the inventors of the neural networks in his fictional universe.[758]

Stanisław Lem offers a version of this intellectually superior supercomputer in his 1981 story *GOLEM XIV*.[759] Originally created for military purposes, *GOLEM XIV* was sent to the Massachusetts Institute of Technology in Boston after some failed tests, where he gives several philosophical lectures on humans, himself, and the meaning of life (the lectures are fictionally edited by "Irving T. Creve"). In his first anthropological thesis, the electronic brain states that humankind's actual meaning is to be a "message"; biological organisms serve only to transmit this message. From GOLEM's perspective, humans are "transitional beings" whose only purpose is to "build rational beings". Finally, GOLEM prophesies that rational humans will sacrifice the human being in its natural, biological state in order to enable evolution from *homo naturalis* to computer.[760] Both *HAL 9000* and *GOLEM XIV* appear as all-powerful, genius-like beings, while humans, in contrast, are characterized as "lemurs and prosimians".[761] Computers in these stories benefit from godlike possibilities: detached from the limits of matter, *GOLEM XIV* as a pure mind can set off for new dimensions of experience, and finally shrouds itself in eternal silence.

Half a cinema century after *HAL 9000*, Wally Pfister's 2014 film *Transcendence* explicitly addresses the futurology of posthumanism. The hero of the story is a charming AI researcher who is about to realize a cybernetic superintelligence: "Some scientists refer to this as the singularity. I call it transcendence." After an assassination attempt by revolutionary technology critics, he is mortally wounded and transfers his mind to a quantum computer. With new powers he subsequently discovers he has developed, he apparently strives for world domination, before being finally destroyed by his opponents (and his widow). Only in the epilogue does it become clear that he actually sought to solve all of the world's problems with the help of controlled nanoparticles. This film contributed significantly to the spread of the concept of singularity.[762]

Luc Besson's film *Lucy* from the same year revolved around a similar idea. By means of a miraculous drug, the heroine rapidly develops into a supremely intelligent being, who can finally arbitrarily shape the form of matter as well as that of her own body. As her evolution continues, by the end of the story she mutates first into a wise supercomputer, and ultimately into a USB flash drive containing the knowledge of all humankind and, beyond that, of all living beings.[763]

The importance of science fiction literature and films can hardly be overestimated, as they reveal cultural ideas about the relationship between humans and computers

---

758 See Kubrick 1968; Clarke 1968.
759 However, some parts of the book are taken from Lem's *Imaginary Magnitude* from 1973. By saying GOLEM (**G**eneral **O**perator, **L**ongrange, **E**thically Stabilized, **M**ultimodelling) Lem alludes, on the one hand, to the Kabbalistic Golem saga. On the other hand, he creates a reference to Norbert Wiener's book *God & Golem, Inc.* (1964). See Gräfrath 1996, 13-14; Lem 1984.
760 See ibid., 39, 49, 82-84.
761 Ibid., 31-32. In the first scene of Kubrick 1968.
762 See Pfister 2014.
763 See Besson 2014.

anticipated over the next few decades. We must be aware that until the middle of the 20th century both Christianity and Darwinism enthroned humankind as the pinnacle of creation. This is reflected in the eugenicist utopia of consciously creating a new, more highly developed type of human. The blind faith in this extreme form of humanism culminated in the Western European and American practice of forced sterilizations, and the murderous racial politics of National Socialism. However, it was shattered by the inherent ethical conflicts that such "selection of inferior life" brought about. In the cybernetic and fictional works of the post-war period, speculation began about the coming, pure and fleshless, and therefore "innocent" utopia of electronic masterminds as the next stage of evolution. They are described as superior, but now also as a threat to humankind (as exemplified by *HAL 9000*). The idea of transferring the human mind into a virtual existence had been described before, but it was not until the late 1980s that Hans Moravec's *Mind Children* included human participation in this superior machine intelligence. Paradigmatically, this change of meaning can be read in Vernor Vinge's publications. Even in his early text from 1983, the singularity merely marks the point in time at which humankind will have created the intelligences that will surpass it. In 1993, Vinge thus designated a posthuman era of *superhumanity*, in which biological and cybernetic life would be immortally interwoven.[764]

This evolutionary model also shapes the metaphorical comparisons that post- and transhumanist authors use to characterize the superiority of superintelligence. For example, according to various explanations, posthuman beings are as incomprehensible to us humans as we are to goldfish,[765] rocks,[766] bacteria,[767] dogs, monkeys, and Neanderthals.[768]

This kind of evolutionary comparison can be found in 19th century racial theories and eugenic propaganda. It is therefore worth examining the cultural components of the posthumanist idea of superintelligence more closely. As described in the previous chapters, from a posthumanist perspective human beings are information-processing systems. The concept of progress – defined as the increase in computing operations per second and storage capacities – is rooted in the Enlightenment idea of increasing work performance and knowledge. Superintelligence now promises the infinite increase of conventional human and cybernetic information processing.

The clearest equivalent to superintelligence is undoubtedly the European and American concept of genius. Until the Romantic period around 1800, genius was reserved exclusively for artistic pursuits such as painting, poetry, and music. The creative genius could guide the creation of nature to perfection, as in the outstanding achievements of individual men such as Petrarch, Shakespeare, Johann Sebastian Bach, or Michelangelo. According to tradition in antiquity, genius was received from inspiration given by the divine eternal. It was only through participating in the divine that a mortal man could create something that could reach beyond his transient

---

764   See Vinge 1983; Vinge 1993.
765   See Bostrom 1998, 401; Hanson 2013, 404-405.
766   See Kurzweil 2005, 136.
767   See ibid., 367.
768   See Yudkowsky 2000; Vinge 1993.

existence and last eternally. This was symbolized throughout antiquity and since the Renaissance by the artist being kissed by the divine muses. Since the 19th century, the concept of genius has been expanded to include philosophers, scientists, and military commanders (such as Napoleon Bonaparte), and since 1900, also inventors such as Thomas Edison and Nikola Tesla.[769] In addition, the concept of the universal genius developed, as applied to Goethe or Leonardo da Vinci. The (auto-)biographical construction of a genius becomes decisive for this categorization, and includes insights into his origin, upbringing, heroic asceticism, as well as strokes of fate. In this way, the doctrine of divine inspiration was replaced by rationalizing theories of genius and achievement, which, however, created a veritable cult of genius at the *fin de siècle*.

One particular indication of this worship of rational brilliance was the cult of chess geniuses, which began in the 1880.[770] It was adopted and continued by posthumanist authors as an indicator of intelligence. They use graphs to illustrate the differences between artificial and human intelligences, such as in the comparison of chess programs like *Deep Thought* and *Deep Blue* with various biological forms.[771] Interestingly, mastering chess was used two centuries earlier to measure the art of automatons striving to perfectly imitate nature. From 1769, the inventor Wolfgang von Kempelen presented his "Mechanical Turk" ("the Chess Turk") an oriental-robed automaton, which apparently could independently and masterfully execute chess games against human players. The enthusiasm for this machine inspired several rulers, such as Napoleon Bonaparte and the Prussian King Frederick II, to play it. However, the automaton was not the mechanical genius it appeared, as von Kempelen and subsequent owners in fact concealed a talented human chess player inside its metal body.[772]

Incidentally, the gender of the genius remains one-sided even after the rationalizations of the 19th century – the muses only kiss men. Thus, today's popular books on the geniuses of humankind seem to struggle with female members in this elitist club.

Francis Galton, the British founder of eugenics first tried to quantify the extraordinary "abilities" of British men in his work *Hereditary Genius* (1869). Impressed by the work of his cousin Charles Darwin, Galton pursued the thesis that, in addition to physical qualities, mental abilities were also inherited biologically:[773] "By natural ability, I mean those qualifications of intellect and disposition, which urge and qualify a man to perform acts that lead to reputation."[774] Galton statistically measures the distribution of intelligence by the number of judges, statesmen, writers, scientists, artists, and theologians produced by individual families and even entire societies. As a result, his

---

769 Kurzweil is described in his English Wikipedia article as "a worthy heir to Edison". He shares the legendary inventor Nikola Tesla's charisma and Kurzweil places his visionary quote at the beginning of his prologue to *The Singularity Is Near*. See Kurzweil 2005, 1. Tesla is considered a misunderstood genius in New Age and related pseudo-scientific movements.
770 See Köhne 2014, 25-33, 58-64.
771 See Moravec 1988, 8-13, 78, 171; Moravec 1999, 66-72, 186-189; Kurzweil 1999a, 74-75, 289-290; Kurzweil 2005, 8, 146, 274-278.
772 See Standage 2003.
773 See Galton 1972, 45-55.
774 Ibid., 77.

universal historical evaluation of all human races attributes the highest realization of these powers and positions to the Attic Greeks, while non-Europeans, and particularly Africans, are found at the bottom of the scale. The latter did not produce any notable personalities and were, according to his personal judgment, so childish, stupid and feeble-minded that Galton was ashamed to belong to the same human species.[775]

One of the most important tools for eugenicists and race theorists at the time was the measurement of the human brain. This was important in two regards: on the one hand, brain weight and brain convolutions were used to explain artistic and scientific genius; on the other hand, such measurements could be used to scientifically legitimize the intellectual and moral development and ranking of human races, social subclasses, and criminals. Originally, only the brains of famous men such as Oliver Cromwell or Lord Byron were dissected and preserved in rare exceptional surgeries. However, in the mid-19th century these developed into a program of systematic research, initially on the brains of famous professors in the German university city of Göttingen. Later it became widespread practice around the time of the First World War (and those so dissected included Carl Friedrich Gauss, Ernst Haeckel, Walt Whitman, Justus Liebig, Franz Schubert, Hermann von Helmholtz, Theodor Mommsen, Robert Schumann, and Wilhelm von Siemens).[776] At the same time, the measurement of the brain and the human skull served as supposed scientific evidence for the different human races. Thus, in many European countries, nationwide random samples were taken to anatomically prove the superiority of one's own nation.

Early brain research had serious implications, especially for the construction of the African "Negro race". It was considered to not only be inferior to all other races, but, according to the polygenists, even belonged to another species. Although scientific evidence already existed to the contrary, during the American Civil War anthropologists such as the British researcher James Hunt claimed that the African's brain was significantly smaller, smoky in color and had fewer twists and turns.[777]

> First, that there is as good reason for classifying the Negro as a distinct species from the European as there is for making the ass a distinct species from the zebra; and if we take intelligence into consideration in classification, there is far greater difference between the Negro and Anglo-Saxon than between the gorilla and chimpanzee.[778]

---

[775] See ibid., 392-395.

[776] Relatives often hoped that such research would anatomically confirm the visible talents of celebrities after death. However, in the end the brains of outstanding scientists did not turn out to be any different from those of "normal" men, women, or other races. As a result, the research into elite brains ceased abruptly at the beginning of the 20th century. The late samples taken from Lenin's (1927) and Einstein's (1955) brains can be attributed more to the cult of personality. See Hagner 2004, 249-264, 296-303.

[777] His book On the Negro's Place in Nature (1865) alludes to Thomas Huxley's Evidence as to Man's Place in Nature (1863) and, during the American Civil War (1861-65), provided important arguments for the legitimation of slavery. See Hunt 1864, XV-XVI., LI-LVI; Hunt 1865, 15-19, 26-27, 53.

[778] Hunt 1864, XVI.

The relationship between Europeans and non-European races thus resembles the former's approach to children. For example, according to proponents of these theories the "Negro brain" only develops until the age of 12, and then remains at this level.[779]

> There is no doubt that the Negro brain bears a great resemblance to a European female or child's brain, and thus approaches the ape far more than the European, while the Negress approaches the ape still nearer.[780]

For this reason, the behavior of so-called "inferior races" was categorized as either choleric or phlegmatic. These other cultures were further deemed incapable of producing a civilization that included scientists and artists, but instead could only know the most brutal barbarism, superstition, torture, and cruelty. Therefore the "Negro's" natural position, it was concluded, was to be subordinate to Europeans, while the journey as a slave from Africa to America was compared to leaving hell and arriving in paradise. Such conclusions can easily be extrapolated to offer a comparison of how the defense of slavery during this period went hand in hand with the political and social disenfranchisement of women in Europe and the United States.[781]

Early brain research in the 19th century thus held immense significance for eugenicist politics in two important ways. According to this logic, representatives of the most biologically valuable group saw themselves as continually threatened by the degeneration of their superior genetic material. The uncontrolled proliferation of lower social classes (in Galton's case the "undesirable classes") and the mixing of whites with the "inferior races" therefore had to be prevented.[782] Forced sterilizations, marriage prohibitions, and, in times of colonialism or National Socialism, the massacre of "unworthy lives", were all implemented with the intent of preventing such "contamination". Eugenicists positively propagated the goal of a pure-bred "ingenious collective" which, as the "master race", would determine the destiny of future humanity. This found its clearest expression in the work of the Germanophile race theorist Houston Stewart Chamberlain.[783] More recent eugenicists, such as Robert K. Graham, who maintained a sperm bank for (male) Nobel Prize winners from 1980 until his death in 1997, subscribed to this fascination with "brilliant brains".[784]

The eugenic fascination with the future development of the brain – toward ever more brain power – continues to be reflected in Teilhard de Chardin's work. In his opinion, the perfection of the human brain will accelerate as a form of "collective cerebralization" through the multiplication of stimuli in global society. It will also experience additional impetus from the "astonishing electronic machines" and the advances in cybernetics, which already existed at that time. The individual human being would thus benefit from the activation of already existing but not yet utilized neurons

---

779 See Hunt 1865, 11, 17, 27, 37, 41, 51, 60.
780 Hunt 1865, 16-17.
781 See Hunt 1864, XV-XVI, LI-LVI; Hunt 1865, 15-19, 26-27, 38, 53.
782 See Galton 1909, 310-313.
783 As Edwin Black shows, this racial ideology has taken root in the United States as well as in Germany. See Köhne 2014, 361-401; Black 2004.
784 In his book *The Future of Man* (1981), Robert K. Graham uses the same arguments as Francis Galton to attempt to prevent the demise of humankind that is threatened by genetic degeneration.

of the brain – "or – who can say ? – by direct (mechanical, biological or chemical) stimulation of new arrangements".[785]

While most of those post- and transhumanist authors who expect the arrival of a cybernetic superintelligence or singularity do not explicitly advocate a renewed eugenics, Nick Bostrom proves to in fact be a proponent. According to him, genetic engineering enhancement could make people healthier, more spiritual, and happier:

> We might speculate, instead, that germ-line enhancements will lead to more love and parental dedication. Some mothers and fathers might find it easier to love a child who, thanks to enhancements, is bright, beautiful, healthy, and happy.[786]

Higher intelligence would afford genetically improved people better professional positions and higher social standing. In contrast to the problematic eugenics programs of the past, the future enhancements possible within liberal society would benefit from the free decision of individuals.[787] The state should, however, consider granting tax incentives for the eugenic enhancement of intelligence, for the common good, and to counteract possible subsequent inequalities.[788] However, it must be considered that, in a liberal democracy, genetic enhancements would instead only be affordable for the already rich, rather than being freely available to everyone. Yet according to Bostrom's logic, the worst possible outcome would in fact be cultural apathy and stagnation, rather than mass inequality: " ... humanity could get permanently stuck in a not-very-good state, having foolishly changed itself to lack any desire to strive for something better."[789]

Ray Kurzweil, for his part, explicitly refers to the results of eugenically motivated brain research when he emphasizes that Einstein's parietal lobe was particularly pronounced and the brains of serial killers contain "errors". In any case, he promises that people of the future will not be limited to mere partial giftedness as Einstein was.[790]

Since Moravec's early writings, all posthumanist authors and many transhumanists have shared a fascination with the artificial intelligence they hope would "transcend" human thought. This admiration of cybernetics is reflected in the metaphorical naming of computers: The first electronic computer conceived by Alan Turing was called *Colossus*, while in his 1949 book the cyberneticist Edmund Berkeley mentions *Giant Brains* – although at that time they were only dwarf brains, as Arthur C. Clarke pointedly notes.[791] This fascination with artificial genius brains emerged historically directly after eugenic breeding fantasies were discredited in 1945 by Nazi racial politics and

---

[785] Teilhard 1966, 111. See ibid., 107-112.
[786] Bostrom 2003, 9. See Loh 2018, 177.
[787] The abortion of millions of female fetuses, now made possible by prenatal diagnostics, is especially prevalent in India and China, even despite government efforts to the contrary. However, Bostrom does not seem to find this worthy of mention, probably because it would counteract the euphemistic logic of complete deregulation.
[788] See Bostrom 2003, 10-15.
[789] Ibid., 20.
[790] See Kurzweil 2005, 202.
[791] See Clarke 1960, 213.

experiments.[792] But it was only with posthumanism and the *transmigration* proposed by Moravec that the idea of human participation in this superhuman intelligence emerged. In Bostrom's case, the sponsorship of historical eugenics is unmistakable. There is a direct connection in the history of ideas via the eugenicist Julian Huxley, whom Bostrom consistently identifies as the originator of transhumanism. The superhuman also influences Bostrom's figures of thought: in an 2016 interview, he describes discovering Nietzsche in his youth as an "epiphany experience," and as awakening from a former somnambulistic life of ignorance, which ultimately led him to philosophy, mathematics, and, finally, transhumanism.[793]

Far be it for me to claim that trans- and posthumanists are generally racists and misogynists. However, it is nonetheless important to recognize that the cultural interpretations of technological posthumanism, as expressed by the fascination with superintelligence, are a direct continuation of those ideas of genius, brain, and race developed in Western Europe and the United States over the last century. The biological metaphors of race theorists around 1900 are comparable to the ideas of modern posthumanists and indicate the persistence of these categorizations. While at that time the brilliant Nordic or Aryan man was posited as evolution's crowning achievement, today this place is occupied by the anticipated superintelligent posthuman. Brain size or quantifiable mental abilities (chess!) remain the best measurement of both these orders of beings.

It is therefore no coincidence that transhumanism is largely a movement of white men. The major transhumanist conferences I attended around the year 2000 had an estimated ratio of one woman to 50 men, with very little ethnic diversification. With the exception of the transgender transhumanist Martine Rothblatt and the artist Natasha Vita-More, hardly any women have regularly contributed to the transhumanist debate. In the important transhumanist *Journal of Evolution and Technology*, in which both activists and some academics publish, only 16 articles by women authors or co-authors (7.8%) can be found among the 203 articles published between 1998 and the latest issue of 2019.[794] Of the 67 contributions at the Extropy Institute's conferences (1994-2004), only 11 were by women (16%). Socrates has conducted only ten out of 251 interviews (3.9%) with women (three of them with Natasha Vita-More alone) on the *Singularity Weblog* since 2010.[795]

It is only to be expected for women and African Americans to react more sensitively when – once again – white men proclaim a new ideal of humanity, even if this time "humanity" is posthuman in scale. In this regard, representatives of post- and

---

[792] See Hagner 2004, 288-296.

[793] However, Bostrom estimates Nietzsche's role in transhumanism to be actually rather minor. See Adams 2016; Bostrom 2005. In contrast, Kurzweil avoids eugenic speculation and bases the medium-term improvement of the human body on nanorobots in the bloodstream. See Kurzweil 2005, 226-258.

[794] However, six of these contributions originate in a scientific conference held at Yale in 2013 on the question of nonhuman personhood, in which several women were involved as animal rights activists and ethicists (Vol 24, 3/2014). If this is taken into account, the proportion of women is reduced to 4.5%.

[795] See www.extropy.org and www.singularityweblog.com (Visited 06/23/2020).

transhumanism who situate superintelligence and singularity at the center of their utopian visions neglect the philosophical, historical, and social implications of these dreams.

6.7 Omega

> Our speculation ends in a supercivilisation, the synthesis of all solar-system life ..., spreading outward from the sun, converting nonlife into mind ... This process, possibly occurring now elsewhere, might convert the entire universe into an extended thinking entity, a prelude to even greater things.[796]
> Hans Moravec

All posthumanist authors consider transferring the human mind into a computer merely an intermediate step on the path to a planetary or even cosmic consciousness. This concept applies elements of a theological history of salvation, which were formulated in their most concise form by Pierre Teilhard de Chardin and prepared for the media discourse by Marshall McLuhan.

The Cosmic Consciousness

According to Marvin Minsky, Gregory Stock, and Kevin Warwick, it is very probable that various identities will exchange and merge into a collective consciousness within this computer memory. This would then become a *new society of mind*: "Some future options have never been seen: Imagine a scheme that could review both your and my mentalities, and then compile a new, merged mind based upon that shared experience."[797]

Hans Moravec believes that the entire Earth will eventually be simulated by a gigantic computer as some kind of digital reserve: All possible pasts would then be reconstructed as permanent simulations to house the last humans and all those who were resurrected.[798] According to Moravec, these unembodied, posthuman individuals would then even be able to dive into the mind of a virtual dolphin or an elephant: "Concepts of life, death, and identity will lose their present meaning as your mental fragments and those of others are combined, shuffled, and recombined."[799]

Frank Tipler, Hans Moravec, and Ray Kurzweil go even further than this vision of networked, virtual personalities. While humans will survive the ages as perfect

---

796 Moravec 1988, 116.
797 Marvin Minsky: *Why Computer Science Is the Most Important Thing That Has Happened to the Humanities in 5,000 Years*. Public lecture, Nara, Japan, 15.05.1996. Cited in Hayles 1999, 244-245. See Warwick 2000, 151; Stock 1993.
798 See Moravec 1999, 164-168.
799 Ibid., 115.

simulations within computers, robots and artificial intelligence shall master the challenges of the real world.[800] Robot probes would then colonize the solar system, the galaxy, and ultimately the entire universe, transforming it into a thinking entity.[801] Once artificial beings have gained initial control, they can go on to master entire galaxies in the interest of humankind and the cosmos. They would thus counteract increasing entropy – the heat death of the universe: " ... life must engulf the entire universe if it is to have the power to force the universe to move in this unlikely way."[802] If the goal of evolution is the preservation of life in the universe, as Tipler argues, then perfecting humans or their descendants via maximizing knowledge is necessarily a part of this plan. Life would therefore attain omnipresence, omnipotence, and omniscience:[803]

> At the instant the Omega Point is reached, life will have gained control of *all* matter and forces ... ; life will have spread into *all* spatial regions in all universes which could logically exist, and we will have stored an infinite amount of information, including all bits of knowledge which is logically possible to know. And this is the end.[804]

Without considering the theistic and anthropocentric context, Moravec connects his own idea of a future "super-consciousness" to Tipler's Omega Point Theory: "We truly exist because our actions lead ultimately to this 'Omega Point' (a term borrowed from the Jesuit paleontologist and radical philosopher Tielhard [sic!] de Chardin)."[805]

Kurzweil first discussed the prospect of such a cosmic expansion in *The Singularity Is Near* in 2005, wherein he acknowledged that there are probably no other intelligent life forms in the universe apart from humanity. He refers to the *Anthropic Principle* as he concludes: "We don't yet see evidence that such a community beyond Earth exists. The community that matters may be just our own unassuming civilization here."[806] Only a few years earlier, in the 1999 *The Age of Spiritual Machines*, he still considered the existence of extraterrestrial, intelligent life probable.[807]

According to his later prognosis, humanity will give birth to a technological civilization, which will travel at least (!) as fast as the speed of light across the universe. As a result, it will transform the formerly stupid matter of the cosmos into intelligent matter. Matter will in fact become so intelligent that it will become capable of overcoming the laws of physics:

> We will determine our own fate rather than have it determined by the current 'dumb,' simple, machinelike forces that rule celestial mechanics ... Such a civilization will overcome gravity ... and other cosmological forces ... and engineer the universe it wants. This is the goal of the Singularity.[808]

---

800 See ibid., 87.
801 See ibid., 116, 164-168.
802 Tipler 1995, 65. See ibid., 55-65.
803 See ibid., 153-154; Barrow / Tipler 1986, 523.
804 Barrow / Tipler 1986, 677.
805 Moravec 1999, 202. See also Moravec 1979.
806 Kurzweil 2005, 362.
807 See Kurzweil 1999, 260.
808 Kurzweil 2005, 29, 364. See ibid., 342-365, 390.

In this way, the entire universe will become saturated with intelligence. Kurzweil therefore deduces the Earth's special significance, and the future creation of the *ultimate computer*. Futurology and the metaphysics of black holes flow together in his work:

> If we increase the mass enough, its gravitational force becomes strong enough to cause it to collapse into a black hole. So a black hole can be regarded as the ultimate computer. Of course, not any black hole will do. Most black holes, like most rocks, are performing lots of random transactions but no useful computation. But a well-organized black hole would be the most powerful conceivable computer in terms of cps per liter.[809]

Anyone assuming that the rational Ray Kurzweil is merely reiterating Tipler's cosmology of salvation history without its theological elements will be sadly disappointed. Kurzweil firmly emphasizes that he is not interested in establishing a new dogma. Rather, Singularitarianism is based on the understanding of purely scientifically recognized trends.[810] However, in numerous places he nonetheless gives precisely the impression that he actually wants to found a new religious faith. In a conversation with "Bill" in his prophetic book, Kurzweil emphasizes that humanity needs a new kind of religion that extends beyond the rationalization of death. In fact, Julian Huxley had already made this demand publicly in his plea for an evolutionary humanism. Similarly, Kurzweil argued that for a charismatic prophet we now require a charismatic operating system:

> BILL: Ha, we've already got that. So is there a God in this religion?
> RAY: Not yet, but there will be. Once we saturate the matter and energy in the universe with intelligence, it will "wake up", be conscious, and sublimely intelligent. That's about as close to God as I can imagine.
> BILL: That's going to be silicon intelligence, not biological intelligence.
> RAY: Well, yes, we're going to transcend biological intelligence. [811]

Kurzweil thus bypasses the concept of the Omega Point and any reference to Christianity or Teilhard de Chardin. However, the phases of evolution (matter, life, mind) and the transformation of the universe into a gigantic computer correspond conceptually to designs by Teilhard de Chardin or Frank Tipler (although the latter is not deemed worthy of mention).

Posthumanist visions of a global or even cosmic conscious entity have developed alongside spiritual and secular interpretations of the Internet since the 1990s. One of the most prominent figures in this context was the American computer scientist Mark Pesce, who established the first widely accepted standard for the visual presentation of virtual reality (*Virtual Reality Modeling Language, VRML*) in 1994. In his numerous publications, presentations at conferences, and media appearances, he not only showcased his technological innovations but also related them to his vivid vision of the future Internet. In his book *Playful World*, during an account of the invention of VRML he

---

809 Ibid., 362.
810 See ibid., 370-374.
811 Ibid., 375.

introduces Teilhard de Chardin as the most significant although long-forgotten prophet of the Internet:

> ... no one foresaw the importance and comprehensive impact of the World Wide Web. But, over fifty years ago, one fairly obscure scientist did predict a coming transformation of the human mind, the birth of collective intelligence, and the emergence of a new way of knowing.[812]

Along with the idea that all human beings will soon be united spiritually, Pesce adopted Teilhard's concept of the noosphere:

> We can't know for sure if the Web is the same thing as the noosphere, or if the Web represents part of what Teilhard envisioned. But it feels that way ... If Teilhard was right, the Web is part of our evolution, as much an essential element of humanity as our acute eyes, our crafty hands, and our wonderful brains.[813]

Equating the Internet with the noosphere, Pesce implied that this technology was no ordinary media innovation, such as radio or television had been during their times. According to Pesce, the outstanding emergence of the Internet actually refers to a spiritual dimension:

> My work around WebEarth has a lot to do with spirituality, with the ideas of Gaia and of the planet as a living being. When I show this work to people for the first time, they usually get it immediately – some even cry ... With VRML the noosphere will become much more tangible. People will recognize it as a real place, even though it is just data.[814]

Pesce thus connects Teilhard's ideas to the Gaia theory, which is of central importance for both many New Age proponents as well as for ecologists. The Internet is therefore conceptualized as an organic part of the Earth, destined to come into existence as part of the natural evolutionary process.

The most comprehensive application of Teilhard's ideas to the area of cyber-discourse can be found in the work of American theologian Jennifer Cobb. In her book, *Cybergrace: The Search for God in the Digital Space* (1998), Cobb – who has more than 15 years of experience as an IT professional – interprets cyberspace as an unlimited avenue for the development of the intellectual, spiritual, and emotional potential of humanity. If human beings could understand the true significance of computer technologies, then, according to Cobb, the world can be experienced anew as a divine reality beyond the dualism of mind and matter.[815]

> In the ongoing process of spiritual evolution, cyberspace has a special role to play ... In this vision, the spiritual basis of the universe is understood as creative events unfolding in time ... Cyberspace can help guide us toward a reconciliation of the major

---

812   Pesce 2000, 164.
813   Ibid., 170.
814   Pesce in interview with Bennahum 1997. Translation by Ali Jones 2020.
815   See Cobb 1998, 8-11.

schisms of our time, those between science and spirit, between the organic world and the world that we create.[816]

Principally, Cobb draws on Teilhard's multi-level evolutionary model, with a particular focus on the leap from the biosphere to the noosphere. However, she is of the opinion that Teilhard's ideas can be accurately understood only in the face of the emergence of cyberspace: "This distinctly non-traditional evolutionary idea may strike us as odd until we consider the phenomenon of cyberspace – that electronically supported layer of human consciousness that now encircles the globe."[817]

Like many other Protestant theologians in the United States, Cobb seeks an alliance between the sciences and Christian theology and legitimates her religious interpretation of cyberspace as the evolution of divine creativity in the universe.[818]

> Creative process forms the soul of cyberspace. The source of richness and potential in this vast, electronic web of experience is spirit. The divine expresses itself in the digital terrain through the vast, global communication networks that are now beginning to display rudimentary self-organizing properties.[819]

From Cobb's viewpoint, humankind must recognize the progress of computer technology as a divine plan: "It is when this knowledge comes fully into our conscious awareness that our deeper journey with cyberspace will truly have begun."[820]

These religiously or spiritually charged media interpretations actually converge with the secular visions of futurologists and postmodern media theorists. As early as 1929, John D. Bernal speculated about a universal, disembodied consciousness (of course, still without reference to cybernetics):

> Finally, consciousness itself may end or vanish in a humanity that has become completely etherealized, losing the close-knit organism, becoming masses of atoms in space communicating by radiation, and ultimately perhaps resolving itself entirely into light. [821]

As early as 1970, the Russian cyberneticist Valentin Turchin adopted Teilhard's idea of the noosphere in his monograph *The Phenomenon of Science – A Cybernetic Approach to Human Evolution*. In this early work, he formulated the idea of a future synthetic consciousness in which human individuals would merge and achieve immortality. Together with Francis Heylighen and Cliff Joslyn, he founded the organization *Principia Cybernetica* in 1989, as well as authoring the *Cybernetic Manifesto* in the same year. However, despite sharing similar goals, such as immortality and a global brain, these

---

816 Ibid., 43.
817 Ibid., 85.
818 Ibid., 12, 51-97.
819 Ibid., 44.
820 Ibid., 239.
821 Bernal 1929, 21. See also Bernal 1969, 855-857.

writers remained largely unnoticed (apart from Ben Goertzel) within the trans- and posthumanist context.[822]

Both Heylighen and the French media philosopher Pierre Lévy interpret the Internet as the first manifestation of this "global brain" or "collective intelligence".[823] By constructing a virtual space, the Internet and other communication methods would thus liberate communication from the material, social, and physical obstacles and limitations posed by "real" space. Cyberspace thus becomes a metaphor for a liberated and egalitarian humanity, which is universal yet also democratically organized:

> Cyberspace gives shape to a new form of the universal: the universal without the totality. Filled with the resonance of Enlightenment philosophy, its universality stems from the fact that it maintains a profound relationship with the idea of humanity.[824]

Without making any reference to Teilhard de Chardin, Lévy sketches his vision of a new, intelligent entity that will emerge from the interaction and communication of the human collective.

> Before you lies cyberspace with its teeming communities and the interlaced ramification of its creations, as if all of humankind's memory were deployed in the moment: an immense act of synchronous collective intelligence, converging on the present, a silent bolt of lightning, diverging, an exploding crown of neurons.[825]

In June 2020 the European Union announced GAIA-X, a comprehensive project to improve data infrastructure, which demonstrates the scope of those techno-utopian ideas that emerged from New Age philosophy.

Teilhard de Chardin, McLuhan, and the Noosphere

Posthumanists, cyberphilosophers, and cybertheologians all venerate Teilhard de Chardin as the great mastermind of the Internet – that global brain for their cybernetic-cosmic history of salvation. Although Samuel Alexander and Alfred N. Whitehead had already developed cosmic theories of evolution, which ultimately led to the realization of God, media discourses only recognized Teilhard's work. In fact, any online search still generates hundreds of academic and popular links idealizing Teilhard as the great mastermind of the Internet.

The dominance of Teilhard's work within media discourse is especially remarkable considering the fact that he almost never discussed the media itself, with the exception of two short notes (see below). I argue that the Canadian media theorist Marshall McLuhan, who eclectically adopted Teilhard's ideas, actually primed media theory for Teilhard's work and cultivated interest in it. Within both popular and sometimes even

---

822   Turchin went into exile in the USA in 1973. He always remained sensitive to the totalitarian tendencies that he had openly criticized in the USSR, even in his cyberutopian works. See Turchin 1977, 85-86, 259-261; Goertzel 2010.
823   See Krüger 2015, 79.
824   Lévy 2001, 100.
825   Ibid., 236.

academic discourses, these two thinkers are often considered to be interchangeable. McLuhan is said to "flirt" with Teilhard's ideas, and their theories are assumed to be congruent.[826] In fact, it is generally accepted that "McLuhan's 'global village' is nothing other than Teilhard's 'noosphere'."[827] Therefore, it is essential in the following section to examine the relation between McLuhan and Teilhard de Chardin, to illuminate the popular and evidently dominating synthesis of McLuhan's idea of the global village and Teilhard's noosphere, a synthesis that anticipates a religious interpretation of the Internet and computer technology and its significance for post- and transhumanism.

As explained earlier, Teilhard depicts the evolutionary process as a continuous unfolding of mind over the stages of *cosmogenesis*, *biogenesis*, and *noogenesis* (the emergence of human consciousness):

> When for the first time in a living creature instinct perceived in itself in its own mirror, the whole world took a pace forward ... A glow of ripples outward from the first spark of conscious reflection. The point of ignition grows larger. The fire spreads in ever widening circles till finally the whole planet is covered with incandescence ... Much more coherent and just as extensive as any preceding layer, the 'thinking layer', which, since its germination, at the end of the Tertiary period, has spread over and above the world of plants and animals. In other words, outside and above the biosphere there is the noosphere.[828]

Teilhard argues that, because of western scientific and philosophical dominance since early Christianity, the "convergence of thinking" and the "planetisation of the noosphere" continued to use communication technology: "thanks to the prodigious biological event represented by the discovery of electro-magnetic waves, each individual finds himself henceforth (actively and passively) simultaneously present, over land and sea, in every corner of the earth."[829]

Teilhard understands this process of evolution as both the ascension of consciousness and as a process of the unification of humanity. That is to say, only if all peoples and all social classes strive for a common goal, can the psycho-biological development of a "mega-synthesis" of a single humanity be realized:

> The idea is that of the earth not only becoming covered by myriads of grains of thought, but becoming enclosed in a single thinking envelope so as to form, functionally, no more than a single vast grain of thought on the sidereal scale, the plurality of individual reflections grouping themselves together and reinforcing one another in the act of a single unanimous reflection.[830]

---

826 See Hickey 2005, 64; Curtis 2005, 164-165.
827 Wolfe 2003.
828 Teilhard de Chardin 1959, 181-182.
829 Ibid., 240.
830 Ibid., 251-252. Although Teilhard is aware of the skepticism that people have towards his utopia, he is absolutely confident that the difficulties of this brief period of rejection will be overcome soon. See ibid., 252-253.

At the "end of the world," the noosphere will finally reach a point of convergence where the totality of all individual consciousness flows together to create a new, super-personal consciousness. According to Teilhard, this Omega Point can be realized only by the power of universal love. Humankind has been chosen to play this extraordinary role, thanks to the appearance of Jesus, and will arrive at the Omega Point through the history of the cosmos.

> If the world is convergent and if Christ occupies its centre, then the Christo-genesis of St. Paul and St. John is nothing else and nothing less than the extension, both awaited and unhoped for, of that noogenesis in which cosmogenesis – as regards our experience – culminates. Evolution has come to infuse new blood ... into the perspectives and aspirations of Christianity. In return, is not the Christian faith destined, is it not preparing, to save and even to take the place of evolution?[831]

Teilhard de Chardin's Christian interpretation thus continues the dynamic understanding of God first developed in German idealism in the 19th century. For example, the German philosopher Friedrich Joseph Schelling described an unfolding God and thus – half a century before Darwin – laid the foundation for a synthesis between metaphysics and evolution. He regarded reason and science as means for the progressive realization of God:

> I situate God as the first and the last, as A and as O, but as A he is not that which he is as the O, and in so far he is only as *this* – God *sensu eminenti*, he cannot also be as *that* God in that sense, nor can he be called God in the strictest sense, unless it is explicitly as the *unevolved* God, *Deus implicitus*, and thus as O the *Deus explicitus* ... But this very existence of God as a personal being is the purpose – in fact quite literally – of science, and not only in general, but as highest, last objective, the goal of all its striving, for which it has struggled for all time ... [832]

The unfolding of the cosmos thus converges with the full realization of God. In contrast to Schelling's romanticist interpretation, Teilhard combines a metaphysical teleology with the unfolding of the noosphere, which itself is conditioned by scientific progress. All scientific endeavors should thus be directed towards the unification of human beings, and thus towards the merging of human and divine consciousness into a "mega-synthesis". According to Teilhard, all movements and layers of evolution will finally culminate in this harmonious unity of all souls: the noosphere's convergence point at Omega.[833]

> The Future-Universal could not be anything else but the Hyper-Personal – at the Omega Point ... It is by definition – in its flower and its integrity – the hoard of

---

831 Ibid., 331.
832 Schelling 1812, 113-114. Translation by Ali Jones 2020. Here Schelling reacts to Friedrich Heinrich Jacobi's traditional and static image of God. In the 18th century the natural philosopher Friedrich Christoph Oetinger had already formulated the basic idea of a God who would manifest in evolution. See Lovejoy 1961, 242-287; McCalla 1998, 29-31.
833 See Teilhard 1976, 254-272.

consciousness liberated little by little on earth by noogenesis adds itself together and concentrates.[834]

Teilhard does not explicitly describe the resurrection of the dead. However, he speaks enigmatically of the "emersion" of the human soul in Omega. Teilhard idealizes Omega as life's space and time in the face of the destructive power of entropy in the universe: "It escapes from entropy by turning back from Omega: the *hominisation* of death itself."[835]

It is thanks to Marshall McLuhan that Teilhard is received so broadly in technological discourse, although the topic of the media is itself largeley irrelevant for his work. In fact, the latter's entire corpus is clearly focused primarily on biological evolution within an explicitly Christian context.[836]

Marshall McLuhan converted to Roman Catholicism in 1937, was employed at three Catholic universities,[837] attended mass every day, and was in close contact with many Catholic theologians, notably including Jesuits. His public commentaries on religious issues were sometimes on the fringe of mainstream discourse. For example, he vigorously criticized the decision of the Second Vatican Council (1961-1965) to abolish Latin as the liturgical language.[838] It is therefore not surprising that a very special bond existed between McLuhan and Teilhard de Chardin. Yet the intellectual bridge between these two thinkers can actually be found in the American theologian, Jesuit, and media theorist Walter J. Ong (1912-2003). Ong studied English literature and philosophy at St. Louis University from 1938 to 1941, where a young McLuhan taught English (1937 to 1944). McLuhan was Ong's adviser for his master's thesis on the Victorian Jesuit and poet Gerald Manley Hopkins, whose works deeply influenced Ong's later idea of a theological connection between evolution and the revelation of god. During this time, Ong and McLuhan cultivated a friendly relationship and frequently exchanged letters. Ong even dedicated the second volume of his dissertation to "Herbert Marshall McLuhan who started all this".[839] While staying in Paris as a Guggenheim fellow in the early 1950s, Ong lived in the same lodgings as Teilhard de Chardin, where he had the opportunity to study the manuscript of *Le Phénomène humain*. This would only be published posthumously in 1955 but would ultimately be recognized as Teilhard's most important work.

---

834 Ibid., 260-261.
835 Ibid., 272. See ibid., 270-272.
836 It is very unlikely that a posthumanist reception of the idea of cosmic consciousness, such as a God-Omega-Point, could be facilitated by science fiction literature. In fact, these themes appear only in the little-known story *The Last Question* (1956) by Isaac Asimov and, peripherally and without any deeper elaboration, in William Gibson's *Neuromancer* (1984). In Asimov's story, the entire universe is populated by humans and intelligent computers, which eventually merge into a single consciousness. In Gibson's book, the hero is confronted with the all-encompassing matrix, "the whole show". See Asimov 1956, 15; Raulerson 2013, 177-183; Gibson 2000, 269; Porush 1992, 132-134. Arthur C. Clarke also uses his non-fictional work to expound the vision of a global brain. See Clarke 1960, 209, 233.
837 McLuhan was employed from 1937-1944 at the Jesuit St. Louis University (Missouri), from 1944-1946 at Assumption College (Windsor, Canada) and after 1946 at St. Michael's College (Toronto).
838 See Eric McLuhan 1999, XXV; Marshall McLuhan 1999a.
839 See Ong 1958.

However, when Ong was assigned to write a review of McLuhan's first book, *The Mechanical Bride* in 1952 he took the opportunity to publish some crucial ideas from Teilhard's work.[840] Following McLuhan's critique of American culture, Ong raises the question of how Catholic theology might respond in an industrial age, before venturing into a discussion of Teilhard's (censored) ideas. Ong introduces the concepts of the cosmosphere and the biosphere, and finally even refers to the promise of the noosphere:

> In a third stage, slowly, man, with human intelligence, has made his way over the surface of the earth into all its parts ... with the whole world alerted simultaneously every day to goings-on in Washington, Paris, London, Rio de Janeiro, Rome and (with reservations) Moscow – human consciousness has succeeded in enveloping the entire globe in a third and still more perfect kind of sphere, the sphere of intelligence, the 'noosphere,' as it has been styled by Father Pierre Teilhard de Chardin, S.J.[841]

Ong later became Teilhard's most important advocate in the Anglophone world.[842] It is therefore evident that McLuhan was familiar with Teilhard's ideas, at least from Ong's review of 1952, even before McLuhan began his own research in communication and media studies. The fact that direct references to Teilhard can only be found in McLuhan's *Gutenberg Galaxy* (1962), appears likely to be due to external critics and his own increasingly skeptical attitude towards Teilhard's work.[843]

At the opening of his *The Gutenberg Galaxy*, McLuhan draws readers' attention to Teilhard's work as "the lyrical testimony of a very Romantic biologist".[844] He even quotes a description of the global unification process and technological progress from *Le Phénomèn humain*, but immediately adds the caveat that Teilhard's optimistic promises have been fiercely criticized by intellectuals. He then introduces Teilhard's notion of the noosphere:

> This externalisation of our senses creates what de Chardin called the 'noosphere' or a technological brain for the world. Instead of tending towards a vast Alexandrian library the world has become a computer, an electronic brain, exactly as in an infantile piece of science fiction.[845]

In the decisive passage where McLuhan refers to Teilhard, electronic media become the "cosmic membrane that has been snapped round the globe".[846] Two further passages in *The Gutenberg Galaxy* connecting the idea of evolutionism and the progress of media technology also refer to Teilhard.[847] McLuhan's subsequent commentaries

---

840 See Farrell 2003.
841 Ong 1952, 84. See McLuhan 1951.
842 See, for example, Ong 1977.
843 See Marchand 1998, 216-218. Media researcher and son of Marshall McLuhan, Eric McLuhan (1942-2018), describes this relationship even more skeptically: "I do know that my father did not find anything in Teilhard's thought that he considered of potential use as regards his own work." E-mail by Eric McLuhan to Oliver Krüger, 02/17/2006.
844 McLuhan 2002, 32.
845 Ibid.
846 Ibid.
847 Ibid., 46, 174.

about Teilhard's work became increasingly diverse, and even contradictory. Although McLuhan does not mention the French Jesuit by name in his third book, *Understanding Media: The Extensions of Man* (1964), he does refer to Henri Bergson's *L'évolution créatrice*, and his utopian harmonic electronic age is guided by Bergson's idea that language is to blame for the separation of humankind:

> Electricity points the way to an extension of the process of consciousness itself, on a world scale, and without any verbalization whatever. Such a state of collective awareness may have been the preverbal condition of men. Language as the technology of human extension, whose powers of division and separation we know so well, may have been the 'Tower of Babel' by which men sought to scale the highest heavens. Today computers hold out the promise of a means of instant translation of any code or language into any other code or language. The computer, in short, promises by technology a Pentecostal condition of universal understanding and unity. The next logical step would seem to be, not to translate, but to by-pass languages in favor of a general cosmic consciousness, which might be very like the collective unconscious dreamt of by Bergson. The condition of 'weightlessness,' that biologists say promises a physical immortality, may be paralleled by the condition of speechlessness that could confer a perpetuity of collective harmony and peace.[848]

However, Bergson's book was also the inspiration for Teilhard's Christian interpretation of evolutionism. McLuhan is far more enthusiastic than even Bergson:

> If the work of the city is the remaking or translating of man into a more suitable form than his nomadic ancestors achieved, then might not our current translation of our entire lives into the spiritual form of information seem to make of the entire globe, and of the human family, a single consciousness?[849]

In other publications and interviews, McLuhan adopts a more analytical attitude, contending that he himself does not see any inherent religious significance in electronic media. Rather he argues "we would not belittle the merely cultural power of the non-literate and the literate forms of life to shape the perceptions and biases of the entire human community."[850]

When he was asked outright in an interview in 1970 about the parallels of his work and Teilhard's ideas, McLuhan offered a sophisticated answer that entirely omitted Teilhard: he rejected all potential predictions of the future impact of media technology as mere speculation. However, he also acknowledged that the omnipresence of the media could offer an incitement for the religious seeker.[851]

On the other hand, McLuhan's explicit critique of religious interpretations of the "electronic age" also reflects his admiration for new communication technologies:

> Electric information environments being utterly ethereal fosters the illusion of the world as a spiritual substance. It is now a reasonable facsimile of the mystical body,

---

848 McLuhan 1994, 80.
849 Ibid., 61.
850 McLuhan 2002, 68. See also the reception of Mircea Eliade in McLuhan's work, Ibid., 67-71.
851 McLuhan 1999b, 87-88.

a blatant manifestation of the Anti-Christ. After all, the Prince of this World is a very great electric engineer.[852]

On other occasions McLuhan disapproves of the idea of a harmonious global community,[853] as per his concept of retribalization. Electronic media supports individualism because of its lack of hierarchies and social centers, and therefore threatens the existence of community life. Indeed, by the end of the 1960s McLuhan no longer advanced a positive opinion on the future impact of electronic media; rather, he declined to make any further evaluations or predictions. The *global village* – a notion inspired by Wyndham Lewis' book *America and Cosmic Man* – became his leading metaphor for media society.[854] McLuhan's book *War and Peace in the Global Village* (1968) shows that he considered this *global village* to also be a place full of conflicts and crises.[855]

McLuhan's differences with Teilhard become apparent in his use of the notion of consciousness. With the exception of a few euphoric predictions in the *The Gutenberg Galaxy* and *Understanding Media*, McLuhan understands *extension of consciousness* as an augmented ability of individual reception, rather than *one* common collective consciousness culminating finally in the Omega Point.[856]

Closer inspection of the relationship between Marshall McLuhan and Pierre Teilhard de Chardin might reveal some significant differences in their theoretical concepts. However, it is even more fruitful to investigate the concrete processes of the reception of Teilhard's work in the recent interpretations of the Internet. Teilhard is by no means a media theorist, and so notions of "information" or "communication" are irrelevant in his idea of a cosmic history. He introduces the noosphere within the context of theological and philosophical considerations of the ascent of human consciousness. Yet, it is also evident that McLuhan's presentation of Teilhard's ideas in *The Gutenberg Galaxy* has become authoritative for later receptions of Teilhard in popular and academic media discourse. First, Teilhard is introduced as a "romantic biologist" and in no way as a Catholic theologian in the Jesuit tradition; second, McLuhan makes no mention of the Christian context of Teilhard's evolutionary model; and third, he keeps quiet about the very core of Teilhard's theory: the convergence of human consciousness in the future Omega Point. Teilhard's ideas are therefore represented as completely secular in McLuhan's works.

Finally, McLuhan clearly reinterprets Teilhard's notion of the noosphere. Paralleling the layer of thought that emerged alongside the first hominids according to Teilhard's

---

852 McLuhan 1999c, 70-72.
853 McLuhan harshly criticizes the emergence of a new oral society: "Terror is the normal state of any oral society, for in it everything affects everything all the time." McLuhan 2002, 32.
854 The well-known painter and author Wyndham Lewis was McLuhan's colleague at the Assumption College in Windsor University. Lewis wrote in *America and Cosmic Man*: " … the earth has become one big village, with telephones laid from one end to the other, and air transport both speedy and safe …" Lewis 1948, 21.
855 See McLuhan 1968.
856 For McLuhan the global village is a village rather than a town because, metaphorically, as in a small town everyone knows everything about everyone else – but without necessarily sharing the views of their fellow human beings. McLuhan 1994, 47.

work, McLuhan determines the noosphere as the "technological brain" – thus the whole world becomes a computer. McLuhan thus performs three modifications that prepared the notion of the noosphere for a broad reception in cyber discourse: first, the noosphere is contextualized as a term of media technology; second, the emergence of the noosphere is dated to the beginning of the "electrical age" – our present time; and third, the noosphere implies, according to McLuhan, a global network that already exists.[857] What was once a slow process of the "planetization" of the noosphere – or a continuous convergence of thinking – suddenly becomes in McLuhan's works a higher level of evolution initiated by the spread of radio, television, and computers in the "electronic age".

In addition to the close connection of media and evolution, another important aspect must be considered for this analysis of the cultural reception of the Internet. When considered holistically, electronic media and the Internet seem to be part of an unfolding organism. In fact, Marc Pesce initially suggested that media are vital elements of Gaia, the Earth. In this context, it is significant that McLuhan took the first steps to consider electronic media as organic. In addition to the basic assumption that media is an extension of our physical senses, McLuhan introduces the biological metaphors of the "electronic brain" and the "cosmic membrane", while Teilhard used the metaphor of the "thinking envelope" (*enveloppe pensante*).[858]

This understanding of technological developments in post- and transhumanism as part of the continuation of organic evolution is possible due to its close connection to Gaia theory. This idea was introduced in the late 1960s by the American biologist Lynn Margulis (1938-2011) and the British physician, geophysicist, and ecologist James E. Lovelock (born 1919). Lovelock founds this theory on the argument that the Earth, together with all its inhabitants, has to be understood as one holistic organism. In his book *Gaia: A New Look at Life on Earth* (1979), Lovelock greatly influenced the emerging environmental movement as well as many holistic thinkers of various religious traditions and innovations:

> The result of this more single-minded approach was the development of the hypothesis that the entire range of living matter on Earth, from whales to viruses, and from oaks to algae, could be regarded as constituting a single living entity, capable of manipulating the Earth's atmosphere to suit its overall needs and endowed with faculties and powers far beyond those of its constituent parts.[859]

The Earth is presented as a threatened planet that must be preserved and should not be recklessly exploited. Lovelock explains that the Earth as a whole reacts to the actions of its inhabitants, in particular to the increasing air pollution caused by humankind.[860]

---

857   Teilhard separated the emergence of the noosphere thousands of years ago from a future "planetization" and "convergence of thinking". See Teilhard de Chardin 1959, 163-212.
858   See Teilhard de Chardin 1959, 251.
859   Lovelock 1991, 9.
860   See ibid., 12, 64-123.

This crucial idea that the totality of all living matter on Earth constitutes one entity has been adopted by a wide range of discourses.[861]

In addition to feminist Christian theologians, such as Anne Primavesi and Rosemary Radford Ruether, prominent New Age thinkers such as Peter Russell, Ken Wilber, and Fritjof Capra adopted elements of the Gaia theory and reunited them with Teilhard's teleological interpretation of evolution. According to Marylin Ferguson, author of the influential New Age book *The Aquarian Conspiracy* (1980), this was no coincidence, as Teilhard de Chardin is actually the author most frequently cited by New Age believers.[862] Russell connects the spiritualized Gaia theory to the emergence of a global brain with a higher consciousness, which itself might be based on the Internet's "interlinking of humanity". In his *Integral Theory*, Wilber refers to many elements of Gaia theory as well as to Teilhard's ideas. The notion of the biosphere, noosphere, and the Omega Point are essential for his theory, albeit not in a Christian sense but rather for an evolutionary teleology. Capra – as well as many other New Age thinkers – combines ecological approaches from Gaia theory with both evolutionism as well as the vision of a spiritual renewal of a unified humanity.[863]

On the other hand, Lovelock's approach is often used in the American context in conjunction with the work of the philosopher and architect Buckminster Fuller (1895-1983), who was very popular during his time.[864] The contemporary and heterogeneous Gaia movement unifies the ideas of well-known thinkers such as Teilhard and Lovelock, along with diverse approaches and practices from ecology, astrology, Buddhism, Hopi culture, neo-shamanism and – last but not least: techno futurism.[865]

The recent reception of Gaia theory in electronic media discourse is mainly due to decisive efforts by James Lovelock himself, aided by McLuhan's postulate of a relation between evolution and media. The ecologist is deeply convinced that progress – particularly that of science and cybernetics – as part of the natural evolution of humankind will also lead to a better understanding of Gaia, but only so long as human beings remain in touch with nature.[866] Although they are concerned about nationalist-inspired resistance, Lovelock and Teilhard share an optimistic outlook regarding the future of life on our planet, since the Earth is now conscious of its own existence:

> Still more important is the implication that the evolution of the homo sapiens, with his technological inventiveness and his increasingly subtle communication network,

---

861 Lovelock's ideas have been adopted within environmentalism primarily by the Brazilian ecologist José Lutzenberger, who initialized the Gaia Foundation in 1987. Lovelock himself was surprised by the religious reception of his work: "I was naïve to think that a book about Gaia would be taken as science only." See Lovelock 2003, 532.
862 See Ferguson 1980, 50-51, 93, 420.
863 See Russell 2000, 64-69; Wilber 1995, 85-87, 111-113; Capra 1982, 284-285.
864 In the 1930s, Fuller proposed a rational vision of a world community that is able to live in accordance with aesthetics and nature on "spaceship earth", as based on scientific-technological progress. See Fuller 1938, 356-360.
865 Judith L. Boice depicted her experiences in Gaian Communities very colorfully. See Boice 1990.
866 Lovelock 1991, 127-140.

has vastly increased Gaia's range of perception. She is now through us awake and aware of herself.[867]

Referring to the analogy of biological brains and networked computers, Lovelock anticipates later cyber theories: "Our brains can be likened to medium-size computers which are directly linked to one another and to memory banks, as well as to an almost unlimited array of sensors, peripheral devices, and other machines."[868]

As demonstrated in these discussions, the super-consciousness as posthumanism's final evolutionary goal is the result of a complex process of receptions and re-interpretations during a long intellectual lineage. It primarily originates in Teilhard de Chardin's teleological theory of evolution, and its specific adaption by Marshall McLuhan in media theory. Technological progress offered the next step of natural evolution and emerged in parallel with James Lovelock's Gaia theory. Thus, when Frank Tipler re-introduced Teilhard's Omega Point, or Hans Moravec and Ray Kurzweil shared their visions of transforming the entire cosmos into one thinking entity, these were in fact only the latest manifestations of a long tradition of ideas that had already been present in New Age philosophy for many decades.

---

867   Ibid., 148.
868   Ibid., 150.

7. Virtuality. Immortality in the Age of Digital Media

> I have heard my teacher say, where there are machines, there are bound to be machine worries; where there are machine worries, there are bound to be machine hearts. With a machine heart in your breast, you've spoiled what was pure and simple, and without the pure and simple, the life of the spirit knows no rest.[1]
> *Zhuangzi (350-280 BCE)*

The previous chapter has approached technological posthumanism from the perspective of the history of ideas. Individual elements, such as the cybernetic image of the human being, visions of immortality, and superintelligence, could be broken down historically. However, in parallel to these individual aspects there are overarching analytical perspectives that are of particular interest for understanding posthumanism. This applies first of all to the economics of futurology: What role does economic thinking play in visions of the future, and who benefits directly from these far-reaching prognoses?

We must also inquire whether a common thread connects all of these themes, in addition to the numerous heterogeneous elements of posthumanist philosophy. These various points of view seem to be unified by the longing for control of that which is indeterminable: the contingencies of human life. Both with regard to the individual and to humanity as a whole, posthumanism offers a clear answer to the fundamental anthropological question: *Where are we going?*

Furthermore, technological posthumanism offers the most recent example of modern theories of progress, the evaluation and classification of which has occupied philosophy, history, and cultural studies since the early 20th century. This is founded upon a discussion of the continuity of, or break with, the Christian history of salvation. This debate will now be traced, in order to formulate a counter-proposal to the dichotomous concepts used so far.

---

1   Zhuangzi 2013, 200. The philosopher is a Daoist.

From a broad cultural-historical perspective, posthumanism does nothing less than overcome the four affronts to humankind introduced in the early chapters of this book. But at what price? The concluding thoughts of this book will address precisely this question.

7.1 Economy

Economics are critical for technological posthumanism on three levels. In the first instance this concerns the dimension of the technological visions themselves. Secondly, we must examine the economic and social conditions of this predicted progress. Finally, we need to consider the economic interests of post- and transhumanism and its actors.

Posthumanism defines life as information processing. In essence, the goal of any posthumanist utopia of progress is to increase the efficiency of this information processing. Increased efficiency means increasing computing and storage capacity while reducing costs. These fundamentals have shaped posthumanism from Moravec's early writings in the late 1970s up to Kurzweil's current prognoses. Progress is associated with the "liberation" of life from inefficient, wasteful, and aimless natural evolution, which, from a cybernetic perspective, has only ever produced the faulty human form. This outdated being must therefore simply be abolished and replaced by an artificial superintelligence. The virtual existence of posthumanity will be characterized by omniscience and infinite wealth, as well as the dazzling prospects described by Moravec, Tipler, and Kurzweil. Strikingly, these are in no way inferior to the promises of modern gangster rap: eternal youth, endless potency, and fantastic sex with supernatural playmates – but now without any threat of disease and fatherhood. Spiritual growth appears only on the periphery. Moral growth – which was so formative for 18th and 19th century theories of progress – no longer plays any role. Economically, this virtual paradise ultimately seems to be no more than the banal dreams of aging men who still lust after eternal youth and wealth.

The necessary social conditions for the spread of artificial intelligence – or even for the production of the hoped-for superintelligence of the singularity – are not seriously examined anywhere by post- and transhumanists. Progress in computer technology only follows the technical law of exponential hardware performance increases. Surprisingly, the problem of software, i.e. of those programs that are actually supposed to produce this superhuman-like artificial intelligence, is never addressed. Posthumanists neglect to even mention that technical progress requires general economic stability, prospering Internet corporations, and an established system of scientific institutions, all of which depend on sustained economic growth. They also ignore the fact that the development of military technology is an important driver for the entire computer and robotics industry.[2] Their limited justifications for this sustained progress instead reflect the posthumanist tendency to view phenomena in isolation from their context, and to avoiding any kind of holistic perspective. Instead, technology and science are seen as independent variables decoupled from the social,

---

2   See Becker 2015, 76-77; Wagner 2015, 29-31, 103-124.

ecological, and cultural environment. The posthumanist vision of future generations of self-improving machines illustrates this paradigm of developing technology in complete indifference to any human factors.[3]

Post- and transhumanism also remain largely silent about what society would look like in the coming decades if these hoped-for technologies of human enhancement do in fact become available. They naively suggest that people will voluntarily adopt these augmentations. Yet any plea for a democratic transhumanism fades away in the dazzling discussion about ever more far-reaching technical visions. Ray Kurzweil occupies the limelight, while James Hughes appears to be an ineffective fig leaf of social conscience.

There also do not seem to be any signs of an egalitarian community of solidarity, neither with regard to future access to these promised technologies, nor in terms of legitimizing this techno-revolution by an increase in efficiency for the benefit of the entire society. Rather, in his economic study of transhumanism, Philipp von Becker identifies the capitalist market as the chief necessary prerequisite for superhuman optimization and freedom: "In reality, however, they enable the individual to better meet the demands of competition, which, by this means, they themselves continue to promote – in short: They encourage optimization of the prevailing compulsion for self-optimization."[4]

There is also no sign of any problem-oriented discussion of the social aspects of trans- and posthumanist visions, despite the knowledge that this conversation is necessary. Instead, such deep reflections are found in the cyberpunk literature of the past four decades, as well as in many popular adaptations in film and television. For example, in the film *Gattaca* (1997), some children in a biotechnologically advanced society are genetically selected and thus have access to social advancement and status, while others are excluded. In the film and book *Cloud Atlas* (2004 / 2012) David Mitchell tells the poignant story of Somni~451, a cloned restaurant waitress who suddenly awakens as a sentient and autonomous being. Yet these clones are trapped in the illusion of social advancement. As soon as they make the slightest attempt to escape their enslavement, they are murdered, and their body parts recycled.[5]

The most disturbing element of these dystopias is not their concrete phenomena, but rather their power structures, as they project the visible tendencies of our present situation. This biotechnological future in fact already exists and rears its ugly head in prenatal diagnostics for the selection of female fetuses, which are aborted by their parents for cultural and economic reasons. This practice is particularly pronounced in China and India, where, in some regions, for every 100 girls born, there are 130-140 boys. Furthermore, in the United States, the Caucasus, and Southeast Europe, gender selection in favor of male offspring is increasingly carried out with the help of abortions and, more recently, in-vitro fertilization.[6] This very real femicide demonstrates how

---

3   See Kroker / Kroker 1996, 75-76.
4   Becker 2015, 70, trans. by AJ. See Wagner 2015, 31; Hayles 1999, 4.
5   See *Orison of Sonmi~451* in Mitchell 2004; Wachowski / Tykwer 2012; Niccol 1997.
6   The social consequences of this femicide, which is sociologically considered as the phenomenon of *missing women*, are enormous. They markedly increase the risk of violence against women,

devastating it is to introduce such biotechnologies without consideration of their pre-existing social and cultural contexts.

With their plea for unlimited genetic and morphological self-determination of the human being, trans- and posthumanism ignore the social reality of the 21st century. However, we can nonetheless anticipate the social consequences of a humanity "optimized" by genetic and cybertechnology, in which inequalities will only be aggravated, despite the celebrated maxims of future liberation.

> This raises the question of a future in which a biological divide between the classes will be established. The super-rich will develop into a completely new species that will live twenty years longer, be more active, will accumulate even more wealth, and finally will then transfer this wealth and the associated power to their descendants, all with even greater consequences than before.[7]

In contrast to the classical utopias of Francis Bacon, Thomas More, or Edward Bellamy, post- and transhumanists do not design a social prospect of coexistence in solidarity with one another. Technology rather than people is central to this futurology. The apparent promise of freedom actually conceals new forms of control and dependence. What is already common in the Internet economy today would indeed become exponentially profitable in the case of a virtual existence:

> The real product of computer capitalism is oneself. And although you are bought, you still pay for it. One pays with what one does or does not do, says or does not say, feels or does not feel, in short: with the loss of intimacy and privacy, with the loss of the integrity of the body and personality.[8]

This raises the question of who would actually own the virtual person stored inside the supercomputer: the person? the storage provider? the uploading software? Furthermore, this promises a perfect economic utopia, as all of a customer's thoughts and actions would be completely transparent. They could even be directly manipulated via small software interventions. This insight applies equally to biotechnologies and cyborg-humans: Frédéric Vandenberghe refers to this as the market-oriented colonization of life.[9]

If tracking ceases to apply only to our smartphones and computers, and instead becomes a part of the body, then the digital control of human beings in their economic and political actions will become limitless. Even now, in the Chinese province of Rongcheng a social credit system is currently being tested to assess the actions and statements of its citizens, and rates these with points leading to either sanctions or privileges. Similarly, facial recognition software can record, and identify, a formerly anonymous pedestrian's non-observance of a red light. The cyborgization of the human

---

trafficking in women, and professional discrimination in these societies. Current data and literature can be found in the article "Sex-selective abortion" on Wikipedia.
7   Krysmanski 2014, 128, trans. by AJ.
8   Becker 2015, 83, trans. by AJ. See ibid., 83-97.
9   See Vandenberghe 2006; Wagner 2015, 56-57.

being, and the subsequent "surveillance, punishment and reward regime"[10] would be the dream of every autocratic and market-based system and could facilitate a completely new form of super totalitarianism. These political and economic utopias complement each other so fruitfully because the analysis, surveillance and steering of human behavior precisely perpetuates the goal of cybernetics and its various descendants: cybernetic psychology, pedagogy, and sociology. Here, too, the English utilitarianism of the 19th century à la Jeremy Bentham continues, according to which the collection of social statistics was intended to enhance legislative control of society.[11]

Therefore, when Ray Kurzweil raves about the possibility of future nanobots embedded in human blood which will re-stock the refrigerator via Wi-fi, this needs to be understood as Google's economic goal of complete customer integration and control. In his foreword to the book *The Eternal E-Customer. How Emotionally Intelligent Interfaces Can Create Long-lasting Customer Relationships* from the year 2000, Kurzweil expands on this vision.[12] However, one must ask, in a world where evading the Apple product universe is already so difficult, how impossible will this become when the entire body is populated by a myriad of nanobots from one particular vendor? In such a case, the corporate fantasy of the "eternal customer" will finally be fulfilled.

Similarly, Martine Rothblatt identifies the inexhaustible source of "the real money" in the immortality business.[13] For Rothblatt, this economic vision is connected to a demand for political rights for *mindclones*, who must not be degraded as second-class citizens. However, she neglects to mention that these *mindclones*' political attitudes can be influenced more efficiently than an armada of Russian bots set loose on social media. At the same time, billions of *mindclones* could be created in a matter of seconds, drastically impacting politics through their suffrage.[14]

The final aspect of this investigation concerns the economy of post- and transhumanism itself. The science writer Dylon Evans raises the incredibly important question: *"Cui bono?* Who profits?" Indeed, those same technological prophets who eagerly welcomed the imminent arrival of superhuman artificial intelligence also later caution against precisely these same entities. On the one hand, such prognoses can be ascribed to a manifest narcissism, as Evans explains: "To regard yourself as one of a select few farsighted thinkers who might turn out to be the saviors of humankind must be very rewarding."[15] On the other hand, these constantly mutating prophecies of imminent risk endorse a range of lucrative future institutes – such as Drexler's Foresight Institute or Bostrom's Future of Humanity Institute, which do nothing but warn of the consequences of their own prognoses.[16] The future never dies – instead, it proves to be an inexhaustible and very profitable resource.

---

10   Becker 2015, 70.
11   See Roszak 1994, 156-158.
12   See Kurzweil 2005, 300-311; Kurzweil 2000, IX-XI.
13   See Rothblatt 2014, 11.
14   See ibid., 183-195.
15   See Evans 2015, 173.
16   See Evans 2015.

This lucrative marketing of the future is also vividly demonstrated at the *Singularity University*, which neither undertakes research nor offers academic qualifications, but rather provides a platform for the marketing of future technologies through its workshops and worldwide events.[17] This is of particular economic relevance for Ray Kurzweil, along with his books and speaking engagements. He seems to have so far failed to accomplish the major *disruptive* and *exponential* technological breakthrough he heralds. In fact, compared to today's Internet entrepreneurs, he remains a relative lightweight with an estimated fortune of merely 27 million US dollar.[18]

Although it seems almost banal to mention here, after praising them in his self-help books, Kurzweil's avid marketing of food supplements has also proven economically significant. These vitamin pills have also become the very profitable focus of events such as *RAADfest*. In the US market – worth about 40 billion US dollar – companies like *Elysium Health* and *Life Extension* have specialized in such supposedly life-prolonging supplements. Ray Kurzweil, Aubrey de Grey, Natasha Vita-More, James Strole, and Bernadeane swear to their followers that in a few years' time therapies to reverse aging will become available, thus finally bringing immortality itself within reach. The message seems almost cynical when one considers that in 2020 the United States' health care system appeared to be completely overwhelmed by attempts to contain the COVID-19 pandemic and has been suffering for years from a massive opioid crisis that takes a toll of 70,000 deaths annually, resulting in a sharp decline in average life expectancy.

Regardless of whether it presents itself as an oracle in academic garb or in a practical lifestyle guide, the future proves to be an inexhaustible resource for a multitude of futurological projects. Despite being inaccessible and unknowable, the virtual future also already translates into very concrete business figures. The practice and message of post- and transhumanism is therefore essentially an economic one: the dystopian "limits to growth" postulated by the *Club of Rome* in 1972 are countered here by visions of unlimited growth for both individuals and humanity: This future is *people unlimited*.

In view of the looming global ecological crisis and the climate change resulting from the unchecked destruction and exploitation of natural resources, the prophecy of infinite, exponential growth, or the *radical abundance* celebrated by Drexler, Kurzweil, and Diamandis instead resembles the last dance on the Titanic. However, this metaphor itself begins to sink when the transhumanist orchestra promises that even this doomed ship can continue to accelerate.[19]

---

17 See Socrates 2015 (video).
18 See https://www.therichest.com/celebnetworth/celebrity-business/men/ray-kurzweil-net-worth/.
19 Peter Diamandis, who heads *Singularity University*, describes this vision in his book *Abundance: The Future Is Better Than You Think* (Diamandis / Kotler 2012), while Eric Drexler does so with an eye to nanotechnology in *Radical Abundance: How a Revolution in Nanotechnology Will Change Civilization* (2013).

7.2 Control and Contingency

In addition to economics, another key concept for all aspects of post- and transhumanist philosophy is control. From this perspective, thinking ultimately serves to control the human system, which must constantly assert itself against external dangers through drugs, meditation, music, feelings, sexuality, or even conversations.[20] Minsky states that progress in knowledge is not based on new experiences, but rather on the acquisition of new means of order and control – and in this case, knowledge is indeed power: "To know the cause of a phenomenon is to know ... how to change or control some aspects of some entities without affecting all the rest."[21] On the other hand, Minsky stresses that control is only possible through possession. The enormous growth in the abilities of artificial intelligences will be accompanied by an increase in their control over the world, which will be reflected in infinite wealth.[22] In Minsky's view, control and possession thus become the general task of intellectual existences, even beyond the limited context of information technology, i.e. human and artificial "thinking machines". Ray Kurzweil also considers that the control and reprogramming of emotions will be an important ability for the human being of the 21st century, who will be equipped with neuronal implants.[23]

In Frank Tipler, Hans Moravec, and Max More's work, the quest for control is reflected in the construction of a deterministic physical worldview. At the core of the posthumanist idea of technological immortalization lies a serious problem: Post- and transhumanists seek to simulate the human personality by recording all of the original body's molecules as a complex computer program – in fact Sandberg and Bostrom speak of *whole brain emulation (WBE)*.[24] A successful simulation would presuppose that atomic and subatomic processes could also be clearly determined. However, at a fundamental level, this is not possible. The development of Werner Heisenberg's *Uncertainty Principle* under the Copenhagen interpretation of quantum mechanics already heralded the end of deterministic physics in 1927, when it was discovered that quantum mechanical processes are neither clearly observable nor predictable. An exact simulation – i.e. the emulation – of real mental processes within a computer will therefore never be possible.[25] In response, some posthumanists have begun to formulate creative ways of addressing this well-known problem.

As an alternative to abandoning the classical-deterministic world view in physics, since his early writings Tipler has advocated the Many-Worlds interpretation. This operates distinctly differently than the Copenhagen interpretation, which makes the topicality of quantum mechanical processes dependent on the observer. Instead, the physicist Hugh Everett's highly controversial Many-Worlds interpretation assumes that a quantum mechanical decision is based on the splitting of the universe, so that many

---

20   See Minsky 1988, 51, 68, 172, 182; Minsky 1994, 113; Minsky 1992a, 24.
21   Minsky 1988, 129. See ibid., 102-105.
22   See ibid., 292-293; Minsky 1994, 108.
23   See Kurzweil 1999a, 150.
24   See Sandberg / Bostrom 2008.
25   See Cassidy 1992.

multiverses are continually being created. Even if we cannot capture the individual processes according to this law, in principle the universe and its parts could still be simulated. Notably, Tipler adheres to this theory even though it produces immense contradictions within his own work upon closer reflection. Indeed, the simulation of *all possible universes* and living beings by the Omega Point seems incompatible with Tipler's exclusively paradisiacal visions.[26] This reintroduction of a pre-modern determinism into physics simultaneously offers an indispensable prerequisite for the simulation of the past in Tipler and Moravec's visions.

In his approach to basic physical questions, Hans Moravec developed ideas under the formative influence of Frank Tipler. Following Tipler and Barrow's *Anthropic Principle*, he emphasizes the observer's role in generating a universe's existence and reality only through his own presence. Moravec develops the solipsistic thesis that, although some of the multiverses (and the beings living in them) are constantly being drowned out of the multitude of all multiverses (for example, by cosmic catastrophes, or a third world war), these are also eliminated from the realm of reality due to the observers being destroyed. The ambitious roboticist therefore suggests a suicide experiment to prove that one's own death is impossible! If a suicide attempt succeeds, the corresponding universe is extinguished, and only those universes – i.e. quantum realities – remain in which the suicide failed or in which no third world war has broken out.[27]

> We lose our ties to physical reality, but, in the space of all possible worlds, that cannot be the end. Our consciousness continues to exist in some of those, and we will always find ourselves in worlds where we exist and never in ones where we don't.[28]

Of course, the question of why Moravec is so concerned with posthuman survival despite his own certainty about immortality remains unanswered.[29] In his dissertation, Max More also invents a fictive means for overcoming the indeterminable quantum processes, as well as the associated, complete control of at least the past, relying for this on a gigantic future computer:

> The 22nd century overthrow of quantum mechanics with its uncertainty principle and replacement by Quantum Super-Determinacy, has allowed (with the aid of vast computational power) the precise determination of the state of the universe at all past times.[30]

The past and all future arbitrary universes therefore become possible via this detour through the Many-Worlds interpretation of quantum mechanics and the subsequent reintroduction of physical determinism, computer simulation, and the emulation of a human being. Only a deterministic approach can guarantee that the original and the emulation do not deviate from each other by indeterminable quantum processes.

---

26   See Tipler / Barrow 1986, 458-506; Tipler 1995, 167-183, 483-488.
27   See Moravec 1988, 153-154, 187-188; Moravec 1999, 193-207.
28   Moravec 1999, 210.
29   See ibid., 13-14, 189, 192-193.
30   More 1995, 6.

In concrete terms, the posthumanist striving for control of indeterminable contingencies manifests itself in many ways. Physical functions become completely controllable in the utopias of cyborgs, and increasingly so in a virtual existence. Age, illness, and physical failure become reversible, or even disappear completely for posthuman beings and their descendants. Sexual desire also becomes controllable. Sexuality itself will happen without physical liability – natural risks, such as AIDS or unwanted pregnancy, which almost all posthumanists mention, are now easily avoidable. In posthumanism bodies and genders become freely selectable and constructible, and it is here that posthumanist discourse and current visions of genetic engineering come together again: In 1952 pioneers in genetic research James Watson and Francis Crick referred to the same sources of cybernetic information theory that were to become the basis of the posthumanist view of humankind. By using the *genetic code* as metaphor, human beings become a hereditary substance that is, in principle, *programmable*.[31] The construction of new, partly virtual bodies is connected to the ideal of a perpetual increase in the intellectual, information-processing performance of the human mind. In posthumanist literature this culminates multiple times in the genius figure of the fictional detective Sherlock Holmes.[32] Compared to these embodied visions, Moravec's confidence in the imminent and total control of earthly weather and the avoidance of natural disasters seems peripheral.[33]

Posthumanist utopias are built upon conquering the greatest contingency of human life: death. This threat is overcome by the expectation of an imminent technological immortality – just as the belief in immediate and all-encompassing progress has always motivated the prophets of progress.[34] Without this prospect of human immortality, advocating an era of artificial intelligence and the end of humanity would sound absurd. Yet through it, attaining immortality, omniscience, beauty, and physical potency appear to be possible, subject only to the human will.

> *Fin-de-siècle* hubristic mania was the desire for perfect knowledge and total power. The goal was complete omnipotence: the power to remake humanity, earth, the universe at large. If you're tired of the ills of the flesh, then *get rid of the flesh*: we can *do* that now. If the universe isn't good enough for you, then *remake* it, from the ground up.[35]

In this way, the posthumanist vision of immortality seems to be the consequence and continuation of a specifically American death repression. None other than Norbert Wiener, the founder of cybernetics, described this with crystal clarity 70 years ago:

> The education of the average American child of the upper middle class is such as to guard him solicitously against the awareness of death and doom. He is brought up in an atmosphere of Santa Claus ... The fact of individual death, the imminence of calamity, are forced upon him by the experiences of his later years. Nevertheless, he tries to relegate these unfortunate realities to the role of accidents, and to build up a

---

31 See Roszak 1994, 16-17; Riegler 1999, 55-56.
32 See Ettinger 1989, 35-37; Moravec 1999, 167.
33 See Moravec 1999, 155-156.
34 See Dawson 1935, 2-3.
35 Regis 1990, 7.

Heaven on Earth in which unpleasantness has no place. This Heaven on Earth consists for him in an eternal progress, and a continual ascent to Bigger and Better Things.[36]

In this context, it is no coincidence that roboticists, cyberneticists, and physicists in particular founded posthumanism, considering their familiarity with the structure of abstract models of reality, such as computer programs. While quantum physics has revealed the limitations of mathematical regularities to model our world, computer-generated virtuality is based on mathematical algorithms that are always unambiguous. John von Neumann's game theory presupposes the quantifiability and rationalizability of human behavior and, from the mathematical model of reality thus obtained, constructs a virtual computer reality that corresponds exactly to these rational conditions.[37] Virtual reality is thus constructed just like a game, according to clear and consistent rules.[38]

Virtuality offers an irresistible attraction through its promises of mastering the flow of time itself and making any conceivable experience freely available, and even more so by the illusion that all human thoughts and experiences can be mathematically determined. Death, which undermines the meaning of a purely this-worldly life, does not exist in virtuality. If the real world can no longer be meaningfully understood and experienced, then virtuality offers a rational and deterministic alternative. The virtual world corresponds to the desire for the perfect logic of calculability. In the 1930s Norbert Elias had already considered the ontological implications of those mathematical world models that are today realized by means of computers. Hidden behind this belief in the mathematical regularity and controllability of the world lies nothing more than a longing for eternity.[39]

The illusion of controlling and repressing death has now come face to face with humanity's increasingly obvious limits in its ability to protect itself against existential threats – in the everyday world and globally. One might even dare to assert that tension is growing between the technological claim to power and powerlessness in the face of the actual uncontrollability of life, society, and nature. Technology is unable to quickly and easily resolve the COVID-19 pandemic, the American opioid crisis, the brutal wars currently raging in Yemen, Afghanistan, and Syria, the natural disasters exacerbated by climate change, or the risk of meltdowns of nuclear reactors. The helplessness of robotics was also paradigmatically revealed in Fukushima in 2011, when remote-controlled devices were unable to cope with high radiation exposure, and human rescue teams had to step in and contain the dangers manually.

Broadly speaking, we can understand posthumanism as a reaction to the crisis of technical utopias at the beginning of the 21st century. Here, for example, an increasing need for control correlates with a decreasing acceptance of risk. Indeed, life today is no more dangerous or risky than in the past (coal energy and coal mining cost more lives

---

36   Wiener 1989, 41.
37   See Neumann / Morgenstern 1966, 34-39.
38   See Weizenbaum 1976, 73-110.
39   Elias 1993, 128-130.

than nuclear energy), but the need for total control has grown enormously, as Arthur and Marilouise Kroker and Hermann Lübbe argue.[40]

However, posthumanism differs from previous technology euphoria in one essential regard: It does not offer individual technical solutions to concrete contemporary problems, which are in fact only marginally considered by posthumanist authors. Instead, an immortal existence in virtuality is the linchpin of the entire posthumanist system. If human biological nature – i.e. the human body – proves to be only partially controllable; if the physical and mental performance of this body can only be increased to a limited extent; and if, on a global scale, the forces of nature and the climate continue to prove to be uncontrollable, then posthumanism's solution will simply be humanity's renunciation of itself and the world.

As Ed Regis has so plainly stated, the simplest solution is: *Get rid of the flesh!* Everything that is beyond simple control and regulation – such as physical weaknesses, age, sexuality, the development of personality, and ultimately death – in other words, a human beings's entire biology and the *wilderness* of the natural environment, should become completely controllable. This can only be accomplished by replacing humans with their mechanical descendants, and by simulating the last generation of humankind as deterministic computer programs. The contingency of the life-world will therefore not be mastered in the conventional sense. Rather, the real human world will be replaced by a completely determinable – i.e. controllable – world. If the world itself is not as regulated or controllable as a computer, then it must be transformed into a computer, as Oswald Wiener and John D. Bernal have already demanded. According to Joseph Weizenbaum, this is the fulfillment of the old cybernetic dream: "The world is full of secrets – and the credo of the AI scene, that everything is predictable, denies the mystery of the living. It instead creates the illusion of complete transparency and suggests that all aspects of our existence can be unraveled."[41]

Technological posthumanism and especially the belief in the almighty singularity promises unambiguous answers in a time of challenging existential risks. As Ray Kurzweil puts it with reference to the history of evolution: "It will continue until the entire universe is at our fingertips."[42] Thus, the prospect of everlasting improvement offers a balm to the spirit.

7.3 Secular Progress and Christian Salvation History

How can we possibly classify and rationalize the entirety of post- and transhumanism in the early 21st century within the history of ideas? First of all, it must be made clear that it is not a question of whether these movements constitute a religion. The heterogeneity of positions they contain – from Christian transhumanists to strong atheist critiques

---

40 See Lübbe 1994, 82–102; Kroker / Kroker 1996, 36–40.
41 Weizenbaum interviewed by Bernhard Pörksen (2000, 276), trans. by AJ.
42 Kurzweil 2005, 487.

– invalidates such a blanket perspective.[43] Indeed, as this book has made clear, it is fruitful to overcome the essentialist binary of whether or not something is a religion. Rather, one should ask what post- and transhumanists do with "religion"?[44] How do they receive and interpret these ideas? How does culture determine this reception? Do overarching, persistent themes show up in these histories?

Post- and transhumanists approach the question of religion from a broad range of angles. Frank Tipler claims that his insights are based on scientific facts alone, although his understanding builds upon the long tradition of natural theology, and the physico-theology of the Protestant theologian William Paley and his contemporaries. Ray Kurzweil and Martine Rothblatt expect new spiritual dimensions to arrive, which will complement the expansion of human abilities in virtual existence. All other post- and transhumanist authors, such as Marvin Minsky, Hans Moravec, Max More, Eliezer Yudkowsky, and Nick Bostrom, consider religion to instead be an obstacle, or even an enemy, of the technological overcoming of the biological human being and its immortalization. In their commentary on the Japanese roboticist Masahiro Mori, *The Buddha in the Robot*, Tipler and Rothblatt illustrate a typical posthumanist interpretation. For Tipler, the book offers proof that all religion can be overcome through technical progress.[45] However, Mori did not understand the future robots to be deified and omnipotent superbeings, but rather referred to "Buddha nature" to describe a robot's potential for evoking human self-knowledge: In his view, in fact, both humans and robots would increase their own levels of freedom if they only accepted the limitations of their abilities.[46]

This example reflects technological posthumanism's highly selective reception of religious ideas. Religion is perceived positively only insofar as it promotes personal self-realization and the expansion of powerful abilities. Thus, Tipler and Rothblatt cite Buddhism as compatible with the posthumanist vision of immortality but avoid naming the central element of Buddhist doctrines of redemption: compassion (*bodhicitta*). Transcendence in Buddhism is not fulfilled in an individualistic fantasy of personal omnipotence. Rather the Buddha Avalokiteshvara has a thousand eyes to observe human suffering, and a thousand hands to comfort those affected by it.

But what are the actual historical contexts of these ideas in detail? The posthumanist conception of the human being is largely determined by a purely materialistic interpretation of Descartes, which itself is based on critical approaches to religion taken from the French Enlightenment and especially adapted from the philosophy of La Mettrie. In concrete terms, this understanding is implemented in early cybernetics, which defines life as information processing and thus creates the indispensable

---

43 Hava Tirosh-Samuelson's attempt to interpret transhumanism as a new religious movement remains inconsistent. The religious scholar and transhumanist William S. Bainbridge, in turn, positions transhumanism as overcoming religion. Both approaches, however, ignore the movement's factual heterogeneity. See Tirosh-Samuelson 2014; Bainbridge 2005.

44 Behind this new perspective lies a paradigm shift in religious studies that replaces the ontological question "What *is* religion?" with the interactionist one "What do people *do* with religion?" See Krüger 2022.

45 See Mori 1980; Tipler 1995, 88; Rothblatt 2014, 264.

46 See Mori 1980, 20-31.

prerequisite for replacing humans with more efficient information-processing systems. However, the dynamic aspect of this human self-improvement is far more complex.

Far beyond the topic of posthumanism, a heated debate still rages about whether secular progress and its goals should be regarded as a secularized expression of Christian salvation history, or as a purely secular product of the Enlightenment, or even as a science that has become religious again. This question refers to an epistemological problem, which itself prevents an adequate assessment of posthumanist philosophy within the history of ideas. This reductive approach implies a bipolar intellectual cosmos of, on the one hand, the theological conception of history and, on the other hand, the secular philosophies that have emerged from it. Yet this cannot do justice to the complex relationship between secular progress and Christian theology, nor can it take the diversity of post- and transhumanist positions into account. Research to date has produced two opposite approaches: in one camp are the English historian John B. Bury, the philosopher Karl Löwith, and the Protestant theologian Rudolf Bultmann, while the philosopher Hans Blumenberg stands in the other.

In 1920, Bury's *The Idea of Progress. An Inquiry into its Origin and Growth* laid the groundwork for the first comprehensive account of modern theories of progress. In clear distinction to a religious history of salvation and the ultimate anticipated moment of divine providence, Bury defines the term *progress* as follows:

> The process must be the necessary outcome of the physical and social nature of man; it must not be at the mercy of any external will; otherwise there would be no guarantee of its continuance and its issue, and the idea of Progress would lapse into the idea of Providence.[47]

Bury traces the idea of progress through the French philosophers Fontenelle, Abbé de Saint-Pierre, Condorcet, and Comte, and presents the English theory of progress as highly dependent on these continental counterparts. England had already experienced political unrest and upheaval before the 18th century, whereas in France the emergence of the theory of progress had immediately preceded the French revolution. Bury therefore judges the English theory of progress only as a "cold reflection" of the French Enlightenment. According to his interpretation, the idea of progress in both France and England is understood as the liberation of reason and rationality from the narrow confines of theological traditions.[48]

> The otherworldly dreams of theologians, which had ruled so long lost their power, and men's earthly home again insinuated itself into their affections, but with the new hope of its becoming a place fit for reasonable beings to live in.[49]

Following Bury, Löwith and Bultmann argued that modern "progress" is Christian in its eschatological expectation of future salvation, yet anti-Christian in its tendency. The idea of progress appears to them as the secularized expression of Christian providence:

---

47 Bury 1955, 5.
48 See ibid., 217-237.
49 Ibid., 349.

> Man has to replace God, and the belief in human progress has to supplant the faith in providence ... To effect this ultimate advance, man has to take up the eternal fight between man and God and decide it; for God or the Absolute is the one great obstacle to human progress and the one great source of all of all kinds of absolutism – economic, political, religious.[50]

Löwith and Bultmann legitimize their theses by predominantly referring to the French, thoroughly anticlerical progress philosophers of the 18th century, such as Voltaire, Turgot, and Condorcet, as well as to Pierre Joseph Proudhon and Auguste Comte in the 19th century. Bultmann regards the European Enlightenment as the secularization of all human life and thought. Just as Christian teleology once promised transcendent salvation, the secular belief in progress now propagates one's mastery of nature, in order to attain worldly happiness. The idea of this-worldly progress, as well as the Christian providence associated with an other-worldly salvation, thus remain ultimately incompatible with Löwith's and Bultmann's conceptions, just as they were with Bury's.[51]

In the recent debate over modern ideas of progress, Reinhart Koselleck and Friedrich Rapp point to this thesis of the secularization of Christian conceptions of history. In modernity, the divine plan of salvation is now fulfilled by the philosophy of history, while secular theories of progress are satisfied by the open horizon of the future. This is reflected terminologically in the conceptual change from the spiritual *profectus* to the secular *progressus*. According to Koselleck, the temporalization of the goal of *perfectio* marks a decisive change in the doctrine of perfection. Once found only in God and the associated *perfectio seu consummatio salutis*, this salvation has now become an earthly goal to strive for. With reference to predominantly French philosophers, it can be understood how, in marked contrast to Christian theology, modern theories of progress transformed the fulfillment of the human being from the eternal into the temporal, and thus relocated the meaning of life to earthly joy. Over the course of the 19th century, the idea of progress became something of a secular religion, but now it is a political, economic, and cultural catchword.[52]

The philosopher Hans Blumenberg has fundamentally criticized this popular thesis of the secularization of Christian salvation. He is adamantly opposed to the overuse of the term "secularization" in historical research. Blumenberg even invokes the category of historical illegitimacy, as he considers the general and infinitely strained thesis of secularization to be permeated by theological implications. For this "whole dimension of hidden meaning" would always ascribe a subliminal theological implication to secular philosophy, politics, science, and culture. For Blumenberg, this was especially problematic for the idea of progress.

> Regarding the dependence of the idea of progress on Christian eschatology, there are differences that would have had to block any transposition of the one into the other. It is a formal, but for that very reason a manifest difference that an eschatology speaks of an event breaking into history, an event that transcends and is heterogeneous to

---

50   Löwith 1949, 62-63.
51   See Löwith 1949, 60-103; Bultmann 1957, 56-73.
52   See Rapp 1992, 58-59, 122-123, 187-190; Koselleck 1975, 371-377, 411.

it, while the idea of progress extrapolates from a structure present in every moment to a future that is immanent in history.[53]

Blumenberg defends the thesis of an independent development of secular, enlightened philosophy in contrast to theological thought. Regarding the modern idea of progress, he states:

> ... the crucial question is still, whether this situation is to be brought about immanently or transcendently, whether man can achieve it by the exertion of his own powers or has to rely for it on the grace, which he cannot earn, of an event breaking in upon him.[54]

Blumenberg thus establishes a clear separation between theological and secular views of history. In reaction to this criticism, Friedrich Rapp offers a moderating thesis that early progress theorists in the 18th century, such as Vico or Herder, remained rooted in Christian concepts of history, but were able to free themselves from these theological premises and implications over the course of the Enlightenment.[55]

The weakness of Blumenberg's criticism is that, like Bury, Bultmann, and Löwith before him, he feels completely committed to the paradigm of the history of effects (*Wirkungsgeschichte*). All the scholars mentioned here believed that modern progress theory originated in 18th century France, and only thereafter began to spread and develop in England and other nations. This prominent role and legacy of the French philosophy of progress is of course by no means to be denied. However, the limitations of this purely effect-historical paradigm have meant that practically no attention has been paid to its reception by English and Scottish philosophers.

Irrespective of its English and French particularities, progress was assumed to be a constant, secular, and enlightened concept. The obvious differences between the French theory of progress and responses by English and Scottish philosophers were largely marginalized. Although general parallels between Christianity's linear understanding of history and the European theory of progress have been proposed, historical sources have never empirically demonstrated how religious theories were transformed into secular ones. Both Bury and Blumenberg developed concepts presupposing a strong demarcation, or even incompatibility, between theological and secular understandings of history. However, the post- and transhumanist reception of religious ideas cannot be explained using such an antagonistic model.

Johannes Rohbeck accuses Blumenberg of ignoring the idea of divine providence and transcendent historical powers in the French and Scottish idea of progress – criticism which also applies to Bury and his successors.[56] In his *Gifford Lectures*, Carl-Friedrich von Weizsäcker had warned against the polarizing separation of religion and science, which a universal secularization thesis would imply. He instead emphasized the manifold solutions offered by the 18th century philosophers.[57]

---

53   Blumenberg 1986, 30.
54   Ibid., 86. See ibid., 27-76.
55   See Rapp 1992, 116-128.
56   See Rohbeck 1987, 244-245.
57   See Weizsäcker 1964, 157-183; Stuckrad 2014, 178-182.

For this reason, it is appropriate to more closely examine the interactions between this-worldly progress and theological providence in English and American historical concepts. As early as the 1960s, the religion scholar Ernst Benz criticized European intellectuals' ignorance of certain important aspects of the Christian understanding of history's supposed secularization.[58] This tendency in the history of ideas is all the more astonishing when one considers that, since the mid-20th century, a whole series of individual studies have been available that question the Enlightenment thesis of a dichotomy between religion and science. Benz and, more recently, Kocku von Stuckrad have extensively discussed how religious discourses since the 17th century have adopted scientific argumentation and legitimation.[59]

Andreas Sommer examines Johann Valentin Andreae's utopian ideal city of Christianopolis, published in the early days of Protestant theology in 1619, which already inextricably linked the discovery of religious truths with the progress of science. Similar to Francis Bacon's *Nova Atlantis* (1626), this rational and experimental natural science is committed to theology. In fact, its very progressiveness is fed by theology. According to Sommer, Protestantism tends to disenchant the world. Yet via human action the profane can be re-divinized, and only thus gains value in the history of salvation. On the other hand, natural science is made sacred by its role in the revelation of the divine creation.[60]

This idea of secular progress as complementing religious salvation history is continued throughout the 17th century in other aspects as well. The Puritan immigrants viewed the conquest of the American wilderness and the building of a new civilization as a religious act – New England became *New Israel*. This movement found literary expression in John Bunyan's *Pilgrim's Progress* (1678) and especially in popular edification literature. Here the believer is taught that progress is a sign of divine grace, as revealed throughout earthly life. In the American context, the literary representation of progress was predominantly religious, missionary, and visionary, and was reinforced by the newly awakening national consciousness as the New World's *manifest destiny*.[61]

Millennialist ideas were also of critical importance for the formation of the American idea of progress. In the 16th century, a renewed interest in Christian eschatology arose alongside the emergence of Protestantism. By relying on the Revelation of John (Rev 20:1-10), the theologians Johann Heinrich Alsted and Johann Piscator argued that the millennium – Christ's millennial reign over the Earth, during which the power of evil over humanity will be banished – would not occur in the present or the past, but rather the future of human history. After Francis Bacon founded his *pansophia*, with reference to Daniel 12:4,[62] this Bible verse subsequently became a Puritan slogan, and they began to emphasize scientific progress as a pre-condition

---

58 See Benz 1965, 157-158.
59 See Benz 1970; Stuckrad 2014, 178-182.
60 See Sommer 1996, 114-124; Dawson 1935, 154-155.
61 See Buchloh 1963, 156-165; Brunotte 2000, 76-85, 273-280.
62 Daniel 12:4 "But thou, O Daniel, shut up the words, and seal the book, *even* to the time of the end: many shall run to and fro, and knowledge shall be increased."

for the dawn of the millennium. The Congregationalist clergyman Josiah Strong (1847-1916) interpreted America's economic and political achievements as an indication of the divine plan that the millennium would begin in his country, since it was precisely these scientific achievements that would distinguish Americans before the world:

> Science is certainly destined to make great progress during the next century ... What if it could be certainly known that during the twentieth century there would be a new revelation of God's will ... What supreme blessings should we expect it to bestow on mankind ... Its truth is evident, but all do not yet perceive that the truths of science are God's truths, that its laws are God's laws.[63]

Here, the necessity of scientific discoveries is interpreted as strengthening religion and defending it against the irreligious tendencies of the natural sciences, in marked contrast to the assumptions of a general secularization thesis.[64]

This popular religious idea of progress led to dynamic improvements and growth in worldly life, but always subordinated these achievements to a religious framework. Religious studies scholar Thomas Hase cites a number of convincing biographical examples illustrating the hopeful potential of the economic and millennialist idea of progress in the 19th century. He argues that the driving force behind these actions was not the fear of eternal damnation, but rather the firm optimism that a better world can be crafted through determined human action.[65]

In light of American millenarianism, we cannot maintain that the Christian concept of providence could simply be replaced by the prospect of a this-worldly improvement in living conditions. The Christian history of salvation is thus not overwritten by modern ideas of progress, but rather was actually its major driving force in the United States. Millenarianism became increasingly popular thanks to its ability to create order amidst a time of many and rapidly appearing innovations. Indeed, it offered an explanation of why such advancement should not only occur, but actually be striven for.[66]

Various historians have identified the weaknesses inherent in Bury's thesis of the incompatibility between the ideas of worldly progress and divine providence. John Baillie, Arthur Ekirch, and especially David Spadafora have all made it clear that, despite the undisputed influence of the French philosophers, the English and American ideas of progress have produced a very peculiar synthesis between this-worldly progress and the Christian history of salvation. The vast majority of British or American philosophers – including well-established thinkers such as Joseph Priestley, David Hartley, Adam Ferguson, and Richard Price – evaluated progress as a divine program evolving in step with humanity's maturity. The full amount of bliss and happiness would only unfold for humankind at the end of time. The complexity, beauty, and well-documented historical development of the world could allow no other conclusion than that the Earth, and humankind with it, cannot be an accidental phenomenon and therefore must be based

---

63   Strong 1893, 11. See Hase 1997, 129.
64   See Ekirch 41-130; Spadafora 1990, 85-104.
65   See Hase 1997, 133-134.
66   See Benz 1965, 157-181; Brunotte 2000, 208-217, 273-280; Hase 1997, 142-148; Spadafora 1990, 105-131.

on a divine plan. According to Priestley, humanity is now responsible for following this path to create a better world, and to use its God-given abilities and powers for the benefit of all. Secular and religious progress are thus merely different sides of one and the same historical process. While English philosophers were no less euphoric than the French in advocating the secular aspects of progress in politics, education, medicine, technology, and science, the semantic context of this concept always remained explicitly Christian:[67]

> But what was the source of all this progress? What could have transformed mankind into beings of ever-greater knowledge, power, happiness, and virtue? For all these believers in the general advancement of the world, the answer was, fundamentally, God: progress appeared to them to be a divine program.[68]

Against this background, it becomes clear why the singularity and the cosmic-divine destination of the Omega Point were integrated into posthumanism. As we have seen, the reception of Teilhard de Chardin's work by posthumanists runs parallel to the philosophical interpretations of the Internet. Frank Tipler invokes the concept of a cosmic history of salvation, ranging from Alpha to Omega, but without any specifically christological components. Hans Moravec adopts the concept only superficially (probably due to Tipler's influence). Ray Kurzweil, on the other hand, precisely adapts the structural elements of Teilhard de Chardin and Frank Tipler's theories, but without using their terminology. For Kurzweil as for Tipler, the realization of God is identical with the transformation of the universe into a single computer made of thinking matter: a cosmic consciousness to counter the threat of entropy. As the only intelligent life in the universe, both Tipler and Kurzweil believe that this ultimate task must therefore fall to humanity. This anthropocentric interpretation also legitimizes the sacrifice of the human being in this pursuit.

The divine Omega Point, towards which biological and technological evolution is heading, supports two important aspects of posthumanist reasoning. 1. Technological posthumanism postulates a unifying idea resembling the secular unification utopias of the *global brain* and the collective intelligence espoused by Turchin and Lévy. 2. This reflects the broad cultural motif of a lost paradise (Book of Genesis) or the dissolution of the human community (Tower of Babel), which echo throughout both Christianity and Judaism. The human endeavor is now characterized by regaining this *Paradise Lost* – which John Milton so strongly established as the mission of the New World – in union with God and all humanity.

As Armand Mattelart and Randy Connolly have pointed out, these ideas are re-invoked again today in interpretations of new communication technologies – in a very broad sense. Over the past centuries, whenever innovations appeared in media technologies, such as the telegraph or radio – or even transport, such as canals or the railroad – certain voices interpreted them as the dawn of a new, liberated age in which humanity would grow together into a harmonious global community.[69] The noosphere

---

67 See Spadafora 1990, 85-132.
68 Ibid., 248.
69 See Connolly 2001, 317-364; Feinberg 1969, 20-21.

and the metaphor of the global village re-create this utopia of an egalitarian, organic community of all people, which was first envisioned in pre-revolutionary France.[70]

The posthumanist concept of salvation is based on a number of highly speculative assumptions, such as the non-existence of extraterrestrial life and the possibility of overcoming quantum mechanics, leading to the technological immortalization of humankind. However, critical observers should not conclude that this vision would thereby lose its wide appeal. To the extent that religions are understood as belief systems, the history of humankind testifies that speculative assumptions eluding any empirical verifiability can prove to be extremely persistent – presumably even more so than many verifiable interpretations of the world. On the one hand, posthumanism's greatest achievement consists in overcoming human calamity. On the other, it also promises what Oswald Wiener calls the "complete solution of all world problems", as well as the "liberation of philosophy through technology" by replacing the world itself.[71] Yet post- and transhumanism's Achilles heel is precisely this tension between its religious and philosophical assumptions and its concurrent claims of scientific argumentation (which should include acceptance of scientific criticism).

It is true that secularly oriented transhumanists, such as Bostrom, Yudkowsky, and More, are visibly uncomfortable with this techno-religious synthesis. However, the discussion has clearly shifted since the turn of the millennium in 2000. While at that time I could describe Frank Tipler's Omega Theory as exotic, its core elements now form the center of post- and transhumanism. Alongside Ray Kurzweil's interpretation of singularity, a teleology of salvation history has developed that is specifically designed to transform the cosmos into a thinking universe. The goal of this process is the realization of God. Posthumanism thus finds itself continuing the tradition of the English moral philosophers of the 18th century, for whom final perfection can only be achieved via union with God. This also blurs the boundaries between the cosmological and the technological concepts of singularity. For popular audiences, Teilhard de Chardin is now celebrated as a prophet of the Internet, superintelligence, transhumanism, and the singularity.[72]

How can this current alliance be explained, despite the fact that early transhumanism was so decidedly critical of religion? To understand this seeming contradiction, one must realize that Christian elements are not actually relevant to the reception and adaption of this christological heritage. Therefore, post- and transhumanism can reach out and speak to both secular and religious audiences in a Janus-faced way.

In my estimation, this approach's notable superiority is due to another element: the persistence – i.e. the permanence – of cultural ideas. As we have seen in our analysis, even the coining of the word *transhuman* (*trasumanar*) in Dante's verses alludes both to the anti-mythological deification of man as well as the Christian view of God. Around 1300, the scholastic John Duns Scotus also introduced the term *virtualiter* into Christian theology. When William Douw Lighthall first invoked the term *transhumanism* in the

---

70 See Mattelart 1996, 85-162, 304.
71 Wiener 1969, CLXXV.
72 See Redding 2016; Kurzweil 2005, 389-390.

mid-20th century, he enriched its religious reading with an interpretation of evolution via the history of salvation, as Teilhard de Chardin and many others also did at that time.

Post- and transhumanism therefore cannot be relegated to merely being a religious philosophy – its techno-centric legitimation of progress remains undisputed. Yet it is also obvious that Tipler, Kurzweil, and their comrades-in-arms succeeded in updating the persistent ideas of (salvation) history, God, humanity, and the cosmos, and connecting them in this new form. Post- and transhumanism therefore do not arise in a cultural vacuum, but rather rely on established interpretations of social reality, which have already been part of Christian thought and western philosophy for two millennia.

In his short story *Accelerando* (2005) the British science fiction author Charles Stross has in fact already anticipated the conclusion of this analyses of the history of ideas and summarized it in only a few words. After rampant debates about the nature of singularity, the two heroes are left with a tired shoulder shrug when faced with the great utopia. One of them sums up it all up tersely:

> "Is not happening yet," contributes Boris. "Singularity implies infinite rate of change achieved momentarily. Future not amenable thereafter to prediction by presingularity beings, right? So has not happened … Singularity is load of religious junk. Christian mystic rapture recycled for atheist nerds."[73]

7.4 The End of the Affronts

In November 2005, I was invited to an exclusive dinner at Princeton University, which was then my academic home, held after a lecture by Nick Bostrom. Around ten interested people sat in an upscale dining room in *Prospect House* (!), discussing bioethics and the future of humankind. As far as I can recall, only one woman was present, while the rest were all white men. During dinner we were served by African American staff. To me, the setting reflected a disturbing continuity of racial-social role distributions in the upper echelons of society, which left me very ill at ease (although the university of course achieves ethnic diversity in many other areas).

Today this dinner with Nick Bostrom seems to have been a symbolic microcosm mirroring the social utopias of trans- and posthumanism. Since the debate over eugenics, it has always been white men who have presented universal blueprints for a renewed and improved humanity. Women and other ethnic groups were, and remain, largely confined to the role of mere spectators. What astonishes me most is that this ethnic and gender homogeneity seems unnoticed by even the wisest adherents to trans- and posthumanism. In fact, many of Bostrom's philosophical studies directly address the question of bias – the attitudes, biases, and inclinations that he believes are often based on selective perceptions of reality:

---

73   Stross 2005, 184. See Raulerson 2013, 33-38. The *rapture* of the nerds is already a fixed topos in the criticism and parody of the Singularitarians. See Sirius / Cornell 2015, 195.

> How big is the smallest fish in the pond? You catch one hundred fishes, all of which are greater than six inches. Does this evidence support the hypothesis that no fish in the pond is much less than six inches long? Not if your net can't catch smaller fish.[74]

However, Bostrom and his colleagues do not realize the degree to which their own trans- and posthumanist utopia is shaped by cultural values, and in particular by their Euro- and androcentric bias. This is most clearly evident in the continuation of the goals of the eugenic cult, particularly regarding geniuses, brains, the superhuman, and the intelligent elites of humanity, which are interpreted in a social Darwinist framework.[75] According to this logic, there can be no solidarity in coexistence, only the survival of the fittest. Of no less momentous importance is the definition of the human being as an information-processing machine, which emerges from a partly utilitarian, partly Protestant interpretation of human life. Finally, these normative elements are fused with further aspects of the Christian and philosophical histories of salvation to form a universal theory of progress, culminating in an almighty singularity and the intelligent colonization of the (divine) cosmos.

The fact that Bostrom is almost exclusively surrounded by white male fish should make him reconsider the mesh of his own "futurological net". The assumption that something like a epitome of creation can exist as the highest stage in the history of evolution, coupled with the belief that this must necessarily be the (Western) man of a technologically advanced civilization, all testifies to an utterly anthropocentric, selective perception. In fact, any other living beings, including sharks, ants, or paramecia, could arrive at the same conclusion.[76] The philosopher Friedrich Rapp points out that the history of evolution itself does not include any hierarchies. In fact, even the criterion that younger species will continue to survive is completely invalidated in light of the possibility of humankind's atomic suicide.

> Scientific observation only leads to the conclusion: some (new) species survive, others do not. However, those species who prove most capable of survival are by no means increasingly differentiated or complex.[77]

In the case of posthumanism, normativity consists of a complex web of assumptions and objectives concerning the economy, society, religion, and gender relations. After analyzing the various individual elements of technological posthumanism, what this vision of the future achieves on a second, more significant level becomes clear.

As described in the early chapters of this book, following Günther Anders, Hannah Arendt, and Sigmund Freud, the philosopher Johannes Rohbeck identified four affronts of humans in the history of modernity: the cosmological affront by Copernicus'

---

74 Bostrom 2002, 1.
75 Eva Hesse has traced the connection between industrialization and the effort to perfect humanity in eugenics. See Hesse 1992, 227-233, 281-336.
76 Sharks have been colonizing this planet for over 350 million years, ants for 100 million years (dinosaurs "only" span a period of about 170 million years). In contrast, the history of hominids began only about five million years ago. The paramecium, in turn, has a genome that is twice as complex as that of humans.
77 Rapp 1992, 84, trans. by AJ. See ibid., 74-87; Dawson 1935, 15-16.

heliocentric worldview; the biological affront by Darwin's theory of evolution; the mental affront by psychoanalysis; and the technological affront by the perfection of humankind's machine creations – the "Promethean shame".[78]

According to Frank Tipler, Hans Moravec, and Ray Kurzweil as well as many transhumanists such as Bostrom and Yudkowsky, technological posthumanism has the ability to "cure" all four of these affronts:

1. Based on the anthropic principle, earthly life is not only located in the meaningful center of the universe (as was the case in Christian cosmology). Rather it has been tasked with no less of a mission than rescuing the entire universe from its otherwise inevitable heat death or entropy.

2. The biological affront is resolved through humanity's role as the creator of artificial intelligence and the singularity. This is especially true since the essence of humankind – our thinking mind – will merge with these posthuman entities, which will overcome the former poor biological existence.

3. & 4. Psychological and technological affronts will be defeated by the complete control and mastery of human mental abilities (via computerization), as well as the subsequent infinite increase in their achievements that comes from fusion with superintelligence. Technology does not degrade humanity, rather it helps humans to achieve transcendental superhumanity and assume total control.

None other than Julian Huxley euphorically welcomed exactly this renewed anthropocentricity of evolution and cosmology in 1963:

> To me, it is an exciting fact that man, after he appeared to have been dethroned from his supremacy, demoted from his central position in the universe to the status of an insignificant inhabitant of a small outlying planet of one among millions of stars, has now become reinstated in a key position, one of the rare spearheads or torchbearers, or trustees – choose your metaphor according to taste – of advance in the cosmic process of evolution.[79]

Technological posthumanism therefore does not signify the end of humanity. However, the development of technological progress that it incorporates does present a substantial challenge to humanism's idea of humankind.[80] From a posthumanist perspective, both humankind and humanism's goals have become obsolete due to a lack of efficiency. This is not because these ideals became obsolete, but rather that the increases in work performance and knowledge according to a posthumanist logic could be realized more efficiently by future artificial intelligences. Critical posthumanism responds to precisely those ideals and goals that technological posthumanism embodies.[81]

From a purely techno-centric perspective, humanity is indeed obsolete – as Günther Anders already knew. Now we simply have to decide whether we as humans wish to

---

78 See Rohbeck 1993, 10.
79 Huxley 1963, 21-22.
80 See Hayles 1999, 286-287.
81 See Bernstein 2019, 19-22; Loh 2018, 130-180.

adopt this techno-centric perspective. Stanisław Lem calls particular attention to this development in terms of the meaning of humankind:

> The more the machine becomes independent from its environment, the better it is from a purely technical point of view. But humans are dependent on their environment (such as the erotic, the social, or bonds of friendship), which creates autonomous rather than goal-oriented (i.e. teleological) values. A cyborg who no longer needs food, drink, or air because he has an atomic energy source built in; a cyborg who can erase any memory from his brain by a simple act of will – this machine will always be more perfect than a human being in terms of performance, because he suffers neither hunger, thirst, shortness of breath, nor pangs of conscience. But in the same way, everything constituting the cultural core of the value of human life is thereby also progressively annulled.[82]

The alternative to posthumanism lies in the uncomfortable acceptance of human imperfection, death, and aging. In this regard, one year before Hans Moravec's work *Mind Children* appeared Ernst Ulrich and Christine von Weizsäcker called for a return to "human measure": including a tolerance of human fallibility, even in the face of "perfect" technology or "perfect" virtual images of humans.[83]

But even this approach remains rooted in posthumanist logic, which, alongside the school of philosophical anthropology or Anders' *Promethean shame*, always interprets human beings as deficient. Perhaps it is worth reversing this perspective, as the novelist Brian Selznick suggests in one of his stories: "You know, machines never have any extra parts. They have the exact number and type of parts they need."[84]

By this approach, (incidentally, the same one which applies to computer programs) the diversity and multiplicity of opportunities inherent to being human must be regarded as an abundance. In comparison, machines and software can be found to be deficient by lacking such possibilities – their processes are determined by (and limited to) a single purpose.[85] Humans on the other hand, are open beings benefiting from an enormous diversity of social relationships and potentials, and constantly developing in their search for identity and meaning. Technological posthumanism, which represents only one of these infinitely many interpretations of meaning, can only construct humans as deficient beings because it imposes utilitarian conditions that reduce them – like a machine – to a single purpose: information processing.

If, on the other hand, we understand humanity as an open question – even as a new venture – then human beings are not deficient; not, as one might say, a *Mängelwesen*.[86] Instead, their curious and free natures benefit from an infinity of possibilities, in direct opposition to cybernetics' deterministic urge for total economic and social control.

---

82 Lem 1972, 183, trans. by AJ.
83 See Weizsäcker / Weizsäcker 1987.
84 Selznick 2007, 342.
85 This is exactly the conceptual problem of a general artificial intelligence – nobody knows how to transition from specialized programs to a universal problem solver.
86 The German philosopher Arnold Gehlen sees the human being as a *Mängelwesen*, a deficient being, in comparison with the physical and morphological superiority of other species.

For Dietmar Kamper, choosing mortality is therefore linked to the freedom to remain human.[87]

> But with freedom comes mortality and absolute uncertainty ... There are indeed incommensurable, terrible truths. Amongst them belongs the momentous assumption that human beings are an open question, to which no possible definite answer – if it has any merit – can ever come close.[88]

---

87 See Kamper 1999, 25-26.
88 Ibid., 96, trans. by AJ. See Gantke 1987, 286-290.

Appendix

List of Abbreviations

AI	Artificial Intelligence
AL	Artificial Life
CPU	Central Processing Unit
Cyborg	Cybernetic Organism
JET	Journal of Evolution and Technology
KZfSS	Kölner Zeitschrift für Soziologie und Sozialpsychologie
MIT	Massachusetts Institute of Technology
SEP	Stanford Encyclopedia of Philosophy
TRE	Theologische Realenzyklopädie
UP	University Press
VR	Virtual Reality
ZfR	Zeitschrift für Religionswissenschaft
ZRGG	Zeitschrift für Religions- und Geistesgeschichte

Bibliography

a) Literature[1]

A

Adams, Tim (2016): Artificial intelligence: 'We're like children playing with a bomb'. In: *The Observer*, 06/12/2016 (online).

Agar, Nicholas (2010): *Humanity's End. Why We Should Reject Radical Enhancement.* Cambridge, MA.

Agar, Nicholas (2015): *The Sceptical Optimist: Why technology isn't the answer to everything.* Oxford.

Ahn, Gregor (2001): Homo religiosus oder künstliche Unsterblichkeit? Vererbung und Anlage in der neueren europäischen Religionsgeschichte. In: *Vererbung und Milieu*, ed. by Michael Wink. Heidelberg, 331-353.

Alcor (1983): Ev Cooper. 1926-1983. In: *Cryonics* (March), 7-9.

Alexander, Samuel (1966)[1920]: *Space, Time, and Deity. The Gifford Lectures at Glasgow 1916-1918*, Vol II. New York.

Altner, Günter (1965): *Schöpfungsglaube und Entwicklungsgedanke in der protestantischen Theologie zwischen Ernst Haeckel und Teilhard de Chardin.* Zürich.

Anders, Günther (^{6}1983)[1956]: *Die Antiquiertheit des Menschen, Bd. 1. Über die Seele des Menschen im Zeitalter der zweiten industriellen Revolution.* München.

Armstrong, Stuart / Kaj Sotala (2012): How We're Predicting AI – or Failing To. https://intelligence.org/files/PredictingAI.pdf.

Asimov, Isaac (1956): The Last Question. In: *Science Fiction Quarterly* (Nov.), 6-15.

Assmann, Jan (^{2}1993)[1983]: Schrift, Tod und Identität. Das Grab als Vorschule der Literatur im alten Ägypten. In: *Schrift und Gedächtnis. Beiträge zur Archäologie der literarischen Kommunikation*, ed. by Aleida and Jan Assmann / Christof Hardmeier. München, 64-93.

Assmann, Jan (2000): *Der Tod als Thema der Kulturtheorie. Todesbilder und Totenriten im Alten Ägypten.* Frankfurt a.M.

---

[1] Square brackets refer to the first edition if the year of publication or translation is different from that of the original.

Ayaß, Ruth (2012): Introduction: Media Appropriation and Everyday Life. In: *The Appropriation of Media in Everyday Life*, ed. by Ruth Ayaß / Cornelia Gerhardt. Amsterdam, 1-15.

B

Bacon, Francis (2017)[1626]: *New Atlantis, and The Great Instauration*. Chichester.
Bacon, Francis (1977)[1638]: *The historie of life and death. With observations naturall and experimentall for the prolonging of LIFE*. New York.
Baedtke, Jan / Christina Brandt / Hans-Ulrich Lessing (Eds.)(2015): *Anthropologie 2.0? Neuere Ansätze einer philosophischen Anthropologie im Zeitalter der Biowissenschaften*. Münster.
Baillie, John (1950): *The Belief in Progress*. London.
Bainbridge, William S. (2005): The Transhuman Heresy. In: *JET* 14/2 (online).
Bainbridge, William S. (2011): *The Virtual Future*. London.
Bainbridge, William S. (2014): *Personality Capture and Emulation*. London.
Barrow, John D. (1997): Frontiers and Limits of Science. In: *How Large is God?* ed. by John M. Templeton. Philadelphia, 203-216.
Barrow, John D. / Frank Tipler (1978): Eternity is Unstable. In: *Nature* 276, 453-459.
Barrow, John D. / Frank Tipler (1979): Analysis of the Singularity Studies of Belinskii, Lifshitz and Khalatnikov. In: *Physical Reports* 56, 371-402.
Barrow, John D. / Frank Tipler (1981): Generic Singularity Studies Revisited. In: *Physical Letters* A 82, 441-446.
Barrow, John D. / Frank Tipler (1985): Closed Universes. Their Future Evolution and Final State. In: *Monthly Notices of the Royal Astronomical Society* 216, 395-402.
Barrow, John D. / Frank Tipler (1986): *The Anthropic Cosmological Principle*. Oxford/New York.
Barrow, John D. / Frank Tipler (1988): Action Principles in Nature. In: *Nature* 331, 31-34.
Barrow, John D. / Frank Tipler / Marie-Odile Monchicourt (1984): *L´homme et le cosmos. Le principe anthropique en astrophysique moderne*. Paris.
Barthes, Roland (1981)[1980]: *Camera Lucida. Reflections on Photography*, trans. by Richard Howard. New York.
Baudrillard, Jean (1993)[1976]: *Symbolic Exchange and Death*, trans. by Iain Hamilton Grant. London.
Baudrillard, Jean (1994): *Die Illusion und die Virtualität*. Bern.
Baudrillard, Jean (1996)[1995]: *The Perfect Crime*. London.
Baumgartner, Hans M. (1994): Zeit und Zeiterfahrung. In: *Zeitbegriffe und Zeiterfahrung*, ed. by Hans M. Baumgartner. Freiburg, 189-211.
Beck, Klaus (1994): *Medien und soziale Konstruktion von Zeit. Über die Vermittlung gesellschaftlicher Zeitordnung und sozialem Zeitbewußtsein*. Opladen.
Becker, Philipp von (2015): *Transhumanismus, Biotechnik und digitaler Kapitalismus*. Wien.
Bellamy, Edward (1888). *Looking Backward: 2000 – 1887*. London.
Bennahum, David (1997): 3-D im Internet: Ein Gespräch mit Mark Pesce, dem Schöpfer von VRML. In: *Die Zeit*, Sept.

Benz, Ernst (1961): Das Bild des Übermenschen in der europäischen Geistesgeschichte. In: *Der Übermensch. Eine Diskussion*, ed. by Ernst Benz. Zürich, 19-161.

Benz, Ernst (1965): *Schöpfungsglaube und Endzeiterwartung. Antwort auf Teilhard de Chardins Theologie der Evolution*. München.

Benz, Ernst (1970): Theologie der Elektrizität. Zur Begegnung und Auseinandersetzung von Theologie und Naturwissenschaft im 17. und 18. Jahrhundert. In: *Abhandlungen der Geistes- und Sozialwissenschaftlichen Klasse der Akademie der Wissenschaften und der Literatur* 1970/12, 1-98.

Benz, Ernst (1977): Akzeleration der Zeit als geschichtliches und heilsgeschichtliches Problem. In: *Abhandlungen der Geistes- und Sozialwissenschaftlichen Klasse der Akademie der Wissenschaften und der Literatur* 1977/2, 1-53.

Berger, Peter L. / Richard Lieban (1963): Kulturelle Wertstruktur und Bestattungspraktiken in den Vereinigten Staaten. In: *KZfSS* 12, 224-236.

Bernal, John D. (1929): *The World, the Flesh, and the Devil. An Enquiry into the Future of the three Enemies of the Rational Soul*. London.

Bernal, John D. (^{3}1969)[1954]: *Science in History*, Vol. 3. *The Natural Sciences in our Time*. New York.

Bernstein, Anya (2015): Freeze, die, come to life. The many paths to immortality in post-Soviet Russia. In: *American Ethnologist* 42/4, 766–781.

Bernstein, Anya (2019): *The Future of Immortality. Remaking Life and Death in Contemporary Russia*. Princeton.

Black, Edwin (2004): *War Against the Weak: Eugenics and America's Campaign to Create a Master Race*. New York.

Bloch, Ernst (1986): *The Principle of Hope*, trans. by Neville and Stephen Plaice / Paul Knight. Cambridge.

Blount, Thomas (1656): *Glossographia: or a dictionary, interpreting all such hard words of whatsoever language, now used in our refined English tongue*. London.

Blumenberg, Hans (1958): Epochenschwelle und Rezeption. In: *Philosophische Rundschau* 8, 94-120.

Blumenberg, Hans (^{3}1986)[1966]: *The Legitimacy of the Modern Age*, trans. by Robert M. Wallace. Cambridge, MA.

Boice, Judith L. (1990): *At One with all Life: A Personal Journey in Gaian Communities*. Forres (Scotland).

Bolle, Fritz (1962): Darwinismus und Zeitgeist. In: *ZRGG* 14, 143-178.

Bollnow, Otto F. (^{8}1997)[1963]: *Mensch und Raum*. Stuttgart.

Bostrom, Nick (1998): Comments on Vinge's Singularity. http://mason.gmu.edu/~rhanson/vc.html#bostrom = Comment by Nick Bostrom: Singularity and Predictability. In: More / Vita-More 2013, 399-401.

Bostrom, Nick (2002): *Anthropic Bias: Observation Selection Effects in Science and Philosophy*. London.

Bostrom, Nick (2003): Human Genetic Enhancements: A Transhumanist Perspective. In: *Journal of Value Inquiry* 37 (4/2003), 493-506.

Bostrom, Nick (2005): A History of Transhumanist Thought. In: *JET* 14/1 (online).

Bostrom, Nick (2008): Letter from Utopia. In: *Studies in Ethics, Law, and Technology*, 2(1). https://nickbostrom.com/utopia.html.

Bostrom, Nick (2014): *Superintelligence. Paths, Dangers, Strategies*. Oxford.

Bostrom, Nick / Rebecca Roache (2008): Ethical Issues in Human Enhancement. In: *New Waves in Applied Ethics*, ed. by Jesper Ryberg / Thomas S. Petersen / Clark Wolf. London, 120-152.

Boussenard, Louis (1890): *Dix mille ans dans un bloc de glace*. Paris.

Braidotti, Rosi (2013): *The Posthuman*. Cambridge.

Brillouin, Leon (^{2}1957)[1956]: *Science and Information Theory*. New York.

Brin, David (2013)[2000]: A Critical Discussion of Vinge's Singularity Concept. In: More / Vita-More 2013, 395-397.

Bringsjord, Selmer / Alexander Bringsjord / Paul Bello (2012): Belief in the Singularity is Fideistic. In: Eden et al. 2012a, 394-408.

Brockman, John (Eds.)(2015): *What to Think About Machines That Think. Today's Leading Thinkers on the Age of Machine Intelligence*. New York.

Broderick, Damien (2000): *The Last Mortal Generation*. New York.

Broderick, Damien (2013)[2000]: A Critical Discussion of Vinge's Singularity Concept. In: More / Vita-More 2013, 397-499.

Brooks, Rodney (2002): *Flesh and Machines. How Robots will Change us*. New York.

Brooks, Rodney (2008): I, Rodney Brooks, Am a Robot. In: *IEEE Spectrum* (June). https://spectrum.ieee.org/computing/hardware/i-rodney-brooks-am-a-robot.

Brooks, Rodney / Luc Steels (Eds.)(1995): *The Artificial Life Route to Artificial Intelligence. Building Embodied, Situated Agents*. Hillsdale.

Brown, Andrew (2005): *J. D. Bernal. The Sage of Science*. Oxford.

Brown, Dan (2013): *Inferno*. New York.

Brown, Dan (2017): *Origin*. New York.

Brunotte, Ulrike (2000): *Puritanismus und Pioniergeist. Die Faszination der Wildnis im frühen Neu-England*. Berlin.

Bryant, Clifton D. / William E. Snizek (1973): The Cryonics Movement and Frozen Immortality. In: *Society* 11/1 (Nov./Dec.), 56-62.

Buchloh, Paul G. (1963): Vom Pilgrim's Progress zum Pilgrim's Regress. Der Fortschrittsgedanke in der englischen und amerikanischen Literatur. In: Burck 1963, 153-178.

Bultmann, Rudolf (1957): *History and Eschatology. The Gifford Lectures 1955*. Edinburgh.

Burck, Erich (Eds.)(1963): *Die Idee des Fortschrittes. Neun Vorträge über Wege und Grenzen des Fortschrittsglaubens*. München.

Burroughs, Edgar R. (1937): The Resurrection of Jimber Jaw. In: *Argosy*, 20 (Feb.).

Bury, John B. (1955)[1920]: *The Idea of Progress. An Inquiry into Its Origin and Growth*. New York.

C

Cassidy, David C. (1992): *Uncertainty: The Life and Science of Werner Heisenberg*. New York.

Capra, Fritjof (1982): *The Turning Point: Science, Society, and the Rising Culture*. New York.

Caygill, Howard (1997): Stelarc and the Chimera. Kant's Critique of Prosthetic Judgment. In: *Art Journal* 56, 46-51.

Ceccarelli, Leah (2013): *On the Frontier of Science. An American Rhetoric of Exploration and Exploitation*. East Lansing.
Cherniavsky, Vladimir (1994): *Die Virtualität. Philosophische Grundlagen der logischen Relativität*. Hamburg.
Clarke, Arthur C. (1956): *The City and the Stars*. New York.
Clarke, Arthur C. (1960): *Profiles of the Future. An Inquiry into the Limits of the Possible*. New York.
Clarke, Arthur C. (1968): *2001. A Space Odyssey*. New York.
Clute, John / P. Nicholls (Eds.)(1999): *Encyclopedia of Science Fiction*. London.
Clynes, Manfred / Nathan S. Kline (1960): Cyborgs and Space. In: *Astronautics* 9/1960, 26-27, 74-75.
Cobb, Jennifer (1998): *Cybergrace. The Search for God in the Digital World*. New York.
Coenen, Christopher (2010): Deliberating Visions: The Case of Human Enhancement in the Discourse on Nanotechnology and Convergence. In: *Governing Future Technologies. Nanotechnology and the Rise of an Assessment Regime*, ed. by Mario Kaiser et al. Dordrecht, 73-87.
Coenen et al. (Eds.)(2010): *Die Debatte über „Human Enhancement". Historische, philosophische und ethische Aspekte der technologischen Verbesserung des Menschen*. Bielefeld.
Coffin, Margaret M. (1976): *Death in Early America*. Nashville.
Collings, Michael R. (1985): The Mechanics of Immortality. In: Yoke / Hassler 1985, 29-38.
Conan Doyle, Arthur (1929): The Disintegration Machine. In: *The Strand Magazine* (Jan.).
Condorcet, Jean-Antoine-Nicolas Marquis de (1970)[1795]: *Esquisse d'un tableau historique des progrès de l'esprit humain*. Paris.
Condorcet, Jean-Antoine-Nicolas Marquis de (1976)[1795]: Sketch for a Historical Picture of the Progress of the Human Mind. In: *Condorcet. Selected Writings*, ed. by Keith M. Baker. Indianapolis, 209-282.
Connolly, Randy (2001): The Rise and Persistence of the Technological Community Ideal. In: *Online Communities. Commerce, Community Action and the Virtual University*, ed. by Chris Werry / Miranda Mowbray. Upper Saddle River, 317-364.
Cryonics Institute (2003): Directors of the Cryonics Institute. http://www.cryonics.org /bio.html#Robert_Ettinger (11/25/2005).
Curtis, James M. (2005): Why World History needs McLuhan. In: Strate / Wachtel 2005, 163-175.

D

Daecke, Sigurd M. (2000): Teilhard de Chardin, Pierre (1881-1955). In: *TRE* 23, 28-33.
Darwin, Charles (1859): *On the Origin of Species. By Means of Natural Selection, or the Preservation of Favoured Races in the Struggle for Life*. London.
Darwin, Mike (1981): An Interview with Saul Kent. In: *Cryonics* (Nov.), 13–20.
Darwin, Mike (1991): Evaluation of the condition of Dr. Bedford after 24 years of cryonic suspension. In: *Cryonics* (Aug.), 22-25.
Davis, Erik (1998): *Techgnosis: Myth, Magic, Mysticism in the Age of Information*. New York.
Dawkins, Richard (1976). *The Selfish Gene*. Oxford.

Dawkins, Richard (1996): *The Blind Watchmaker. Why the Evidence of Evolution Reveals a Universe without Design*. New York.

Dawson, Christopher (1929): *Progress and Religion. A Historical Inquiry*. London.

De Grey, Aubrey (2008): *Ending Aging: The Rejuvenation Breakthroughs that Could Reverse Human Aging in Our Lifetime*. London.

Deitch, Jeffrey (1996): Menschliches und Künstliches. In: *Kunstforum International* 132, 112-123.

Derham, William (^{4}1721)[1714]: *Astro-theology. Or a Demonstration of the Being and Attributes of God, from a Survey of the Heavens*. London.

Derham, William (1754)[1713]: *Physico-theology, or a Demonstration of the Being and Attributes of God, from His Works of Creation*. London.

Dery, Mark (1996): *Escape Velocity. Cyberculture at the End of the Century*. New York.

Descartes, René (1824)[1637]: *Discours de la méthode*, ed. by Victor Cousin. Paris.

Descartes, René (1967a): *Oeuvres philosophiques de Descartes*, Vol. I, ed. by Ferdinand Alquié. Paris.

Descartes, René (1967b): *Oeuvres philosophiques de Descartes*, Vol. II, ed. by Ferdinand Alquié. Paris.

Descartes, René (1985): *The Philosophical Writings of Descartes*, Vol I, trans. by John Cottingham / Robert Stoothoff / Dugald Murdoch. Bath.

Descartes, René (1985b): *The Philosophical Writings of Descartes*, Vol II, trans. by John Cottingham / Robert Stoothoff / Dugald Murdoch. Bath.

Diamandis, Peter / Steven Kotler (2012): *Abundance: The Future Is Better Than You Think*. New York.

Dobrée, Bonamy (1959): *English Literature in the Early Eighteenth Century 1700-1740*. Oxford.

Dolliver, Mark (2019): US Time Spent with Media 2019. Digital Time Keeps Rising as Growth Subsides for Total Time Spent. In: *eMarketer* 05/30/2019 (online).

Dotzler, Bernhard J. / Peter Gendolla / Jörgen Schäfer (1992): *MaschinenMenschen. Eine Bibliographie*. Frankfurt a.M.

Doyle, Richard (2003): *Wetwares. Experiments in Postvital Living*. Minneapolis.

Drexler, K. Eric (1996)[1986]: *Engines of Creation. The Coming Era of Nanotechnology*. London.

Drexler, K. Eric (2013): *Radical Abundance: How a Revolution in Nanotechnology Will Change Civilization*. New York.

Dühring, Eugen (^{2}1877)[1865]: *Der Werth des Lebens. Eine Denkerbetrachtung im Sinne heroischer Lebensauffassung*. Leipzig.

Dyson, Esther et al. (1994): Cyberspace and the American Dream. A Magna Carta for the Knowledge Age. http://www.pff.org/issues-pubs/futureinsights/fi1.2magna carta.html.

Dyson, Freeman (1988): *Infinite in all Directions*. New York.

E

Edelhart, Mike (1983): Immortality through Science. In: *Psychology Today* 8/1983, 40-41.

Eden, Amnon H. et al. (Eds.)(2012a): *Singularity Hypothesis. A Scientific and Philosophical Assessment*. Berlin.

Eden, Amnon H. et al. (2012b): Singularity Hypothesis: An Overview. In: Eden et al. 2012a, 1-14.
Ekirch, Arthur A. (1944): *The Idea of Progress in America, 1815-1860*. New York.
Elias, Norbert (1993)[1984]: *Time. An Essay*. Oxford.
Elias, Norbert (1982)[1939]: *The Civilizing Process*, Vol II, *State Formation and Civilization*, trans. by Edmund Jephcott. New York.
Esfandiary, Fereidoun M. (1959): *The Day of Sacrifice*. New York.
Esfandiary, Fereidoun M. (1965): *The Beggar*. New York.
Esfandiary, Fereidoun M. (1966): *Identity Card*. New York.
Esfandiary, Fereidoun M. (1970): *Optimism One. The Emerging Radicalism*. New York.
Esfandiary, Fereidoun M. (1973): *Up-Wingers*. New York.
Esfandiary, Fereidoun M. (1977): *Telespheres*. New York.
Ettinger, Robert C. (1948): The Penultimate Trump. In: *Startling Stories* (Mar.).
Ettinger, Robert C. (1964): *The Prospect of Immortality*. New York.
Ettinger, Robert C. (1967): Cryonics and the Purpose of Life. In: *The Christian Century* 84/40, 1250-1253.
Ettinger, Robert C. (1989)[1972]: *Man into Superman*. New York.
Evans, Dylan (2015): The great AI swindle. In: Brockman 2015, 172-173.

F

Farrell, Thomas J. (2003): In Memoriam Walter J. Ong, S.J. In: *Christianity and Literature* 52, 451-457.
Feinberg, Gerald (1966): Physics and life prolongation. In: *Physics Today* 19/11, 45-50.
Feinberg, Gerald (1969): *The Prometheus Project. Mankind's Search for Long-Range Goals*. New York.
Ferguson, Adam (1789): *An Essay on the History of Civil Society*. London.
Ferguson, Marilyn (1980): *The Aquarian Conspiracy: Personal and Social Transformation in the 1980s*. Los Angeles.
Flessner, Bernd (1991): *Weltprothesen und Prothesenwelten. Zu den technischen Prognosen von Arno Schmidt und Stanisław Lem*. Frankfurt a.M.
Flessner, Bernd (1996): Archäologie im Cyberspace. Anmerkungen zu Stanisław Lems Phantomatik. In: Lem 1996, 7-22.
Flessner, Bernd (Ed.)(1997a): *Die Welt im Bild. Wirklichkeit im Zeitalter der Virtualität*. Freiburg.
Flessner, Bernd (1997b): Das Finis mundi als museale Agonie. Zu Herbert W. Frankes Orchideenkäfig. In: Flessner 1997a, 97-115.
Flessner, Bernd (Ed.)(2000a): *Nach dem Menschen. Der Mythos einer zweiten Schöpfung und das Entstehen einer posthumanen Kultur*. Freiburg.
Flessner, Bernd (2000b): Antizipative Diffusion. Science Fiction als Akzeptanzbeschleuniger und Wegbereiter einer multitechnokulturellen Gesellschaft. In: Flessner 2000a, 245-264.
Flusser, Vilém (2011)[1985]: *Into the Universe of Technical Images*, trans. by Nancy Ann Roth. Minneapolis.

Flusser, Vilém (1993): Vom Virtuellen. In: *Cyberspace. Zum medialen Gesamtkunstwerk*, ed. by Florian Rötzer / Peter Weibel. München, 65-71.

FM-2030 (1989): *Are You a Transhuman? Monitoring and Stimulating Your Personal Rate of Growth in a Rapidly Changing World*. New York.

Foucault, Michel (1977)[1975]: *Discipline and Punish. The Birth of the Prison*. New York.

Franke, Herbert (1973)[1961]: *The Orchid Cage*. New York.

Franke, Herbert (1974)[1970]: *Zone Null*. New York.

Franke, Herbert W. (1997): Bilderwelten – Weltbilder. In: Flessner 1997a, 359-366.

Franklin, Benjamin (1780): Letter to Joseph Priestley, 02/08/1780. https://founders.archives.gov/documents/Franklin/01-31-02-0325.

Freese, Peter (1997): *From Apocalypse to Entropy and Beyond. The Second Law of Thermodynamics in Post-War American Fiction*. Essen.

Fredericksen, Dick (1971): A Word in Edgewise 6 (February). https://digital.library.illinois.edu/items/4127ea80-29ac-0136-4d81-0050569601ca-f.

Freyermuth, Gundolf (1998): *Cyberland. Eine Führung durch den High-Tech-Underground*. Reinbek.

Fukuyama, Francis (2002): *Our Posthuman Future. Consequences of our Biotechnology Revolution*. New York.

Fuller, Buckminster R. (1938): *Nine Chains to the Moon*. Philadelphia.

Funk, Isaac K. (Ed.)(1949): *New Standard Dictionary of the English Language*. New York.

G

Gadamer, Hans-Georg (^{2}2004)[1960]): *Truth and Method*, trans. by Joel Weinsheimer / Donald G. Marshall. New York.

Galouye, Daniel F. (1964): *Simulacron-3*. New York.

Galton, Francis (^{3}1909): *Memories of my Life*. London.

Galton, Francis (1972)[1869]: *Hereditary Genius. An Inquiry into Its Laws and Consequences*. Gloucester.

Gantke, Wolfgang (1987): *Die Bedeutung des hermeneutischen Ansatzes Otto Friedrich Bollnows für die Religionswissenschaft*. Dissertation. Bonn.

Garreau, Joel (2005): *Radical Evolution. The Promise and Peril of Enhancing Our Minds, Our Bodies – and What it means to Be Human*. New York.

Gebauer, Gunter (1984): Hand und Gewißheit. In: Kamper / Wulf 1984a, 234-260.

Gendolla, Peter (1992a): *Anatomien der Puppe. Zur Geschichte des MaschinenMenschen bei Jean Paul, E. T. A. Hoffmann, Vielliers de l'Isle-Adam und Hans Bellmer*. Heidelberg.

Gendolla, Peter (1992b): *Zeit. Zur Geschichte der Zeiterfahrung. Vom Mythos zur ‚Punktzeit'*. Köln.

Gestrich, Christof (1981): Deismus. In: TRE 8, 392-406.

Gibbon, Edward (1925)[1788]: *The History of the Decline and the Fall of the Roman Empire*, Vol. 4, ed. by John Bury. London.

Gibson, William (1986): *Count Zero*. New York.

Gibson, William (1988): *Mona Lisa Overdrive*. New York.

Gibson, William (2000): *Neuromancer*. London.

Giddens, Anthony (1990): *The Consequences of Modernity*. Cambridge.

Godwin, William (1793): *An Enquiry Concerning Political Justice and Its Influence on General Virtue and Happiness*, 2 volumes. London.

Goertzel, Ben (2010): *A Cosmist Manifesto. Practical Philosophy for the Posthuman Age*. N.P.

Good, Irving J. (1962): The Social Implications of Artificial Intelligence. In: *The Scientist Speculates: An Anthology of Partly-Baked Ideas*, ed. by Irving J. Good. London, 192-198.

Good, Irving J. (1965): Speculations Concerning the First Ultraintelligent Machine. In: *Advances in Computers* 6, 31-88.

Gouhier, Henri (1962): *La pensée métaphysique de Descartes*. Paris.

Gove, Philip B. (Ed.) (1993): *Webster's Third New International Dictionary of the English Language*, Vol. 3. Springfield (Ma.).

Gräfrath, Bernd (1996): *Lems 'Golem'. Parerga und Paralipomena*. Frankfurt a.M.

Gräfrath, Bernd (2000): Erlösung durch Überwindung des Menschen? Stanisław Lems Philosophie transbiologischer Personen. In: Flessner 2000a, 281-300.

Graham, Elaine L. (2002): *Representations of the Post/Human. Monsters, Aliens and others in Popular Culture*. New Brunswick.

Graham, Elaine L. (2015): The Final Frontier? Religion and Posthumanism in Film and Television. In: Hauskeller / Philbeck / Carbonell 2015, 361-370.

Graham, Jenny (1995): *Revolutionary in Exile. The Emigration of Joseph Priestley to America 1794-1804*. Philadelphia.

Gray, Chris H. (2002): *Cyborg Citizen. Politics in the Posthuman Age*. New York.

Großklaus, Götz (^{2}1997): *Medien-Zeit. Medien-Raum. Zum Wandel der raumzeitlichen Wahrnehmung in der Moderne*. Frankfurt a.M.

Groys, Boris (2005): Unsterbliche Körper. In: Groys / Hagemeister 2005, 8-18.

Groys, Boris / Michael Hagemeister (Eds.)(2005): *Die neue Menschheit. Biopolitische Utopien in Russland zu Beginn des 20. Jahrhunderts*. Frankfurt a.M.

Gruman, Gerald J. (1966): A History of Ideas about the Prolongation of Life. The Evolution of the Prolongevity Hypothesis to 1800. In: *Transactions of the American Philosophical Society* 56/9, 1-102.

Gunderson, Keith (1964): Descartes, La Mettrie, Language and Machines. In: *Philosophy* 39, 193–222.

H

Haeckel, Ernst (^{2}1902): *Gemeinverständliche Vorträge und Abhandlungen aus dem Gebiete der Entwicklungslehre*, Vol. 1. Bonn.

Haeckel, Ernst (1905): *Last Words on Evolution. A Popular Retrospect and Summary*. New York.

Haeckel, Ernst (1913)[1899]: *The Riddle of the Universe. At the Close of the Nineteenth Century*. London.

Hagemeister, Michael (1989): *Nikolaj Fedorov. Studien zu Leben, Werk und Wirkung*. München.

Hagemeister, Michael (1997): Russian Cosmism in the 1920s and Today. In: *The Occult in Russian and Soviet Culture*, ed. by Bernice Glatzer Rosenthal. Ithaca, 185-202.

Hagemeister, Michael (2012): Konstantin Tsiolkovskii and the Occult Roots of the Soviet Space Travel. In: *The New Age of Russia. Occult and Esoteric Dimensions*, ed. by Birgit Menzel / Michael Hagemeister / Bernice Glatzer Rosenthal. München, 135-150.

Hagner, Michael (2004): *Geniale Gehirne. Zur Geschichte der Elitegehirnforschung*. Göttingen.

Halacy, Daniel S. (1965): *Cyborg – Evolution of the Superhuman*. New York.

Haldane, J. B. S. (1924): *Daedalus; or, Science and the Future*. London.

Halberstam, Judith / Ira Livingston (Eds.)(1995): *Posthuman Bodies*. Bloomington.

Hammel, Eckhard (1994): Medien, Technik, Zeit. Zur Geschichte menschlicher Selbstwahrnehmung. In: *Zeit – Medien – Wahrnehmung*, ed. by Mike Sandbothe / Walther Zimmerli. Darmstadt, 60-79.

Hanson, Robin (2013): A Critical Discussion of Vinge's Singularity Concept. In: More / Vita-More 2013, 404-406.

Harari, Yuval N. (2016)[2015]: *Homo Deus. A Brief History of Tomorrow*. London.

Haraway, Donna (1985): A Cyborg Manifesto. Science, Technology and Socialist-Feminism in the Late Twentieth Century. In: Socialist Review 80, 65-107.

Haraway, Donna (1991): *Simians, Cyborgs and Women. The Reinvention of Nature*. New York.

Harrington, Alan (1977)[1969]: *The Immortalist*. Millbrae.

Harrison, Peter / Joseph Wolyniak (2015): History of 'Transhumanism'. In: *Notes and Queries* 62/3 (Sep.), 465-467.

Hase, Thomas (1997): Die religiöse Deutung von Fortschritt und Expansion im amerikanischen Postmilleniarismus. In: ZfR 5, 115-148.

Hassan, Ihab (1977): Prometheus as Performer: Toward a Posthumanist Culture? A University Masque in Five Scenes. In: *Georgia Review* 31/4, 830-850.

Hassler, Donald M. (1985): Introduction. In: Yoke / Hassler 1985, 3-6.

Hatfield, Gary (2014): René Descartes. In: *SEP* (online).

Hauskeller, Michael / Thomas D. Philbeck / Curtis Carbonell (2015)(Eds.): *The Palgrave Handbook of Posthumanism in Film and Television*. New York.

Hawking, Stephen / Roger Penrose (1970): The Singularities of Gravitational Collapse and Cosmology. In: *Proceedings of the Royal Society*, Vol. 314, 529–548.

Hayles, N. Katherine (1999): *How We Became Posthuman. Virtual Bodies in Cybernetics, Literature and Informatics*. Chicago.

Heil, Reinhard (2010a): Trans- und Posthumanismus. Eine Begriffsbestimmung. In: Hilt / Jordan / Frewer 2010, 127-149.

Heil, Reinhard (2010b): Transhumanismus, Nanotechnologie und der Traum von Unsterblichkeit. In: *Visionen der Nanotechnologie*, ed. by Arianna Ferrari / Stefan Gammel. Heidelberg, 25-49.

Heil, Reinhard (2010c): Human Enhancement – Eine Motivsuche bei J. D. Bernal, J. B. S. Haldane und J. S. Huxley. In: Coenen et al. 2010, 41-62.

Heil, Reinhard (2018): Der Mensch als Designobjekt im frühen Transhumanismus und Techno-Futurismus. In: *Designobjekt Mensch. Die Agenda des Transhumanismus auf dem Prüfstand*, ed. by Paul Göcke / Frank Meier-Hamidi. Freiburg, 53-79.

Heil, Reinhard / Christopher Coenen (2014): Transhumanistische Visionen und Computertechnik. In: *Computertechnik und Sterbekultur*, ed. by Knut Böhle et al. Münster.

Heim, Michael (1993): *The Metaphysics of Virtual Reality*. New York.
Heims, Steve J. (^{3}1981): *John von Neumann and Norbert Wiener. From Mathematics to the Technologies of Life and Death*. Cambridge.
Helmholtz, Hermann von (1885): On the Interaction of Natural Forces. In: *Popular Lectures on Scientific Subjects*. New York, 153-196.
Herbrechter, Stefan (2009): *Posthumanismus. Eine kritische Einführung*. Darmstadt.
Herbrechter, Stefan (2013): *Posthumanism. A Critical Analysis*. London.
Hesse, Eva (1992): *Die Achse Avantgarde-Faschismus. Reflexionen über Filippo Thomaso Marinetti und Ezra Pound*. Zürich.
Hickey, Neil (2005): McLuhan in the Digital Age. In: Strate / Wachtel 2005, 61-66.
Hilt, Annette / Isabella Jordan / Andreas Frewer (Eds.)(2010): *Endlichkeit, Medizin und Unsterblichkeit. Geschichte – Theorie – Ethik*. Stuttgart.
Hobbes, Thomas (1839)[1655]: Of Identity and Difference (The First Grounds of Philosophy 11). In: *The English Works of Thomas Hobbes of Malmesbury*, ed. by William Molesworth. London, 132-138.
Hobsbawm, Eric (2000): Introduction: Inventing Traditions. In: *The Invention of Tradition*, ed. by Eric Hobsbawm / Terence Ranger. Cambridge, 1-14.
Hölscher, Lucian (2018): Future Thinking – A Historical Perspective. In: *The Psychology of Thinking about the Future*, ed. by Gabriele Oettingen / A. Simur Sevincer / Peter M. Gollwitzer. New York, 15-30.
Holmes, Oliver W. (1859): The Stereoscope and the Stereograph. In: *Atlantic Monthly* 3 (6/1859), 738-748.
Hooper, Joseph (2005): The Prophet of Immortality. In: *Popular Science*, 01/01/2005 (https://www.popsci.com/scitech/article/2005-01/prophet-immortality).
Houellebecq, Michel (2000)[1998]: *The Elementary Particles*, trans. by Frank Wynne. New York.
Hruska, Joel (2017): The ISS is Getting the Most Powerful Computer Ever Sent to Space. In: *Extreme Tech* 08/14/2017 (online).
Hufeland, Christoph W. (1854)[1797]: *Art of Prolonging Life*, ed. by Erasmus Wilson. Boston.
Hughes, James (2004): *Citizen Cyborg. Why Democratic Societies must respond to the Redesigned Human of the Future*. Cambridge.
Hunt, James (1864): On the Negro's Place in Nature. In: *Journal of the Anthropological Society of London*, Vol. 2, XV-LVI.
Hunt, James (1865): On the Negro's Place in Nature. In: *Memoirs of the Anthropological Society of London*, 1863-64, Vol. 1, 1-64.
Huntington, Richard / Peter Metcalf (^{2}1991): *Celebrations of Death. The Anthropology of Mortuary Ritual*. Cambridge.
Husserl, Edmund (1991)[1928]: *On the Phenomenology of the Consciousness of Internal Time*, trans. by John Barnett Brough. Dordrecht.
Huxley, Julian (1923): *Essays of a Biologist*. New York.
Huxley, Julian (1929): *Religion without Revelation*. New York.
Huxley, Julian (1951): Knowledge, Morality and Destiny. In: *Psychiatry* XIV, 127-151.
Huxley, Julian (1957a): *New Bottles for New Wine. Essays by Julian Huxley*. London.
Huxley, Julian (1957b): Transhumanism. In: Huxley 1957a, 13-17.

Huxley, Julian (1957c): A Re-definition of Progress. In: Huxley 1957a, 18-40.
Huxley, Julian (1957d): Evolutionary Humanism. In: Huxley 1957a, 18-40.
Huxley, Julian (1963): The Future of Man – Evolutionary Aspects. In: *Man and his Future. A Ciba Foundation Volume*, ed. by Gordon Wolstenholme. London, 1-22.
Huxley, Julian (1976)[1958]: Introduction by Sir Julian Huxley. In: Teilhard de Chardin 1976, 11-28.

I

Immortality Institute (Ed.)(2004): *The Scientific Conquest of Death. Essays on infinite Lifespans*. Buenos Aires.
Innerhofer, Roland (1996): *Deutsche Science Fiction 1870-1914. Rekonstruktion und Analyse der Anfänge einer Gattung*. Wien.
Innerhofer, Roland (2003): Von Frankensteins Monster zu Edisons Eva. Die Geburt des künstlichen Menschen aus dem Geist der Maschine. In: *Mythen der Kreativität. Das Schöpferische zwischen Innovation und Hybris*, ed. by Oliver Krüger / Refika Sariönder / Annette Deschner. Frankfurt a.M., 269-297.
Irrgang, Bernhard (2005): *Posthumanes Menschsein? Künstliche Intelligenz, Cyberspace, Roboter und Designer-Menschen*. Wiesbaden.
Irrgang, Bernhard (2014): *Handling technical Power. Philosophy of Technology*. Stuttgart.
Iser, Wolfgang (1990): *Fingieren als anthropologische Dimension der Literatur*. Konstanz.
Iser, Wolfgang (1991): *Das Fiktive und das Imaginäre. Perspektiven literarischer Anthropologie*. Frankfurt a.M.
Iserson, Kenneth V. (1994): *Death to Dust. What Happens to Dead Bodies?* Tuscon.

J

Jastrow, Robert (1981): *The Enchanted Loom. Mind in the Universe*. New York.
Jauss, Hans Robert (1982): *Toward an Aesthetic of Reception*, trans. by Timothy Bahti. Minneapolis.
Joll, James (1960): *Three Intellectuals in Politics*. New York.
Jones, Neil R. (1931): The Jameson Satellite. In: *Amazing* (July).
Jordan, Isabella / Andreas Frewer (2010): Todesverdrängung, (Un-)Sterblichkeit und Medizin. Theoretische und soziale Aspekte des Transhumanismus. In: Hilt / Jordan / Trewer 2010, 151-169.
Joy, Bill (2000): Why the Future doesn't need us. In: *Wired* 8.04, 1-11.

K

Kamper, Dietmar (1976): Einleitung: Vom Schweigen des Körpers. In: *Zur Geschichte des Körpers*, ed. by Dietmar Kamper / Volker Rittner. München, 7-12.
Kamper, Dietmar (1995): *Unmögliche Gegenwart. Zur Theorie der Phantasie*. München.
Kamper, Dietmar (1999): *Die Ästhetik der Abwesenheit. Die Entfernung der Körper*. München.
Kamper, Dietmar / Christoph Wulf (Eds.)(1984a): *Das Schwinden der Sinne*. Frankfurt a.M.
Kamper, Dietmar / Christoph Wulf (1984b): Blickwende. Die Sinne des Körpers im Konkurs der Geschichte. In: Kamper / Wulf 1984a, 9-17.

Kapell, Matthew W. (2016): *Exploring the Next Frontier. Vietnam, NASA, Star Trek and Utopia in 1960s und 1970s American Myth and History.* New York.

Kapuściński, Ryszard (1992)[1990]: *Lapidarium. Notizen und Reflexionen.* Frankfurt a.M.

Katz, Elihu / David Foulkes (1962): On the use of mass media as 'escape': Clarification of a concept. In: *Public Opinion Quarterly* 26/3 (1962), 377-388.

Keller, Christoph (2003): *Building Bodies. Der Mensch im biotechnischen Zeitalter. Reportagen und Essays.* Zürich.

Kent, Saul (1983): The first Cryonicist. In: *Cryonics* (Mar.), 4-12.

Kephart, William M. (1950): Status after Death. In: *American Sociological Review* 15/5, 635–643.

Kerr, Philipp (1998): *The Second Angel.* London 1998.

Kirkinen, Heikki (1960): *Les Origines de la Conception Moderne de l'Homme-Machine. Le Problème de l'Ame en France a la Fin du Regne de Louis XIV (1670-1715).* Helsinki.

Klein, Jürgen (1986): Materialismus – Evolution – Induktion. Wissenschaft im neunzehnten Jahrhundert. In: *ZRGG* (38), 249-258.

Klemperer, Victor (1998)[1995]: *I Will Bear Witness. A Diary of the Nazi-Years. 1933-1941,* trans. by Martin Chalmers. New York.

Kluge, Sven (2014): Menschenverbesserung in einer Welt ohne Mensch? Zur Aktualität und Kritikwürdigkeit von Günther Anders' Diagnose einer Antiquiertheit des Menschen. In: *Jahrbuch Pädagogik 2014. Menschenverbesserung. Transhumanismus,* 83-104.

Köhne, Julia B. (2014): *Geniekult in Geisteswissenschaften und Literaturen um 1900 und seine filmischen Adaptionen.* Wien.

Koselleck, Reinhart (1975): Fortschritt. In: *Geschichtliche Grundbegriffe. Historisches Lexikon zur politisch-sozialen Sprache in Deutschland,* Vol. 2, ed. by Otto Brunner / Werner Couse / Reinhart Kosselleck. Stuttgart, 351-423.

Koplos, Janet (1993): Stelarc in the Kitchen. In: *Art in America* 81 (10/1993), 104.

Kröner, Magdalena (2020): Digital Bodies. Virtuelle Körper, politisches Embodiment und alternative Körperphantasmen. In: *Kunstforum International* 265, Jan. / Feb. 2020, 48-71.

Kroker, Arthur / Marilouise Kroker (1996): *Hacking the Future. Stories for the Flesh-Eating 90s.* Montreal.

Krüger, Oliver (2004): *Virtualität und Unsterblichkeit. Die Visionen des Posthumanismus.* Freiburg i.Br.

Krüger, Oliver (2005): Gnosis in Cyberspace? Body, Mind and Progress in Posthumanism. In: *JET* 14 (Aug.)(online).

Krüger, Oliver (2010): The Suspension of Death. The Cryonic Utopia in the Context of the U.S. Funeral Culture. In: *Marburg Journal of Religion* 15 (online).

Krüger, Oliver (2015): Gaia, God, and the Internet – revisited. The History of Evolution and the Utopia of Community in Media Society. In: *Online – Heidelberg Journal for Religions on the Internet* 8 (online).

Krüger, Oliver (2017): "Religion" definieren. Eine wissenssoziologische Analyse religionsbezogener Enzyklopädistik. In: *Zeitschrift für Religions- und Geistesgeschichte* 69/1, 1-46.

Krüger, Oliver (2018): The 'Logic' of Mediatization Theory in Religion: A Critical Consideration of a New Paradigm. In: *Marburg Journal of Religion* 20/1 (online).

Krüger, Oliver (²2019)[2004]: *Virtualität und Unsterblichkeit. Gott, Evolution und die Singularität im Post- und Transhumanismus*. Freiburg i.Br.

Krüger, Oliver (2022): From an Aristotelian Ordo Essendi to Relation. Shifting Paradigms in the Study of Religions in the Light of the Sociology of Knowledge. In: *Numen* 69/1, 1-36.

Krüger, Oliver / Andrea Rota (2015): Die Verkündigung von Jehovas Königreich in Hörfunk und Internet. Ein Beitrag zur Medienhermeneutik. In: *Religion, Staat, Gesellschaft* 16 1/2, Sonderheft *Zum Bibel- und Weltverständnis christlicher Religionen*, 75-108.

Krysmanski, Hans Jürgen (2014): Der ganz alltägliche Transhumanismus. In: *Jahrbuch Pädagogik 2014. Menschenverbesserung. Transhumanismus*, 123-142.

Kuny, Terry (1997): A Digital Dark Ages? Challenges in the Preservation of Electronic Information. In: *3RD IFLA Council and General Conference*. https://archive.ifla.org/IV/ifla63/63kuny1.pdf.

Kurzweil, Ray (1990): *The Age of Intelligent Machines*. Cambridge.

Kurzweil, Ray (1993): *The 10% Solution for a Healthy Life*. New York.

Kurzweil, Raymond (1999a): *The Age of Spiritual Machines. When Computers Exceed Human Intelligence*. New York.

Kurzweil, Ray (1999b): Spiritual Machines. The Meaning of Man and Machine. In: *The Futurist* 33/11, 16-21.

Kurzweil, Ray (2000): Foreword. In: *The Eternal E-customer: How Emotionally Intelligent Interfaces Can Create Long-lasting Customer Relationships*, by Bryan Bergeron. New York, IX-XI.

Kurzweil, Ray (2005): *The Singularity Is Near. When Humans Transcend Biology*. New York.

Kurzweil, Ray (2010): How My Predictions Are Faring. http://www.kurzweilai.net/images/How-My-Predictions-Are-Faring.pdf

Kurzweil, Ray (³2012a): Foreword to the Third Edition. In: *The Computer / the Brain*, von John von Neumann. New Haven, 11-28.

Kurzweil, Ray (2012b): *How to Create a Mind. The Secret of Human Thought Revealed*. New York.

Kurzweil, Ray / Terry Grossman (2004): *Fantastic Voyage. Live Long Enough to Live Forever*. New York.

Kurzweil, Ray / Terry Grossman (2009): *Transcend: Nine Steps to Living Well Forever*. New York.

L

Laderman, Gary (1996): *The Sacred Remains. American Attitudes Towards Death 1799–1883*. New Haven.

La Mettrie, Julien Offray de (1953)[1747]: *Man a Machine*. La Salle (IL).

Larsen, Dave (1967): Cancer Victim's Body Frozen for Future Revival Experiment. In: *Los Angeles Times*, 01/19/1967.

Lavery, David (1992): *Late for the Sky. The Mentality of the Space Age*. Carbondale (IL).

Leary, Timothy F. (1994): *Chaos and Cyber Culture*. San Francisco.
Leary, Timothy F. / R. U. Sirius (1997): *Design for Dying*. San Francisco.
Lem, Stanisław (1969) [1955]: Are You There, Mr. Jones? In: *Vision of Tomorrow* (Aug.), 55-58.
Lem, Stanisław (1972): Roboter in der Science Fiction. In: *Science Fiction. Theorie und Geschichte*, ed. by Eike Barmeyer. München, 163-186.
Lem, Stanisław (1974)[1971]: *The Futurological Congress*. New York.
Lem, Stanisław (1976)[1971]: *The Star Diaries*. New York.
Lem, Stanisław (1980)[1957]: *Dialoge*. Frankfurt a.M.
Lem, Stanisław (1982)[1971]: *Memoirs of a Space Traveller. Further Reminiscences of Ijon Tichy*. New York.
Lem, Stanisław (1984)[1981]: Golem XIV. In: *Imaginary Magnitude*, trans. by Marc E. Heine. New York, 97-248.
Lem, Stanisław (1987)[1982]: *Lokaltermin*. Frankfurt a.M.
Lem, Stanisław (1996): *Die Entdeckung der Virtualität*. Frankfurt a.M.
Lem, Stanisław (2010)[1964]: *Summa Technologiae*, trans. by Joanna Zylinska. Minneapolis.
Le Roy, Édouard (1928): Les origines humaines et l'évolution de l'intelligence. XVI. Conclusion. In: *Cours et Conférences* 29 (16/1928), 696-724.
Lévy, Pierre (2001): *Cyberculture*. Minneapolis.
Lewis, Wyndham (1948): *America and Cosmic Man*. London.
Lighthall, William D. (1930): *The Person of Evolution. The outer Consciousness. The Outer Knowledge. The Directive Power*. Toronto.
Lighthall, William D. (1940): The Law of Cosmic Evolutionary Adaptation. An interpretation of recent thought. In: *Proceedings and Transactions of the Royal Society of Canada* 34, section 2, 135–41.
Liversidge, Anthony (1994): Interview: Frank Tipler. A Physicist proposes a Theory of Eternal Life that Yields God. In: *Omni* 17 (10/1994), 89-109.
Loh, Janina (2018): *Trans- und Posthumanismus zur Einführung*. Hamburg.
Lovejoy, Arthur O. (1961): *The Great Chain of Being. A Study of the History of an Idea*. Cambridge (MA).
Lovelock, James E. (1991)[1979]: *Gaia. A new Look at Life on Earth*. Oxford.
Lovelock, James E. (2003): God and Gaia. In: *Worldviews, Religion, and the Environment: A Global Anthology*, ed. by Richard C. Foltz. Belmont, 531-540.
Löwith, Karl (1949): *Meaning in History. The Theological Implications of the Philosophy of History*. Chicago.
Lübbe, Hermann (^{2}1994)[1992]: *Der Lebenssinn der Industriegesellschaft. Über die moralische Verfassung der wissenschaftlich-technischen Zivilisation*. Berlin.
Luckmann, Thomas (1986): Zeit und Identität: Innere, soziale und historische Zeit. In: *Zeit als Strukturelement von Lebenswelt und Gesellschaft*, ed. by Friedrich Fürstenberg / Ingo Mörth. Linz, 135-174.
Lüdeking, Karlheinz (1996): Das Vergnügen des Körpers. In: *Kunstforum International* 133, 56-67.
Luetke, Joachim (2000): *Posthuman. The Art of Joachim Luetke*. Stuttgart.

Luhmann, Niklas (1979): Zeit und Handlung – Eine vergessene Theorie. In: *Zeitschrift für Soziologie* (1/1979), 63-81.

Lyotard, Jean-Franois et al. (1985): *Immaterialität und Postmoderne*. Berlin.

M

Maaßen, Helmut (1991): Offenbarung, Mythos und Metaphysik: Drei Gottesbegriffe der Tradition und Whiteheads bipolarer Gott. In: *Die Gifford Lectures und ihre Deutung. Materialien zu Whiteheads 'Prozess und Realität'*, Vol. 2., ed. by Michael Hampe / Helmut Maaßen. Frankfurt a.M., 217-233.

MacCorquodale, Duncan (Ed.)(1996): *This is my body... this is my software*. London.

Macho, Thomas (1994): Vom Skandal der Abwesenheit. In: *Anthropologie nach dem Tode des Menschen. Vervollkommnung und Unverbesserlichkeit*, ed. by Dietmar Kamper / Christoph Wulf. Frankfurt a.M., 417-436.

Mann, Laurie D. (1981): How the Cryonics Movement Thawed Out. In: *Cryonics* 16 (Nov.), 9-12.

Marchand, Philip (1998): *Marshall McLuhan. The Medium and the Messenger. A Biography*. Toronto.

Martin, George M. (1971): Brief proposal on immortality: an interim solution. In: *Perspectives in Biology and Medicine* 14/2, 339.

Marvin, Carolyn (1987): Information and History. In: *Ideology of the Information Age*, ed. by Jennifer Daryl Slack / Fred Fejes. Norwood, 49-62.

Mattelart, Armand (1996): *The Invention of Communication*. Minneapolis.

Mayr, Otto (1986): *Authority, Liberty, and Automatic Machinery in Early Modern Europe*. Baltimore.

McCalla, Arthur (1998): Evolutionism and Early Nineteenth-Century Histories of Religions. In: *Religion* 28, 29-40.

McGinn, Colin (1999): Hello, HAL. In: *New York Times Book Review*, 01/03/1999.

McInerny, Ralph / John O'Callaghan (2014): Saint Thomas Aquinas. In: *SEP* (online).

McLuhan, Eric (1999): Introduction. In: McLuhan 1999a, IX-XXVIII.

McLuhan, Marshall (1951): *The Mechanical Bride: Folklore of Industrial Man*. New York.

McLuhan, Marshall (1968): *War and Peace in the Global Village. An Inventory of Some of the Current Spastic Situations That Could Be Eliminated by More Feedforward*. New York.

McLuhan, Marshall (1994)[1964]: *Understanding Media. The extensions of Man*. Cambridge.

McLuhan, Marshall (1999a): *The Medium and the Light. Reflections on Religion*, ed. by Eric McLuhan / Jacek Szlarek. Toronto.

McLuhan, Marshall (1999b): Electric Consciousness and the Church. In: McLuhan 1999a, 78-88.

McLuhan, Marshall (1999c): Letter to Jaques Maritain 5/6/1969. In: McLuhan 1999a, 70-73.

McLuhan, Marshall (2002)[1962]: *The Gutenberg Galaxy. The Making of Typographic Man*. Toronto.

Mehlhausen, Joachim / Daniela Dunkel (1994): Monismus/Monistenbund. In: *TRE* 23, 212-219.

Meyer-Drawe (2014): Mit 'eiserner Inkonsequenz' fürs Überleben – Günther Anders. In: *Jahrbuch Pädagogik. Menschenverbesserung. Transhumanismus*, 105-122.

Miller, Perry (^{8}1979): *The Transcendentalists. An Anthology.* Cambridge (MA).

Miller, R. Bruce / Milton T. Wolf (Eds.)(1992): *Thinking Robots, An Aware Internet, and Cyberpunk Librarians: A Collection of Background Essays Prepared for the 1992 LITA President's Program, "Tools for Knowing, Environments for Growing: Visions of the Potential of Information Technology for Human Development".* Chicago.

Minsky, Marvin L. (1954): *Neural Nets and the Brain Model Problem.* Dissertation. Princeton.

Minsky, Marvin L. (1965): Matter, Mind and Models. In: *Proceedings of IFIP Congress 1965*, I, May. Washington, 45-49.

Minsky, Marvin L. (1967): *Computation. Finite and Infinite Machines.* Englewood Cliffs.

Minsky, Marvin L. (1977): Plain Talk about Neurodevelopmental Epistemology. In: *Proceedings of the Fifth International Joint Conference on Artificial Intelligence*, ed. by P. Winston / R. Brown. Cambridge (MA), 421-450.

Minsky, Marvin L. (1981): Music, Mind and Meaning. In: *Computer Music Journal* 5/3.

Minsky, Marvin L. (1982): Why People Think Computers Can't. In: *AI Magazine* 3/4.

Minsky, Marvin L. (1984): Communication with Alien Intelligence. In: *Extra-terrestrial. Science and Alien Intelligence*, ed. by Edward Regis, Jr. Cambridge (MA).

Minsky, Marvin L. (1988)[1985]: *Society of Mind.* New York.

Minsky, Marvin L. (1992a): Alienable Rights. In: *Discover* 14/7, 24-26.

Minsky, Marvin L. (1992b): Future of AI Technology. In: *Toshiba Review* 47/7.

Minsky, Marvin L. (1992c): A Conversation with Marvin Minsky. In: *AI Magazine* 14/3, 31-45.

Minsky, Marvin L. (1994): Will Robots Inherit the Earth? In: *Scientific American* 271/10, 108-113.

Minsky, Marvin L. (1996)[1986]: Foreword. In: Drexler 1996, IV-VII.

Minsky, Marvin L. (2006): *The Emotion Machine: Commonsense Thinking, Artificial Intelligence, and the Future of the Human Mind.* New York.

Mitchell, David (2004): *Cloud Atlas.* New York.

Moravec, Hans (1979): Today's Computers, Intelligent Machines and Our Future. In: *Analog. Science Fiction/Science Fact* 99 (Feb.), 59-84.

Moravec, Hans (1988): *Mind Children. The Future of Robot and Human Intelligence.* Harvard.

Moravec, Hans (1992): Pigs in Cyberspace. In: Miller / Wolf 1992, 15-22.

Moravec, Hans (1996a): Körper, Roboter, Geist. In: *Kunstforum International* 133, 98-112.

Moravec, Hans (1996b): Die Evolution des postbiologischen Lebens. Szenarien der Entwicklung von intelligenten Robotern und Agenten. http://www.heise.de/tp/deutsch/special/vag/6055/1.html.

Moravec, Hans (1996c): Geisteskinder. Universelle Roboter. In vierzig Jahren haben sie uns überholt. In: *C'T Magazin für Computer und Technik* (6/1996), 98-104.

Moravec, Hans (1998): When will Computer match the human brain? In: *Journal of Transhumanism* 1 (Online).

Moravec, Hans (1999): *Robot. Mere Machine to Transcendent Mind.* New York.

Moravec, Hans (2009)[2008]: Rise of the Robots – The Future of Artificial Intelligence. In: *Scientific American*, 03/23/2009. https://www.scientificamerican.com/article/rise-of-the-robots.

Moravec, Hans / Frederic Pohl (1993): Souls in Silicon. In: *Omni* 16/11, 66-76.

Moravec, Hans / Stuart Shieber (1997): Will Researchers Develop a Computer that Duplicates Human Intelligence in the Foreseeable Future? In: *CQ Researcher*, 11/14/1997, 1001.

More, Max (1990): Transhumanism. Towards a Futurist Philosophy. https://web.archive.org/web/20051029125153/http://www.maxmore.com/transhum.htm.

More, Max (1994): On Becoming Posthuman. http://www.maxmore.com/becoming.htm (12/15/2003).

More, Max (1995): *The Diachronic Self: Identity, Continuity, Transformation.* http://www.maxmore.com/disscont.htm (12/15/2003).

More, Max (1996): Transhumanism. Towards a Futurist Philosophy. http://www.maxmore.com/transhum.htm (12/15/2003).

More, Max (1997a): Virtue and Virtuality. From Enhanced Reality to Experience Machines. http://www.maxmore.com/virtue.htm (12/15/2003).

More, Max (1997b): Beyond the Machine. Technology and Posthuman Freedom. http://www.maxmore.com/machine.htm (12/15/2003).

More, Max (1998a): Extropian Principles. Version 3.0. A Transhumanist Declaration. http://www.maxmore.com/extprn3.htm (12/15/2003).

More, Max (1998b): Dynamic Optimism. An Extropian-Emotional Virtue. http://www.maxmore.com/optimism.htm (12/15/2003).

More, Max (1999): A Letter to Mother Nature. http://www.maxmore.com/mother.htm (15.12.2003).

More, Max (2000a): Extropy Institute. Successful Memetic Incubator, 1988-2000 Onward! http://www.extropy.com/success.htm (12/15/2003).

More, Max (2000b): Embrace, Don't Relinquish, the Future. http://www.maxmore.com/maxview.htm (12/15/2003).

More, Max (2000c): Transhumanists vs. Mysterians on the Posthuman Condition. http://www.maxmore.com/feedmag1.htm (12/15/2003).

More, Max (2009): Why Catholics Should Support the Transhumanist Goal of Extended Life. http://strategicphilosophy.blogspot.com/2009/09/why-catholics-should-support.html.

More, Max (2010): The Overhuman in the Transhuman. In: *JET* 21 (online).

More, Max (2013a): A Critical Discussion of Vinge's Singularity Concept. In: More / Vita-More 2013, 406-409.

More, Max (2013b): The Philosophy of Transhumanism. In: More / Vita-More 2013, 2-17.

More, Max / Natasha Vita-More (Eds.)(2013): *The Transhumanist Reader.* Chichester.

Morgan, Richard K. (2002): *Altered Carbon.* London.

Mori, Masahiro (1980)[1974]: *The Buddha in the Robot. A Robot Engineer's Thoughts on Science and Religion.* Tokyo.

N

Nassehi, Armin (1993): *Die Zeit der Gesellschaft. Auf dem Weg zu einer soziologischen Theorie der Zeit.* Opladen.

Neesham, Claire / Caroline Smith (1995): Beyond Flesh / Blood. In: *New Scientist* 148/11, 28-29.

Negroponte, Nicholas (1996): *Being Digital.* New York.

Neilson, William A. (Eds.)(1959): *Webster's New International Dictionary of the English Language.* Springfield (MA).

Nelson, Robert (1968): *We Froze the First Man. The Startling True Story of the First Great Step toward Human Immortality.* New York.

Neumann, John von (1966): *Theory of Self-Reproducing Automata.* Urbana.

Neumann, John von (^{5}1964)[1958]: *The Computer and the Brain.* New Haven.

Neumann, John von / Oskar Morgenstern (^{9}1966)[1944]: *Theory of Games and Economic Behaviour.* Princeton.

Newman, Lex (2019): Descartes' Epistemology. In: *SEP* (online).

Ni, Siobhan (2007): 'Why may not man one day be immortal?' Population, perfectibility, and the immortality question in Godwin's political justice. In: *History of European Ideas* 33, 25-39.

Nielsen, Michael (2013)[2000]: A Critical Discussion of Vinge's Singularity Concept. In: More / Vita-More 2013, 409-411.

Nicholls, Peter (1999a): Cyberpunk. In: Clute / Nicholls 1999, 288-290.

Nicholls, Peter (1999b): Virtual Reality. In: Clute / Nicholls 1999, 1285-1286.

Nowlan, Philip F. (1928): Armageddon 2419 AD. In: *Amazing* (Aug.).

Nozick, Robert (1989): *The Examined Life.* New York.

O

O'Bryan, Jill (2005): *Carnal Art. ORLAN's Refacing.* Minneapolis.

Oliver, Myrna (1981): Families Awarded Nearly $ 1 Million in Cryonics Suit. In: *Los Angeles Times*, 6/6/1981.

O'Neill, Gerard K. (1977): *The High Frontier. Human Colonies in Space.* New York.

Ong, Walter J. (1952): The Mechanical Bride. Christen the Folklore of Industrial Man. In: *Social Order* 2, 79-85.

Ong, Walter J. (1958): *Ramus and Talon Inventory*, Vol 2. Cambridge.

Ong, Walter J. (1977): *Interfaces of the Word: Studies in the Evolution of Consciousness and Culture.* Ithaca.

ORLAN (1999): *Self-Hybridation*, ed. by Laurent Cauwet. Paris.

ORLAN (2000): Manifesto of Carnal Art. www.orlan.eu/texts/#manifestefr.

Ossege, Barbara (1999): Tod, wo ist dein Stachel? Zur Herstellbarkeit von Leben und Tod. In: Riegler / Lammer / Stecher 1999, 172-180.

P

Paley, William (1802): *Natural Theology.* London.

Paley, William (1842): *The Works of William Paley, D. D., Archdeacon of Carlisle, to which is prefixed The Life of the Author.* Edinburgh 1842.

Pannenberg, Wolfhart (1968)[1961]: *Revelation As History*. New York.
Pannenberg, Wolfhart (1995): Breaking a Taboo. Frank Tipler's The Physics of Immortality. In: *Zygon 30*, 309-314.
Passmore, John (1970): *The Perfectibility of Man*. London.
Philipkoski, Kristen (2002): Ray Kurzweil's Plan: Never Die. In: *Wired* 11/18/2002, https://www.wired.com/2002/11/ray-kurzweils-plan-never-die.
Pepperell, Robert (1995): *The Post-Human Condition*. Oxford.
Perry, R. Michael (1991): For the Record – First Suspension no 'Blue Sky' Event, in: *Cryonics* 12 (July), 11-12.
Perry, R. Michael (1992): For the Record. Gerald Feinberg, Scientific Cryonics Advocate. In: *Cryonics* 13 (June), 4-11.
Perry, R. Michael (2000): *Forever for All. Moral Philosophy, Cryonics, and the Scientific Prospects for Immortality*. N.P.
Pesce, Mark (2000): *The Playful World. How Technology is Transforming Our Imagination*. New York.
Piaget, Jean (1952)[1936]: *The Origins of Intelligence in Children*. New York.
Platt, Charles (1996): "The Man who Named Cryonics." In: Cryocare Report No. 8 (July). http://www.cryocare.org/index.cgi?subdir=/url=ccrpt8.html (11/28/2005).
Plessner, Helmuth (1952): Über die Beziehung der Zeit zum Tode. In: *Eranos-Jahrbuch 1951*, ed. by Olga Fröbe-Kapteyn. Zürich, 349-286.
Plessner, Helmuth (1980): *Gesammelte Schriften III. Anthropologie der Sinne*, ed. by Günter Dux / Odo Marquard / Elisabeth Ströker. Frankfurt a.M.
Pohl, Frederik (1964): Intimations of Immortality. In: *Playboy* (June), 158.
Pohl, Frederik (1989): When Machines Surpass People. Review of *Mind Children* by Hans Moravec. In: *New Scientist* (Feb.), 65.
Polkinghorne, John (1995): I am the Alpha and the Omega Point. Review. In: *New Scientist* 2/4/1995 (online).
Poinsett, Joel R. (1834): *Inquiry into the Received Opinions of Philosophers and Historians, on the Natural Progress of the Human Race from Barbarism to Civilization*. Charleston.
Pörksen, Bernhard (2000): Das Menschenbild der Künstlichen Intelligenz. Ein Gespräch mit Joseph Weizenbaum. In: Flessner 2000a, 265-280.
Porush, David (1992): Transcendence at the Interface: The Architecture of Cyborg Utopia – or – Cyberspace Utopoids as Postmodern Cargo Cult. In: Miller / Wolf 1992, 127-135.
Press, William H. (1986): A place for teleology? In: *Nature* 320, 315-316.
Priesner, Claus (2011): *Geschichte der Alchemie*. München.
Priestley, Joseph (^{2}1771): *An Essay on the First Principles of Government, and on the Nature of Political, Civil, and Religious Liberty*. London.
Proudfoot, Diane (2012): Software Immortals: Science or Faith? In: Eden et al. 2012a, 367-394.

Q

Quigley, Christine (1998): *Modern Mummies. The Preservation of the Human Body in the Twentieth Century*. Jefferson.

R

Randow, Gero von (1998): *Roboter. Unsere nächsten Verwandten*. Hamburg.

Rapp, Friedrich (1992): *Fortschritt. Entwicklung und Sinngehalt einer philosophischen Idee*. Darmstadt.

Raulerson, Joshua (2013): *Singularities. Technoculture, Transhumanism, and Science Fiction in the 21st Century*. Liverpool.

Redding, Micah (2016): The Jesuit Priest Who Believed in God and the Singularity. In: Motherboard 3/8/2016 (online).

Regis, Ed (1990): *Great Mambo Chicken and the Transhuman Condition. Science Slightly over the Edge*. Reading (MA).

Reitmeier, Heidi (1996): 'I Do Not Want To Look Like...' Orlan on becoming-Orlan. In: *MAKE. The magazine of women's art*, 72 (10/11 1996).

Richard, Birgit (2000): Vergehen Konservieren Uploaden. Strategien für die Ewigkeit. In: *Kunstforum International* 151, 51-84.

Richards, Earl Jeffrey (1997): Vergangenheitsbewältigung nach dem Kalten Krieg. Der Fall Hans Robert Jauß und das Verstehen. In: *Germanisten. Zeitschrift schwedischer Germanisten* 1, 28-43.

Riegler, Johanna (1999): Schrecklich gut! Zum Verhältnis von Revolution und Reaktion, Monster und Puppe, Faszination und Schrecken. In: Riegler / Lammer / Stecher 1999, 52-59.

Riegler, Johanna / Christina Lammer / Marcella Stecher et al. (Eds.) (1999): *Puppe. Monster. Tod. Kulturelle Transformationsprozesse der Bio- und Informationstechnologien*. Wien.

Rievman, Ellen B. (1976): *The Cryonics Society. A Study of Variant Behavior among the Immortalists*, Diss. Florida Atlantic University.

Roco, Mihail C. / William S. Bainbridge (2003): Converging Technologies for Improving Human Performance: Nanotechnology, Biotechnology, Information Technology and Cognitive Science. Dordrecht (http://www.wtec.org/ConvergingTechnologies /Report/NBIC_report.pdf).

Rohbeck, Johannes (1987): *Fortschrittstheorie der Aufklärung. Französische und englische Geschichtsphilosophie in der zweiten Hälfte des 18. Jahrhunderts*. Frankfurt a.M.

Rohbeck, Johannes (1993): *Technologische Urteilskraft. Zu einer Ethik technischen Handelns*. Frankfurt a.M.

Roszak, Theodore (^{2}1994)[1986]: *The Cult of Information. A Neo-Luddite Treatise on High Tech, Artificial Intelligence, and the True Art of Thinking*. Berkeley.

Rothblatt, Martine (2014): *Virtually Human. The Promise – and the Peril – of Digital Immortality*. New York.

Rottensteiner, Franz (1997): Unsterblichkeit im Computer? In: Flessner 1997a, 367-381.

Rötzer, Florian (1989): Technoimaginäres – Ende des Imaginären? In: *Kunstforum International* 98, 54-59.

Rötzer, Florian (1996a): Die Zukunft des Körpers. In: *Kunstforum International* 132, 54-71.

Rötzer, Florian (1996b): Traum von der Ewigkeit oder: Von der digitalen Endlichkeit. In: *KörperDenken. Aufgaben der Historischen Anthropologie*, ed. by Frithjof Hager. Berlin, 232-236.

Rötzer, Florian (1997): Als Cyborg ewig leben. In: *Spiegel special* (3/1997), 72-78.
Rucker, Rudy (1982): *Software*. New York.
Rucker, Rudy (2007): *Postsingular*. New York.
Russell, Peter (2000): *The Global Brain Awakes. Our next evolutionary Leap*. Boston.
Russell, William C. (1974)[1887]: *The Frozen Pirate. Volumes 1 and 2*. New York.
Rutsky, R. L. (1999): *High Techné. Art and Technology from the Machine Aesthetic to the Posthuman*. Minneapolis.

S

Sampson, Ronald V. (1956): *Progress in the Age of Reason. The 17th Century to the Present Day*. London.
Sandberg, Anders (1998): My Thoughts and Comments on the Omega Point Theory of Frank J. Tipler. In: *Anders Sandberg's Pages*, http://www.aleph.se/Trans/Global/Omega/tipler_page.html.
Sandberg, Anders (2013a)[2010]: An Overview of Models of Technological Singularity. In: More / Vita-More 2013, 376-394.
Sandberg, Anders (2013b)[2000]: A Critical Discussion of Vinge's Singularity Concept. In: More / Vita-More 2013, 411-416.
Sandberg, Anders / Nick Bostrom (2008): Whole Brain Emulation. A Roadmap. Technical Report #2008-3, Future of Humanity Institute. Oxford. http://www.fhi.ox.ac.uk/reports/2008-3.pdf.
Sanders, Olaf (2014): Echte Menschen? Posthumanistische Spuren in populärer Serienkultur und ihrer filmischen Vorgeschichte. In: *Jahrbuch Pädagogik 2014. Menschverbesserung. Transhumanismus*, 219-233.
Sandomir, Richard (2002): Williams Children Agree to Keep Their Father Frozen. In: *New York Times*, 12/21/2002.
Sass, Hans-Martin (1968): Daseinsbedeutende Funktionen von Wissen und Glauben im Jahrzehnt 1860-1870. In: ZRGG 20, 112-138.
Schäfer, Daniel (2010): Auf der Suche nach der Überwindung des Todes. Medizinische Spekulationen im kulturellen Kontext. In: Hilt / Jordan / Frewer 2010, 20-32.
Schelling, Friedrich W. von (1812): *Denkmal der Schrift von den göttlichen Dingen und des Herrn Friedrich Heinrich Jacobi und der ihm in derselben gemachten Beschuldigung eines absichtlich täuschenden, Lüge redenden Atheismus*. Tübingen.
Schenkel, Oskar (2000): Literatur als Labor. Posthumane Welten bei H. G. Wells. In: Flessner 2000a, 101-114.
Schivelbusch, Wolfgang (1977): *Geschichte der Eisenbahnreise*. München.
Schiwy, Günther (2001): *Ein Gott im Wandel. Teilhard de Chardin und sein Bild der Evolution*. Düsseldorf.
Schöner, Gregor (2014): Embodied Cognition, Neural Field Models of. In: *Encyclopedia of Computational Neuroscience*. Berlin, 1084-1092.
Schröter, Jens (2002): Biomorph. Anmerkungen zu einer neoliberalen Gentechnik-Utopie. In: *Kunstforum International* 158, 84-95.
Schutz, Alfred / Thomas Luckmann (1974)[1973]: *The Structures of the Life-World*, Vol. I, trans. by Richard M. Zaner / H. Tristram Engelhardt. London.

Schutz, Alfred / Thomas Luckmann (1989)[1983]: *The Structures of the Life-World*, Vol. II, trans. by Richard M. Zaner / David J. Parent. London.

Seltzer, Mark (1994): *Bodies and Machines*. New York.

Selznick, Brian (2007): *The Invention of Hugo Cabret*. New York.

Shannon, Claude E. / Warren Weaver (1964)[1949]: *The Mathematical Theory of Communication*. Urbana.

Sheskin, Arlene (1979): *Cryonics. A Sociology of Death and Bereavement*. New York.

Shultz, Suzanne M. (1992): *Body Snatching. The Robbing of Graves for the Education of Physicians in Early Nineteenth Century America*. Jefferson.

Sill, Oliver (1997): 'Fiktionale Realität' versus 'reale Realität'? Zu den kunst- bzw. literaturwissenschaftlichen Reflexionen Niklas Luhmanns und Wolfgang Isers. In: *Soziale Systeme* 3/1997, 137-155.

Simakova, Marina (2016): No Man's Space. On Russian Cosmism. In: *e-flux* 74. https://www.e-flux.com/journal/74/59823/no-man-s-space-on-russian-cosmism/.

Simpson, J. A. / E. Weiner (Eds.)(^{2}1989): *The Oxford English Dictionary*. Oxford.

Sirius, R. U. / Jay Cornell (2015): *Transcendence. The Disinformation Encyclopedia of Transhumanism and the Singularity*. San Francisco.

Snyder, Don (1967): "Couple who Nursed Cancer Victim Doubt Return-to-Life." In: *Los Angeles Times*, 01/19/1967.

Socrates (2012): 17 Definitions of the Technological Singularity. In: *Singularity Weblog*. https://www.singularityweblog.com/17-definitions-of-the-technological-singularity/.

Sommer, Andreas U. (1996): Religion, Wissenschaft und Politik im protestantischen Idealstaat. Johann Valentin Andreaes 'Christianopolis'. In: *ZRGG* 48, 114-137.

Sorgner, Stefan L. (2009): Nietzsche, the Overhuman and Transhumanism. In: *Journal of Evolution and Technology* 20 (March 2009) (online).

Sorgner, Stefan L. (2016): Transhumanismus. "Die gefährlichste Idee der Welt"!? Freiburg i.Br.

Spadafora, David (1990): *The Idea of Progress in Eighteenth-Century Britain*. New Haven.

Stableford, Brian (1999a): Cryonics. In: Clute / Nicholls 1999, 283-284.

Stableford, Brian (1999b): Immortality. In: Clute / Nicholls 1999, 616.

Stambler, Ilia (2014): *A History of Life-Extensionism in the Twentieth Century*. Rison Lezion. www.longevityhistory.com.

Standage, Tom (2003): *The Turk: The Life and Times of the Eighteenth-Century Chess-Playing Machine*. New York.

Stapledon, Olaf (1930): *Last and First Men. A Story of the Near and Far Future*. London.

Staudinger, Hugo (1986): Die Nebenwirkung einer Reise? Darwins Theorie und die Folgen. In: *ZRGG* 38, 167-185.

Stausberg, Michael (1998): *Faszination Zarathushtra. Zoroaster und die Europäische Religionsgeschichte der frühen Neuzeit*. Berlin.

Steels, Luc (1994): The Artificial Life Roots of Artificial Intelligence. In: *Artificial Life* 1 (1/2 1993/1994), 75-110.

Steels, Luc (1996): Die Zukunft der Intelligenz. In: *Kunstforum International* 133, 84-89.

Stelarc (1996): Von Psycho- zu Cyberstrategien: Prothetik, Robotik und Teleexistenz. In: *Kunstforum International* 132, 72-81.

Stelarc (1998): From Psycho-Body to Cyber-Systems: Images as Post-Human Entities. In: *Virtual Futures. Cyberotics, Technology and Post-Human Pragmatism*, ed. by Joan B. Dixon / Eric Cassidy, 116-123.

Stelarc (2000): Obsolete Zeit? Ein Gespräch mit Sven Drühl. In: *Kunstforum International* 151, 117-124.

Stephens, Charles A. (1920): *Immortal Life. How it will be achieved*. Norway Lake.

Stephenson, William (2014): Timothy Leary and the Trace of the Posthuman. In: *PostHumains. Frontières, évolutions, hybridités*, ed. by Elaine Déspres / Hélène Machinal. Rennes, 281-298.

Sterling, Bruce (1985) [1979]: *Schismatrix*. New York.

Stock, Gregory (1993): *Metaman. The Merging of Humans and Machines into a Global Superorganism*. Toronto.

Stock, Gregory (2002): *Redesigning Humans. Our Inevitable Genetic Future*. Boston.

Strate, Lance / Edward Wachtel (Eds.)(2005): *The Legacy of McLuhan*. Cresskill.

Strong, Josiah (1893): *The New Era or the Coming Kingdom*. New York.

Stross, Charles (2005): *Accelerando*. London.

Strugatsky, Arkady / Boris Strugatsky (1978)[1961]: Candles before the Control Board. In: *Noon: 22nd Century*. New York, 209-230.

Stuckrad, Kocku von (2014): *The Scientification of Religion. An Historical Study of Discursive Change, 1800-2000*. Berlin.

T

Tabbert, Thomas T. (2004): *Menschmaschinengötter. Künstliche Menschen in Literatur und Technik*. Hamburg.

Tandy, Charles (Eds.)(2003): *Death and Anti-Death, Vol. 1: One Hundred Years After N. F. Fedorov (1829-1903)*. Ann Arbor.

Teilhard de Chardin, Pierre (1966)[1956]: *Man's Place in Nature. The Human Zoological Group*. London.

Teilhard de Chardin, Pierre (1976)[1955]: *The Phenomenon of Man*. New York.

Times (1997): Still Frozen after all these Years. In: *New York Times*, 01/12/1997.

Tipler, Frank J. (1980): General Relativity and the Eternal Return. In: *Essays in General Relativity. A Festschrift for Abraham H. Taub*, ed. by Frank Tipler. New York, 21-38.

Tipler, Frank J. (1981): Extraterrestrial Intelligent Beings Do Not Exist. In: *Quarterly Journal of the Royal Astronomical Society* 21, 267-282.

Tipler, Fank J. (1986): Cosmological Limits on Computation. In: *International Journal of Theoretical Physics* 25, 617-661.

Tipler, Frank J. (1989): The Omega Point as *Eschaton*. Answers to Pannenberg's Questions for Scientists. In: *Zygon* 24, 217-253.

Tipler, Frank J. (1991): Alien life. In: *Nature* 354, 334-335.

Tipler, Frank J. (1994): Sophistry and Illusion. In: *Nature* 369, 198.

Tipler, Frank J. (1995)[1994]: *The Physics of Immortality. Modern Cosmology, God and the Ressurection of the Dead*. New York.

Tipler, Frank J. (2007): *The Physics of Christianity*. New York.

Tipler, Frank J. (2015): If you can't beat'em, join'em. In: Brockman 2015, 30-31.

Tirosh-Samuelson, Hava. (2014): Religion. In: *Post- and Transhumanism: An Introduction*, ed. by Robert Ranisch / Stefan L. Sorgner. Frankfurt a.M., 49-71.

Torr, James D. (2002): *The American Frontier*. San Diego.

Trésor de la Langue Française. Dictionnaire de la langue du XiX^e rt du XXe siècle (1789-1960), Vol. 16, ed. by Centre National de la Recherche Scientifique. Institut National de la Langue Française. Paris 1994.

Turchin, Valentin F. (1977)[1970]: *The Phenomenon of Science – A Cybernetic Approach to Human Evolution*. New York.

Turing, Alan M. (1950): Computing Machinery and Intelligence. In: *Mind* 59, 433-462 = Turing 1992, 133-160.

Turing, Alan M. (1992): *Collected Works of A. M. Turing. Mechanical Intelligence*, ed. by Darrel C. Ince. Amsterdam.

U

Ulam, Stanisław (1958): John von Neumann 1903–1957. In: *Bulletin of the American Mathematical Society* 64, 1-49.

V

Vandenberghe, Frédéric (2006): *Complexités du posthumanisme. Trois essais dialectiques sur la sociologie de Bruno Latour*. Paris.

Van Velzer, Ryan (2014): Immortality eludes People Unlimited Founder. In: *AZCentral*, 11/28/2014.

Vauvenargues, Luc de Clapiers (1857): Œuvres de Vauvenargues, ed. by D.-L. Gilbert. Paris.

Veatch, Robert M. (1975): The Whole-Brain-Oriented Concept of Death. An Outmoded Philosophical Foundation. In: *Journal of Thanatology* 3, 13-30.

Vernadsky, Vladimir I. (1997)[1926]: *The Biosphere*. New York.

Verne, Jules (1893)[1892]: *The Castle of the Carpathians*. London.

Villiers de l'Isle-Adam, Auguste de (2000)[1886]: *Tomorrow's Eve*. Champaign.

Vinge, Vernor (1983): First Word. In: *Omni*, January 1983, 10.

Vinge, Vernor (1992): *A Fire Upon the Deep*. New York.

Vinge, Vernor (1993): The Coming Technological Singularity. How to Survive in the Post-Human Era. http://mindstalk.net/vinge/vinge-sing.html.

Vinge, Vernor (2008): Signs of the Singularity. In: *IEEE Spectrum* (June). https://spectrum.ieee.org/biomedical/ethics/signs-of-the-singularity

Vinge, Vernor (2013)[2003]: Technological Singularity. In: More / Vita-More 2013, 365-375.

Virilio, Paul (1995)[1993]: *The Art of the Motor*. Minneapolis.

Vita-More, Natasha (1983): Transhuman Manifesto. https://humanityplus.org/transhumanism/transhumanist-manifesto/

Vita-More, Natasha (1990): Cryonics as a Safety Net. http://www.natasha.cc/cryonics.htm.

Vita-More, Natasha (1995): Recreating Reality – Redifining Art. A Continuous Process. Paper given at *Extro2*. http://www.natasha.cc/extro.htm.

Vita-More, Natasha (1997a): Future of Sexuality. http://www.extropicart.com/-sex.htm (1/1/1997).
Vita-More, Natasha (1997b): Extropic Art Manifesto. http://www.extropic-art.com/extropic.htm (12/15/2003).
Vita-More, Natasha (2000a): The Transhumanist Art Centre. http://www.extropic-art.com/history.htm (12/15/2003).
Vita-More, Natasha (2000b): Create/Recreate. The 3rd Millenial Culture. Typescript.
Vita-More, Natasha (2013): Aesthetics: Bringing the Arts / Design into the Discussion of Transhumanism. In: More / Vita-More 2013, 18-27.
Volpicelli, Gian (2014): The Transhumanist Church that has Faith in Technology. In: Motherboard, 12/31/2014 (online).
Vonnegut, Kurt (1991)[1966]: *Slaughterhouse-Five or the Children's Crusade. A Duty-Dance with Death.* New York.

W

Wagner, Thomas (2015): *Robokratie. Google, das Silicon Valley und der Mensch als Auslaufmodell.* Köln.
Walford, Roy L. (1983): *Maximum Life Span.* New York.
Walford, Roy L. (2000): *Beyond The 120-Year Diet.* New York.
Wallace, Alfred R. (1912)[1903]: *Man's Place in the Universe. A Study of the Results of Scientific Research in Relation to the Unity or Plurality of the Worlds.* London.
Warwick, Kevin (1997): *March of the Machines. Why the New Race of Robots Will Rule the World.* London.
Warwick, Kevin (1998): *In the Mind of the Machine. The Breakthrough in Artificial Intelligence.* London.
Warwick, Kevin (2000): Cyborg 1.0. In: *Wired* 2, 144-151.
Warwick, Kevin (2004): *I, Cyborg.* Chicago.
Weber, Max (1968)[1920]: *Economy and Society.* New York.
Weindling, Paul (2012): Julian Huxley and the Continuity of Eugenics in Twentieth-century Britain. In: *Journal of Modern European History* 10/4, 480-499.
Weizenbaum, Joseph (1976): *Computer Power and Human Reason. From Judgement to Calculation.* New York.
Weizsäcker, Carl-Friedrich (1964): *The Relevance of Science. Creation and Cosmogony.* London.
Weizsäcker, Christine / Ernst U. von (1987): Warum Fehlerfreundlichkeit? In: *Das Ende der Geduld. Carl Friedrich von Weizsäckers 'Die Zeit drängt' in der Diskussion.* München, 97-101.
Wells, Herbert G. (1895): *The Time Machine. An Invention.* London.
Wells, Herbert G. (1899): *When the Sleeper awakes.* London.
West, Patrick (2000): The secret lives of our Walter Mitties. In: *New Statesman*, 10/30/2000. https://www.newstatesman.com/node/193765
Whitehead, Alfred N. (1929): *Process and Reality. An Essay in Cosmology.* New York.
Wiener, Norbert (^{2}1961)[1948]: *Cybernetics: or Control and Communication in the Animal and the Machine.* Cambridge (MA).

Wiener, Norbert (1985): *Collected Works with Commentaries. Vol. IV. Cybernetics, Science and Society; Ethics, Aesthetics, and Literary Criticism; Book Reviews and Obituaries*, ed. by Pesi R. Masani. Cambridge.
Wiener, Norbert (1989)[1950]: *The Human Use of Human Beings: Cybernetics and Society.* London.
Wiener, Oswald (1969): *die verbesserung von mitteleuropa, roman.* Reinbek.
Wilber, Ken (1995): *Sex, Ecology, Spirituality: The Spirit of Evolution.* Boston.
Williams, Thomas (2001): John Duns Scotus. In: *SEP* (online).
Wittgenstein, Ludwig (1969): *Über Gewißheit. On Certainty*, ed. by Gertrude E. M. Anscombe / Georg H. von Wright. Frankfurt a.M. / Oxford.
Wolfe, Cary (2010): *What is Posthumanism?* Minneapolis.
Wolfe, Tom (2003): The All-in-One-Global-Village. In: *Grey Lodge Occult Review* 6 (June). http://www.greylodge.org/occultreview/glor_006/global.htm (1/12/2006).
Worthington, William (^{2}1748): *Essay on the Scheme and Conduct, Procedure and Extent of Man's Redemption.* London.
Wujastik, Dagmar / Suzanne Newcomb / Christèle Barois (Eds.)(2017): Introduction. In: *Transmutations: Rejuvenation, Longevity, and Immortality Practices in South and Inner Asia.* Special Issue in: *History of Science in South Asia*, I-XVII.
Wulf, Christoph (1984): Das gefährdete Auge. Ein Kaleidoskop der Geschichte des Sehens. In: Kamper / Wulf 1984a, 21-45.

Y

Yoke, Carl B. (1985): List of Works on Immortality in Science Fiction. In: Yoke / Hassler 1985, 209-222.
Yoke, Carl B. / D. Hassler (Eds.) (1985): *Death and the Serpent. Immortality in Science Fiction and Fantasy.* Westport.
Yudkowsky, Eliezer S. (2000a): *Singularitarian Principles. Version 1.0.2. Extended Edition.* https://web.archive.org/web/20070613190005/http://yudkowsky.net/sing/principles.ext.html#preface.
Yudkowsky, Eliezer S. (2000b): *Singularitarian Principles. Version 1.0.2. Extended Edition.* http://yudkowsky.net/obsolete/principles.html.

Z

Zachary, G. Pascal (1997): *Endless Frontier. Vannevar Bush, Engineer of the American Century.* Cambridge.
Zhuangzi (2013)[1968]: *The Complete Works of Zhuangzi*, trans. by Burton Watson. New York.
Zons, Raimar (2001): *Die Zeit des Menschen. Zur Kritik des Posthumanismus.* Frankfurt a.M.

b) Movies, TV series, and documentaries

Allen, Woody (1973): *Sleeper.* USA.
Amenábar, Alejandro (1997): *Abre los Ojos.* Spain.

Bloch, Robert (1966): *What Are Little Girls Made Of?* Star Trek episode 9.
Besson, Luc (2014): *Lucy*. France.
Brambilla, Marco (1993): *Demolition Man*. USA.
Cameron, James (1984): *The Terminator*. USA.
Cronenberg, David (1999): *eXistenZ*. USA.
Daniels, Greg (2020): *Upload*. USA.
Fassbinder, Rainer W. (1973): *Welt am Draht*. WDR/Germany.
Kalogridis, Laeta (2018): *Altered Carbon*. USA.
Kosinski, Joseph (2010): *Tron Legacy*. USA.
Kouba, Robert (2017): *Singularity*. USA.
Kubrick, Stanley (1968): *2001. A Space Odyssey*. USA.
Lukacevic, Damir (2010): *Transfer*. Germany.
Leonard, Brett / G. Everett (1991): *The Lawnmower Man*. USA.
Lisberger, Steven (1982): *Tron*. USA.
Miner, Steve (1992): *Forever Young*. USA.
Molinaro, Edouard (1969): *Hibernatus*. France, Italy.
Niccol, Andrew (1997): *Gattaca*. USA.
Nelson, Garry (1979): *The Black Hole*. USA.
Pfister, Wally (2014): *Transcendence*. USA
Ptolemy, Barry (2009): *Transcendent Man*. USA.
Roach, Jay (1997): *Austin Powers. International Man of Mystery*. USA.
Rusnak, John (1999): *The Thirteenth Floor*. USA.
Sasdy, Peter (1976): *Welcome to Blood City*. UK, Canada.
Shatner, William (1989): *The Final Frontier*. USA.
Sussberg, Jason (2014): *The Immortalist*. UK, USA, India.
Trumbull, Douglas (1982): *Brainstorm*. USA.
Verhoeven, Paul (1990): *Total Recall*. USA.
Wachowski, Andy / Larry Wachowski (1999): *The Matrix*. USA.
Wachowski, Lana / Lilly / Tom Tykwer (2012): *Cloud Atlas*. Germany, USA.

c) Videos (online)

- Kurzweil, Ray (1965): I've Got a Secret. https://www.youtube.com/watch?v=X4Neivqp2K4
- Kurzweil, Ray (2016): Ray Kurzweil Remembers Marvin Minsky, 04/04/2016. https://www.youtube.com/watch?v=FIK3X2fKJrE
- Kurzweil, Ray (2017): Interview. Human-Level AI is Just 12 Years Away. https://www.youtube.com/watch?v=JiXVMZTyZRw
- Minsky, Marvin L. (2010): Ray Kurzweil interviews Marvin Minsky, 2010. https://www.youtube.com/watch?v=RZ3ahBm3dCk
- Minsky, Marvin L. (2013): Marvin Minsky on AI: The Turing Test is a Joke! Interview with Socrates / Nikola Danaylov of the SingularityWeblog, 07/12/2013. https://www.youtube.com/watch?v=3PdxQbOvAlI

- Socrates (2015): The Emperor Has No Clothes: Socrates Deconstructs Singularity University. https://www.singularityweblog.com/socrates-deconstructs-singularity-university/, 11/29/2015.
- Tipler, Frank (2013): The Laws of Physics Say The Singularity is Inevitable! Interview with Socrates / Nikola Danaylov of the SingularityWeblog 10/29/2013, https://www.singularityweblog.com/frank-j-tipler-the-singularity-is-inevitable/
- Vinge, Vernor (2011): We Can Surpass the Wildest Dreams of Optimism. Interview with Socrates / Nikola Danaylov of the SingularityWeblog, 04/15/2011. https://www.singularityweblog.com/vernor-vinge-on-singularity-1-on-1-we-can-surpass-the-wildest-dreams-of-optimism/

Index of Names[1]

A

Abbé de Saint Pierre, 213, 303
Abbott, Lyman, 182
Agar, Nicholas, 24
Alexander, Samuel, 182, 184–187, 281
Allen, Ethan, 194
Allen, Woody, 245
Alsted, Johann Heinrich, 306
Amenábar, Alejandro, 242
Anders, Günther, 24, 35, 37, 39, 44, 47, 51–56, 91, 119, 164, 311–313
Andreae, Johann Valentin, 306
Anselm of Canterbury, 155, 208
Arendt, Hannah, 51, 52, 311
Aristotle, 128, 129, 133, 139, 140, 170, 178, 192
Asimov, Isaac, 74
Assmann, Jan, 34, 55
Augustine of Hippo, 128, 140, 155

B

Bach, Johann Sebastian, 270
Bacon, Francis, 63, 155, 164, 213, 214, 226, 228, 294, 306
Bacon, Roger, 225
Badmington, Neil, 21
Baillie, John, 307
Bainbridge, William S., 79, 82, 85, 224
Barad, Karen, 21
Barcelo, Elia, 242
Barnes, Ernest William, 182, 186, 196
Barrow, John D., 96, 120, 129, 160, 161, 170, 185, 191–193, 195, 196, 199, 298
Barthes, Roland, 35, 55
Bateson, Gregory, 163
Baudrillard, Jean, 24, 45–47
Beck, Klaus, 31, 34, 36
Becker, Philipp von, 24, 258, 293
Bedford, James H., 251, 255
Bennet, James C., 83
Bentham, Jeremy, 156, 177, 295
Bentley, Richard, 170, 194
Benz, Ernst, 214, 306
Berger, Peter L., 34
Bergson, Henri, 31–33, 64, 162, 183, 185, 286
Berkeley, George, 137, 192, 197, 237
Bernal, John D., 63, 67, 231–233, 240, 261, 280, 301
Besson, Luc, 269
Bigelow, Julian, 141
Blackford, Russel, 79
Bloch, Ernst, 117, 118
Bloch, Robert, 240
Blount, Thomas, 92
Blumenberg, Hans, 116, 303–305
Boethius, 170
Bogdanov, Aleksandr, 229
Bollnow, Otto Friedrich, 38
Boltzmann, Ludwig, 162

---

1   For pragmatic reasons, the four most common authors (Ray Kurzweil, Marvin Minsky, Frank Tipler, and Hans Moravec) are not listed in the index.

Bonnet, Charles, 178
Bostrom, Nick, 61, 66, 78, 80, 85, 86, 201, 205, 211, 222, 223, 249, 264–267, 274, 275, 295, 297, 302, 309–312
Braidotti, Rosi, 21
Brillouin, Leon, 163
Brin, David, 267
Brin, Sergey, 210
Bringsjord, Selmer, 266
Broderick, Damien, 211
Brown, Bernadeane, 87, 89, 296
Brown, Charles Paul, 87
Brown, Dan, 20
Bruno, Giordano, 249
Büchner, Ludwig, 186
Buffier, Claude, 127
Bultmann, Rudolf, 303–305
Bunyan, John, 168
Burroughs, Edgar R., 245
Bury, John B., 303, 305, 307
Bush, George W., 215
Bush, Vannevar, 202, 214, 217

C

Calvin, John, 176
Capra, Fritjof, 289
Carter, Brandon, 192
Carus, Paul, 181
Cary, Henry Francis, 64
Chamberlain, Fred & Linda, 247
Chamberlain, Houston Stewart, 273
Cherniavsky, Vladimir, 48
Chislenko, Sasha, 98, 149
Christie, Agatha, 192
Cicero, 170
Clark, Nancie, 75
Clarke, Arthur C., 88, 98, 160, 233, 234, 237, 268, 274
Clarke, Richard, 226
Cobb, Jennifer, 279
Coenen, Christopher, 23
Columbus, Christopher, 214
Comte, Auguste, 213, 229, 303, 304

Condorcet, Antoine Marquis de, 153, 154, 213, 226, 303
Connolly, Randy, 308
Cooper, Evan, 246
Copernicus, Nicolaus, 53, 67, 311
Cornaro, Luigi, 226, 228
Crick, Francis, 299
Cromwell, Oliver, 272
Cronenberg, David, 242

D

da Vinci, Leonardo, 271
Daguerre, Louis, 39
Danaylov, Nikola, 210
Dante, 64, 65, 67, 215, 309
Darwin, Charles, 53, 179, 189, 283
Darwin, Erasmus, 156, 178
Davis, Erik, 265
Dawkins, Richard, 101, 126, 173, 188
de Funès, Louis, 245
de Grey, Aubrey, 78, 79, 84, 85, 87, 223, 224, 248, 250, 296
de Val, Jaime, 80
Deitch, Jeffrey, 22
Denis, Jean Baptiste, 228
Derham, William, 170, 194, 195
Dery, Mark, 22
Descartes, René, 117, 120, 125–129, 131, 134–137, 140, 145, 150, 302
Diamandis, Peter, 210, 296
Dick, Philip K., 242
Diderot, Denis, 167, 178, 196
Dilthey, Wilhelm, 41, 50
Drexler, Eric, 74, 78, 82, 83, 85, 86, 98, 250, 295, 296
Dühring, Eugen, 167
Duns Scotus, John, 48, 309
Dyson, Freeman, 97, 161, 233

E

Edelhart, Mike, 236
Eden, Amnon H., 23
Edison, Thomas Alva, 237, 271
Edwards, John, 156
Ehricke, Krafft, 74

Einstein, Albert, 274
Eisenhower, Dwight D., 73
Ekirch, Arthur, 307
Elias, Norbert, 33, 43, 54, 151, 300
Ellis, Bret Easton, 162
Engels, Friedrich, 162
Esfandiary, Fereidoun M., 61, 68, 70, 71, 73–75, 105, 222
Ettinger, Robert, 61, 68–70, 72, 74, 83, 117, 222, 234, 245–248, 250, 252, 255, 262, 263
Ettinger, Robert C. W., 245, 248
Evans, Dylon, 295
Everett, Hugh, 297

F

Faloon, William, 88
Fassbinder, Rainer W., 48, 240
Fedorov, Nikolai, 88, 228–230
Feinberg, Gerald, 234
Ferguson, Adam, 153, 213, 307
Ferguson, Marylin, 289
Feuerbach, Ludwig, 76, 229
Finot, Jean, 230
Fiske, John, 182, 186
Flessner, Bernd, 31, 91
Flusser, Vilém, 42, 49
FM-2030, 61, 70, 72, 74, 81, 105
Fontenelle, Bernard le Bovier de, 154, 213
Foucault, Michel, 43
Franke, Herbert W., 44, 47, 238–240, 243, 258
Franklin, Benjamin, 63, 154, 156, 194, 226, 263
Fredericksen, Dick, 235
Freud, Sigmund, 52, 230, 311
Freyermuth, Gundolf, 22
Fromm, Erich, 249
Fukuyama, Francis, 23
Fuller, Buckminster, 93, 289

G

Gadamer, Hans-Georg, 116
Gafsou, Matthieu, 112

Galen, 112, 170
Galouye, Daniel F., 240
Galton, Francis, 186, 271, 272
Garreau, Joel, 22
Gauss, Carl Friedrich, 272
Gehlen, Arnold, 41, 154
Gerhoh of Reichersberg, 155
Gibbon, Edward, 213
Gibson, Mel, 245
Gibson, William, 29, 241
Giddens, Anthony, 39
Gilbert, William, 155
Gilgamesh, 69, 225
Giraud, Fabien, 112
Gobel, David, 84
Godwin, William, 177, 227
Goertzel, Ben, 78, 85, 92, 230, 250, 281
Goethe, Johann Wolfgang von, 180, 271
Good, Irving, 198, 203, 209, 267, 269
Graham, Elaine, 21, 217
Graham, Robert K., 273
Gray, Asa, 181, 186, 196
Gray, Chris Hables, 84
Gross, Daniel, 177
Großklaus, Götz, 24, 31, 36–38
Grossman, Terry, 104, 261
Groys, Boris, 56

H

Haeckel, Ernst, 128, 180, 229, 272
Halacy, Daniel, 262
Haldane, John B. S., 63, 67, 186, 232
Hanson, Robin, 79, 266
Harari, Yuval, 23
Haraway, Donna, 21
Harbisson, Neil, 111
Harrington, Alan, 249
Hartley, David, 156, 307
Hassan, Ihab, 92
Hawking, Stephen, 199
Hayles, N. Katherine, 23, 49, 94, 119, 120, 130, 146
Heil, Reinhard, 23, 198
Heine, Heinrich, 38

Heinlein, Robert, 74, 98
Heisenberg, Werner, 297
Helmholtz, Hermann von, 162, 272
Helvétius, Claude-Adrien, 177, 196
Herbert, Frank, 98
Herbrechter, Stefan, 21
Herder, Johann Gottfried, 154, 178, 305
Hesse, Eva, 54
Heylighen, Francis, 280
Hitler, Adolf, 98
Hobbes, Thomas, 125, 127, 129
Hobsbawm, Eric, 62
Holbach, Paul-Henri T., 196
Holmes, Oliver Wendell, 40
Holmes, Sherlock, 69, 299
Hölscher, Lucian, 117
Home, Henry, 153
Homer, 225
Houellebecq, Michel, 20
Hufeland, Christoph W., 227, 228
Hughes, James, 63, 66, 68, 79, 85, 87, 250, 293
Hume, David, 153, 213
Hunt, James, 272
Husserl, Edmund, 31–33, 51
Huxley, Aldous, 63, 66, 186
Huxley, Julian, 63, 65, 67, 72, 76, 186, 187, 189, 233, 261, 275, 312
Huxley, Thomas, 186

I
Ingarden, Roman, 116
Iser, Wolfgang, 45–47
Istvan, Zoltan, 88
Itskov, Dmitry, 210

J
Jackson, Andrew, 169
Jackson, Michael, 22
Jastrow, Robert, 168, 235
Jauß, Hans Robert, 116
Jefferson, Thomas, 194
Jones, Neil R., 245
Jung, C. G., 249

K
Kac, Eduardo, 111
Kamper, Dietmar, 24, 43, 49, 57, 139, 150, 314
Kant, Immanuel, 63, 178
Kapuściński, Ryszard, 158
Kempelen, Wolfgang von, 271
Kent, Saul, 88, 247
Kepler, Johannes, 170
Kerr, Philip, 241
King, Stephen, 242
Klemperer, Victor, 37
Kohl, Helmut, 47
Kroker, Arthur & Marilouise, 91
Kubrick, Stanley, 268

L
La Mettrie, Julien Offray de, 63, 120, 127, 129, 227, 302
Lactantius, 155
Lafitau, Joseph-François, 169
Lahontan, Louis Armand de Lom d'Arce, 169
Lamarck, Jean-Baptiste, 178
Lavery, David, 22, 74
Law, Edmund, 156, 176, 178
Le Roy, Édouard, 229
Le Sage, Georges-Louis, 127
Leary, Timothy, 56, 61, 73–75
Leibniz, Gottfried Wilhelm, 127, 178
Lem, Stanisław, 24, 29, 44, 50, 237, 238, 243
Levandowski, Anthony, 89
Lévy, Pierre, 281
Liebig, Justus, 272
Lighthall, William Douw, 64, 65, 309
Lincoln, Abraham, 88, 253
Linde, Carl von, 252
Locke, John, 127, 137, 178
Loh, Janina, 21
Lovejoy, Arthur Oncken, 129, 178
Löwenthal, Eduard, 181
Lower, Richard, 228
Löwith, Karl, 303–305
Lübbe, Hermann, 301

Luckmann, Thomas, 34, 35
Luhmann, Niklas, 33
Lyotard, Jean-François, 24, 41

M

MacClaurin, Colin, 194
Macho, Thomas, 36, 56
Maes, Pattie, 212
Mandeville, John, 225
Marinetti, Filippo Thomaso, 105–107, 109, 112
Martin, George M., 234
Marvin, Carolyn, 148
Marx Hubbard, Barbara, 74
Marx, Karl, 76
Mather, Cotton, 168
Mattelart, Armand, 308
Mayr, Otto, 146
McCalla, Arthur, 178
McCarthy, John, 144
McCosh, James, 181
McCulloch, Warren, 99, 142
McGinn, Colin, 128
McKay, Donald, 148
McLuhan, Marshall, 30, 73, 93, 276, 281, 282, 284–289
Mead, George Herbert, 33
Merkle, Ralph, 83, 86, 248, 250
Mechnikov, Ilja, 230
Michelangelo, 271
Millar, John, 154
Milton, John, 308
Mitchell, David, 293
Mommsen, Theodor, 272
Monchicourt, Marie-Odile, 96
Moore, Gordon, 206
More, Max, 61, 66, 75, 76, 85, 88, 105, 118, 124, 129, 132, 138, 160, 161, 166, 174, 175, 211, 222, 248, 250, 262, 297, 298, 302
Morgan, Richard, 242
Morgenstern, Oskar, 141
Mori, Masahiro, 302
Morrow, T. O., 76, 80, 81, 161
Morse, Samuel, 39

Mukařovský, Jan, 116
Muñoz, Manel, 112
Murphy, Joseph, 77

N

Napoleon Bonaparte, 271
Nassehi, Armin, 33
Nayar, Pramod K., 21
Negroponte, Nicholas, 48, 98
Nelson, Robert, 248
Neumann, John von, 99, 120, 140–146, 149, 163, 171, 201–203, 300
Newton, Isaac, 31, 155, 186, 194
Nielsen, Michael, 211, 266
Nietzsche, Friedrich, 63, 69, 76, 160, 162, 229, 262, 275
Nowlan, Philip F., 245
Nozick, Robert, 243

O

Obama, Barack, 215
Oetinger, Friedrich Christoph, 178
Ong, Walter J., 284, 285
Oppenheimer, Robert, 202
Origen of Alexandria, 155, 197
ORLAN, 22, 109–112
O'Connor, Max Terence, 75, 105
O'Neill, Gerard, 74, 83, 215
Ovid, 64

P

Page, Larry, 210
Paine, Thomas, 194
Paley, William, 126, 154, 156, 157, 177, 186, 189, 194, 195, 302
Parfit, Derek, 132
Peale, Norman Vincent, 77
Pearce, David, 61, 78, 79, 85
Penrose, Roger, 171, 199
Pepperell, Robert, 21, 93, 106, 260
Perry, R. Michael, 248
Pesce, Mark, 278
Petrarch, 270
Piaget, Jean, 41

Piscator, Johann, 306
Pitts, Walter, 142
Plato, 128, 140, 170, 178, 237
Plessner, Helmuth, 30–32
Pliny the Elder, 225
Plutarch, 129
Pohl, Frederick, 234
Poinsett, Joel Roberts, 169
Pope, Alexander, 178
Portman, Adolf, 67
Powell, Colin, 217
Price, Richard, 156, 176, 177, 226, 307
Priestley, Joseph, 156, 176, 177, 307, 308
Prisco, Giulio, 85, 89
Protagoras, 192
Proudfoot, Diane, 198, 208
Putin, Vladimir, 230

R
Ray, John, 193, 194
Regis, Ed, 22
Régis, Pierre Sylvain, 127
Ribas, Moon, 111
Roco, Mihail, 82, 224
Rohbeck, Johannes, 52, 305, 311
Roosevelt, Franklin D., 214
Rosenblueth, Arturo, 140, 141
Ross, John, 156
Rostand, Jean, 246
Rothblatt, Martine, 79, 80, 85, 89, 92, 222, 223, 226, 248, 250, 275, 295, 302
Rottensteiner, Franz, 23
Rötzer, Florian, 22, 56
Rousseau, Jean-Jacques, 169
Rucker, Rudy, 241
Russell, Pee Wee, 246
Russell, Peter, 289
Russell, William Clark, 244

S
Sandberg, Anders, 61, 78, 79, 86, 198, 201, 205, 211, 223, 250, 265, 266, 297
Savage, Minot Judson, 181

Schelling, Friedrich Wilhelm, 185
Schubert, Franz, 272
Schumann, Robert, 272
Schütz, Alfred, 30–33
Selznick, Brian, 313
Shakespeare, William, 270
Shannon, Claude, 99, 120, 140, 146–148, 162, 237
Shatner, William, 217
Siboni, Raphaël, 112
Siemens, Wilhelm von, 272
Sirius, R.U., 22
Smith, Adam, 153, 154
Smyth, Garret, 75
Socrates, 198, 199, 210, 275
Sorgner, Stefan Lorenz, 24, 66, 79, 80, 85, 262
Spadafora, David, 155, 307
Spencer, Herbert, 162
St. Jude, 74
Stableford, Brian, 236
Stalin, Joseph, 98
Stambler, Ilia, 224
Stapledon, Olaf, 233, 268
Steels, Luc, 22, 84, 98
Steinach, Eugen, 230
Stelarc, 22, 29, 105, 107, 109, 111, 112, 166, 168, 222
Stephens, Charles A., 231, 233
Sterling, Bruce, 84, 93
Stock, Gregory, 78, 276
Strabo, 225
Strole, James Russel, 87–89, 296
Stross, Charles, 310
Strugatsky, Arkadi & Boris, 230, 239, 258
Stuckrad, Kocku von, 306
Szilard, Leo, 163

T
Tandy, Charles, 230
Teilhard de Chardin, Pierre, 63, 66, 67, 93, 118, 182–189, 192, 197–199, 229, 273, 276, 279–282, 284–289, 308, 309

Tertullian, 155
Tesla, Nikola, 271
Theseus, 129
Thiel, Peter, 84, 210
Thomas Aquinas, 128, 129, 133, 140, 197
Thomson, William, 162
Tillich, Paul, 197
Toynbee, Arnold, 67
Triptree, James, 240
Turchin, Valentin, 280
Turgot, Anne R., 154, 213
Turing, Alan, 120, 140, 144, 145, 237, 267, 274

U
Ulam, Stanisław, 201–203

V
Vandenberghe, Frédéric, 24, 294
Vauvenargues, Luc de Clapiers, 33, 34, 37
Veatch, Robert M., 235
Venzmer, Gerhard, 230
Vernadski, Vladimir, 229
Verne, Jules, 230, 237, 243, 257
Vico, Giovanni B., 305
Villiers de l'Isle-Adam, Auguste, 237, 257
Vincent of Lérins, 155
Vinge, Vernor, 78, 104, 198, 201, 203–205, 209, 211, 215, 218, 260, 263, 266, 267, 270
Vita-More, Natasha, 75, 78, 85, 88, 89, 109, 112, 250, 275, 296
Vodička, Felix, 116
Voltaire, François-Marie Arouet, 170, 304
Vonnegut, Kurt, 11, 162
Voronoff, Serge, 230

W
Wachowski, Andy & Larry, 242
Wagner, Thomas, 24
Walford, Roy L., 78, 84, 223, 250
Wallace, Alfred Russel, 179
Warburton, William, 156
Warwick, Kevin, 83, 86, 111, 153, 166, 168, 174, 262, 276
Washington, George, 194
Watson, James, 299
Weaver, Warren, 146, 148, 162
Weber, Max, 176
Weizenbaum, Joseph, 145, 301
Weizsäcker, Carl-Friedrich, 305
Weizsäcker, Christine & Ernst Ulrich, 313
Wells, H. G., 12, 162, 230
Werner, Karl, 247
Wesley, John, 176, 226
Wheeler, John A., 192
Whitehead, Alfred North, 33, 64, 182–186
Whitman, Walt, 272
Wiener, Norbert, 99, 120, 140–146, 148, 149, 163, 237, 246, 257, 261, 299
Wiener, Oswald, 239, 240, 301, 309
Wilber, Ken, 289
Williams, Ted, 248
Wittgenstein, Ludwig, 136
Wolfe, Bernard, 240
Wolfe, Cary, 21
Woltmann, Ludwig, 54
Wonder, Stevie, 217
Worthington, William, 156, 176–178
Wright, George Frederick, 181
Wulf, Christoph, 24, 48, 151

Y
Yoke, Carl B., 236
Yudkowsky, Eliezer, 79, 80, 85, 198, 204, 205, 209, 215, 302, 309, 312

Z
Zhuangzi, 291
Ziolkowski, Konstantin, 229
Žižek, Slavoj, 43
Zons, Raimar, 23

Social Sciences

kollektiv orangotango+ (ed.)
This Is Not an Atlas
A Global Collection of Counter-Cartographies

2018, 352 p., hardcover, col. ill.
34,99 € (DE), 978-3-8376-4519-4
E-Book: free available, ISBN 978-3-8394-4519-8

Gabriele Dietze, Julia Roth (eds.)
Right-Wing Populism and Gender
European Perspectives and Beyond

April 2020, 286 p., pb., ill.
35,00 € (DE), 978-3-8376-4980-2
E-Book: 34,99 € (DE), ISBN 978-3-8394-4980-6

Mozilla Foundation
Internet Health Report 2019

2019, 118 p., pb., ill.
19,99 € (DE), 978-3-8376-4946-8
E-Book: free available, ISBN 978-3-8394-4946-2

**All print, e-book and open access versions of the titles in our list
are available in our online shop www.transcript-publishing.com**

Social Sciences

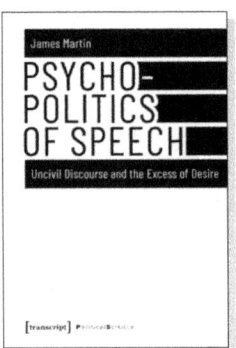

James Martin
Psychopolitics of Speech
Uncivil Discourse and the Excess of Desire

2019, 186 p., hardcover
79,99 € (DE), 978-3-8376-3919-3
E-Book:
PDF: 79,99 € (DE), ISBN 978-3-8394-3919-7

Michael Bray
Powers of the Mind
Mental and Manual Labor
in the Contemporary Political Crisis

2019, 208 p., hardcover
99,99 € (DE), 978-3-8376-4147-9
E-Book:
PDF: 99,99 € (DE), ISBN 978-3-8394-4147-3

Ernst Mohr
The Production of Consumer Society
Cultural-Economic Principles of Distinction

April 2021, 340 p., pb., ill.
39,00 € (DE), 978-3-8376-5703-6
E-Book: available as free open access publication
PDF: ISBN 978-3-8394-5703-0

**All print, e-book and open access versions of the titles in our list
are available in our online shop www.transcript-publishing.com**

GPSR Authorized Representative: Easy Access System Europe, Mustamäe tee
50, 10621 Tallinn, Estonia, gpsr.requests@easproject.com

www.ingramcontent.com/pod-product-compliance
Lightning Source LLC
Chambersburg PA
CBHW080213040426
42333CB00044B/2647